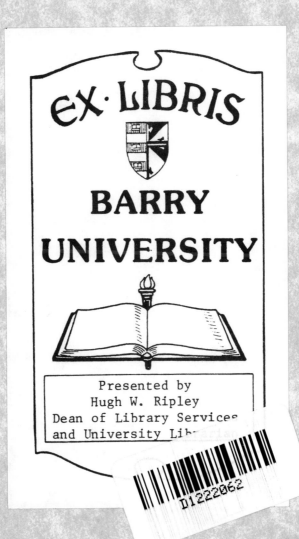

DATE DUE

The Civil War Journal of
Colonel William J. Bolton

Colonel William J. Bolton

The Civil War Journal of Colonel William J. Bolton

51st Pennsylvania

April 20, 1861–August 2, 1865

edited by
Dr. Richard A. Sauers

COMBINED PUBLISHING
Pennsylvania

PUBLISHER'S NOTE

The headquarters of Combined Publishing are located midway between Valley Forge and the Germantown battlefield, on the outskirts of Philadelphia. From its beginnings, our company has been steeped in the oldest traditions of American history and publishing. Our historic surroundings help maintain our focus on history and our books strive to uphold the standards of style, quality and durability first established by the earliest book-makers of Germantown and Philadelphia so many years ago. Our famous monk-and-console logo reflects our commitment to the modern and yet historic enterprise of publishing.

We call ourselves Combined Publishing because we have always felt that our goals could only be achieved through a "combined" effort by authors, publishers and readers. We have always tried to maintain maximum communication between these three key players in the reading experience.

We are always interested in hearing from prospective authors about new books in our field. We also like to hear from our readers and invite you to contact us at our offices in Pennsylvania with any questions, comments or suggestions, or if you have difficulty finding our books at a local bookseller.

For information, address:
Combined Publishing
P.O. Box 307
Conshohocken, PA 19428
E-mail: combined@combinedpublishing.com
Web: www.combinedpublishing.com
Orders: 1-800-418-6065

Cataloging-in-Publication Data available from the Library of Congress

ISBN 1-58097-039-7

Printed in the United States of America.

Contents

Introduction   7
List of Abbreviations   11
1. The 4th Pennsylvania (April 20–July 28, 1861)   13
2. The 51st Pennsylvania (September 10–December 31, 1861)   27
3. The Burnside Expedition (January 1–July 5, 1862)   37
4. Second Manassas (July 6–September 4, 1862)   67
5. The Maryland Campaign (September 5–November 8, 1862)   79
6. Fredericksburg (November 9, 1862–February 4, 1863)   97
7. The Department of the Ohio (February 5–June 5, 1863)   107
8. Vicksburg and Jackson (June 6–August 17, 1863)   121
9. The Department of the Ohio (August 18–November 3, 1863)   137
10. Knoxville (November 4, 1863–February 9, 1864)   147
11. The Ninth Army Corps (February 10–May 3, 1864)   187
12. The Overland Campaign (May 4–June 15, 1864)   197
13. Petersburg (June 16–December 31, 1864)   217
14. Petersburg (January 1–April 22, 1865)   241
15. Final Duty (April 23–August 2, 1865)   261
Appendix: Field, Staff, and Company Officers of the 51st PA   273
Bibliography of the 51st PA   278
Index   283

Introduction

Of the many famous Pennsylvania units of the Civil War, one of the best-known is the 51st Pennsylvania Volunteer Infantry. Formed in the fall of 1861 by Colonel John F. Hartranft, this unit remained in service as a veteran volunteer regiment until mustered out of service in July 1865. It served in the Ninth Army Corps under Ambrose E. Burnside, fighting in North Carolina, Virginia, Maryland, Tennessee, and Mississippi.

The second, and last, colonel of the regiment was William J. Bolton. He was at first captain of Company A, then was promoted to major after Antietam. After Lieutenant Colonel Edwin Schall was killed at Cold Harbor, Bolton was promoted to colonel after Hartranft finally received a long-overdue promotion to brigadier general.

Colonel Bolton was born in Norristown, Montgomery County, Pennsylvania, on October 22, 1833. He was named after the Reverend William Jordan, a Baptist minister from North Carolina then preaching at the Norristown Baptist Church. The colonel's four siblings included his older brother Joseph K. Bolton, who also served in the 51st Pennsylvania.

After early schooling in a variety of locales, young Bolton graduated from Tremont Seminary in 1851. Bolton's first regular employment was learning the machinist trade at William Jamison & Sons in Norristown. When he left his apprenticeship, Bolton worked at iron fence-making, as an engineer at the Lucinda Furnace, at the Schall and Dewees Nailworks, and finally as an engineer at James Hooven & Sons. While working at Hooven's, Bolton became involved in a political difference with another militia officer, the result of which was his discharge from Hooven's in October 1860.

Bolton was able to work as a substitute at another mill, but he was penniless when the rebellion opened in April 1861. He had been interested in military matters ever since the age of seven, when he would drill with neighborhood pals, Winfield Scott Hancock among the number. In 1855, Bolton enlisted in the Wayne Artillerists, one of Norristown's uniformed militia companies. In June 1859, he was commissioned second lieutenant in that organization. A month later, Bolton was commissioned Judge Advocate of the Second Brigade, Second Division. He was appointed paymaster on the staff of the division commander in April 1860. When President-elect Lincoln stopped in Harrisburg and made a speech in front of the capitol building on February 22, 1861, Captain Bolton served as officer of the guard for the day's ceremonies.

When the conflict started, the company offered its services to Governor Andrew G. Curtin. However, all the officers had resigned when the company tendered its offer, and so Bolton, even though no longer an active member, was elected captain. The Wayne Artillerists became Company A, 4th Pennsylvania Volunteer Infantry, led by Colonel John F. Hartranft. This regiment saw no active service; its term of service expired on July 20, and even though the

Union army was moving toward the enemy at Bull Run, most of the men in the 4th voted to return home.

Bolton later recalled that he had come to the conclusion that the war would last longer than three months even before his first term of service had expired. As soon as he returned home to Norristown, Captain Bolton began recruiting a company for the three years' service. This new organization became Company A, 51st Pennsylvania Volunteer Infantry, again led by Hartranft.

Bolton served in the 51st until the regiment was mustered out of service in July 1865. He was twice wounded. At Antietam, a bullet hit him in the face, passed through both cheeks, fractured his jaw, and cut his tongue. Bolton recuperated and returned to duty as major of the regiment, then was promoted to colonel in June 1864. On July 30, 1864, during the fighting at the Crater, an iron ball from a spherical shell hit him in the same place, but passed under the jawbone and lodged behind it. Surgeons were unable to locate it, but during a fit of coughing seventeen years later, the ball dropped into Bolton's hand.

Following the war, Bolton and his brother John started a wallpaper business that remained in the two brothers' hands until Colonel Bolton sold it in 1882. The previous year, Governor Hartranft had appointed him a customs house inspector in Philadelphia. Bolton held this position until the administration changed in 1886; he was a Republican and lost the job. After a year's unemployment, Bolton became a watchman at the grand depot of John Wanamaker's, then was elevated to Special Officer at the depot until he resigned in October 1889. At this time, he was appointed a customs inspector in Philadelphia by Collector Thomas V. Cooper. In December 1894, Bolton was appointed a U.S. Storekeeper and stationed at Spreckel's Bonded Warehouse in Philadelphia. Until his death on August 2, 1906, Bolton served in this capacity at other warehouses in Philadelphia.

During the war, the Montgomery County Republicans nominated Bolton for Clerk of County Courts. Bolton learned of this while home on a leave of absence and was influenced to remain in the contest even though his opposition was stronger. He was defeated. In the fall of 1865, he was nominated for County Treasurer but suffered another defeat; in 1867 he lost the race for County Sheriff.

On February 25, 1868, Bolton married Emma Rupert of Columbia County. The couple was on their honeymoon when the man who had defeated him as sheriff died suddenly and Governor John W. Geary appointed Bolton to fill out the term. Bolton's remaining political career consisted of terms as a member of the Town Council of Norristown and city Burgess, coupled with an 1878 defeat in a contest for state legislator from Norristown.

Mr. and Mrs. Bolton had six children, only one of whom, Mary, survived until adulthood. Mrs. Bolton died on May 26, 1897. The couple and their children were all buried in Riverside Cemetery in Norristown.

Bolton reentered military service in September 1869, when he was commissioned captain of the Bolton Guards. Two years later, Governor Geary commissioned him colonel of the 16th Pennsylvania Infantry Regiment. In 1873, Governor Hartranft appointed him a major general in the National Guard of Pennsylvania. Bolton was placed in command of the Second Division, composed of units from Bucks, Montgomery, and Delaware counties. The division was reorganized in 1874 to include units from Montgomery, Bucks, Berks, Lehigh, and Northampton. Bolton held this rank until his commission expired in 1878.

The veteran was also interested in his Civil War comrades. He became a charter member of the Grand Army of the Republic Post in Norristown which became the General Zook Post 11. He was its commander for a time and was a delegate to several national conventions. He organized posts in Conshohocken and Pottstown, and was voted a member of the prestigious Post 2 in Philadelphia. Bolton was also elected to the Union Veteran Legion and attended some of its national conventions.

In September 1880, the survivors of the 51st Pennsylvania organized their first annual reunion and elected Colonel Bolton president of the association for its first three years. On February 5, 1890, Bolton was elected a Companion of the First Class of the Military Order of the Loyal Legion of the United States, Commandery of Pennsylvania. This veterans' organization restricted its membership to those who had participated in the Civil War as Union officers.

Bolton also was a member of two Pennsylvania commissions organized to supervise the acquisition of land and erect monuments on the Antietam battlefield. The first commission was organized by Governor Robert E. Pattison in 1894 and the second by Governor Samuel W. Pennypacker in 1903.

At some point after the war, Bolton took his wartime diaries and began to recopy them, adding orders and reports received during the conflict. He filled two ledger-sized volumes of over twelve hundred pages with his handwriting. His daily chronicle included the services of both the 4th and 51st Pennsylvania regiments. Bolton added a family and personal history, then followed the daily log with transcriptions of 51st Pennsylvania soldier letters published by Norristown newspapers and miscellaneous material pertaining to the war and the 51st regiment. He also included a detailed regimental roster of the 51st.

Following Bolton's death, these ledger books were acquired by the Pennsylvania Commandery of MOLLUS and today are still owned by the Civil War Library and Museum at 1805 Pine Street in Philadelphia. I discovered the Bolton "War Journal" several years ago while researching my doctoral dissertation, General Burnside's 1862 North Carolina Campaign. Since that time, the library allowed me to borrow the books so that I could transcribe the entire journal section. I have deposited a complete transcription of this section of Bolton's journal in the library for use by patrons.

I first transcribed Bolton's manuscript exactly as he wrote it. I next divided the manuscript into campaign chapters and prefaced each with a brief explanatory paragraph. Then, I broke the longer daily entries into paragraphs for ease of reading. I also standardized capitalization and added commas where necessary. Footnotes provide background on people, places, and terms, as well as identifying Bolton's sources for some passages. I have rarely used [sic] after misspelled or misused words; [sic] has been used only when I felt it was necessary for understanding. In many cases, I have corrected Bolton's spelling of personal names, indicating at times when he consistently used an alternate spelling.

When reworking his diary, Bolton made liberal use of the *Official Records*. I have deleted most of his quotes and paraphrases from the *Official Records* when I felt such material was extraneous and did not pertain directly to the 51st Pennsylvania and its daily operations. Bolton was not an admirer of Generals Irvin McDowell and George B. McClellan; I have also deleted much of his criticism of these two generals. Bolton also used Thomas Parker's regimental history; the notes indicate when he did so, and when he repeated mistakes that Parker had made.

Bolton added a lengthy regimental roster to his journal. I have used Bolton's notations from this roster to upgrade his casualty listings for the battles and engagements in which the 51st participated. Usually, Bolton's list of casualties in his journal failed to match those included in the official lists of casualties; thus I used his roster to correct his initial listings. I have used different abbreviations than Bolton did for ranks of those listing in the casualties in order to show where my corrected lists appear. Also, the names followed by an asterisk (*) for the June 18, 1864, Petersburg casualty list were names provided by Bolton as a supplement of casualties for the entire June 15-18 period. I was not able to break the entire list of wounded into specific days and thus arbitrarily placed these names under the June 18 heading.

A number of people aided me in this project. Albert M. Gambone provided contacts for me at the Historical Society of Montgomery County and helped with my contact with General Hartranft's descendants. Judith A. Meier of the Historical Society of Montgomery County provided background on area citizens mentioned by Bolton and provided other research help. Ronn Palm graciously allowed me to use his numerous images of 51st Pennsylvania soldiers. The United States Army Military History Institute also granted me permission to use photos from its archives. Robert T. Lyon also provided an image from his collection of Civil War photographs. Brian Pohanka provided background material on the duties of regimental officers.

Dr. Richard A. Sauers
June 1999

Abbreviations

A.A.A. Gen.	Acting Assistant Adjutant General
A.A.I.G.	Acting Assistant Inspector General
A.A.Q.M.	Acting Assistant Quartermaster
A.C.	Army Corps
A.C.S.	Assistant Commissary of Subsistence
Adj.	Adjutant
Art, Arty.	Artillery
Asst.	Assistant
Brig. Gen.	Brigadier General
Bty	Battery
Btys	Batteries
Capt.	Captain
Cav	Cavalry
Co.	Company
Cos.	Companies
Col.	Colonel
Com. Sgt.	Commissary Sergeant
Corpl.	Corporal
Cpl.	Corporal, editor's use
G.O.	General Orders
Gen., Genl.	General
Hd. Qrs.	Headquarters
Hvy	Heavy
Inst.	Instant
Lieut.	Lieutenant
Lt. Col.	Lieutenant Colonel
Maj. Gen.	Major General
Mus.	Musician
No.	Number
Priv., Prv.	Private
Pro. Mar.	Provost Marshall
P.V.	Pennsylvania Volunteers
P.V.V.	Pennsylvania Veteran Volunteers
Pvt.	Private, editor's use
Q.M.	Quartermaster
Q.M.S.	Quartermaster Sergeant
Serg. Maj.	Sergeant Major
Sergt.	Sergeant
Sgt.	Sergeant, editor's use
S.O.	Special Orders
Surg.	Surgeon
USCT	United States Colored Troops

Chapter 1

The 4th Pennsylvania

April 20–July 28, 1861

On April 15, 1861, President Abraham Lincoln issued a call for 75,000 three-month militia to suppress the rebellion. By the end of April, the Commonwealth of Pennsylvania had raised and equipped almost 21,000 eager volunteers. The 4th Pennsylvania, led by Colonel John F. Hartranft, joined Brigadier General Irvin McDowell's army in Washington. McDowell was not anxious to engage the Southern troops confronting him until his own volunteers were better trained. However, faced with the expiration of enlistment of most of his soldiers, McDowell was forced to attack. As the Union army marched toward Manassas, the 4th's enlistment expired on July 20; patriotic speeches and pleas failed to coerce the rank and file to remain for the battle. Colonel Hartranft and another officer remained behind as volunteer aides; the rest of the 4th marched toward Washington while their comrades fought at Bull Run.

Apr 20—Left Norristown for Harrisburg Pa. as Captain of Company A, one-hundred and fifteen men (115). Arrived in Harrisburg at 2 1/2 o'clock P.M., and proceeded at once to the camp ground at the Fairground which was afterwards known as Camp Curtin. The regiment was known as the 4th Regiment Volunteer State Militia, and was organized from the First Regiment, Second Brigade, 2d Division, State Militia.

A meeting had been held in Norristown on the evening of April 16th in the Odd Fellows Hall, and the result was, on the following day, the 17th, the services of the regiment was tendered to Gov. A. G. Curtin, for the term of three months, and on this day with about six-hundred (600) officers and men we left Norristown. On the morning of our departure, the ladies of the town, through Judge Daniel M. Smyser, presented the regiment with a stand of colors, in front of the Court House, before a dense and weeping assembly.[1]

I had been thrown out of employment in October 1860, by my action with the taking of a cannon from the Wide Awakes and in the meantime from October 1860 to April 20th, 1861,

---

1. Judge Daniel M. Smyser was president judge of the Seventh Judicial District. The flags presented to the regiment consisted of a 33-star national color and a blue regimental color painted with the state coat of arms.

had had but four weeks employment, and consequently I was bankrupt. Elected Captain, just two days before, unexpectedly, all the other officers resigning but myself. My uniform had to be remodeled to suit my new grade, and otherwise fitting myself out for a three months campaign, and not one cent in my pocket, to do it with, made matters look very serious with me, but I was bound to go, so I ordered what was necessary and trusted in God for the result.

The evening before I left home (April 19th) while drilling the company the last time before our departure from our Armory in the Humane Engine House, and as I was about to dismiss the company with the order to meet early next morning for our departure for the seat of war, Mr. E. B. Moore steped [sic] forward and placed a sum of money in my hands. It turned out to be forty-eight dollars ($48.00). It was a God send. Knowing that I was embarking in a dangerous expedition, and my brother Joe with me in the same racket, and my father and mother in advance ages, I gave the whole amount to them.

I consequently left my home on that Saturday morning without one cent of money in my pocket, or a change of clothes to my back. All I took with me was my honor, my sword and the many kind wishes of dear friends. After leaving the front of the Court House where the flags were presented, and on marching down Main Street, and in passing Lawyer Bonsall's[2] law office, he kindly placed a banknote in my hands, and further on down the street on our way to Bridgeport, Daniel Longaker also did the same thing. I was also presented with a Bible on marching down the street by Mr. Wm. Shives, and carried it with me in my trunk through the three-months and three-years service, and have it still. On reaching Bridgeport this money, together with my gold watch, I handed to my brother John, who took them home to my mother.

The following is the roster of the companies that left town on this day:

Captain Wm. J. Bolton	Co. A	115 men
Captain Rob. E. Faylor	Co. B	76 men
Captain John R. Brooke	Co. C	77 men
Captain R. T. Schall	Co. D	77 men
Captain Geo. Amey	Co. E	77 men
Captain Wm. Allabaugh	Co. I	78 men
Captain Walter H. Cook	Co. K	76 men

Company C belonged to Pottstown and joined us at that point. During the day, three more companies were added to our strength, which made a regiment of ten companies as follows:

Captain Geo. Dunn	Co. F	78 men
Captain John W. Chamberlin	Co. G	76 men
Captain Austin B. Snyder	Co. H	77 men

Company F was from Delaware, Company G from Union, and Company H from Centre, counties.

Apr 21—Today we elected regimental officers and were as follows:

Colonel John F. Hartranft	Norristown
Lt. Col. Edward Schall	Norristown
Major Edwin Schall	Norristown
Adj. Charles Hunsicker, Appointed	Norristown

---

2. Henry C. Bonsall.

Q.M. Wm. H. Yerkes	Norristown
Surg. James B. Dunlap	Norristown
Asst. Surg. Chas. W. Rodgers	Norristown
Chaplain T. W. McDaniels	Doylestown
Serg. Maj. Martin Malony, Appt.	Norristown
Q.M.S. Wm. M. Mintzer	Pottstown
Drum Major Geo. W. Arnold	Norristown

Regimental Band

D. H. Stubblebine, Leader	James Longan
Edmund Smith	Jacob F. Gauger
Alfred Calwell	Alpheus Mixell
Samuel Weis	John Peterman
George Evans	Andrew Peterman
Daniel Ruck	Hammond Winters
Ephraim Hale	William Gibson

During the day the regiment was mustered into the State service, and later on into the United States service as a Volunteer regiment. We were all engaged in drilling our companies all day.

During the afternoon we received marching orders, and left Camp Curtin at 7 o'clock P.M. and took the cars for Philada. arriving there at Broad & Prime [present-day Washington Avenue] at 12 o'clock in the morning. We had not been provided with haversacks or canteens, but were each given a blanket which was rolled up and strung over our shoulders. We were all very hungry, and the boys discovered barrels of dried beef cut into pieces of about four inches square (they all declared it to be horseflesh) which they appropriated to their use. We all had very sore mouths the next morning.

While we were at Harrisburg, we all slept in sheep pens, on heaps of straw. This was a great change from the soft beds we had just left. On leaving camp, our pockets were filled with crackers so hard that they could not be broken by ordinary means, the teeth, so other means were used.

We were crowded in freight cars, without seats, but on arriving at Philada. It was much worse. Marching to the P.W. & B.R.R.[3] and there lay down on the platforms, and in the baggage rooms and other places, and slept until 4 1/2 o'clock in the morning.

When we left Norristown, we all carried the Minie rifle musket, a good arm, but the state had no ammunition on hand to suit that class of guns, so we left them in the sheep pens, and were given old condemned Harper Ferry muskets which had once been flintlocks. It was very discouraging, but this was no time to rebel. On arriving at Philada. we were ordered by Genl. Patterson[4] to report to Col. [Charles P.] Dare of the 23d Regiment, and taking one (1) company of his own, and the 4th Regiment, at 4 1/2 o'clock in the morning, proceeded by rail to Perryville, Maryland, and took possession of the town, thus saving the place from falling into the hands of the rebels. On passing through Wilmington, the citizens furnished us all with good substantial food, which we all thought very kind. Wrote a letter home to my mother.

---

3. Philadelphia, Wilmington & Baltimore Railroad, with station at Broad Street and Washington Avenue.

4. Major General Robert Patterson commanded the Department of Pennsylvania.

Apr 22—My company occupied quarters in a shed and I myself had quarters on board of the Steamer *John Schiver*. We all drilled our companies for several hours. Had religious service on board the Steamer led by John Moore, a private of my company at his request. Camp alarmed during the night (to try us, we afterwards found out). My voice gave out from constant drilling. Could not speake above a whisper.

Private Wm. Rapine of Company B was shot and killed on the spot by Col. Dare under very sad circumstances. We all hold that Dare was not justifiable in doing what he did. Rapine was a sentinel, and on duty, with orders. This officer attempted to pass. Rapine challenged him. The challenge was unheeded. Rapine fired, which he had a right to do. Dare returned the fire and killed Rapine on the spot. Wm. S. Rapine was a good soldier, and was only doing his duty as a sentinel when he was shot down. Had he lived, he would have made his mark in the service.

None of us had much to eat during the day, except the horseflesh, so called, captured at Broad and Prime. Wrote a letter home to my sister.

Apr 23—During the day took up new quarters for my company. All hands drilling their companies for several hours. My voice very bad, and a very sore throat. Rations very scarce. Private William Biggs Company I committed suicide in an out-of-away place along the river by shooting himself. His body was sent to Norristown. Can see the rebel flag flying across the river at Havre-de-Grace, Md.

Apr 24—Left Perryville late in the afternoon on board of the steamer *Annapolis* with the right wing of the regiment, Companies A, C, D, F and I. In going up the river at night, which was very dark, we were hailed by the commander of the frigate *Constitution*, he thinking that we might be the enemy immediately opened his Port-Holes, and ordered his men to mand the guns. We could hear his command distinctly ringing in the stillness of the night. He demanded to know who we were. Dr. Dunlap replied "Right wing of the 4th Regiment Penna. Vols. bound for Annapolis." We were allowed to proceed, but might have been blown to pieces, as we had not signaled the Frigate, although we had seen her lights, an oversight of the commander of the Steamer *Annapolis*. It was a very stormy night. Prayer meeting on board, conducted by John Moore. Arrived in Annapolis at 2 o'clock in the morning.

Apr 25—Disembarked during the day and were assigned quarters in the magazine of the Naval Grounds, an octagonal shape. Its walls were pierced with port-holes at intervals of six feet. Cannon were in position on the side commanding the river. We were on the top floor and the magazine under us contained 3,000 pounds of powder. While on the river, and before landing, a great many of the boys took the Magazine for a big bake oven. Rations became more plenty here, and we felt more like men, and made up for lost time. Distributed through the grounds were to be seen a large number of old Mexican guns, captured as we were told from the Mexican war. The guns were covered with representations of live heads, horses and warriors, &c. They were a sight for us all, not having seen such a sight before. The regiment was ordered to report to Major General Benjamin F. Butler, who was in command. Drilled our companies for several hours. At the request of Moore, prayer meeting was held during the evening, which were always well attended.

Apr 26—Arose very early in the morning and took a stroll through the grounds looking at the sights. Drilled my company for four hours. Wrote a letter to my sister. The usual prayer meeting held by Moore.

Apr 27—Drilled my company for about five hours. Took a stroll through the grounds and buildings. Moore held his usual prayer meeting during the evening. Having some trouble with Geo. De Haven. Disposed to be insubordinet.

Apr 28—Drilled my company for several hours. Strolled through the grounds as usual. Clothing arrived for us, and they are all kinds of fits. Moore has his usual prayer meeting. Wrote a few letters home.

Apr 29—Drilled my company as usual. Received a number of letters from friends at home. Moore held his usual prayer meeting. Long roll beat during the night, and the whole regiment turned out under arms in a very short time and formed line. Afterwards learned it was a trick of Butler to try the men.

Apr 30—Drilled my company for several hours and wrote several letters home. The men are all impromptu tailors altering their clothes to make them fit.

May 1—Appointed officer of the Guard for the next twenty-four hours, and reported to Genl. Butler for orders.[5] Was up all night. Wrote several letters to friends. Usual prayer meeting by Moore. De Haven still very insubordinet, and inclined to make trouble.

May 2—Slept a good part of the day. Drilled my company several hours. Compelled to place De Haven in irons. Usual prayer meeting in the evening.

May 3—Drilled my company for several hours. Regimental drill in the afternoon. Large details made from the regiment to unload commissary stores, and to repair the railroad. Received a letter from my sister and from several friends from home.

May 4—Companies all drilling in the morning and afternoon. Usual details for unloading commissary stores and repairing railroad. Received a number of newspapers from home. Usual prayer meetings.

May 5—Engaged all day in issuing the new uniforms, shoes, caps &c. to the company. Gray pants, blue blouses and caps. All hands looking very grotesque in their ill fitting clothes, and quite all of the men had to have their pants and blouses, also their caps altered. Fortunately I had a number of tailors in the company, and I put them to good work, and they did it very willingly, and the men in a day or two looked more presentable. Wrote a letter home to my sister. During the day changed my company quarters from the magazine to one of the brick school buildings within the Naval grounds. Usual prayer meeting in the evening.

May 6—Drilled my company in the morning and afternoon for several hours, and they are getting along very well. Wrote a letter to my sister. A detail made from the company to unload commissary stores.

May 7—Paid a visit to the city on a pass given me by Genl. Butler. Visited the Capitol building and saw everything of note. Changed our quarters.

May 8—In pursuance to orders, the regiment broke camp and left Annapolis for Washington about 12 o'clock M. All along the whole route sentinels were stationed. Arrived in Washington about 6 1/2 o'clock P.M. A great crowd was at the depot to meet us expecting to find a splendid equipped regiment, but they were disappointed. All our dirty clothes bundled up in our dirty white blankets (once white) strapped on our backs, as we had no knapsacks. We were indeed a sorry set of looking objects, and a great deal of fun was poked at us as we marched up Pennsylvania Avenue. There were friend and foe on the side walks, but we kept our temper, knowing that if we should be attacked, we had our guns, and plenty of ammunition, and the hearts and

5. Bolton here referred to his assignment as Officer of the Day. Among other things, the Officer of the Day was responsible for maintaining a proper line of pickets around a camp. For details, see United States War Department, *Revised Regulations for the Army of the United States, 1861* (Philadelphia: J. G. L. Brown, Printer, 1861; reprint edition, Gettysburg: Civil War Times Illustrated, 1974), 62-65, 84-87.

the courage to use them should it be required, but all passed off well. My company, and Company F Captain Dunn, were quartered in a Church (First Congregational Church) on Seventh Street. The other eight companies were quartered in the Assembly buildings closeby.

May 9—Received a number of letters from home from old friends. Drill my company in the church yard. Rations plentiful and of the best kind. Wrote a few letters home.

May 10—Drilled my company in the morning and afternoon for several hours. The close confinement in the crowded quarters we had is begining to show bad results. Many of my men are sick.

May 11—Drilled my company in the morning and afternoon in the church yard. Paid a visit to the Smithsonian Institute, also to the Washington Monument. Have had a great deal of trouble with Geo. De Haven again. Am compelled to put him in irons several times a day. He has threaten to shoot me on several occassions, but do not fear him.

May 12—Drilled my company morning and afternoon. Wrote letters to my sister and brother.

May 13—Drilled my company morning and afternoon. Read the Articles of War to the company.[6]

May 14—Drilled my company morning and afternoon. Read the Articles of War to the company.

May 15—Drilled my company morning and afternoon. Received a letter from my sister, and from several Norristown friends.

May 16—Regimental drill on Penna. Avenue. Received some papers from Norristown. Was taken a little sick.

May 17—Was not very well all day.

May 18—Drilled my company and wrote several letters to friends in Norristown.

May 19—Rained all day. Paid a visit to the Old Capitol Prison.

May 20—No drilling to day. The men all engaged in writing letters and visiting notable places about the city.

May 21—Drilled my company for several hours. By an invitation of the Secretary of State, William H. Seward, all the Officers of the regiment attended a levee given by him at his residence in Washington. We all had a good time, and returned to our quarters late in the evening.

May 22—Paraded my company to the banks of the Potomac River, near the Washington Monument, for the purpose of bathing.

May 23—Drilled my company for several hours. Received a large package towels &c. from a Mr. Burr, a citizen of Washington, who took a great interest in myself and company. Wrote a letter to my sister.

May 24—The regiment left their quarters in Washington, and marched a few miles to the outskirts of the city, near Bladensburg, and went into camp, naming it Camp Montgomery. The camp was on high elevated ground, and the drainage and outlook splendid, as we could see for miles around.

May 25—Drilled my company for several hours. Received a letter from my new made friend Burr, who kindly invited me to his house on "I" street.

May 26—Drilled my company for several hours. Wrote a letter to my sister, and several friends. Moore had his usual prayer meeting in the company street.

---

6. The Articles of War covered topics such as the conduct of officers, furloughs, punishment, and grievances. See *Revised Army Regulations, 1861*, 499-516, for a complete listing of all 101 articles.

May 27—Drilled my company morning and afternoon. During the day, I was presented with a number of Haverlocks [sic] for my men, by a citizen of Washington.[7]

May 28—Drilled my company as usual. Received a letter from my sister, and from a number of other friends. Some friend sent me a package of smoking tobacco, and some eggs, and papers. Called on my friend Burr on "I" street, and took dinner with him.

May 29—Drilled my company as usual. Was invited, and took dinner with Geo. Randall and his father at Willards Hotel.

May 30—Was in command of the camp, as all the field officers were absent. Wrote a letter to my sister, and to other friends. Was presented with two one dollar gold pieces by my friend Wm. H. Slingluff of Norristown.[8]

May 31—Drilled my company as usual. Received and wrote several letters. Genl. Adam Slemmer of the Regular Army paid our camp a visit.[9]

Jun 1—Drilled my company as usual. Received a number of articles from a Mr. Stickney living at Kendell Green just back of our camp, who formed a great friendship for me. Paid a visit to Washington.

Jun 2—Was detailed as Officer of the Day, to serve twenty-four hours. Company drilled by Lieut. Bolton.

Jun 3—Drilled my company as usual. About dark, received orders to have my company to fall in and to await orders. Ordered to go on picket about three miles out from camp on the Bladensburg road. Slept on the ground all night when we had a chance to sleep. Our principal duty was to watch and guard a certain house. Had a good mess of strawberries and cream, out in the patch picked just from the vines.

Jun 4—Returned to camp about 6 o'clock in the morning. Received letters from my sister and brother. Some kind friend sent me a box of eggs.

Jun 5—Had company drill and inspection. Wrote letters to my sister and brother.

Jun 6—Drilled my company as usual. Received and wrote several letters.

Jun 7—Company drill and inspection.

Jun 8—Company drill. In the evening was ordered out with my company to go several miles in the country to guard a certain cross-road.

Jun 9—Returned to camp early in the morning. Company drill in the afternoon.

---

7. Havelocks were cloth (cotton or canvas) hat covers which were draped over the neck and shoulders in an effort to ward off sunstroke. They could be worn either over or under the kepi or forage hat. Havelocks were popular during the early days of the war until soldiers found that they also cut off air circulation. Perhaps the most widespread popular notion of havelocks comes from their use by the French Foreign Legion.

8. William H. Slingluff was a long-time employee of the Montgomery Bank (president of it in 1868) and a founder of the Norristown Water Company. Although originally a Whig, Slingluff joined the Democratic Party in 1860; he also served on the local school board and borough council.

9. Adam J. Slemmer, a Montgomery County native, was an 1850 West Point graduate. When Florida withdrew from the Union, Slemmer moved his company of the 1st U. S. Artillery to Fort Pickens, across the bay from Pensacola, which he held until reinforced. Slemmer was promoted to major of the new 16th U. S. Infantry on May 20. [Ezra J. Warner, *Generals in Blue* (Baton Rouge: Louisiana State University Press, 1964), 450-1.]

Jun 10—Company drill. Was detailed as Officer of the Day, for twenty-four hours. Received a letter from Mrs. Benjamin E. Chain of Norristown.[10]

Jun 11—Company drill. Received and sent several letters.

Jun 12—Company drill and inspection. Was ordered out on picket to guard a certain cross-road. During the night arrested a suspicious looking man and sent him under guard to camp.

Jun 13—Company drill. Received a lot of red shirts and gum blankets, and six bottles of whiskey. By an invitation, took dinner with Mr. Stickney at Kendell Green.

Jun 14—Company drill. Wrote a letter to my brother. Regimental Band arrived.

Jun 15—Company drill and inspection. Received a lot of news-papers from Norristown.

Jun 16—Company drill and inspection.

Jun 17—Company drill. Received a number of letters. Paraded with the regiment to Washington to be reviewed by the President.

Jun 18—Broke camp at Camp Montgomery and marched through Washington to the Long Bridge. Left camp at 2 o'clock P.M. and after a long and tedious march of fourteen miles, passed through Alexandria, Va., and at 9 o'clock P.M. came to a halt and went into bivouac, one and half miles west of Alexandria, on ground known as Shooters Hill, which was surrounded by a high pannel fence and the ground strewn with new mown grass. It took twenty-eight army wagons to move our camp baggage. We were very tired and slept well on our new bed of grass.

In passing out King street Alexandria, the Marshall House, a hotel kept by John S. Jackson was pointed out to us as the place where Col. E. E. Ellsworth, commanding the New York Fire Zouaves, was killed by Jackson, and he in turn was killed by Private Brownell of the Zouaves on May 24/61, on the occassion of Ellsworth entering the town. Great indignation was indulged in by the men, and one word from the officers, the house would have been gutted. Ellsworth had cut down a rebel flag that floated from a staff on the building, which we could plainly see from Washington.

Jun 19—Pitched our tents this morning. Fence, post, grass and every thing else in the shape of boards were appropriated for beds and flooring, and we soon had a splendid camp, and a fine view, overlooking Alexandria and Washington. During the day orders were issued naming our new home, Camp Hale. To the south of us was Fort Ellsworth, a very strong and formidable fort. Close by us were encamped the Ellsworth Zouaves, 5th Mass., 5th Penna., and 1st Mich. Received a new military coat from home to-day.

Jun 20—Detailed as Officer of the Day. Had charge of the surrounding camp. Wrote a letter to Mrs. Benj. E. Chain.

Jun 21—Off of duty all day. Wrote and received several letters. Received some papers from Norristown.

Jun 22—Off of duty all day. Received a number of letters. Received a lot of papers from John Wood, M. C. member of Congress from our district.[11] Private Geo. M. Randall of my company discharged to receive a Lieut. commission in the United States Regular Army, through Senator John P. Hale.[12]

---

10. Benjamin E. Chain was a district attorney from Norristown.

11. John Wood was a Democratic congressman representing the Fifth District.

12. George M. Randall entered the 4th U. S. Infantry as a 1st Lieutenant. In August 1864, he was commissioned a major in the 14th New York Heavy Artillery, then promoted to lieutenant colonel in 1865. [Frederick Phisterer, *New York in the War of the Rebellion 1861 to 1865*, 5 volumes (Albany: J. B. Lyon Company, 1912), 2:1494.]

Jun 23—Company drill, morning and afternoon. Received and wrote several letters.

Jun 24—Company drill, morning and afternoon.

Jun 25—Company drill, morning and afternoon. Received a letter and papers from sister.

Jun 26—Company drill and inspection.

Jun 27—Detailed as Officer of the Day. The regiment made a parade to Alexandria. Received a letter from my brother.

Jun 28—Company and regimental drill. Received a letter from Geo. M. Randall, now of the Regular Army. In the evening myself and company were sent out on picket to Clouds Mills, several miles from camp, and on the pike leading to Centreville. We barricaded the road with flour barrels filled with sand and stones, and laid behind them all night in the rain. We imagined that every bush and tree was a rebel. Randall is 2d Lieut., 4th U.S. Infantry.

Jun 29—Returned to camp in the morning. Company and regimental drills, and dress parade in the evening. Answered some letters.

Jun 30—Our pickets under command of Lieut. McClennan were attacted during the night. Sergt. Haines of the rebel army was killed, and his body was brought into camp in a cart. We had one man killed Thomas Murray of Company E and one man wounded Chas. H. Rhumer of Company E. Wrote a letter to my sister, and to several other persons.[13]

Jul 1—Drilled my company, and had regimental drill, and dress parade in the evening.

Jul 2—Drilled my company. Regimental drill in the afternoon and dress parade in the evening. Received some papers.

Jul 3—Drilled my company. Regimental drill and dress parade. Received some letters.

Jul 4—Dress parade in the evening. Received a letter from Geo. M. Randall.

Jul 5—Drilled my company in the skirmish drill. Dress parade in the evening.

Jul 6—Detailed as Officer of the Day.

Jul 7—Company and regimental drills. Dress parade in the evening.

Jul 8—Company and regimental drills. Dress parade in the evening.

Jul 9—Company and regimental drills, and dress parade. Wrote letters to Randall and to my brother.

Jul 10—Company and regimental drills, and dress parade. Went to the city of Washington and received a check from Paymaster David Taggart for $189.90 and drew the money. Received several letters. In the evening received a visit from the daughter of Jackson of the Marshall House fame, in regard to a dog belonging to the family, said to be harbored in my company.

Jul 11—Company and regimental drills, and dress parade. Companys of the regiment all paid to-day by Major David Taggart. During the day received orders to move my company, and to occupy Fort Ellsworth.[14]

Jul 12—Spent the day very pleasantly. Gave Col. Hartranft $160.00 to place in the Montgomery County Bank to my credit.

---

13. Lieutenant M. Robert McClennan was from Company B. Bates wrote that the wounded man was Llewelyn Rhumer, not Charles H. Rhumer. [Samuel P. Bates, *History of Pennsylvania Volunteers, 1861-5,* 5, volumes (Harrisburg: B. Singerly, 1869-71), 1:41.

14. Fort Ellsworth was located on the site now occupied by the George Washington Masonic National Memorial. [Benjamin F. Cooling and Walton H. Owen, *Mr. Lincoln's Forts* (Shippensburg, PA: White Mane Publishing Company, 1988), 38.

Jul 13—Detailed as Officer of the Day for the garrison of the fort. The fort contains 17 guns and 255 men to mand them. Total garrison 843 men.

Jul 14—Drilled my company. Wrote and received several letters.

Jul 15—Company drill. Late in the afternoon received orders to vacate the fort, and to report with my company to the old camp and rejoin the regiment.

Jul 16—Detailed as Officer of the Day. During the day received orders to march. Leaving all of our baggage, including knapsacks and overcoats, but retaining our blankets and haversacks and very little in them, we started on our march, and after a tedious march of fourteen miles went into bivouac late at night on the banks of the Pohick Creek, and laid on the ground all night.

The camp fires of the different regiments looked grand, as far as the eye could reach they could be seen. Our regiment was assigned to the 1st Brigade, 3d Division, McDowell's Army. The division was commanded by Genl. S. P. Heintzelman, and the Brigade by Genl. Wm. B. Franklin. The brigade consisted of the following:

> 5th Mass.—Col. [Samuel C.] Lawrence
> 11th Mass.—Col. [George] Clark
> 1st Minn.—Col. [Willis A.] Gorman
> 4th Penna.—Col. [John F.] Hartranft.
> Company I, 4th U. S. Artillery

The 5th Regiment Penna. Vols. also belonged to our brigade but were detached, and remained at Alexandria to garrison that place.

Jul 17—Left our bivouac early in the morning and marched nearly all day, reaching Sangster's Station late in the afternoon. The county Poor House was located here, and we found ourselves among a lot of crazy people, many of them negroes. We had very little to eat. Some of the colored cooks made us some corn daggers, but they were made without salt. Some of the boys caught a big rooster, and soon dispatched him, and was very soon in the pot. He must have been ten years old, for we could hardly eat him. Besides we had no salt to cook him with.

Before we had finished him, my company was ordered to go out on picket that night, about two miles from camp in a very lonely place. A guide was sent with me, but the miles seemed to be very long and I naturally became very anxious, and kept my eye fixed on him. We at last reached the place. It was now quite dark, and had but little time to reconnoiter the surroundings, but I lost no time, and soon had my pickets and vedettes posted keeping a reserve with me, establishing my headquarters in front of the mansion under a big tree. I did not trust the guide, and much less the owner of the mansion and I therefore kept them in view.

The owner of the mansion professed to be very hospitable and urged me very often to take one of his rooms and go to bed, but I declined knowing that it would not be proper for me to do so. I remained awake the whole night and visited the pickets very often. During the night he brought out a smoked ham, and we ate it raw with a relish. He also gave us plenty of milk. The time seemed very long, but all things ended well with us.

Jul 18—Returned to camp at the Poor House about daylight, and without getting anything to eat, took up our line of march. The road we were on intersected with the Warrenton Turnpike and on reaching that point, we waited there for the passage of Hunter's division. It having passed, we again moved forward, and turned from the pike just beyond Cub Run and reached Bull Run at Sudley's Stream early in the afternoon, with nothing in our haversacks, and no place to get something to eat.

Laid on the ground all night in the rain. The sight that night was grand. Thousands of camp fires could be seen as far as the eye could reach. The water we had to drink was hardly fit to bathe in, much less to drink, and when daylight dawn upon us, we were surprised when we looked at the place we had used our water from during the night. We were worn out, from the loss of sleep and for something to eat, and we were a very sorry looking crowd. Heintzelman's Division is now all in bivouac here and is made up of three brigades, commanded by Cols. Willcox, Franklin, and Howard, and its strength is 9,500 men.[15]

Jul 19—Remained in bivouac all day and night near Centreville, and in about the same condition as the day before, nothing to eat.

Jul 20—Laid in bivouac all day and night near Centreville with nothing to eat. The term of the enlistment of the regiment expired to-day. General McDowell has made an appeal in a Special Order, asking the regiment to remain a few days longer, and pledgeing that the time of muster-out of service should not exceed two (2) weeks. Difference of opinion prevailed throughout the whole regiment, but there were no concert of action. Many were willing to remain, I among the number.

The fact of the matter was, the men had been badly used. They had a right to their discharge. Many had already made provisions to reenlist in the service after a short stay at home. I myself had a part of a company already enlisted for the new call of three years men. The General seeing that nothing could be done, in Special Orders, ordered the regiment to retire to their old camp to report to General Runyon to be mustered-out.[16] General McDowell very unjustly censured the regiment for a part of his failure in his official report. A scape-goat had to be had, and this regiment and battery formed the food for it. The rebels were as badly whipped as our army was, but he did not know it and had another general officer been in command other than him, results would have turned out far different with the Union Army. A great many of his army that did remain were in Alexandria as soon as we were, and very many of them were regulars.[17]

Col. John F. Hartranft remained behind and was assigned to Franklin's brigade as a volunteer aide-de-camp, and was complimented for his services by that officer. Captain Walter H. Cook of Company K remained behind and was in Hunter's division as a volunteer aide-de-camp, and was also complimented by that officer for his services.[18]

The following is a true copy of McDowell's S.O. to the regiment:

---

15. Colonel Samuel P. Heintzelman's Third Division was composed of brigades led by Colonels William B. Franklin, Orlando B. Willcox, and Oliver O. Howard.

16. Brigadier General Theodore Runyon commanded McDowell's Fourth Division, which covered Washington.

17. For the mention of the 4th Pennsylvania in McDowell's report, see United States War Department, *The War of the Rebellion: A Compilation of the Official Records of the Union and Confederate Armies*, 70 volumes in 128 parts (Washington: Government Printing Office, 1880-1901), Series 1, Volume 2, 325. Hereafter, all references will be cited as *O.R.*, followed by the appropriate volume and part. Unless noted, all references are to Series 1.

18. Hartranft received a Congressional Medal of Honor for his services at Manassas. The award was made in 1886.

Special Orders	Hdqrs. Dept. Northeastern Va.
No. 37	Centreville July 20, 1861.

The general commanding has learned with regret that the term of service of the Fourth Regiment Pennsylvania Volunteers is about to expire. The services of this regiment have been so important, its good conduct so general, its patience under privations so constant, its state of officering so good, that the departure of the regiment at this time can only be considered an important loss to the Army.

Fully recognizing the right of the regiment to its discharge and payment at the time agreed upon when it was mustered into the service, and determined to carry out literally the agreement of the Government in this respect, the general commanding nevertheless requests the regiment to continue in service a few days longer, pledgeing himself that the postponement of the date of muster out of service shall not exceed two weeks. Such members of the regiment as do not accede to this request will be placed under the command of proper officers to be marched to the rear, mustered out of service, and paid as soon as possible after the expiration of their term of service.

By command of Genl. McDowell:
James B. Fry,
Assistant Adjutant-General.

General McDowell finding that the regiment did not take up with his S.O. later in the day issued another order, ordering the regiment to Alexandria Va., to be mustered-out. The following is the true copy:

Special Orders	Hdqtrs. Dept. N.E. Va.
No. 39	Centreville July 20 1861.

I. The Fourth Regiment Pennsylvania Volunteers, having completed the period of its enlistment, is hereby honorably discharged from the service of the United States. The regiment will, under the command of the Lieutenant Colonel, take up the march tomorrow for Alexandria, and on its arrival at that place will report to General Runyon to be mustered out of service.

II. Colonel Hartranft, Fourth Regiment Pennsylvania Volunteers, having volunteered his services, is assigned to duty on the staff of Colonel Franklin, commanding brigade.

x x x x x
By order of General McDowell:
James B. Fry,
Assistant Adjutant-General.[19]

Jul 21—The regiment left their bivouac early in the morning under the command of Lieut. Col. Schall, and after a march of twenty-four miles reached Camp Hale late in the afternoon. Found quite a number of letters in camp for me on my return.

---

19. See *O.R.*, volume 2, 745, for both special orders.

Jul 22—The regiment remained in camp all day and rested. During the day they were mustered out of the United States service.

Jul 23—Broke camp and left for home. Marched through Alexandria and arrived during the day in Washington. Left there in the evening. Met my friend Burr at the depot, who was glad to see me.

Jul 24—The regiment arrived in Baltimore in the morning, and left for Harrisburg arriving there about 8 o'clock in the evening, and bivouaced in the Capitol grounds.

Jul 25—Remained in bivouac in the Capitol grounds. Very busy all day in making out muster-out rolls and discharge for the company.

Jul 26—The regiment still in bivouac at the same place. A lawyer kindly let me have the use of his office for my quarters. Still busy in making out muster out rolls and discharges. A very distressing tragedy occurred to-day. Private George Reiff of Company B was mortally wounded today in a melee among some soldiers and citizens, and was carried in the house of a Mrs. Hulmes on North 3d at Harrisburg.

Jul 27—Muster out rolls and discharges all looked over and compared. Regiment mustered out of the State service. I made out to secure a frame building for quarters for my company and moved them into it, and had a good nights rest under cover.

Jul 28—Left Harrisburg during the early morning for Norristown, and arrived in Bridgeport at 3 o'clock A.M., crossed the DeKalb Street bridge to Norristown, and after a short street parade, was drawn up in line in front of the court house, and an address of welcome was delivered by Judge Daniel M. Smyser. It was Sunday morning and the streets were lined with people, who gave us a hearty welcome. Word received of the death of Geo. A. Reiff.

A complete Muster-in roll of Company A, 4th Regiment Pennsylvania Volunteers:

Captain William J. Bolton	Priv. Culp, George
1st Lieut. Joseph K. Bolton	Priv. Deem, John
2d Lieut. William S. Ensley	Priv. Dehaven, Geo. W.
2d Lieut. Abraham L. Ortlip	Priv. Doud, James M.
1st Sergt. George W. Guss	Priv. Earle, William P.
2d Sergt. John A. Wills	Priv. Ellis, Jon. B.
3d Sergt. Thomas B. Garner	Priv. Ely, Jonathan T.
4th Sergt. William T. Roberts	Priv. Ensley, Wm. C.
1st Corpl. Samuel S. Fries	Priv. Feather, Augustus
2d Corpl. George Keen	Priv. Fitzgerald, Chas. H.
3d Corpl. C. Jones Iredell	Priv. Fitzgerald, John P.
4th Corpl. Charles Yost	Priv. Garner, Sylvester
Mus. William A. Lambert	Priv. Gilbert, Theodore
Mus. Samuel G. Doud	Priv. Hartranft, Abr
Priv. Aikens, Samuel	Priv. Holt, Joseph
Priv. Banks, Benjamin	Priv. Jenkins, Major L.
Priv. Bath, David B.	Priv. Johnson, John M.
Priv. Boyer, Edwin	Priv. Jones, John
Priv. Brookes, John	Priv. Jordan, John
Priv. Carpenter, George T.	Priv. Kanause, John

Priv. Kelley, Henry S.

Priv. Kelley, John S.

Priv. Kelley, Thomas

Priv. Kirkbride, Abra. H.

Priv. Knipe, Benjamin F.

Priv. Kulp, George H.

Priv. Lewis, Elijah

Priv. Lightcap, Michael

Priv. Mather, William L.

Priv. Moore, John S.

Priv. Moyer, Joseph R.

Priv. McCoy, William

Priv. McCartney, James

Priv. Nungesser, William B.

Priv. Pugh, Reese

Priv. Randall, George M.

Priv. Reiff, Thomas J.

Priv. Richards, John

Priv. Robbins, Jacob

Priv. Roberts, Robert

Priv. Saylor, James C.

Priv. Saylor, Josiah

Priv. Schrach, Val.

Priv. Selah, Theodore

Priv. Server, Mathias T.

Priv. Shainline, Henry C.

Priv. Shainline, John Y.

Priv. Shainline, Wm. H.

Priv. Shoffner, George W.

Priv. Shoffner, John R.

Priv. Slemmer, Adam

Priv. Smedley, Isaih [sic]

Priv. Smedley, Mifflin

Priv. Smith, Henry S.

Priv. Spencer, James

Priv. Stephens, Jacob R.

Priv. Sutch, Abraham B.

Priv. Sutch, Charles

Priv. Thompson, Benj. P.

Priv. Tippen, Henry

1st Lieut. Joseph K. Bolton was commissioned Captain and transferred to Company F. Company A furnished the following named persons as officers afterwards in the three (3) years service: Bolton, Wm. J.; Bolton, Jos. K.; Ensley; Ortlip; Guss; Wills; Feather; Moore; Thompson; and Randall. Regular army, ten persons. 1st Lieut. Jos. K. Bolton was elected Captain of Co. F June 14th 1861, and Chas. Hunsicker 1st Lieut. on the same date. Capt. Dunn and Lieut. Cooper both resigning on that date. Wm. C. Ensley was elected 1st Lieut. June 14/61 in the place of 1st Lieut. Jos. K. Bolton, promoted.

Chapter 2

The 51st Pennsylvania

September 10–December 31, 1861

Anxious to clear the name of the old 4th Pennsylvania, Colonel Hartranft quickly began organizing a new regiment of three-year volunteers. Many of his three-month soldiers reenlisted and became members of the new 51st Pennsylvania. The regiment organized at Camp Curtin, then was assigned to the command of Brigadier General Ambrose E. Burnside, headquartered at Annapolis, Maryland.

The interval between July 29th 1861, and September 9th 1861, I imployed my time in recruiting a company for the three years service, visiting friends and relatives and attending balls and parties, and tea parties to which many of us were invited before our final departure for the seat of war.

Sep 10—Left Norristown with my company with ninety-nine (99) men and officers amid the plaudits of an admiring populous, who lined the side walk, as the company marched through the town to take the cars at Bridgeport for Harrisburg, to be mustered into the State, and United States service for three years, or during the war. Amid the sobbing and crying and handshaking of men, women and children, and the many God speedes to us, the train pulled out from the station with its living freight, many of them never to return again. Arrived in Harrisburg about 2 o'clock P.M. and immediately proceeded to Camp Curtin and went into camp. The company was the first military organization to leave Montgomery County for the three years service, and was the first company on the ground, what afterwards became the 51st Reg. P.V.V.[1]

Sep 11—The company were all examined by the Surgeon to-day, and all of the men were passed by him, and they were immediately sworn into the State service by the mustering officer James A. Beaver.[2]

---

1. Camp Curtin was located just north of Harrisburg, Pennsylvania. For an excellent detailed study of this important military post, see William J. Miller, *The Training of an Army: Camp Curtin and the North's Civil War* (Shippensburg, PA: White Mane Publishing Company, Inc., 1990).

2. Lieutenant Colonel James A. Beaver of the 45th Pennsylvania was assigned as second in command of Camp Curtin on September 9. [Miller, *Camp Curtin*, 54.]

Sep 12—The company was sworn into the United States service to-day for three years or during the War, and was known as Company A, 51st Regiment, Pennsylvania Volunteers. Attended school for the instruction of officers at Capt. Taggart quarters.[3]

Sep 13—Company drill. Spent a part of the day in Harrisburg.

Sep 14—Received a leave of absence for three days and left for Norristown.

Sep 15—Spent the day at home, and went to church in the evening.

Sep 16—Returned to Harrisburg. Company drill. Captain George R. Pechin arrived in camp to-day with eighty-one men.

Sep 17—Company and regimental drills. Regimental dress parade in the evening for the first time.

Sep 18—Company drill. Regimental drill under Captain Taggart. The regiment was made up promiscuously of the different companies in camp. Received a few letters.

Sep 19—Company drill. Received and wrote several letters. Was presented with a pistol by my old friends in Hoovers Rolling Mill.

Sep 20—Moved my camping ground to a better groun [sic] and location.

Sep 21—Received twenty gum blankets from a number of ladies of Norristown. Wrote them a letter acknowledging their receipt.

Sep 22—Company and regimental drills. Wrote a letter to Mrs. Benj. E. Chain and to several other persons.

Sep 23—Company and regimental drills, under the charge of Captain Tarbutton. Wrote several letters. Two of my men deserted, Joseph Divers and Samuel Foreman.[4]

Sep 24—Company and regimental drills as usual under Captain Tarbutton. Communicated with Constable Londsdale at Norristown about the two deserters.[5]

Sep 25—Company and regimental drills as usual.

Sep 26—As to-day is Thanksgiving day, there was no drilling of any kind.

Sep 27—Rained all day. Received a letter from Constable Londsdale informing me that he had caught my two deserters and had lodged them in the county jail.

Sep 28—Company and regimental drills as usual. A number of my company were marched to the city of Harrisburg to be mustered into the United States service by Lieut. W. Piper 5th United States Artillery. Received a number of letters.

Sep 29—Company and regimental drills as usual. Whole regiment struck their tents for several reasons--sanitary, policing the grounds, and to learn them to strike and to pitch their tents.

Sep 30—Company and regimental drills as usual. Received a dispatch about my two deserters.

Oct 1—Company and regimental drills as usual. Am not feeling very well.

Oct 2—Company and regimental drills as usual.

---

3. Bolton here referred to Captain William A. Tarbutton, whose job it was to train new recruits, officers and men alike. See Miller, *Camp Curtin*, 71-73, for more details.

4. Divers remained with the regiment until his term of enlistment expired, while Foreman was discharged in January 1863. See Thomas H. Parker, *History of the 51st Regiment of P. V. and V. V.* (Philadelphia: King & Baird, Printers, 1869), 626-27.

5. Bolton probably referred to Thomas Longsdale.

Oct 3—Drills as usual. Caught another of my deserters, John D. Smith. Have them all in irons.[6]

Oct 4—Moved our camp for sanitary reasons, and to discipline the men in the striking and pitching of tents.

Oct 5—Drills as usual. Not feeling very well.

Oct 6—Drills as usual. Received some letters.

Oct 7—Drills as usual. Wrote a few letters.

Oct 8—Held an election in the company, acted as Judge of the election. Left camp in the evening for Norristown on a leave of absence.

Oct 9—Spent the day at home with my father and mother.

Oct 10—Went to Port Kennedy to recruit men for the regiment. Company received new army blankets.

Oct 11—Went to the Trappe to recruit for the regiment.

Oct 12—Left Norristown for Camp Curtin, arriving there in the afternoon.

Oct 13—Drills as usual. Received some letters.

Oct 14—Drills as usual. Wrote some letters.

Oct 15—Received a check for $196.50 from Col. Potts for the pay of rations, that amount being allowed me while recruiting and furnishing my men with meals while in camp at Norristown.

Oct 16—Drew from the Harrisburg Bank the $196.50 and paid the men who furnished their own meals. Company drill.

Oct 17—Received my mothers picture in a Madalion which I carried on my watch chain. Also received a pot of preserves from my mother.

Oct 18—Drills as usual. Received my guns from the State Arsenal.

Oct 19—Company and regimental drills as usual.

Oct 20—Company and regimental drills as usual. Priv. George Bond of Company A died very suddenly in camp to-day.

Oct 21—Company and regimental drills as usual. Received the news in camp of the killing of Col. E. D. Baker, commanding the California or 71st Regiment Pennsylvania Volunteers, at Ball's Bluff, or sometimes called Edwards Ferry.

Oct 22—Being my birthday, spent the morning in Harrisburg.

Oct 23—Company and regimental drills as usual. Received a letter from my sister.

Oct 24—Company and regimental drills as usual. Attended school for officers.

Oct 25—Company and regimental drills as usual, and dress parade in the evening. Attended school for officers.

Oct 26—Company drills, and dress parade in the evening. Attended school for officers.

Oct 27—Company drills as usual. Received and wrote several letters. Attended school.

Oct 28—Company drills as usual. Attended school.

Oct 29—Company and regimental drills and dress parade in the evening. Went to Harrisburg.

Oct 30—Company and regimental drills. Attended school. Wrote a few letters.

Oct 31—Company and regimental drills as usual.

Nov 1—Company and regimental drills as usual, and dress parade in the evening.

---

6. Smith remained with the 51st until the unit disbanded in July 1865. See Parker, *51st PA*, 630.

Nov 2—Rained all day. Spent the day in reading up tactics and the army regulations.

Nov 3—Company and regimental drills, and dress parade in the evening. Attended school.

Nov 4—Company drills, and dress parade in the evening. Attended school.

Nov 5—Drills as usual. Attended school. Regiment paraded and were drawn up in line closed en-masse, forming three sides of a square. Gov. A. G. Curtin then presented us with a stand of colors, saying among other things, "return with them with honor, or return not at all." From this we made up our minds that we would soon receive marching orders. A great crowd was present, as two other regiments, the 52nd and 53d were also presented with colors. Visitors were present from the city and the adjoining camps, Cameron and Greble. All hands felt in a good humor, as they were anxious to get away from Harrisburg.

Nov 6—Company and regimental drills as usual. Attended school.

Nov 7—Company and regimental drills, and dress parade in the evening. Attended school.

Nov 8—Regimental drill, and dress parade. Attended school.

Nov 9—Detailed as Officer of the Day, for the next twenty-four hours. Company drill.

Nov 10—Slept nearly all day. Company drills. Priv. Adolph Sanders of Company A died in camp to-day.

Nov 11—Company and regimental drills as usual. Attended school.

Nov 12—Company and regimental drills and dress parade in the evening. Left for Norristown on a leave of absence.

Nov 13—Took a ride in the country and recruited one man for the regiment.

Nov 14—Left Norristown for Harrisburg, arriving there in the afternoon. Company drills, and dress parade in the evening. Our dress parades were generally witnessed by the citizens of Harrisburg who generally came out to the camp towards evening, and remained until after dark. Rumors in camp that we will soon leave here.

Nov 15—Rained all day. Received a letter from T. Sanders, father of Adolph Sanders, concerning the death of his son. Early in the day received orders to prepare to breake camp. The 51st Regiment Pennsylvania Volunteers was composed of troops organized at Harrisburg, from the Counties of Montgomery, Northampton, Centre, Snyder, Union, and Lycoming, five of the companies coming from Montgomery. The following composed the regimental staff and non-commissioned staff:

Lt. Col. Thomas S. Bell	Col. John F. Hartranft	Chap. D. G. Mallory
Adg't. Daniel P. Bible	Sgt. Maj. C. Jones Iredell	Asst.Surg. James D. Noble
Hos.-Stu'd.Martin H. Dunn	Q.M.Sgt. Wm. L. Jones	Major Edwin Schall
Quar.-Mas. Jno. J. Freedley	Surg. J. A. Livergood	Com.Sgt. Saml. P. Stephens

* Company A, Captain Wm. J. Bolton, with a full company was the first to arrive on the ground, and was the first company to be mustered into the State, and National service. The other companies from Montgomery arrived soon after. In the three months service, we drilled Coopers tacticts, but here in Camp Curtin, we changed to Hardee,[7] and commenced at once

---

7. Bolton referred to two of the tactical manuals used by the Union army. The first was Samuel Cooper, *A Concise System of Instructions and Regulations for the Militia and Volunteers of the United States* (Philadelphia: Charles Desilver, 1861). The original edition was published in 1836. The primary manual used by both armies was William J. Hardee, *Rifles and Light Infantry Tactics*, 2 volumes (Philadelphia: J. B. Lippincott Company, 1855).

to make ourselves familiar with the new drill by attending school of instructions and constant practices at drill on the field. Many of us had seen service with the three months volunteers, and of course were not totally ignorant of our duties, so we had a start in the art of war.

We had a great deal of wet weather, and consequently a great deal of mud. Some of the men became dissatisfied, and some few deserted. I remember the second night after the arrival of my company. The rain poured down in torrents. I thought myself that the bottom had fallen out, everything was submerged, and we all looked like drownded rats, but I knew it would not do for me to grumble. I soon had my men in good humor. I always made it a point to take good care of my men, for I knew it would pay in the future, and it turned out so, to the close of the war. They never went without anything to eat over night if I could devise a plan to get it either by fare, or foul means, as many of the boys of old Company A well remember to this day, and I know I never regretted it while I was in command of Company A. The other companies did not get along so well for a time, but good feeling soon prevaled and all went on as well as could be expected among so many men, as it takes all kind of men to make a crowd, and they would play their little tricks, and have their little fun, and they could not well be blamed, for it was destined for them to see some terrible times as events will show further on in this journal.

A great deal of trouble existed in Captain Pechin's company, from various causes, and desertions were more frequent from that company. Indeed it looked as if he would not be able to get enough men to be mustered into the United States service, and was not able until the regiment had left Harrisburg, but they were finally mustered in at Annapolis, November 28th 1861. Very soon after our arrival in camp, the soldiers troubles commenced, comfortless clothing, and scanty rations. Many of the men had left home without one cent in their pockets, and very many in their shirt sleeves. In fact the worse clothing they could put on as they reasonable supposed on their arrival in camp, new uniforms would be provided. They were doomed to disappointment, for they did not receive anything until about the 1st of October, and then only a lot of worn out old blankets and old quilts, alive with vermin, the same having been used in the three months service. They were piled in the company streets and set on fire, but with it all, there was some little scratching done.[8]

In the evening after dress parade, the boys would have their fun in many ways, wrestling, jumping, running, but the most practiced, the tossing up in the air in the blanket which was always kept up until the close of the war. The boys were always on the lookout for a change of grub. I remember that one night the boys made a raid on a cattle train, the consequence was a hog was captured and very soon dispatched, carried on a litter into camp as a sick man. The pickets were none too wise. Another trick was to purchase a watermellon, hollow it out, and fill it full of whiskey.

A great many of the soldiers suffered greatly from diarrhoea, dysentery, rheumatism, change of home comforts, food, and the change of water, and bad sleeping quarters, were perhaps the cause. Several men died while we were in camp, and some we left there who died afterwards. While recruiting my company in Norristown during August and September, I rationed the men in the camp I had established in the town, located on the commons at the foot of West Jacoby Street. Having had possession of the tents of the old Wayne Artillerists, I pitched them on the ground mentioned. I could have quartered them in the old armory, the Humane Engine House, but I wanted to familiarize them in camp duty, cook their meals, police duty, &c &c. as I knew it would be to their benefit in the near future. My brother or I would go to market close by and purchase what was needed for the camp and would make all the provi-

8. Bolton here followed Parker, *51st PA*, 17.

sions for the cooking of the same. Sometimes the neighbors adjoining the camp would do some cooking for the boys. Mrs. H. S. Stephens was particularly kind in this way. Sometimes the market men would send us rotten fish, the same oft told tale. Anything good enough for the soldier. The consequence was my brother and I would advance to the market, raise thunder and the boys would bury the fish and fire a salute over the once fresh fish. Pour devels, and myself included would have been glad to have had them later on during the war.

We had a little gun in camp, and always fired a gun at sunrise and sunset. The girls would come to see us of course. Sometimes I would dress in citizens clothes and sometimes in military. I generally slept in camp with the boys. Being out late one night little late calling on some ladies, and as usual, returned to camp, and went to bed. In the morning got up and changed my clothing, and on putting on my military clothes, found my pants had been sewed up at the bottom of each leg, watch-fob and arm holes of my vest the same—good joke. The evening I left camp with my company, September 9th 1861, myself and two Lieutenants were publicly presented with swords and belts in the Court House. Carried mine through the war up to the battle of Antietam, where I lost it after being wounded in the face.

Nov 16—After being under arms nearly all day, the regiment left Harrisburg about 4 o'clock P.M. marched through the city and crossed the Susquehanna River to the depot of the Northern Central Railroad, and embarked on thirty-seven box or cattle cars without seats. The weather was very bad, snowing and raining and very cold, and the cars was filthy with manure. The trains pulled out from the station at 5 o'clock P.M. reaching Glen Rock about midnight, laying over there for about two hours. The boys found a field of corn fodder and made use of it for beds in the cars.[9]

Nov 17—Regiment arrived in Baltimore about 8 o'clock in the morning, after a very cold and disagreeable ride, and all hands out of humor. During the night, Corp. John C. Brannon, through mischief, set fire to the car that a portion of my company was in, whose conduct I will speak of hereafter. Regiment marched through the Monumental City to the Washington Depot, and were treated to some good coffee, bread and butter, &c. Marched back to the Pratt Street wharf, and loaded our baggage, where we also had some good refreshments. At 6 o'clock P.M. we marched back to the Washington depot, and embarked on board the cars, bound for Annapolis, Md. Passed the "Relay House" and Annapolis Junction during the night.

Nov 18—Regiment arrived in Annapolis about 1 o'clock in the morning, and it was as dark as pitch, and after daylight, we were all put in comfortable quarters in the St. Johns College Buildings, which were all built of brick and very commodious. Was detailed for the next twenty-four hours, Officer of the Day.

Nov 19—All of the companies now commenced to go down to hard drilling, officers making themselves familiar with the tactics and the army regulations. The lettering of the companies was completed to-day and are as follows:

Capt. Wm. Allebaugh, C	Capt. James M. Linn, H	Capt. Rob. F. Taylor, F
Capt. Ferdinand Bell, B	Capt. Geo. R. Pechin, I	Capt. John Titus, K
Capt. Wm. J. Bolton, A	Capt. Edward Schall, D	
Capt. Geo. H. Hassenplug, E	Capt. Austin Snyder, G	

Nov 20—Left the College Buildings and went into camp a short distance from the College grounds, and named our new quarters Camp Burnside. It was a beautifully located camp and

---

9. Following Parker, *51st PA*, 27-28.

was on the banks of the Severn River, and when the boys were not drilling, they were out on the river boating, fishing, and oystering, therefore we lived grand in our new quarters. Surg. J. A. Livergood was to-day transferred from the 51st P.V. to the 101st P.V. and Surg. John A. Hossack transferred from the 101st P.V. to the 51st P.V. The French troops during the Revolution encamped on this very same ground. There were stoneheads and foot-marks on our drill grounds.

Nov 21—Regimental and company drills and dress parade in the evening. Wrote several letters.

Nov 22—Regimental and company drills, and dress parade in the evening. Received several letters.

Nov 23—Company drills, and dress parade in the evening. Wrote several letters.

Nov 24—Company inspection. Company attended church in the evening.

Nov 25—Company drill, and dress parade in the evening.

Nov 26—I reduced to the ranks Corp. John C. Brannon of my company (the first person in the regiment reduced) for setting fire to the cars on our way from Harrisburg to Annapolis. Company drill. Detailed a a member of a General Court Martial. The Court met in one of the College Buildings, and elected Col. Ed. Harland, 8th Conn. Vols. as President of the Court.

Nov 27—Company drill, and dress parade in the evening. Attended a meeting of the General Court Martial in one of the Naval Buildings, and after doing some little business, the Court adjourned at 2 o'clock P.M. Received and wrote several letters to friends at home.

Nov 28—Company drills, and dress parade in the evening. Attended a session of the Court Martial.

Nov 29—Company drill and dress parade in the evening. Attended a session of the Court Martial. Received a letter from my mother.

Nov 30—Company drill and dress parade. Attended a session of the Court Martial. Wrote a letter to mother.

Dec 1—Company and regimental drills, and dress parade in the evening. Regimental Band organized to-day, and are composed of the following persons:

George A. Arnold (Leader)	William Earl	Joseph C. Millhouse
Samuel G. Arnold	Alexander Earls	Benjamin Rowland
Jesse S. Baird	John Earp	Charles A. Thompson
Simon Britton	Wilson Foster	Benjamin Watkins
Jeremiah W. Buck	James Haas	William Williams
Jesse M. Buckis	George V. Hansell	William Workizer
Charles Day	Philip Jacobs	

George A. Arnold was not mustered into the United States service but was paid from the regimental fund.

Dec 2—Company and regimental drills and dress parade. Court Martial not in session.

Dec 3—Company and regimental drills and dress parade. Attended a session of the Court Martial.

Dec 4—Company and regimental drills and dress parade. Attended a session of the Court Martial.

Dec 5—Company and regimental drills and dress parade. Attended a session of the Court martial.

Dec 6—Attended a session of the Court Martial. Received a box of good things from my mother. Regiment struck tents and moved their camp about two miles up along the railroad near Annapolis Junction. The ground is beautifully situated, and our new camp is called Camp Union.[10]

Dec 7—Company drills and dress parade. Received and wrote several letters. The men of the regiment when not otherwise engaged, spend a great deal of their time in beautifying the camp with evergreens, pines, and laurels &c in which the country around abounds. Each company endeavor to excell the other, and the result is, we have a most beautiful camp. Arches sprung across the company streets, and a fine large arch at the main entrance to the camp.

Dec 8—Company inspection. Received and wrote several letters. Dress parade in the evening.

Dec 9—Company drills and dress parade. Attended a session of the Court Martial. Finished up all business that was before it, and adjourned sine die.

Dec 10—Company and regimental drills, and dress parade in the evening. Received several letters.

Dec 11—Company drills and inspection.

Dec 12—Company drills. Detailed as Officer of the Day for the next twenty-four hours. Our Sutlers arrived to-day, Rodermel & Hartranft.

Dec 13—Company drills. In the afternoon the whole Burnside Coast Division was reviewed by Brig. Gen. John D. [sic] Foster and Staff. The regiment did handsomly for the first time.

Dec 14—Company drills. The whole Coast Division again reviewed this afternoon by Genl. Foster and Staff. We were to have been reviewed by Genl. Burnside, but for some reason he did not make his appearance. Received some letters.

Dec 15—Company drills. Regimental inspection in the afternoon. Judgeing by the surroundings, things look like a movement of the Coast Division. Received a letter from my mother.

Dec 16—Company drills, and dress parade in the evening. Attended school of instructions.

Dec 17—Company drills, and dress parade in the evening. Received some letters and papers.

Dec 18—Company drills, inspection and dress parade. Attended school of instructions for officers. Received a box of good things from my mother, and several letters from lady friends.

Dec 19—The whole Coast Division was reviewed by Genl. Foster, Gov. [Thomas H.] Hicks and the Legislature of Maryland, and was a grand affair.

Dec 20—The whole Coast Division again reviewed by Major Genl. A. E. Burnside and Staff.

Dec 21—Company drills and dress parade in the evening. Received a letter from my mother, and wrote her one.

Dec 22—Company drills and regimental inspection. Wrote a letter to my mother.

Dec 23—Company drills and dress parade in the evening. Received from the Paymaster $227.69.

Dec 24—Company drills and dress parade in the evening. Our regiment was assigned to-day by official orders to Brig. Genl. Jesse L. Reno's Brigade and was composed of the following troops:

---

10. Parker, *51st PA*, 30, wrote that the regiment moved its camp on December 3. He is supported by the December 3 diary entry of Henry Gangewer, Company K. See Mary S. Dix (editor), " 'And Three Rousing Cheers for the Privates': A Diary of the 1862 Roanoke Island Expedition," *North Carolina Historical Review* 61 (January 1994): 66.

51st New York Vols.	Col. Robert B. Potter
51st Penna. Vols.	Col. John F. Hartranft
21st Mass. Vols.	Lt. Col. [Alberto C.] Maggi
9th New Jersey Vols.	Col. J. W. Allen

Dec 25—Company drills, inspection, and dress parade. Sent home through the hands of Major Schall, $200.00 to my mother, also a large amount belonging to the members of Company A to their families.

Dec 26—Company drills and dress parade. Regiment received new uniforms. Regiment inspected by members of Genl. [George B.] McClellan's staff.

Dec 27—Company drills, and dress parade. Received and wrote several letters.

Dec 28—Company and regimental drills. While on regimental drill we received orders to report at 12 o'clock M next day on board of one of the fleet awaiting us at the wharves of the Naval School at Annapolis with three days cooked rations.[11]

Dec 29—Company and regimental drills, and dress parade in the evening. Wrote a letter to my mother.

Dec 30—Company and regimental drills, and dress parade in the evening. Received a letter from my sister.

Dec 31—Company drills. Regiment inspected by members of Genl. McClellan's staff and mustered for two months pay. Regimental band complemented me with a serenade.

---

11. Parker, *51st PA*, 39, wrote that these orders came on December 29.

Chapter 3

The Burnside Expedition

January 1–July 5, 1862

The objective of General Burnside's Coast Division was coastal North Carolina. After a harrowing ordeal at Hatteras Inlet, during which the passage was delayed by two fierce storms, Burnside's ships entered Pamlico Sound. Then followed victories at Roanoke Island (February 7-8) and Newbern (March 14). The 51st Pennsylvania fought in the engagement at Sawyer's Lane (April 19) and then remained in camp near Newbern until Burnside went north to Virginia in July. During this time, the regiment was part of Brigadier General Jesse L. Reno's Second Brigade, which was expanded into a division in April.

Jan 1—Company and regimental drills and dress parade. Very heavy storm during the night, blew down the tents and sent the canvas, poles and pins in all directions. We had standing orders to be ready to march at a moments notice. Very heavy details are made every day to go to the City of Annapolis to load the vessels laying at the Naval School wharves. Provisions, ammunition, coal, wood, cattle, horses, artillery &c all this labor was done by the soldiers of the Coast Division. Drew new caps and distributed them to the men.

Jan 2—Company and regimental drills and dress parade. Detailed as Officer of the Day for the next twenty-four hours.

Jan 3—Detailed as Officer of the Day for the next twenty-four hours. Received a box from my mother and a letter from my brother John.

Jan 4—Again detailed as Officer of the Day. Received several letters. Generals Foster, Reno, and Parke commenced this morning to embark their horses and teams at the wharves designated for each brigade.[1]

Jan 5—Again detailed as Officer of the Day for the next twenty-four hours. Received letter from my mother. Received from Paymaster Brown $262.50. The three brigades completed the embarkation of their horses and teams and other stores to-day.

---

1. The Coast Division was organized as follows:
   First Brigade, Brig. Gen. John G. Foster: 23rd, 24th, 25th, 27th MA, 10th CT
   Second Brigade, Brig. Gen. Jesse L. Reno: 21st MA, 6th NH, 9th NJ, 51st NY, 51st PA
   Third Brigade, Brig. Gen. John G. Parke: 4th, 5th RI, 8th, 11th CT, 53rd, 89th NY
   Artillery: 1st NY Marine Arty.; Bty F, 1st RI; Co. B, 99th NY
In addition, the new Department of North Carolina contained the garrison troops at Hatteras Inlet. Here, Brig. Gen. Thomas Williams had command of the 48th PA, 9th NY, and Bty C, 1st US.

Jan 6—The whole Coast Division struck tents at an early hour this morning and marched through the snow to Annapolis to embark, as follows: Foster's Brigade marching to the upper wharf at the Naval School yard, Reno's Brigade to the lower wharf of the Naval School yard, Parke to the small wharf north of the Hospital at the Naval School yard. Each man carried forty rounds of buck and ball in their cartridge boxes. The sick who were convalescent had all been put on board a few days before, and the more critical ones were sent to the hospitals at Washington and Annapolis, and when sufficiently recovered to rejoin their regiments.

Companies A, C, F, and K embarked on board of the Schooner *Scout*, Toney Master, all under the command of Lieut. Col. Bell. Companies B, D, E, G, H, and I embarked on board of the S.S. *Cossack*, Bennett Master, all under the command of Col. Hartranft. The *Cossack* carried two steel three inch Wiard rifle guns. After the regiment had all embarked, the two vessels, the *Cossack* and *Scout* dropped out into the stream, and rode at anchor off Annapolis.[2]

The whole fleet was composed of seventy-five or eighty vessels made up of steamships, barks, brigs, and schooners, and presented a splendid sight while riding at anchor, particularly at night when all had their lights out on the riggin. The masters of our two vessels were very good men. Before going on board I sent home to my mother through the hands of Maj. Snyder who was visiting us $240.00. We were all perfectly ignorant as to our destination. Was detailed as Officer of the Day.

Jan 7—The fleet still laying at anchor in the stream off Annapolis. Received and wrote several letters. *Scout* towed up to the *Cossack*.

Jan 8—The fleet still laying at anchor in the stream off Annapolis. Blue flags to the fore.

Jan 9—At 8 1/2 o'clock A.M. the whole fleet weighed anchor and steamed down the Chesapeake, the S.S. *Cossack* having in tow the Schooners *Scout* and *Recruit*. Steamed down the Bay about one hundred miles and at 12 o'clock M. heaved anchor on account of the fog. The men enjoyed themselves in dancing during the day, bands playing.

Jan 10—The whole fleet weighed anchor about 10 o'clock A.M. and steamed on our way. Arrived at Fortress Monroe about 3 o'clock P.M. and heaved anchor off the Rip-Raps and laid there all night. All hands still ignorant of our destination. Our journey so far has been very pleasant. The decks are always crowded, the men are either dancing or playing cards.

Jan 11—The whole fleet laid at anchor all day. At 9 o'clock P.M. the whole fleet weighed anchor, we of the *Scout* in tow of the *Cossack*. On our reaching the ocean, our hauser was dropped, the *Scout* hoisted their canvas, and from that time on, we had to look out for ourselves. Sea sickness began to attack the men. Each vessel has its own sealed orders.

Jan 12—At daylight none of the fleet was to be seen. The North Carolina coast was to be seen, but far distant. Early in the morning the wind blew a terrible hurricane, and the sea ran very high and consequently many of us on the *Scout* became very seasick. About noon it died away somewhat, but the sea was rolling mountains high, and every moment we thought we would be dashed to pieces, but the noble little craft rode the waves splendidly, but oh! our stomachs!

The *Cossack* reached Hatteras Inlet, N.C. about 5 o'clock P.M. but the *Scout* and *Recruit* did not fare so well. It was impossible for the *Cossack* to enter Pamlico Sound on account of the treacherous channel so she was compelled to put to sea again and on the next morning found herself forty miles out at sea from the Inlet. As for us on the *Scout* no land can be seen. Foggy, sea rough, blowing hard.[3]

---

2. The ships captains were N. Torrey of *Scout* and J. W. Bennett of *Cossack*.

3. This story is not true. *Cossack* reached the inlet as stated and rammed through the breakers to reach the anchorage in safety. Here, Bolton relied on Parker, *51st PA*, 52.

Jan 13—Weather clear, but a very heavy wind and very rough sea, causing our vessel to labor very heavily, and many of the smaller vessels were compelled to cut loose from the steamers that were towing them. It has rained all day and still no land in sight for us. The Master tells us that he has run pass the Inlet, along the Carolina coast, and came near being captured, mistaking that point for Hatteras. The *Cossack* crossed the bar and entered the Inlet about 11 o'clock A.M. Very few vessels in sight.

Jan 14—Sea running very high more so than yesterday. In my birth all day and somewhat seasick. The Master tells us that we are thirty miles out of our course. Very heavy rain and no land in sight. Blowing fearfully.

Jan 15—The weather to-day is more calm. Remained in my birth all day. The Master tells us that we are now fifty-two miles out of our course south of Hatteras. It has been raining all day, and we are out of water, coffee and tea. Men are drinking water caught from the sails. Not very palatable, but it is the best we can do.

Jan 16—The sea still running very heavy, and after beating around for a long time, at last came in sight of land and the fleet in the inlet, this about 11 o'clock A.M. Still nothing to eat or drink. Passed the wreck of a steamer. The Master ran up signal reading "out of water." We dropped anchor about 8 o'clock P.M. Received four barrel of water from a passing vessel, which relieved our wants in that direction for a short time. Priv. James Conway Company D died at Hatteras Inlet. Lowered into a boat, band playing a dirge, to be taken ashore and buried in the sand beach. Cold and windy.

Jan 17—Arrived off Hatteras Inlet about 12 o'clock M. and after a great deal of work, running aground on the bar several times, we finally reached Pamlico Sound about 2 1/2 o'clock P.M.[4] While laying off the inlet we could plainly see Forts Hatteras and Clark.[5] Received some more water from other vessels of the fleet. For several days we were given vinegar to drink. We would catch the rain water on the sails, or whenever we could scoop it up. Although rather salty, we could drink it with a relish.

Our men on board of the *Cossack* we learned had given us up as lost, as we were six days behind them when we should not have been more than a day behind. But the steamer had hugged the shore, and could make better time,but on account of the storm we were driven to sea and were tossed about a great deal, and at one time were caught in the Gulf Stream. So sick were the men sometimes that they wished the schooner would go down. Our meeting was a joyous one after we met the balance of the regiment in the Sound. Have not seen the sun for three days.

Jan 18—The *Scout* was on the bar several times during the day on account of the storm, many of the vessels dragging their anchors and running into each other. Wrote letters to my brother and sister.

Jan 19—The men were employed nearly all day in throwing overboard about forty tons of ballast, consisting of pig iron. The vessel was found to be drawing too much water and had to be lightened up so as to be able to pass over the many bars and to pass up the sound to a safter anchorage. We suffered a great many inconveniences, insufficient rations, no water, and no

---

4. *Scout* did not reach Pamlico Sound, but merely the safe anchorage just outside the "swash" channel that led through the inlet to the sound. Several of Burnside's ships drew too much water to pass through this shallow waterway, and consequently had to be lightened before attempting the passage.

5. These two forts had been captured by a Union attack in August 1861 and had been occupied since that time.

mail. We had several members of the regiment to die here. Their bodies were put in rude coffins, such as could be made on board of ship, and taken ashore and buried on the beach near Fort Clark.

Jan 20—We are still laying at anchor in the sound. Wrote several letters to my friends at home, and spent a part of the day in reading. Inspected my company on deck. Water still scarce. We are having violent thunder storms nearly every night. Rations very scarce and we all think that we have it very hard. Very little drilling is being done, and what is done is done without arms, as they injure the deck by their use. The men amuse themselves by playing cards and when the weather is fine by dancing on the deck. Wrote several letters. A lovely day.

Jan 21—We are still laying at anchor in the sound. Company drills on deck, two companies at a time. Although we are laying apparently idle, Burnside is busy in getting his fleet over the various bars, by transporting the troops from one vessel to the other and returning them to their own vessels. Sgt. Theo. H. Gilbert Company A reduced to the ranks for insubordination.

Jan 22—Rained all day. Spent a good part of the day in playing euchre.[6] We learned to-day that the last vessel of the fleet entered the inlet. Rumor has it that upwards of one hundred and sixteen vessels are in and about the inlet.

The Master of the *Scout* is a very good kind hearted little irishman, but was very close with his liquor, and in the absence of no fighting and nothing else to do, Capt. Taylor and myself would enter into a conspiracy to relieve him of some of his liquor in this use. The Captain would on some pretence get the Master into conversation on deck long enough for me to go to my state room to provide myself with a quart coffee pot. I would then make for the Master's state room, fill my pot, and take it to my own room, and in due time Taylor and one or two other officers who were in the secret would punish the contents of the coffee pot. The Master remarked in the cabin several times in our presence that his demijohn was getting darn light, but he never knew how it came to get light. We afterwards heard while laying at Newbern N.C. that he had fallen down his hatchway and had broken his neck.

Priv. George Shaffer, Company D, died on board of the *Cossack* and was buried on the beach, his name cut on his rough box "I.O.O.F." [International Order of Odd Fellows].

Jan 23—We had violent storms all day. Company drills on deck, and in the evening played euchre.

Jan 24—Spent the day in reading up tactics, and drilling my company. Stormed during the night.

Jan 25—Company drills. Reading tactics and playing cards in the evening. Clear and cool.

Jan 26—By the looks of things, there will be a movement of the fleet very soon. The gunboats are all now mostly over the bars and are practicing target, but the only drawback are the transports containing the troops, they are makingbad headway. The steamers *Admiral*[7] and *George Peabody* after many attempts have at last succeeded in crossing the bar. While this is going on we are having very fine weather generally. *Pautuxent* pulls the *Scout* out and puts us in safe anchorage.

Jan 27—Reading up tactics nearly all day and played euchre in the evening and otherwise enjoyed ourselves. Fine weather.

Jan 28—Reading up tactics all day and playing euchre in the evening. The splendid steamer *Eastern Queen* succeeded in getting over the bar to-day making thirty-five vessels directly be-

---

6. Euchre was a card game.

7. This steamer was also known by its original name, *Guide*.

longing to the fleet. Genl. Burnside has just arrived, having been on business at Washington. A rebel schooner would run down towards our fleet during the day to spy out what she could see, as we supposed, and our gunboats would give chase after her, and would be very exciting. Wrote a letter to my sister.

Jan 29—Our four companies were taking on board of the steamer *Union* (better known as the *Wheelbarrow*, a name the 51st gave her) to lighten up the *Scout* so that she could cross the bar. We were put on board of the steamer *Cossack*. We have now forty-one vessels belonging to the fleet over the bar. Five tug-boats arrived to-day from Baltimore and are being used in towing the vessels over the bars. Band of the 24th Mass. playing "Dixie."

Jan 30—Have a very sick headache all day. A rebel boat came within sight and some of our vessels put after her and captured her with a number of rebels on board.[8] The *Cossack* took on board to-day four hundred barrels of condensed sea water.

Jan 31—We are still on board of the *Cossack*. Received some papers from Mr. Auge[9] of Norristown, also a number of letters. We now have sixty-two vessels of all classes over the bar. Guard duty, drilling in the manual and policing was done every day, the same as we were in camp. Water is very scarce. From six to ten men wash in the same water and use the same towel. The sutler is on board and is asking fabulous prices for his goods. Quite early this morning a sail was observed approaching towards our fleet from the opposite side of the Sound. One of our picket gunboats steamed after her and captured her. She proved to be a schooner from Middletown, a point directly opposite. Was loaded with wood and five deserters from the rebel camp at Middletown.

Feb 1—The four companies this morning left the steamer *Cossack* about 11 o'clock A.M. and were put on board of the steamer *Phoenix*, from whence we were again put on board of the *Scout*, she having at last been gotten of the bar. We were all very glad to return to our old home.

Feb 2—Wrote a few letters and spent the rest of the day in reading. There appears to be a great deal of sickness in Company D and some little in the other companies.

Feb 3—Spent the day very pleasantly in playing euchre and reading. A small boat captured to-day with nineteen negroes on board. Wrote a few letters home and received several. Rained all day.

Feb 4—Detailed as Officer of the Day. All of the fleet now over the various bars that is likely to get over and things look like business, as we have learned on board of the *Scout* that Burnside has reported to Commodore Goldsborough[10] that he was in readiness to start.[11] Corpl. George W. Bowman of Company D died on board of the *Cossack*. Sailing orders received on board.

Feb 5—The whole fleet weighed anchor at 7 o'clock A.M. and after a pleasant passage without accident arrived off Stumpy Point, about six miles from the entrance to Croatan Sound, about 5.30 P.M. when the signal to anchor was given from Burnside's flag ship for the whole fleet to

---

8. *O.R.*, vol. 9, 357.

9. Moses Auge was the publisher of the *Norristown Republican*.

10. Commodore Louis M. Goldsborough, the commander of the North Atlantic Blockading Squadron, accompanied Burnside as naval commander. His tactical officer was Commander Stephen C. Rowan.

11. *O.R.*, vol. 9, 75.

anchor for the night.[12] It was a most beautiful day as the fleet steamed up the sound in three lines of battle, the *Scout* as usual in tow of the *Cossack*. It was indeed a grand sight. The Flag Ship *Philadelphia* was closely watched during the day, for on board of her was Burnside, for up to this date we were still ignorant as to our destination. It was all surmise with us but we felt and knew by the preparations there would be a racket within the next twenty-four hours.

Feb 6—At 6.30 A.M. the signal was run up from the Flag Ship to weigh anchor, and at 8 1/2 A.M. the whole fleet was in motion, proceeded by the gunboats, the whole fleet moving very cautiously, fearing masked batteries on either shore. The forts on Roanoke Island were within plain sight, and besides the sound was filled with sunken obstacles. The weather was very dull and gloomy with a very heavy fog. Passed Croatan Light House and soon entered Croatan Sound the fog becoming so heavy we were compelled to drop anchor about dark off Roanoke Island, before the fog became so heavy we could not see from the decks of our vessels, the whole rebel fleet at anchor, and in line of battle off Pork Point.

A demand was made by Genl. Burnside for the surrender of the Island which was rejected on the part of Col. Jordan, then in command of the Island.[13] Orders were immediately passed to all of the vessels of the fleet, and preparations were made for an attack in the morning. The signal corps were actively employed all day. The decks of the gunboats were cleared for action and all preparations were made during the night for the safe landing of the troops.

The excitement ran high and there was very little sleeping done through the night. All knapsacks were to be left on board and all other luggage, so as not to incumber the troops. We all felt anxious for the coming morning. Rain and becoming very misty.

Feb 7—The signal was given from Burnside's flag ship early in the morning to weigh anchor, coffee having been served us at 5 o'clock in the morning. The fleet was soon in motion and moved in three lines and each steamer had from two to three schooners in tow, the whole proceeded by the gunboats. It was a grand sight, the distance between the three lines were unbroken through the entire length, extending two miles, except perhaps Burnside's boat the *Picket*, which was dashing along everywhere. After getting under weigh Commodore Goldsborough hoisted his signal from his flag ship, which at the time being was all greek to us, but on being deciphered by the Master of our schooner read as follows: "The country expects every man to do his duty."

The head of the naval fleet arrived off Pork Point battery[14] at 9 o'clock A.M. when the first gun was fired. At 10.30 the action became general, and continued in most gallant style until about 6.30 P.M. The rebel fleet retreated as our fleet advanced, behind a barricade of sunken vessels and piles. The first assault was made on Fort Bartow. Previous to this five or six of the armed propellers containing the infantry were sent forward with the *Picket* to anchor in line of battle with the naval fleet, the whole under the command of Capt. Hazard[15] of the Navy. The rest of the propellers containing troops were ordered by Genl. Parke to anchor some distance below to act as a guard. A great deal of amusement was afforded the infantry portion of the

---

12. *O.R.*, vol. 9, 75.

13. Brigadier General Henry A. Wise was the commander of Roanoke Island. Wise was sick at his headquarters at Nag's Head. The actual field commander was Colonel Henry M. Shaw of the 8th North Carolina. Colonel John V. Jordan led the 31st North Carolina. Here, Bolton followed Parker, *51st PA*, 70-71.

14. Fort Bartow.

15. Captain Samuel F. Hazard commanded Burnside's army gunboats.

fleet at the movement of a little slope, *Granite,* with one gun, 32-pounder, she would run right up under the guns of Fort Bartow, discharge her gun, tack around in a circle, and bang away, and then go through the same movement. The gallant little sloop was not struck once.[16]

While all this was going on we received orders to prepare to land, and everything was in a bustle. We were placed in smaller boats and with eight or ten of them in line were towed by light draugh steamers to the Island, jump out and wade to shore. It was a very tedious operation, and at this time the rain was falling and a cold wind was blowing. We were all huddled together in a small place along the beach and bivouacked on the ground all night without any protection and nothing to eat as we could not build any fires as we were too near the enemies works. We had been on shipboard thirty-three days, and when we landed we thought the land was going from under us.

Before landing the men would watch every shot that was fired from our gunboats, and when they would strike the magazine of a building within the forts and set them on fire or blow them up the scene on board of the transports was animated beyond description, wild cheers would go up from a thousand throats. It rained all night and the fine white sand ran down our backs and everything generally was disagreeable. A heavy detail was made from the regiment for picket duty, and there was more or less fireing all night.

The point of landing was at Ashby's Harbor. Foster's troops landed first and we of Reno's brigade soon followed with Parke on our heels. The *Picket* and the Flagship *Delaware* covered our landing. An armed force was discovered at the point designated for our landing and we were compelled to move to another point opposite Hammond's House, but a few well directed shots from the *Picket* and *Delaware* soon dispersed the enemy. The landing of the troops was a beautiful sight, in less than twenty-five minutes from the time of landing of the boats at least four thousand troops were passing over the marshes at a double-quick and formed in grand order on the dry land near the house. By 12 o'clock midnight the entire coast division (except one regiment the 24th Mass. whose steamer had grounded, together with Porter's battery of Dahlgren howitzers had been landed.)[17] While we were resting a careful reconnaissance was made and the troops were posted in case of an night attack. The day clear but rather cold, rained all night.[18]

Feb 8—Formed in line of battle at 8 o'clock A.M. and marched in the direction of the fireing, and not a morsal of food of any kind in our stomachs. Our course was through a dense forest of pines all undergrown and all swamp land. We finally struck a very narrow road-way made of corduroy. Two teams could not have passed each other on it. The wounded were now being carried pass us on stretchers andleaning on the arms of their comrades who had been more fortunate.

Before daylight Genl. Foster had been ordered to advance and up to 8 o'clock A.M. Genls. Reno and Parke's brigades had been held in reserve and kept ready to move at a moments notice. About 10 o'clock A.M. the battle raged in all of its fury, we driving the enemy as we advanced. About one and a half miles on the road from the Hammond's House Foster's troops encountered a battery across the road, which was very narrow and winding and leading through a deep marsh full of small pines and very thick brush, looking to the eye impenetrable. The timber in front was cleared away that their guns might have a full sweep.

---

16. Here, Bolton generally followed *O.R.*, vol. 9, 75 (Burnside's report).

17. Midshipman Benjamin H. Porter commanded a six-gun battery of boat howitzers landed to assist the infantry attack.

18. This paragraph generally followed *O.R.*, vol. 9, 76-77.

Foster at once moved to the attack through the morass on our right for the purpose of turning the enemies left. We of Reno's brigade soon came up and proceeded to turn the right of the enemies position through the swamp on that side. Genl. Parke followed next and was ordered to the right. Things now commenced to get warm and Parke was ordered to charge which was done at a run with yells and cheers. The enemy abandoned their battery and commenced to retreat, hastened along by Reno's brigade of which we formed a part, having turned the enemies right, and we were now fireing into the rear of their battery, and charging into them at the same time. About the same moment Parke's column turned the other flank, and the consequence was that the enemy retreated in precipitation, leaving guns unspiked and their caissons and the dead and wounded in the fort.

Our brigade, Reno's, went in immediate pursuit, Foster following soon after and passed us, as we were engaged in securing many fugitives who were attempting to escape in boats across the Nag's Head. Foster soon came up to the retreating enemy and received the surrender of Col. Shaw, who commanded the forces on the Island, and Reno received the surrender of Col. Jordan's camp, the 31st North Carolina, which consisted of well-built quarters, store houses and hospitals, all new. In the charge on the fort the 21st Mass. and 51st New York of our brigade was simultaneous with that of the 9th New York, but the 21st Mass. claimed that they entered first, and it is generally conceeded that it did. Not a horse had been landed and consequently all ammunition and stores were transported to the front by the soldiers. We had no field artillery, and the only thing in that line that we had was the two light marine howitzers and they were dragged along by hand.[19]

Taking a view of ground that we had to go over one would think that it was impenetrable, swamps, bogs, fallen trees &c. My Company A and Company F were ordered to the left of the road, the enemies right and we soon found ourselves in a deep swamp, followed by a detachment of the 4th R.I. We all found as we advanced we were getting in a muddy swamps waist deep and no solid ground near us. It had rained all night the night before and that made it still worse. Members of Companies A and F climbed the trees so that the guns could be located. The balance of the 51st was on the right of the corduroy road.

In following up the retreat of the enemy, the roads were strewn with canteens, blankets, haversacks, knap-sacks, clothing of all kind, swords, pistols, arms, bowie knives, &c. They shot the horses and mules rather than let them fall into our hands. Our march to Jordan's camp was about fifteen miles. On our way we passed the "Wise Legion" a fine looking body of men, all over six feet high, who all wore long, white overcoats. They looked splendid as they stood in line as we passed them. Jordan's camp was a large village as it were, made up of wooden barracks and commodiously quartering our whole regiment. Here we captured large quantities of commissary stores of all kinds, and we made up for lost time and lived very good. By the time that we reached this camp we were soaked through and through but dried ourselves as best we could. I was detailed to take charge of one of the stores houses and received the captured arms and ammunition &c.

The prisoners were a hard looking crowd, many of them could not spell their names and those who belonged to companies that were not assigned to any regiment had very curious names for their companies some of which were as follows—"Co. A O.K. Boys," "Co. C Hatteras Avengers," "Co. D Jeff Davis Boys" &c. Nearly all of them were armed with bowie knives, about twelve inches long. Many of them after they found that the Island had been captured threw them in the swamps, not wishing to be captured with them on their persons.[20]

---

19. The naval battery consisted of six boat howitzers.

20. Generally from Parker, *51st PA*, 81.

One of our regiment left the main road and captured some sixty prisoners in their attempt to escape through Shallow Bag Bay among them being Capt. O. Jennings Wise who was severely wounded and soon afterwards died. Gov. Wise made good his escape to Nag's Head, thus deserting his dying son. Of the 51st Priv. James Dolan, Co. G, was wounded. By an order of Genl. Burnside each regiment engaged on the Island should inscribe on their flags ROANOKE ISLAND, N.C. FEB. 7 & 8, 1862.

Feb 9—Not feeling very well, spent the best part of the day in my quarters. Towards evening walked around to take a look at the prisoners. They were a hard set of ragamuffins, dirty and full of vermin, as I found out after occupying their quarters. They looked upon us with suspicion, but we endeavor to cinvince them otherwise, and were kind to them as they were our own countrymen, but away off in their estimate of our indurance and fighting qualities, as they found out later.

Feb 10—Rained and snowed nearly all day. Confined in my quarters nearly all day with a sore throat, foot and ankle. On the night of our landing in the darkness, I got in a bog with my left foot and went in over knee deep, and could not get out myself. Priv. George Bodey of my company, a man of over six feet and well built and strong, pulled me out, minus a boot. After some digging I recovered the boot, but the murky mud I never could get off my clothes. We have it to-day and it is indisputable, that state colors of the 21st Mass. was the first flag planted on Fort Defiance, then the flag of the 51st New York, and soon after the regimental flag of the 21st Mass.

Feb 11—Rained and snowed all day. Wrote a letter to my mother. The men of the regiment are out on a little tramp to-day, and are taking their guns along with them, and have brought into camp quite a number of prisoners who had been hiding themselves in the bushes since the battle. Quite one hundred and seventy-five have been captured in this way, and with the prisoners not a few hogs that the men had found running at large around the island. A great many pits were found in their rambles over the island, filled with sweet potatoes, kegs of molasses, salt-fish and tobacco. They had buried them to keep them from us. The island was of a sandy soil but the looks of the soil in many places appeared to have been disturbed from its natural state and the boys suspected something wrong, and out would come the ramrods, and each pit would be probed and the consequence was something would be struck. Tin plates, and tin cups would be used for shovels and soon out would come the contents, and they were carted to camp, much to the delight of the boys, and they would live well for some time, and make up for lost time. The process with the ramrod business was always thereafter kept up until the close of the war, where the grounds were found in the same condition.

Feb 12—A most beautiful day. Wrote several letters and sent home a box of shells I had picked up along the beach. From the time we landed on the island our conveniences for cooking were not of the best, but a soldier could always find a way as they had plenty to cook. Slap-jacks were a favorite thing among the boys. To-day all baggage and cooking utensils were brought off of the transports where they had been since we embarked at Annapolis, and we now began to feel more like ourselves. Was announced to-night on dress parade in General Orders by Genl. Burnside that Elizabeth City had surrendered to our forces on the 10th of February and of course the boys all feel jubilant. To-day a large number of captured officers and men were put on board of transports and sent to N.Y.

Feb 13—Received letters from my sister and brother, and several other friends, also made some answers. Company drills.

Feb 14—Am not feeling very well. Regiment fell in line and marched several miles over the island for observation and recreation more than anything else. The high white sand hills are immense, and are a sight to see. The sand is very fine.

Feb 15—Wrote several letters. The regiment again formed in line and marched to the different forts and intrenchments on the island, and were well received by the different garrisons occupying the works. We had a good opportunity to learn much about the island and the people. The island is surrounded by Roanoke, Croatan, Pamplico and Albemarle Sounds, and is situated a short two miles from the mainline, and is about twelve miles long and three miles wide, and lies very low, and a good part of it an impassable swamp, and in this swamp we fought our first battle, and it is here where the rebel fort (now Fort Russell) stands with her three spiked guns. Standing on the ramparts of the fort, and looking towards the position of the assaulting column, one could not believe that the position could be taken, but we did get there.

The centre of the island is much drier, and has immense sand hills, many as high as several hundred feet, and the sand is fine and as white as snow. On one end of the island is a very large windmill. The people live by fishing and hunting as game is very plenty here. The horses are very small also the cows. The harness they use for their teams is made of rope, and the whole team would make you laugh. We returned to our quarters at a late hour, having enjoyed our tramp very much as it was instructive and gave us an idea how our southern friends lived. As game and fish are plenty we are living at the top of the heap.[21]

By an order issued by Burnside, whenever possible divine service will be held by the chaplains on Sundays, and all work cease, and sanitary orders issued as to certain hours for bathing and the washing of clothes in swamp water.

Feb 16—Wrote several letters. Regimental drill. The men have just discovered that the rebels in trying to escape from the island relieved themselves of everything in the shape of firearms &c in trying to make there escape to their boats, and in wading to them. They threw away in deep water all their arms and the men would go along the beach and grapple up immense bowie knives, pistols and muskets. The knives were terrible looking weapons, and it is supposed that they intended to butcher us if the chance presented. Very many of the knives were sent home by our men. Heavy details are made every day from the regiment for camp and garrison duty and unloading vessels. Burnside issued a Proclamation to-day to the people of North Carolina, urging them to return to their allegiance.[22]

Feb 17—Am not feeling very well. Regiment formed and escorted a large number of rebel prisoners to the beach to be embarked on board of steamers to be exchanged at Elizabeth City. The fishing season is now in its prime and as there are plenty of fishing nets on the island the men hire them at a very small amount and the consequence is, we are having plenty fresh shad and herrings, and are living grand.

Feb 18—Company and regimental drills and dress parade. To-day Burnside sent a detachment of the 9th New York on an expedition up the Chowan River for the purpose of destroying the bridge over the Norfolk and Weldon railroad.

Feb 19—Company and regimental drills and dress parade. The men are getting to be expert fishermen. Large quantities are brought into camp every night, and are sold to the men very cheap. Burnside to-day sent a joint expedition of the army and navy on the steamer *Union* and three naval launches up Currituck Sound for the purpose of reconnoitering the shores and destroying some salt-works said to be there.

---

21. These two paragraphs were taken from Parker, *51st PA*, 87-88.

22. See *O.R.*, vol. 9, 363-64, for the text of this proclamation.

Feb 20—Company and regimental drills and dress parade.

Feb 21—Detailed as Officer of the Day for the next twenty-four hours. Company and regimental drills and dress parade. Wrote a letter to my sister.

Feb 22—Not feeling very well. Company drills and dress parade.

Feb 23—Company inspection. Regiment attended divine service out in the open air. Wrote several letters.

Feb 24—Have a very bad cough and am not otherwise well. Received a package of papers from Mr. Rob Iredell[23] of Norristown. Received and wrote a few letters. Company drills and dress parade.

Feb 25—Not feeling at all well. Regiment received a very large mail and the boys are correspondingly happy. Regiment very much displeased and out of humor with the newspaper account of the battle of Roanoke Island. By their account there seemed to have been nobody there in that battle except the 9th New York. Great indignation among the troops.[24]

Feb 26—All the companies are being drilled in the skirmish drill over the sand hills. Took a stroll along the beach. Observed that the rebels had driven a large number of piles across the sound (Croatan) from a point near Fort Bartow, now Foster, to the North Carolina shore near Fort Forrest, but our fleet are removing them. Strolled on further and found the soldiers were digging out in the swamps large quantities of brier roots in which the island abounds, and in their leisure time convert them into smoking pipes and loads of them are sent home to their friends.

Feb 27—Companies all drilling the skirmish drill. Wrote a letter to my brother and friends in Norristown.

Feb 28—Skirmish drills as usual, and during the day the regiment was mustered for pay, after which the whole regiment was detailed for guard and picket duty. The health of the regiment is now very good.

Mar 1—All of Company A on guard duty. In the evening all of the forces on the island were called in line and received the news that Savannah, Nashville, Memphis, Forts Henry and Donelson had been taken by our forces. General Reno, our commander, came out before us and made a speech to the men, after which there was great jollification. Our quarters were illuminated, bands were playing, and great rejoicing all around until after midnight.[25]

Mar 2—Rained nearly all day. The boys are still keeping up their rejoicing over the good news received last evening.

Mar 3—Regiment received orders to prepare themselves with three days cooked rations and pack up all baggage and be ready to move at a moments notice. Early in the morning the regiment fell in on the color line and at 8 o'clock A.M. marched towards the beach, and immediately embarked on board of the steamer *Union* (*Wheelbarrow*) and steamed to our old floating quarters, the schooner *Scout* and *Cossack* and all safely put on board by 3 o'clock P.M.

---

23. Robert Iredell was publisher of the *Norristown Herald and Free Press*. Two of his sons, Charles and James, served in the 51st.

24. Immediately after the battle, a controversy began regarding which Union troops captured the battery. Reno's 21st Massachusetts and 51st New York claimed the honor, but the belated frontal attack by the 9th New York under Colonel Rush C. Hawkins, captured headlines and angered many Union soldiers.

25. From Parker, *51st PA*, 92.

Mar 4—Detailed as Officer of the Day. The whole regiment received new arms, Enfield rifled-muskets, and were a great improvement over our old ones. We were to have received new arms at Hatteras before we made the attack on Roanoke Island, but the steamer *City of New York* went down off the Inlet with everything on board. We received a large mail just after getting on board which always cheered up the men. On leaving the island we were compelled to leave some of our men behind in the hospital sick. Priv. Benj. P. Thompson was the only man left out of my company.

Mar 5—Spent a good part of the day reading and playing euchre in the evening.

Mar 6—Companies took their turns in drilling on deck and otherwise spent the day in reading and playing euchre in the evening. A terrible storm broke in to-day. Some of the vessels dragged their anchors and were driven around among the other vessels of the fleet promiscuously and doing some little damage. The small-pox has began to show itself among the regiment, and when the case demanded it they were taken to the island for treatment.

Mar 7—Company drills. Spent the day in reading and playing euchre.

Mar 8—This being the eight of the month, we are all celebrating the victory of Roanoke Island on board of the *Scout*. In trying to play a trick on Asst. Surg. Noble, I succeeded in playing one on myself. In lighting his pipe I attempted to put some powder in his pipe, and the consequence was that the flask exploded in my hand and blew a ring off my finger, and I had a swoolen hand for several days to nurse. The storm has abated, and is now more calm.

Mar 9—A most beautiful day. Wrote a letter to my sister. Company drills. Received orders for the fleet to prepare to leave the anchorage but later on during the day was countermanded.

Mar 10—Company drills and inspection.

Mar 11—The whole fleet at a given signal left their anchorage about 8 o'clock A.M. the *Scout* again in tow of the *Cossack* and steamed down Croatan Sound in the direction of Hatteras Inlet in a terrible rain storm, all hands compelled to keep below decks. Received letters from my mother and sister and a large number from friends. The fleet heaved anchor about 4 o'clock P.M. in sight of Hatteras.

Mar 12—A lovely morning and the Sound as smooth as ice and the fleet looks grand riding at anchor. At 7 o'clock A.M. the signal flags began to wave from the decks of the fleet and we learned from the Master of the *Scout* that it all means to weigh anchor and to proceed. The transports escorted by a flotilla of fourteen armed gunboats under the command of Commodore Stephen Clegg Rowan proceeded across Pamplico Sound and then up the Neuse River and when up the river about twenty-five miles, we came to a halt for about an hour while the gunboats reconnoitered the shore, as columns of smoke were seen at intervals of a mile or two, which proved to be the enemy's mode to signal the approach of our flotilla. Three days rations and sixty rounds of ammunition were issued to each man before hand in case that a forced landing should have to be made, but no enemy appeared and the whole fleet at eight o'clock P.M. heaved anchor at the mouth of Slocum's Creek, about sixteen miles below the City of Newberne.[26]

Mar 13—At 6.30 A.M. a preparatory signal was hoisted to make preparations to land and the naval vessels, with the gunboat *Picket*, moved in towards the mouth of the creek, and commenced to shell the woods some distance in advance of us. A reconnaissance was made to ascertain the depth of the water by the gunboat *Delaware*, Captain [S. P.] Quackenbush, and by Mr. H. H. Helper, with the boats crew of the *Alice Price*. Very soon afterwards, the signal for

26. Although Civil War-era soldiers used several different spellings of the city's name, the correct spelling was "Newbern."

the troops to land was hoisted, and at 8.30 A.M. the regiment commenced to disembark at Slocum's Creek, and in less than twenty minutes three regiments were on shore. Some of the steamers having grounded the men leaped overboard and waded to the shore, holding their cartridge boxes out of the water. The enthusiasm while all this was going on could not have been excelled.[27]

The three brigades were soon formed and put in motion, Foster with his brigade moved up the main county road, Reno with his brigade moved up along the railroad, Parke following up along the county road in supporting distance of the other two brigades, the whole marching column abreast of Commodore Rowan's flotilla of gunboats, who were engaged in shelling the woods as we advanced. It was raining in torrents and the roads were ankle deep in mud. The enemy were now fleeing before us.[28]

After a march of some six miles the head of our column reached the first intrenchments of the rebels at Otter Creek. It had been a cavalry encampment and had only been deserted but a short time, and by appearances, very hastily, as we captured all their camp equipage, and rations still cooking on the fires, and some already on the tables, and of course the 51st boys took a little rest here and partook of a good meal without any labor on their part to prepare it. Of course the camp was ransacked and the boys took what they wanted. The deserted intrenchments were a mile long, broken by redans for field pieces along the river bank. At this point communication was held with the fleet.

After obstructing the railroad at this point the three columns moved on, the gunboats still keeping abreast of the head of the column. The 51st had not proceeded far when they came up to a number of marines tugging away at a six gun naval boat howitzer battery under the command of Lieut. [R. Sheldon] McCook. The marines were played out and so were we, but McCook hailed us and showed us an order from Burnside, giving him permission to impress the first regiment that came along into his service to help along with his howitzers. We were the first. You can imagine our situation, marching with a heavy knapsack, three days rations in their haversacks, sixty rounds of ammunition and all the paraphernalia of a common soldier, and then tugging away with these six howitzers and caissons full of shot and shell for fourteen miles, you can imagine what each soldier had to do, and very often the wheels went down in the mud up to the axles.[29]

They do say that misfortune never comes signally, if I may be permitted to use the expression for low and behold after a march of a few miles we came up to Capt. Bennett & Dayton of the *Cossack* and *Highlander* with their two steel twelve pound Wiard-rifle guns fast in the mud and sand clear up to the hubbs, and his eighteen men completely played out. He begged for God's sake to the 51st to give him a hand and not to let him stick. There was no orders on our part for such action. We nevertheless gave him our assistance as we were very much attached to each other, and after a long and fatiguing march of sixteen miles, we had reached a point within one mile of the enemies picket at 9 o'clock P.M., with our guns, pretty well used up, and bivouacked for the night in a thick pine forrest in the mud and deep swamp. It rained all night as it had done during the entire day. We were wet through and through, fatigued and muddy from head to foot, but we crowded around the camp fire and passed a cheerless and a uncomfortable night, knowing the coming morrow there would be a racket.

27. Generally followed Burnside's report in *O.R.*, vol. 9, 201.

28. *O.R.*, vol. 9, 202.

29. Parker, *51st PA*, 100.

Mar 14—After passing a sleepless night, we were astir at sunrise and found ourselves full of pitch from head to foot. Our loaded muskets were examined and the charges all withdrawn, being wet could not be fired. Soon after sunrise, the three columns were in motion. Genl. Foster moved up the country road and attacked the enemy's front and left. Genl. Reno moved up the railroad to turn the enemy's right, and Genl. Parke move up the country road as a reserve.[30] A thick fog was prevailing at the time about a foot from the ground, and it was almost impossible to see anything in advance of us.

The 51st again tugged away on the ropes of the boat howitzers but were soon relieved by the Eleventh Connecticut and we advanced along the railroad and shortly left the road and soon came in full view of the rebel fortifications, and then filed to the left and entered a very rough piece of woods on a "double quick" over everything and found ourselves in front of a three gun battery, and we were immediately ordered to lie down, and did so in time, for soon a perfect shower of grape,shrapnel, and canister, came flying over our heads.

The engagement had now become general all along the line. About one o'clock Genl. Burnside ordered Foster on the right to charge and the gunboats on the Neuse River to follow up as the infantry advanced. The movement proved to be a success. Orders soon followed from Burnside for the 51st P.V. to charge the works in their immediate front near the brick-kiln. The order was soon given to the regiment and through fallen timber and a deep swamp the fort was taken and the flag of the 51st P.V. was planted on the works by Color Corporal George W. Foote of Co. E. It was the national colors that Foote so gallantly planted on the rebel works and it happened to be the old flag of the 4th Reg't. Penna. Vols. of which he had been a member, belonging to Co. G and was the first flag on any of the rebel works. Foote was assisted in climbing up on the top of the works by Lieut. [James A.] Beaver, who with several others of the regiment had reached the fort in advance of Foote. A small national flag carried by the "daughter of the regiment of the 4th Rhode Island" had been placed on the fort really first, but remained only a short time.[31]

The ground over which the regiment had to charge was over a deep swampy ravine in which the water had been dammed up some thirty or forty inches and it was over waist deep and the felled trees laid in all kinds of positions. It would seemed rather impossible for any human being to have pass over it, but the men, without reserve plundged into the water, and deliberately picked there way over the fallen timbers and reached the fort as discribed.

The battle took place at a point called Woods Brickyard, a few miles from the City of Newberne. Bennett of the *Cossack* with his two guns had done terrible work on our right, his very first shot dismounting one of the enemy's guns. In fact all of the marine howitzers had done splendid work, and the 51st boys did not regret the labor they had given to bring them up. On our reaching the fort, the rebels deserted their works in great confusion, leaving their three guns unspiked and all of their dead and wounded in our hands. Our guns must to have played sad havoc with their horses as very many were found dead within the fort.

This charge and taking of the fort virtually ended the battle for at this juncture Foster appeared in their rear with one of his regiments thus cutting off their retreat, and he Foster received the surrender of Col. Avery and some two hundred men.[32] The 21st Mass. of our

---

30. *O.R.*, vol. 9, 202-3.

31. Generally followed Parker, *51st PA*, 105-6. General Reno, in his report (*O.R.*, vol. 9, 221) wrote that he, not Burnside, sent the order for the 51st to attack.

32. Colonel Clark M. Avery commanded the 33rd North Carolina.

brigade was left in charge of all the prisoners and the remaining forces moved along the railroad directly for Newberne in pursuit of the flying enemy and at the crossing of the county road and railroad the columns came together. Foster's brigade consolidated and moved on, Reno's brigade following. Parke's brigade followed the county road and was ordered, if possible, to save the bridge, 1840 ft. long, over the Trent River from distruction, but we were too late, the bridge and part of the City was on fire, also found that the draw of the county bridge had been destroyed by the fleeing rebels, and after some consultation Burnside had with his Generals and Commodore Rowan, Foster was ordered to cross the river and occupy the City, and at 5 o'clock P.M. Burnside was in full possession of the City of Newberne and all of its fortifications. The enemy flew in all directions leaving everything behind even the meals on their tables. As there were a great many firemen among us, the fire in the city was soon subdued, but the splendid railroad bridge over the Trent was a total wreck. The rebels had also sent down the Neuse River fireships to burn our fleet but they did no damage.[33]

The 51st towards evening marched up the railroad and went into bivouac near the burning bridge on the banks of the Neuse River, and laid out all night without shelter in a drenching rain, and the air cold and chilling and the ground soaked with rain, with only a cup of coffee to go to sleep on. The regiment only had nine men wounded seven of whom were very slight, so slight that the company commanders did not think of such importance as to place their names on the rolls. The following were the only two who were seriously wounded: Privates John Johnson and Owen Rex of Company D.[34]

Mar 15—Early in the morning the regiment left their bivouac and marched some two miles to the enemies barracks and went into cantonment formally Camp Lane of the rebel forces. The day was a most beautiful one, and after getting well fixed we took advantage of it by looking over the ground we had fought the day before. The peach trees were out in full bloom, and the trees in the forest were hanging with Spanish moss, and the whole county looked indeed grand. No one would have thought that a deadly battle had been fought here the day before. On our rounds we found a fort on wheels. An eight wheel car truck on which was mounted a gun, the sides of the platform having been iron plated with loop-holes inserted at intervals for the use of muskets. We found out from the prisoners that the intention was to run it down the track about sunrise the morning before (as the 51st bivouacked along the railroad that night) and give us a surprise, but we were all too early for them and they never had a chance to put it into use. In looking over the ground where we had made our charge, we discovered thirteen finished redans and five guns bearing on our front, and an almost impassible morass, fallen timber &c. We could not but think and look in amasement at what we had accomplished, and if the surroundings had been told us before the charge, we would have said no, it cannot be done.

We found that our new quarters were filthy dirty and filled with vermine and about the same as we found them at Roanoke Island, and to add to it, it was now raining, but there happened to be fire-places built in the barracks, so the men set to work and built themselves fires and did some little cooking, but there was very little sleeping done that night on account

---

33. Following *O.R.*, vol. 9, 204.

34. The official casualty list included the following wounded men: Francis Young, Co. B; David Kane and Michael Mullin, Co. C; Owen Rix and John Johnston, Co. D; David Pierse, Co. E; Henry White and James Gruter, Co. F; James Dolan, Co. G. Casualty list is from Entry 652, Civil War Regimental Casualty Lists, Records of the Adjutant General's Office, Record Group 94, National Archives. Additionally, in the 51st PA roster, Bolton recorded the name of Pvt. William H. Weidner, Co. D, who died of wounds on April 16.

of the vermin. By an order of Burnside, Genl. Foster was appointed Military Governor of Newberne and its suburbs, and was directed to open the churches to-morrow the 16th at a suitable hour, the bells to be rung, the chaplains of the different regiments may hold divine service in them.[35] To-day Genl. Burnside issued the following order to the troops of the Coast Division:

> General Orders   Hdqrs. Dept. of North Carolina
> No. 17   New Berne, March 15, 1862
>
> The general commanding congratulates his troops on their brilliant and hard-won victory on the 14th. Their courage, their patience, their endurance of fatigue, exposure, and toil cannot be too highly praised. After a tedious march, dragging their howitzers by hand through swamps and thickets; after a sleepless night, passed in a drenching rain, they met the enemy in his chosenposition, found him protected by strong earthworks, mounting many heavy guns, and although in an open field themselves, they conquered. With such soldiers, advance is victory.
>
> The general commanding directs with peculiar pride that, as a well-deserved tribute to valor in this second victory of the expedition, each regiment engaged shall inscribe on its banner the memorable name "New Berne."
>
> By command of Brig.Genl. A. E. Burnside:
> Lewis Richmond.
> Assistant Adjutant-General.[36]

Mar 16—Rumors reached our camp this morning that Richmond had been taken and the boys are consequently happy and are hoping for the close of the war. The regiment is out of rations, except a small lot of raw pork which some of the men had found hid away about the barracks. Foraging very soon commenced, and large quantities of all kind were found and soon put to use. A general cleaning up of the arms &c which had become very rusty began to-day, and those that could, visited the battle ground and fortifications.

Mar 17—Wrote a letter to my sister. Received orders to prepare ourselves for a march. Left our cantonment early in the morning on a reconnaissance in light marching order, and without rations, all we had was some little salt, and the boys took the hint that we were after something for the inner man, and I am sure that it was needed. We were the only regiment on the march.

After three or four miles march, we came upon a line of breastworks and came to a halt, and took a survey of the situation and surroundings. We found that the trees had all been cut down and had fallen across the road, and at this point a foot-bridge had been distroyed, in fact every thing done to impede any troops that might want to pass in that direction, but our pioneers soon put things in passable condition and we again resumed our march through the swamps and mud and soon on an open plain of nearly four thousand acres which was a cotton plantation and belonged to a man by the name of Peter G. Evans, who we are told by the slaves on the place was a captain in the cavalry regiment we had driven out of the intrenchments on the morning of the 13th. It was about dusk when we arrived here, and we were pretty well used up from fording streams and wading through swamps but now what a feast we had. We found about eighty slaves and an immense amount of cotton, horses, cattle, hogs, goats, mules, a

---

35. *O.R.*, vol. 9, 371-2.

36. *O.R.*, vol. 9, 207.

saw-mill, a flour-mill, and any quantity of flour and corn meal, and about five thousand bushels of corn.[37]

We went into bivouac, but tired as the men were, they began to skirmish around and about one and a half miles from camp, they found over one thousand bushels of sweet potatoes buried in three different holes. Hard and trying march as it had been, the men could not resist the temptation. Out came the potatoes, fires were built and fifteen or twenty hogs and two bullock were killed, and I can assure you that the boys had a good repast and afterwards a good nights rest.

Mar 18—All hands rose early in the morning and after a hearty meal, began to load up the cotton and other captured property, and proceeded to our cantonment and after a long hard march, reached our camp about dark, pretty well used up. On leaving the plantation, one of the slaves told me that this Captain Evans was in the battle on the 14th and had been wounded and had died from his wound three days later. The boys cooked themselves a good meal on their return and soon after found themselves all in bed.

Mar 19—Rained nearly all day. Wrote several letters home. Received our trunks and other camp equipage from off shipboard, and as we had not had a change of clothing for seven days the treat was appreciated. The men indulged in a day of rest, talked over their march of the two days before, and many visited the water batteries along the Neuse. Fort Ellis was a splendid piece of engineering, the whole sides fronting the Neuse were lined with gabions and were splendidly made and the interior was perfection. It mounted eight (8) guns but they never had the chance to use one of them against our fleet.

Burnside has made the following dispositions of all the troops: Foster to guard all the approaches to the city, throwing out his pickets from four to five miles; Reno to guard the line of the Trent and railroad as far as the Brickyard, also throwing out his pickets from four to five miles; Parke to guard the Croatan down his line, throwing out pickets as far as the other brigades.[38] Indications clearly point to the fact that Burnside does not intend that the grass shall not grow under the feet of the Coast Division.

Mar 20—Rained all day. Wrote several letters. The men were left off in squads to pay a visit to the City of Newberne.

Mar 21—The whole regiment left their cantonment at 7 o'clock A.M. and moved up the Trent River about twenty-four (24) miles from Newberne and bivouacked near Pollocksville about dark. The purpose was to burn three bridges, and all several miles apart. The one at Pollocksville was burned first, the one at Trenton about midnight, and the other later. Not feeling very well, I was left behind in command of the camp. A report reached us towards evening that the regiment had been surrounded by the enemy's cavalry, and had been cut off, which of course created some little excitement with us all who had remained in camp.

Mar 22—Wrote a letter to my brother. We are all feeling very bad about the reported capture of the regiment, but about 3 o'clock P.M. stragglers began to come in, who set our minds at rest about the regiment, which was a great relief to us who had remained in camp. The whole of the regiment reached camp about dark, and reported that they had forded eight (8) streams of water waist deep and the roads muddy and in an awful condition. Having marched forty-eight (48) miles in the two days they were ready to take a good rest.

---

37. Following Parker, *51st PA*, 113.

38. *O.R.*, vol. 9, 372. General Parke had taken his brigade south toward Beaufort harbor, which was guarded by Fort Macon.

Mar 23—Vessels are arriving to-day with supplies and are now being unloaded and we begin to think that we are ourselves again.

Mar 24—Detailed as Officer of the Day. Wrote several letters home.

Mar 25—All the men of our regiment who were left back at Roanoke Island as invalids joined the regiment to-day except a few who were down with the small-pox. With the steamer came also a very large mail, the first since the capture of Newberne, and as it rained all day, we enjoyed reading our letters and gave us a good chance to make answer to many of them.[39]

Mar 26—Am not feeling very well. Wrote several letters to friends in Norristown.

Mar 27—Regiment mustered for pay.

Mar 28—Early this morning the regiment packed up and left their cantonment and moved to within one mile of Newberne and went into camp having received a lot of new Sibley tents. Our new home was named Camp Hartranft.[40]

Mar 29—Regiment slept in tents for the first time since the expedition left Annapolis a period of sixty-three (63) days.

Mar 30—A most beautiful day. Spent the day in reading the news. To-day we received some reinforcements, the steamer *Admiral* landing the 17th Mass., the steamer *Cossack* the 2d Md. and the steamer *George Peabody* the 79th N.Y. regiments.[41]

Mar 31—Detailed as Officer of the Day.

Apr 1—Not feeling very well. The weather is grand, the trees are out in full bloom, and the surrounding country indeed looks beautiful.

Apr 2—Not feeling very well. Weather very warm. Regiment ordered under arms to proceed to the wharf to escort the 2d Md. regiment to their quarters. By a General Order #23 of this date the corps d'armee now in occupation of this department will at once be organized into three divisions to be commanded according to seniority as follows, viz:

First Division by Acting Major General Foster Second Division by Acting Major General Reno Third Division by Acting Major General Parke.[42]

Apr 3—Regiment struck tents this morning and about 2 o'clock P.M. left Camp Hartranft and marched to the Trent River, embarked on board of a ferry-boat and crossed the river and landed in the City of Newberne, marched to the outskirts of the City, pitched our tents, and named our new home "Camp Franklin." More reinforcements arrived to-day the 3d N.Y. Artillery and 103d N.Y. regiment of infantry. Our forces are now guarding 36 miles of rail-roads between here and Beaufort.

Apr 4—Weather still very warm. Heavy detail made from the regiment to go down to the river to unload commissary stores.

---

39. Parker, *51st PA*, 120.

40. Parker, *51st PA*, 120, wrote that the regiment moved to the new camp on March 29. Gangewer, "Roanoke Island Island," 81, recorded in his diary on March 29-30 that it took two days to move the entire regiment.

41. The reinforcements sent to Burnside at this time included the 3rd New York Artillery, 2nd Maryland, 17th Massachusetts, and 103rd New York. The 79th New York was then serving in South Carolina.

42. *O.R.*, vol. 9, 375.

Apr 5—Weather still very warm. Received a letter from my sister. Company drills.

Apr 6—Wrote several letters. Regiment formed on the color line and proceeded by our Band marched to Newberne and attended church our Chaplain Mr. Mallory officiating.

Apr 7—Detailed as Officer of the Day.

Apr 8—Company and regimental drills.

Apr 9—Company drills. Regiment were paid two months pay. I received $259.50. Wrote a letter to my mother.

Apr 10—Not very well. Company and regimental drills. The sun very hot, a great deal of sickness in the regiment. Men have the diarrhoea, dysentery, ague, rheumatism, and some few the small-pox.

Apr 11—Still not feeling very well. Company drills. Sent home through the hands of Chaplain Mallory to my mother $210.00.

Apr 12—Still not very well. Company and regimental drills.

Apr 13—Still not very well but keep on duty. Company inspection. Whole regiment attended church in the morning.

Apr 14—Still not very well. Detailed as Officer of the Day. Also received notice detailing me as a member of a General Court Martial.

Apr 15—Attended a session as a member of the General Court Martial held in the jail at Newberne. Received several letters.

Apr 16—Attended the session of the Court Martial. During the morning was relieved as a member and ordered to report to the regiment as they had received marching orders. The regiment formed on the color line and left camp about 4 o'clock P.M. marched through the city to the wharf and embarked on board of a steamboat and steamed down the Neuse about two miles and were transferred to the steamer *Admiral*. Am not feeling very well. The 21st Mass. was also with us on board of the steamer *Guide*. The two steamers lay at anchor at this point two miles below the city all night. All ignorant of our destination.[43]

Apr 17—The two steamers *Admiral* and *Guide* weighed anchor about 5 o'clock A.M. and proceeded on our way, the troops still ignorant of their destination. The two steamers soon entered Pamlico Sound, passed into Croatan Sound, and after running aground several times, about dark anchored off Roanoke Island for the night.

Apr 18—The two steamers weighed anchor late in the afternoon and steamed towards Elizabeth City N.C. Our steamer ran aground several times. Three tug boats came to our assistance and succeeded in hauling us off, but again going out of Croatan Sound into the waters of Albemarle Sound we grounded again, so hard that we were compelled to remain in that position all night.

Apr 19—In the early morning by the aid of several tugs we were again pulled off and proceeded on our way, reaching a point on the Pasquotank River about 3 miles below Elizabeth City about 5 o'clock in the morning and commenced to disembark immediately. Owing to the deep draugh of the *Admiral* she could not get nearer than three hundred feet of shore, and the consequence was all hands, officers and men cheerfully sprang into the water and waded to land at a given signal. They lowered themselves down the side of the steamer without disrobing, guns on their shoulders, with cartridge box fastened on the end of their bayonets, and

---

43. The 21st Massachusetts sailed on the steamer *Northerner* (Colonel Clark's report in *O.R.*, vol. 9, 320). The 51st was on the steamer *Admiral*, also known as *Guide*.

through water up to their necks, made for the landing, which they all made in safety, all hands taking it good naturedly. Our sister regiment fared somewhat better. They were transferred to the light-draught steamers *Ocean Wave* and *Massasoit* and afterwards to small row-boats and launches, which were run in as near the shore as possible, but with it all they too had to do some wading. It was a beautiful sight to see the landing of the troops.[44]

The troops built fires and began to dry themselves as best they could but very soon by order of Genl. Reno the two regiments the 51st P.V. and the 21st Mass. were formed in line in an open field and Lieut. Col. Bell placed in command of the brigade.[45] Company A was sent forward as the advance guard of the column. The wagons hauling the ammunition and two boat howitzers from the steamer *Virginia* were next put in line. The brigade took up the line of march about 8.30 A.M. The Fourth Brigade composed of the 9th New York, 89th New York and the 6th New Hampshire and two boat guns belonging to Company K 9th New York all from Roanoke Island under the command of Col. Rush C. Hawkins had effected a landing about 2.30 A.M. the same morning at a place opposite Cobb's Point about four miles below Elizabeth City on the Pasquotank River with orders to proceed us and take possession of and occupy a bridge near South Mills where there were extensive stone locks on the Dismal Swamp Canal. It was presumed that Hawkins was well on his way when Bell's column was put in motion.

Our column advanced rapidly along an excellent road through a level and fertile district, halting only a few moments at a time for water and rest. The water we found very stagnant and very scarce at that and the sun was beating down on our devoted heads at a terrible rate, and the way we were marching it was evident that it was a forced one. Company A kept some three fourths of a mile in advance of the main column with skirmishers well advanced on the road and to the right and left of it. After marching some sixteen miles and about 10 o'clock A.M. Company F, Captain Hart, was sent forward to re-enforce me, and none too soon. The weather was now becoming very oppressive and the men began to suffer from the heat and for the want of water, canteens all empty and no opportunity to refill them. No halt had been made for breakfast, and the hard bread and salt beef could not well be eaten without water, and the men were faint from want of food.

Shortly we came up to a draw well, the first we had seen on the march. As we had taken all of the water we had got from the pools along the road, I determined to halt the two companies for a short spell for them to refill their canteens. While lying here for the few moments by the roadside we were astonished to see a large body of troops coming down on our left flank. To our dismay it was none other than Hawkins with his brigade, and we came very near to firing into one another. Reno was very much vexed at this state of affairs, for he had supposed that Hawkins was well in advance. Hawkins had taken the wrong road and had marched 12 miles out of his road.

Reno finding his [Hawkins's] men very much jaded by this long march ordered them in rear of our brigade and it was now evident what Reno intended Hawkins to do would now fall to our lot. After filling our canteens I put Companies A and F in motion again. We had not proceeded far when I noticed a number of stakes about three feet heigh driven in the ground along the roadway at intervals of about one hundred feet. They of course excited my suspicion

---

44. Bolton generally followed Colonel Clark's report in *O.R.*, vol. 9, 320, for this entry. He also used Reno's report in *ibid.*, 305-6.

45. Colonel Hartranft was in Norristown on a leave of absence. Two of his children, Ada and Wilson, were both very ill and died within a week of each other.

and after consulting with Capt. Hart I advanced more cautiously, doubling my skirmishers on the right and left of the road. As we advanced the stakes continued along the road. At this juncture Reno sent me word by an orderly that he would halt the main body of troops all on the main road and some three fourths of a mile in my rear for a short rest and cook something to eat.

The orderly had not left me more than five minutes when suddenly a solid twelve pound cannon ball struck the road about one hundred and fifty feet in advance of my company and between my advance skirmishers and my company and ricochetting passed over their heads and landed in a field in my rear near the main column. Others soon followed in quick succession. Hearing the report and seeing the ball strike the road, I ordered my men to break to the right and left and protect themselves by a worm fence that was on either side of the road. My pickets kept the enemy employed until the main body of our troops came up, which was about 12 o'clock M. Previous to this we had observed some eight or ten horsemen watching our movements but at so great a distance from us that we were unable to fire at them with any effect. During this time Reno was not idle. We also observed a dense smoke arise along our whole front lying close to the ground and blowing towards us, which entirely concealed the enemy from us. Reno on reconnoitering their position found that they were posted in an advantageous position in a line perpendicular to the road, their infantry in ditches and their artillery commanding all the approaches and their rear protected by a dense forest.

Companies A and F still holding their position on the main road, the other eight companies of the 51st P.V. were immediately ordered to file to the right and pass over to the edge of the woods for the purpose of turning their left. The 21st Mass. following the same course and in reserve. Hawkins' brigade coming up was also with the 9th and 89th New York was ordered to our support. The 6th New Hampshire were formed in line to the left of the road and ordered to support our four pieces of artillery. Col. Howard of the Coast Guard had two of his boat howitzers with A and F and was keeping the enemy employed.[46]

The engagement now became general, and shot and shell fell thick and fast, but the 51st P.V. and the 21st Mass. at last succeeded in turning the enemies left. They opened a brisk musketry fire and about the same time the 9th N.Y. also coming up in range and being too eager to engage, very unfortunately charged upon the enemy's artillery. The charge was a gallant one, but they were exposed to a most deadly fire of canister, grape and musketry and were compelled to retire, but immediately rallied on the 89th N.Y. Both regiments were then ordered to form a junction with the 21st Mass.

In the meantime the 51st P.V. and 21st Mass. kept up an incessant fire upon the rebels who had now withdrawn their artillery and were retiring. In the meantime the 6th New Hampshire had steadily advanced in line to the left of the road, and when within about two hundred yards poured in a most deadly volley, fired as it were by one man, which completely demoralized the enemy, which about finished the battle.

The engagement lasted about three and half hours. The men were completely fagged out by the intense heat and their long march that we could not pursue them. Before the engagement had ended, it had commenced to rain. Pickets were thrown out men rested under arms in line of battle. Some little cooking was done but the rails were so wet that they would not burn. We took only a few prisoners, some 10 or 15, most of whom belonged to the 3d Georgia Regiment.

During the early part of the night, Reno held a consultation with the officers, and it was finally decided, as the object of the expedition had been accomplished, and that a rumor had

---

46. Colonel William A. Howard commanded the 1st New York Marine Artillery, a unit which accompanied the Burnside Expedition to provide artillery support for the army troops.

gained ground that the rebels were expecting re-enforcements, that the expedition would return to their vessels. Accordingly the 51st P.V. were selected to find a place to bury a wagon load of intrenching tools.[47] The dead of both armies had already been gathered together and buried. The wounded of both armies had also been gathered together and placed under charge of a number of surgeons, who had established a field hospital in an old barn on the battlefield. Orders finally came for us to prepare to march. The pickets were withdrawn, and at 10 o'clock at night we were again on the move, taking a road leading to Currituck Court House,[48] the 51st P.V. covering the rear, with the Pioneers of the regiment in the rear of all under the command of Lieut. Ortlip. Nearly all of our wounded we were compelled to leave in the field hospital under the care of Dr. O. Warren, assistant surgeon of the 21st Mass. The rebel prisoners Reno paroled. On leaving the bivouac, a deep wide ditch ran diagonally across the field, it had commenced to rain during the battle and it still continued and the night was as dark as pitch, and in the darkness of the night, the men nearly all plunged into the ditch. On reaching the road, and after the last man had crossed, the bridge that spanned the Dismal Swamp Canal was cut away by our pioneers and off we started marching all night. The casualties in the regiment killed, wounded and missing as follows:

Killed:

Pvt. Benjamin H. Brouse, Co. E   Pvt. William R. Hoffman, Co. E
            Pvt. Adam Robinson, Co. I

Wounded:

Pvt. John Clare, Co. A   Pvt. Fred Kreamer, Co. F
Pvt. Monroe Nyce, Co. A (also captured)   Pvt. Theophilus Baird, Co. G
Pvt. Harvey Pinch, Co. A (also captured)   Pvt. James Powers, Co. G
Pvt. Joseph H. Zearfoss, Co. A (also captured) Pvt. Jacob Lennig, Co. H
Pvt. Lewis H. Young, Co. B (also captured)   Cpl. H. C. McCormick, Co. H
Pvt. Abraham Custer, Co. C   Lieut. George Shorkley, Co. H
Pvt. John Plunkett, Co. C (also captured)   Sgt. Matthew Vandine, Co. H
Lieut. Lewis Hallman, Co. D (also captured)   Cpl. Richard Martin, Co. I
Pvt. Owen Rex, Co. D   Pvt. Lewis Patterson, Co. I
Pvt. Robert H. Irwin, Co. E   Pvt. Abraham Wampole, Co. I
Pvt. Nathaniel Casselman, Co. F (also captured)

The 51st P.V. perhaps fared better than her sister regiments with her wounded and overmarched men, and here true companionship was shown by the members of the regiment. The slightly wounded were assisted along, leaning on the shoulders between two companions, the same also with the fatigued and worn out men.

Reno fully expected that the rebels would parole our wounded immediately on their being captured, as Burnside had done with theirs, but it was not done and it was some time before they were returned to the regiment.

The rebel troops that opposed us in this engagement were the Third Georgia Regiment said to have been 1800 strong under Col. Wright, some drafted militia under the command of

47. Instead of intrenching tools, the wagon held the gunpowder and related apparatus that was to be used to destroy the Dismal Swamp Canal locks at South Mills. The 51st did not do a good job burying this material. Colonel Ambrose R. Wright's 3rd Georgia returned after Reno fell back and discovered the gunpowder. Here again, Bolton followed Parker, *51st PA*, 144.

48. Bolton here followed the common error of mistaking Currituck Court House for its actual name, Camden Court House.

Col. Ferebee of North Carolina, Thirty-second North Carolina Regiment Colonel Brabble's, and the First Louisiana Regiment Colonel Vincent's, McComa's battery of artillery and one company of cavalry, Capt. Gillett's Southampton Cavalry, the whole under the command of Brig. Genl. Blanchard. The Third Georgia was reported to have been pretty well cut up and the rebel loss has been reported to have been something over 400.[49] The rebels were under the impression that the whole of Burnside's forces were marching upon them. After our forces had routed them, they fell back in great confusion on Joy's Creek some two miles to the rear of their former position, thinking perhaps that we would follow them in the morning. We took complete possession of the field and their works, a discription of which will be found in foot note below, and the manner in which they intended to roast us alive.*

---

*It was the skirmishers of Co. A who brought on, and opened this engagement. The right of the skirmishers rested on "Old Road," and the left rested on the Pasquotank River. The road leading to South Mills passed through the centre of the skirmish line at which point I had doubled the skirmishers, and kept them somewhat in advance of the main line. On the right there was a dense forest of heavy pines, and on the left the river, and our skirmishers covered the whole front of the rebel forces, and held the line until Reno reconnoitered the position and brought up the main column.

Immediately upon the report of the first gun, Col. Wm. A. Howard of the First New York Marine Artillery, who had followed in the rear of Companies A and F immediately run up his two boat howitzers and took position at the intersection of a narrow lane that ran off of "Old Road" to the main road leading to South Mills, and without cover for his guns commenced a rapid fire, which kept the enemy engaged until Reno made disposition of his troops. Howard's coolness in working his guns greatly inspired our men. Standing in the open road, unprotected reconnoitering the enemys position with his glasses, was indeed cool. A part of Company A and the whole of F was in support of him, and the only protection they had from the enemys shot and shell were the worm fences that were on either side of the road, and they were completely covered with the limbs of the trees that had been shot off by the guns of the enemy.

On the report of the first shot, a little incident occurred at this point is worth mentioning, as it was very amusing and in the midst of our racket with the enemy, made us all laugh. It appears that Quartermaster Freedley in the early morning on our column marching through Currituck Court House, captured a contraband, and one as black as the ace of spades, partly for his own use, and partly as a guide for our column. The weather was very warm, and it appears one of the drummers of the band thought that he would make use of him also, so he gave him the big base drum to carry. He was following along in rear of Company A when the first shot came flying down the road. The first thing we heard was an unearthly yell, and here was the poor darkey exclaiming Whar-is-de-man-dat-ownes-dis-banjo, repeating it several times. He found him at last, and leaping the worm fence like a deer was out of sight in an instant. We found him next morning at the landing twenty-one miles away.

Another incident I may relate here although it occurred later in the day near the close of the battle. Company A had changed its position to a yard to the left of the road in which stood a frame house whose occupants had fled at our approach. A long row of bee-hives stood in a line, and a huge pile of old fence rails close by. On this pile of rails were perched Privates Charles and John Henniss, and John Clare all of Company A setting there unconcernedly, thinking perhaps about making a raid on the bee-hives. The rebels were firing their shot and shell around rather carelessly. Noticing their dangerous position I call to them, and ordered them to a more secure position. They complied none too soon. A solid shot struck the rail pile about near where they had been setting, and in a second the rails, bee-hives, bees and honey was flying in all directions. Their timely leave reduced the casualties in Company A by at least three.

Apr 20—After marching all night, the regiment arrived at Currituck Court House about 5 o'clock A.M. A more wearisome march has seldom been made by any troops. The night was

---

49. Colonel Ambrose R. Wright had in action part of his 3rd Georgia, three guns of Captain McComas's battery, a company of cavalry, and some local militia which guarded the flanks. Wright's strength was about 400 men; his casualties amounted to approximately 32 soldiers.

dark, the soft, clayey mud from three to twelve inches in depth, and the men worn out by the labors of the day, having marched forty-two miles, besides passing through the excitement and fatigue of the battle. We were now only three miles from the point of our landing the morning before. All this we had done inside of twenty-four hours, besides fighting a battle lasting one hour and a half, gathering the killed and wounded, burying the dead and a wagon load of tools, caring for the wounded, and taking about three hours rest.

But tired as the men were, they must have a little fun. They visited the jail and opened all the cell doors, and let every convict escape. While some were attending to this racket another party took possession of a large well-stocked country store near the prison. The owner being a bitter secessionist they got the que and they made short work of him and the contents of his store—a hogshead of molasses, sugar, groceries, meats of all kind, boots, shoes, and hats. It was rather a grotesque procession as they moved on towards the landing three miles away, but the boys reach there with their booty about sunrise pretty well used up.

The *Admiral* rode at anchor at the same spot we had left her on the morning before, some 300 yards from shore. We at once commenced to embark on board again by wadeing out to her in some three or four feet of water. In a few hours all hand were on board and the first thing in order was to dry their clothes and afterwards prepare something to eat. We had had no good water for twenty-four hours. All along the road the water was stagnant and in the small streams. The water was as dark as logwood, caused it is supposed by the roots of the trees.

Are march back was a very rapid one, and as the last man crossed the numerous bridges they were cut away by our pioneers, and many a poor fellow was carried on the backs of his more fortunate companion rather than to be left behind to fall into the hands of the rebels. About 10 A.M. the *Admiral* weighed anchor and moved off to the music of the regimental band, bound for Newberne but we had not proceeded far before we run hard aground and the whole regiment was compelled to embark on another vessel of lighter draught and proceeded towards Roanoke Island, arriving there late in the afternoon and anchored off the Island for the night. In the meantime three tugs were sent to haul the *Admiral* off, which they succeeded in doing, and she followed after us.

Apr 21—The *Admiral* came along side of us this morning, and we were again placed on board of her, and she soon got under way, and with very cautious running reached Brant Island Shoals about 9 o'clock P.M. where, owing to the intense darkness it was not considered safe to proceed farther on account of the distruction of the light house. She dropped her anchors, and remained here all night. It rained inceasantly all day which kept the boys all below decks but they amused themselves by playing cards, and reading.

Apr 22—At daybreak the *Admiral* was signaled to hoist her anchors and be prepared to proceed on her way. Again the signal was given and she was steaming on her way through Pamlico Sound, and soon made the mouth of the Neuse River and moved along gallantly with her noble living freight towards the city of Newberne, where we arrived safely about 2 o'clock P.M. and after some delay, we disembarked and about 4 o'clock P.M. On the wharf to the great surprise of us all there stood Col. Hartranft, who had just arrived from Norristown, having been home on a leave of absence. He was of course very glad to see us after our grand achievements in the demonstration on Norfolk Va. and our success at Camden. After a short march, we reach our old camp, receiving the plaudits as we marched along, from the soldiers along the side-walks. A mail having arrived during our absence, the boys were all correspondingly happy on the receipt of letters from home.

Apr 23—Boys all taking a good rest and cleaning up muskets and clothing. Another mail arrived to-day. Received a letter from my brother.

Apr 24—Company drills in the morning, and regimental inspection in the afternoon. Oil cloth blankets issued to the regiment.[50] Was in command of the regiment and took charge of dress parade.

Apr 25—Company and regimental drills, and dress parade.

Apr 26—Company and regimental drills, and dress parade. The good news reached us that a part of our forces under Gen. Parke had reduced and taken Fort Macon, N.C. which caused much rejoicing among the troops of the expedition. By the order of Burnside, a large enclosed bastioned field work, capable of holding 1,000 men and mounting thirty guns is being constructed near our camp. It commands the town, also the Neuse River. It is being built principally by contraband labores who are paid and rationed by the government.[51]

To-day, Burnside issued the following General Order, which was read before the regiment on dress parade:

> General Orders Hdqrs. Dept. of North Carolina
> No. 30 April 26th, 1862.
> The general commanding desires to express his high appreciation of the excellent conduct of the forces under command of Brigadier-General Reno in the late demonstration upon Norfolk. He congratulates them as well upon the manly fortitude with which they endured excessive heat and extraordinary fatigue on a force march of 40 miles in twenty-four hours as upon the indomitable courage with which, notwithstanding their exhaustion, they attacked a large body of the enemy's best artillery, infantry, and cavalry in their own chosen position, achieving a complete victory. It is therefore ordered, as a deserved tribute to the perseverance, discipline, and bravery exhibited by the officers and soldiers of the Twenty-first Massachusetts, Fifty-first Pennsylvania, Ninth New York, Eighty-ninth New York, and Sixth New Hampshire, on the 19th of April--a day already memorable in the history of our country--the above regiments inscribe upon their respective colors the name "Camden, April 19."
> The general commanding desires to express his approbation of General Reno's strict observance of orders when the temptation to follow the retreating enemy was so great.
> By command of Maj. Gen. A. E. Burnside:
> Lewis Richmond,
> assistant Adjutant-General.[52]

Apr 27—Detailed as Officer of the Day. Regimental inspection.

Apr 28—Company and regimental drills. Wrote several letters home.

Apr 29—Company and regimental drills, and dress parade. Weather very warm.

---

50. Parker, *51st PA*, 158, wrote that this was the first time the 51st received gum blankets.

51. Bolton referred to Fort Totten, the primary Union fort guarding Newbern.

52. This order is in *O.R.*, vol. 9, 307.

Apr 30—Regimental inspection and muster for pay. In command of the regiment, and drilled them in regimental drill and dress parade.

May 1—Company and regimental drills. Received a letter from my mother, and from several friends.

May 2—Company and regimental drills and dress parade in the evening.

May 3—The 51st Penna. Vols. and the 21st Mass. Vols. were reviewed to-day on the banks of the Trent, about three miles from camp by Genls. Burnside and Reno. The day was very warm and sultry, and it was after dark when the regiment reached camp.[53]

May 4—Detailed as Officer of the Day. Regimental drill and dress parade.

May 5—Company and regimental drills, and dress parade. During the night the rain poured down in torrents, completely washing out the camp, and we were all looking like drownded rats.

May 6—Company and brigade drills.

May 7—Company and regimental drills and dress parade. Received a letter from my brother.

May 8—Company and regimental drills. Received a lot of news papers from Mr. Robert Iredell of Norristown, Pa.

May 9—Company and regimental drills, acted as Lieut. Col. on regimental drill. During the day the whole regiment struck tents for the purpose of policing the quarters. The regiment received new Sibley tents.

May 10—Regiment fell in on the color line and were marched to church. Wrote a letter to my sister.[54]

May 11—Company drill and inspection.

May 12—Detailed as Officer of the Day.

May 13—Company and brigade drills. Fort Totten was finished to-day and is now occupied by troops.

May 14—Company and regimental drills and dress parade.

May 15—Company drills. Received a lot of papers from Mr. Iredell. Regiment received orders to prepare to march with sixty rounds of ammunition and three days cooked rations. After waiting several hours the order was countermanded.

A reconnaissance under the command of Col. Thomas J. C. Amory of the 17th Mass. consisting of the 17th Mass., 25th Mass., 3d N.Y. Cavalry, and two pieces of artillery all belonging to Foster's Division left camp this morning at 2.30 o'clock A.M. and proceeded towards Trenton. Met the enemy at Trenton Bridge and had a skirmish with them with some small loss to ourselves. Lt. Col. J. Eugene Duryee, 2d Md. of Reno's Division was also sent out to operate with the troops above named and succeeded in having a brush with the enemy at Pollocksville and Young's Cross Roads, and on his return to camp destroyed the bidge at haughton's Mills. His loss was small.[55]

May 16—Company and regimental drills and dress parade. Wrote several letters.

May 17—Company inspection, and the Articles of War read in front of the company.

May 18—Regiment formed on the color line and proceeded to church. Dress parade.

---

53. Parker, *51st PA*, 161-2, wrote that the review occurred on May 2.

54. Bolton may be in error here; May 10 was Saturday.

55. *O.R.*, vol. 9, 335 (Amory's report).

May 19—Detailed as Officer of the Day. Received several letters and papers.

May 20—Company and brigade drills.

May 21—Not feeling very well. Pvt John C. Brannon, Co. A, died at newberne.

May 22—Company and regimental drills. Made out a list of the effects of Pvt. John C. Brannon, also wrote a letter to his wife.

May 23—Not feeling very well. Wrote a few letters.

May 24—Appointed as a member of a Council of Condemnation to pass on certain articles in the regiment. The members met at the quarters of Lieut. Col. Bell in the afternoon.

May 25—Company and regimental drills and dress parade. Wrote several letters to Norristown.

May 26—Detailed as Officer of the Day. Board of Survey met and condemned 22 boxes of crackers. Was elected president of the board.

May 27—Company and regimental drills. Signed the company pay-rolls. received letters from my brother and sister.

May 28—Company and regimental drills. receive orders to prepare to move our camp.

May 29—Regiment struck tents and marched about 4 miles to the left bank of the trent River. The camp is on beautiful ground and is the shape of a horse shoe. Our new quarters is named "camp Reno."[56]

May 30—The men spent the day fixing up their new quarters.

May 31—Regiment left camp at 7 o'clock A.M. and marched to a large field on the Trent River to be reviewed. After reaching there, a heavy rain set in, and we were all ordered back to camp. At 3 o'clock P.M. we made another attempt, and marched to Newberne, where the whole Coast Division was reviewed by Genl. Burnside and Gov. [Edward] Stanly, who had just been appointed Provisional Governor of North Carolina. The weather was very hot. We reached our camp long after dark wet through and through, and pretty well used up generally.

June 1—Company inspection. Received and wrote several letters.

June 2—Company and regimental drills. Regiment paid to-day, I receiving from the Paymaster $262.50.[57]

June 3—Detailed as Officer of the Day. Wrote a letter to my sister. Met with the Board of Survey.

June 4—Company drills and dress parade. Wrote a letter to my mother, sent her $200.00.

June 5—Company drills and dress parade. Not feeling very well.

June 6—Company and regimental drills and dress parade. Not feeling very well. The camp is full of green snakes, and the boys are kept busy in killing them. The county around the camp abounds in blackberries, mountain plums, grapes and mulberries. There is also plenty of eggs, poultry and milk to be had at fare prices, and consequently we are all living grand.[58]

June 7—Company drills and dress parade. Not feeling very well.

June 8—Company drills and inspections. Read the Articles of War to the company.

June 9—Detailed as Officer of the Day. Brigade drill lasting nearly all day. All of the pioneers belonging to the regiment were sent about 15 miles in the country for the purpose of destroy-

---

56. Camp Reno was located in a horseshoe bend of Brice's Creek just south of where it entered the Trent River.

57. Parker, *51st PA*, 175-6, wrote that this was the regiment's initial payment in greenbacks.

58. Parker, *51st PA*, 175.

ing bridges and felling trees across the roads leading into Newberne. They remained away four days.[59] Received several letters from home.

June 10—Company and regimental drills and dress parade. Wrote a few letters home.

June 11—Company drills and dress parade. Paid a visit to Newberne.

June 12—Brigade drill. Drew a sketch of my headquarters in the pines and sent it home to my mother. Gov. Stanley paid our camp a visit. A heavy detail from the regiment commenced to build a ferry across Bries' Creek, and cut a road through the pines, and soon cleared a fine place for a drill ground.

June 13—Company and regimental drills, and dress parade. Received a letter from my brother.

June 14—Company drills and dress parade. Drew several more sketches of my headquarters to send home to friends.

June 15—Detailed as Officer of the Day. Company inspection and dress parade.

June 16—Company, regimental, and brigade drills. Detailed as a member of a regimental Court Martial.

June 17—Regimental Court met, organized and adjourned. Not feeling very well. The regiment was paid an official visit by Gen. Burnside.

June 18—Company and regimental drills and dress parade. Wrote several letters home.

June 19—Regiment inspected by Col. Hartranft. Dress parade.

June 20—The First and Second Divisions was reviewed to-day by Genls. Burnside, Reno, and Parke. The occasion was the presentation of a sword to Gen. Burnside by the state of Rhode Island. The sun was excessively hot, and in marching to the parade ground, the rain poured down in perfect torrents, and the sky was as black as ink, but as Burnside appeared at a distance, and in nearing the two divisions drawn up in lines and wet to the skin, a beautiful rainbow spanned the heavens, forming a triumphant arch of gorgeous splender. The review and sword presentation was a magnificent affair, and the two divisions did grand in their marching and general deportment. The regiment reached their camp long after dark, pretty well used up.

June 21—Detailed as Officer of the Day. Captain Blair Co. G with his company **was sent** several miles in the country for picket duty, and did not return for several days.[60] Wrote a letter to my brother.

June 22—Company and regimental drills. During the week I offered prizes of $5.00, $2.50, and $1.00 to the three persons who had the cleanest arms, accouterments, and the most soldierly appearance in the company. The following were chosen the judges: Col. Hartranft, Major Schall, and Capt. Bell, who awarded the prizes as follows: Private James M. Botton, 1st prize Private Daniel Stout, 2d Prize Private Theo. H. Gilbert, 3d Prize.[61]

June 23—Company and regimental drills, and dress parade.

June 24—Company, regimental and skirmish drills.

June 25—Company drills and dress parade. Paid a visit to Newberne and while there bought a field glass paying $25.00 for it. Wrote several letters home.

June 26—Company and brigade drills and dress parade.

June 27—Company and regimental drills.

---

59. Parker, *51st PA*, 176.

60. Parker, *51st PA*, 179.

61. Parker, *51st PA*, 180.

June 28—Company drills and dress parade. Wrote a letter to my sister.

June 29—Detailed as Officer of the Day. Company inspection. Received orders to prepare to move in eight hours notice.

June 30—Regiment packed up all baggage and it was all sent to the wharf this morning and put on board of transports.

July 1—Towards evening the regiment struck tents, which were all rolled up and hauled to Newberne and immediately put on board of the transports that we were to embark on. After dark all the wood that had been in use about the camp was gathered up and placed in several large piles and set on fire, and the men during the night engaged in all kinds of amusements to wild away the night.

July 2—About 4 o'clock a.m. the "assembly" was beat, and the regiment formed on the color line and at once took up the line of march to Newberne and immediately embarked on board of the steamer *Excelsior*, and at 7 o'clock a.m. dropped down the river some few miles, and the regiment was transferred to the schooner Recruit. By 12 o'clock M. the two divisions of Parke and Reno had assembled at a point two miles below the city, and about that hour the whole fleet steamed down the Neuse River unconscious as to our destination. Near dark the whole fleet came to an anchor for the night, off the mouth of Slocum's Creek (called by the rebels Fisher's Landing) 18 miles below Newberne. Foster with his 1st Division was left in command of the Department of North Carolina.

July 3—The whole fleet weighed anchor at daylight, and at the signal, moved off, but the *Recruit* had some difficulty in getting off, and when we did get under way, the whole fleet was out of sight. The regiment had spent a miserable night, and it was not much better this morning, as the rain was pouring down in torrents, and everything was soaking wet, ammunition damaged and all our rations in the same condition, and all hands in the worse kind of humor. Besides the schooner was short of sailors and a detail of some six or eight men was made from the regiment to take the place of sailors. The was about 800 of us on board, when one half of that number would have been a load.

Well we had not proceeded far when we were hailed by the steamer *Alice Price*, Burnside's dispatch boat, when Col. Hawkins of the 9th N.Y. informed us that Richmond had fallen into the hands of McClellan, and that we were to return to Newberne. Of course wild cheers filled the air, and orders were given for our return to Newberne, where we arrived about 6 o'clock p.m. and dropped anchor for the night. From this move it was very evident that our mission was to go to the refitt of McClellan.

July 4—The troops began to disembark about 11 o'clock a.m. six of the companies reached their old camping ground about noon, and the balance about 4 o'clock p.m. Towards evening the tents arrived and we at once commenced to pitch them, but now we found the loss of our boards and woods we had destroyed, but the men made the best of it. At this juncture a large hog came running through the camp, and there was soon a running of soldiers, tents and boards forgotten. The porker was captured and soon dispatched, and in less than no time, was cooking over the fires.

July 5—Regiment spent the day in putting the camp in its orginal condition again, and rejoicing over the downfall of Richmond–but behold, before taps were sounded we learned to our dismay that the city had not fallen into our hands, and before any sleep reached our eyes, orders again was received to prepare to march at a moments notice. This time the orders were explicit, and that Richmond was our destination.

Chapter 4

Second Manassas

July 6–September 4, 1862

Burnside's troops landed at Newport News, Virginia, as reinforcements for Major General George B. McClellan and the Army of the Potomac. However, with the Peninsula Campaign ended, Burnside's North Carolina detachment was combined with a division from South Carolina as the Ninth Army Corps and sent to report to Major General John Pope and the new Army of Virginia. The 51st, part of the Second Division, took part in the Second Manassas Campaign which culminated in the battle of the same name on August 29-30, 1862. After being present at Chantilly (September 1), the regiment entered the Washington defenses as the Union army retreated.

July 6—Regiment struck tents at 3 o'clock A.M. and marched to Newberne and by 6 1/2 o'clock A.M. were again on board of the *Recruit*, and at 11 o'clock A.M. in tow of the *Excelsior*, proceeded down the river. The two same divisions were again afloat, and looked gayly as they steamed away. The men singing and otherwise enjoying themselves. We proceeded on our way all night, and the ride was a very pleasant one.

July 7—The fleet arrived at Hatteras Inlet about 7 1/2 o'clock A.M. and at once prepared to put to sea, and they all succeeded but the *Recruit*, she having run aground on the swash opposite Forts Hatteras and Clark, and it became necessary to put all hands ashore on Hatteras Island. While the tugs were employed in getting the steamer over the Swash the men enjoyed themselves in sea bathing and collecting sea shells and otherwise enjoying themselves. By 1 o'clock we were again on board, and crowding on all her sails, and like a thing of the air, we were soon sailing on the ocean. The advance with Burnside arrived at Fort Monroe about 4.30 P.M. and immediately informed Stanton of his arrival, and he in turn was inform that the President was on his way to meet him, and to hold all troops at that point until his arrival.

July 8—After a very pleasant ride on the ocean the regiment arrived at Fortress Monroe at 12.30 o'clock P.M. We were the last to arrive. The whole fleet rode at anchor off the Fortress all day, 8,000 well tried troops awaiting orders. Wrote a letter to my sister and spent the day in reading war news.

July 9—The whole fleet weighed anchor at 5 o'clock P.M. and left the Fortress, arriving at Newport News Va. about 8 o'clock P.M. all hands remaining on board all night. While laying at the Fortress, the President in company of Burnside passed by the *Recruit.* The President was saluted by the guns of the Fortress and by the man-of-war in Hampton Roads.

July 10—Regiment disembarked about 9 o'clock A.M. marched about one mile from the point of landing, pitched our tents, and called our new home "Camp Lincoln." This movement practically ended our connection with the Department of N.C.*

---

* The success of the Burnside Coast Division must have been very gratifying to the loyal people of the North. Leaving Annapolis early in January, their destination only being known to those in high command, braving the tempestuous sea, and worse still, treacherous Hatteras, driven to sea, and lost, as some of them supposed us to be, (the *Scout* with four companies aboard) getting the whole fleet, with few exceptions over the numberless swashes and bars that had to be encountered. Preparing to attack a strongly fortified, and intrenched island was no small undertaking. Landing under the protection of our gunboats, and laying all night in the rain, right under the guns of our foe, and within range. Up at daybreak and in line ready for action. Although the 51st P.V. did some daring work in this engagement, but for some reason unexplained, they failed to receive the credit that was justly due them.

After a rest, on the 8th of March, we again embarked on our fleet of vessels, and lay at anchor ready for another movement. On the 11th of the same month, the fleet left their anchorage, and steamed for Newberne, and under the guns of Commodore Rowan landed at Slocum's Creek, or Fisher's Landing, and after a short march, encountered the enemy on the 14th, routed him, and proceeded by our gunboats, overtook him on the outskirt of Newberne, engaged him, which resulted in the capture of an immense amount stores and public property. The rebels had obstructed the Neuse River just below the city with a fleet of sunken schooners loaded with stone, but the commodore ran through them and kept abreast of the army as they advanced. Here as at Roanoke Island we had to encounter (said to be by the rebels) impenetrable swamps, but we got through them, and it is doubtful whether they had ever been passed over by any human being before. Parke's troops broke the enemy's centre and Reno and Foster charged on either flank and the day was ours. At Camden also a detachment of the Coast Division did splendid work. Again returning to Newberne our forces were continually occupied. Thus it will be seen the result of our expedition can be summed up as follows: the capture of Roanoke Island with many prisoners and guns; Newberne with immense stores; the reduction of Fort Macon, giving us the control of one of the best harbors on the southern coast; capturing Washington, Kingston, Morehead City, Beaufort, Goldsborough, and Elizabeth City; and the entire command of Albemarle and Pamlico sounds, and destroyed all the rebel fleet in those waters.

Burnside had a very warm place in the affections of his soldiers, which but a few of the officers of the army ever had. Often he could be found riding into our camp unattended either by aid or orderly, inquiring of the men about their camp kitchens, and as to the quality of their rations, and the cleanliness of all the cooking utensils &c and the sanitary condition of the camp. He generally appeared in his loose blue Rhode Island blouse and check shirt, and always had a pleasant smile for all, and a kind word for everyone. At the bombardment of Roanoke Island, he could be seen up aloft on the rigging of his flag ship watching the shells from our fleet, and when one would do some good work, he would join in the cheers of his men. In all independent commands, it can be said of him, he never lost a battle.

July 11—Company drills and dress parade. I find myself in command of the regiment.

July 12—Company drills and dress parade. Wrote several letters home.

July 13—Company inspection and the Articles of War read in front of the companies in the company streets.

July 14—Company and brigade drills, and dress parade. A detail made from the regiment to day for guard duty at the Parrish farm three miles from camp on the road leading to the small town of Hampton.

July 15—Company and regimental drills and dress parade. Detailed as Officer of the Day. Received a letter from my brother.

July 16—Find myself in command of the regiment. Company drills and dress parade. The weather very warm, and all spare time is spent in fishing for crabs, bathing, foraging, as our rations are short and very scarce. Base-ball is the principal amusement and is enjoyed by both officers and men.

July 17—Company, regimental and brigade drills and dress parade. Wrote several letters.

July 18—Company and regimental drills and dress parade. Made out my Brigade Guard Report to headquarters.

July 19—Company and brigade drills, and dress parade. Was officially notified by letter from Beaufort N.C. that Prv. David Schrack of Co. A died at that place. During the day paid a visit to Fortress Monroe, and had a very pleasant time, visiting the fortress and meeting with many prominent officers.

July 20—Company inspection and the Articles of War read to the companies in the company streets. Details made from the regiment to proceed home to recruit men for the regiment.

July 21—Company and Brigade drills, and dress parade. Wrote a letter to Beaufort N.C. in regard to the death of Private David Schrack, Co. A. Wrote a letter to my brother. Asst. Surg. James D. Noble resigned. Recruiting detail left for home under Capt. J. Merrill Linn.

July 22—Company and regimental drills, and dress parade. Wrote a letter to my sister. An official order read on dress parade on camp duty, which will keep us pretty well occupied.

July 23—Company and regimental drills and dress parade. Received a letter from my sister.

July 24—Company and regimental drills and dress parade. Received a large bundle of news-papers from my friend Iredell.

July 25—Company and regimental drills, and dress parade. The 1st Brigade and part of the 3d, with a battery of six pieces left Newport News to go to Yorktown.

July 26—Company drills and dress parade. Paid a visit to Fortress Monroe and met with Generals Halleck, Dix, Burnside, Parke, Reno, and Meggs.[1]

July 27—Detailed as Officer of the Day. Received a letter from my mother. From three to four hundred wounded, sick, and well prisoners arrived here to-day from Richmond. They looked as if they had had rough treatment. They were put in the hospital and are receiving kind treatment from the lady nurses. All our connection with the Coast Division was severed to-day. By G.O. No. 84, War Department, the troops now under Gen. Burnside is now known as the 9th Army Corps.

July 28—Company and brigade drills and dress parade. Was detailed as a member of a regimental Court Martial. All the sick and convalescents belonging to the regiment left at Newberne arrived to-day.

July 29—Company and regimental drills and dress parade. Made out my Brigade Guard Report. Wrote a letter to my mother.

July 30—Company and regimental drills and dress parade. Whole regiment marched out about three miles from camp and engaged in target practice.

---

1. The other generals mentioned here, in addition to Burnside, Parke, and Reno, were Major General Henry W. Halleck (General in Chief of Union armies), Major General John A. Dix (Department of Virginia commander), and Brigadier General Montgomery C. Meigs (Quartermaster General).

July 31—Company and regimental drills and dress parade. Wrote several letters to friends in Norristown.

Aug 1—Company and regimental drills, and dress parade. During the day practiced signalling with flags. Received orders to prepare to march. Received a letter from my sister and a bundle of news-papers from Mr. Iredell. Dr. Jon. R. Rineholdt reported for duty and was mustered in as Asst. Surg.

Aug 2—Regiment struck tents at 8 o'clock A.M. and marched to the wharf and immediately embarked on board of the schooner *Restless* and sailed down the James River, arriving at Fortress Monroe at 8 o'clock P.M. and dropped anchor for the night.[2]

Aug 3—Weighed anchor about 1 o'clock A.M. and sailed through Cheasapeake Bay, and soon entered the mouth of the Potomac. Burnside passed us on the way and we all gave him a hearty cheer. We came to an anchor near Mount Vernon, about 9 o'clock P.M. for the night.

Aug 4—Weighed anchor and started again at 2 o'clock A.M. and arrived at the mouth of Aquia Creek at 1 1/2 o'clock P.M. and at 10 o'clock P.M. disembarked and immediately embarked on board of the cars of the "Aquia Creek and Fredericksburg Railroad," and arrived at the depot opposite Fredericksburg at 12 o'clock midnight, disembarked and bivouacked on the ground all night.[3]

Our trip had been a pleasant one, and nothing of particular note occurred except that the boys declare and swear that they had been drinking rat coffee during their trip. After it was too late it appears that a large cauldron had been filled with ship's water during the night to have ready for the next morning. During the night it was discovered that two rats had in some way fallen into the cauldron, and unable to get out had drowned. It remained a standing joke for some time with the boys. Dr. Chas. S. Duffell reported for duty and was mustered in as Asst. Surg.

Aug 5—Moved our position about one mile further back from the depot to a wheat field belonging to the Phillips farm, pitched our tents and named our new home "Camp Ferrero." The paymaster arrived and paid us two months pay, I receiving $262.50. Camp rumor had it that the two divisions of the 9th Army Corps will operate with Pope's army.[4]

Aug 6—Company and regimental drills. Sent home $190.00 to my mother. Brigade dress parade in the evening. Commission officers drill every day.

Aug 7—Detailed as Officer of the Day. Went on the Grand Rounds at 12 o'clock midnight. Another detail made from the regiment to proceed to Pennsylvania to recruit for the regiment, all under the command of Lieut. Jacob P. Brooke. The detail left the camp the same day.

Aug 8—Company and regimental drills, and dress parade. Received and wrote several letters. Paid a visit to Falmouth.

Aug 9—Company drill and dress parade. Received a letter from my mother, and a bundle of news-papers from Mr. Iredell. Our two divisions received marching orders, and to be ready to march in three hours notice, and to pack up all surplus baggage, and send it to Aquia Creek for safe keeping. The roar of artillery can be heard from a distance in our camp to-day. There will be work for us soon. Rumor reached camp late to-night that Genl. Pope moved from Sperryville, Little Washington, and Warrenton, with the corps of Banks, Sigle, and one division of McDowell

---

2. Parker, *51st PA*, 191, wrote that the regiment embarked on board of *Recruit*.

3. Parker, *51st PA*, 191-2, wrote that the 51st arrived at Aquia Creek at 9 a.m., departed an hour later, and reached Fredericksburg at 1 p.m. Companies C and G arrived the next day.

4. Parker, *51st PA*, 193, wrote that the 51st used Sibley tents during the campaign.

corps, numbering in all 32,000 men, to meet the enemy who had crossed the Rapidan and was moving on Culpepper. This we all suppose accounts for the artillery firing.[5]

Aug 10—Company drills and regimental inspection. Wrote a letter to my brother.

Aug 11—Company and brigade drills, the latter under the command of Col. Hartranft, his first attempt, and did very well. Many of the officers expressed home their surplus baggage, as a long campaign is expected. Sent home through the hands of Philip Jacobs $50.00 company funds, of which I was treasurer.

Aug 12—Company drills. Served as a member of a Court Martial. Received marching orders. At 6 o'clock P.M. the regiment fell in on the color line and shortly after stacked arms to await further orders. They had no more than done so, when a violent storm swept over this section of country tearing our tents from their fastenings and sending them in all directions. Our orders were to leave them standing, as we were to move without tents. They were collected together again and pitched, but in a very delapidated condition.[6]

At 7 o'clock P.M. we formed on the color line, and moved off, the rain pouring down in perfect torrents swelling all the creeks and ravines to overflowing, as we soon discovered. Our line of march was along the Rappahannock River, and we marched all night. The night was as dark as pitch, and our marching very slow. The roads were obstructed with upset wagons and the artillery stuck in the mud, and the mud knee deep and all hands soaked through and through, and out of humor. Our command consisted of 12 regiments of infantry, 4 batteries of artillery, and 2 companies of cavalry, all under Gen. Reno, with orders to report to Gen. Pope, commanding the Army of Virginia, to which the detachment of the 9th A. C. was now attached. Our old commander Burnside remained at Falmouth.[7]

Aug 13—After a most tedious march all night we came to a halt about 4 o'clock A.M. and went into bivouac without any shelter and nothing to eat, as we were too tired to prepare it. Left our bivouac at 9 o'clock A.M. came to a halt at noon for rest near a peach orchard, and the boys soon made short work of the fruit. This was near the Yellow House, some eight miles from Fredericksburg. After our short rest we started again. The heat had now become intense, but kept up our march until 9 o'clock P.M. when we came to a halt, and bivouacked in an open field for the night.

Soon after our halt, a very distressing rumor reached our camp of an accident on the Potomac, in which four men of the 51st P.V. lost their lives. Later news brought the truth. It

---

5. The Army of Virginia contained three corps. The First was led by Major General Franz Sigel, the Second by Major General Nathaniel P. Banks, and the Third by Major General Irvin McDowell. A small reserve corps under Brigadier General Samuel Sturgis also was attached to the new army.

6. Parker, *51st PA*, 195.

7. *O.R.*, vol. 12, part 3, 566. The Ninth Corps was organized as follows:
   First Division, Brig. Gen. Isaac I. Stevens
       First Brigade, Col. Benjamin C. Christ: 50th PA, 8th MI
       Second Brigade, Col. Daniel Leasure: 46th NY, 100th PA
       Third Brigade, Col. Addison Farnsworth: 28th MA, 79th NY
       Artillery: 8th MA Bty; Bty E, 2nd US
   Second Division, Maj. Gen. Jesse L. Reno
       First Brigade, Col. James Nagle: 6th NH, 48th PA, 2nd MD
       Second Brigade, Col. Edward Ferrero: 21st MA, 51st NY, 51st PA
       Artillery: PA Bty D; Bty E, 4th US

appears by a collision on the Potomac River, off Ragged Point, between the steamers *Peabody* and *West Point*, the latter sunk She was loaded with convalescent soldiers of Burnside's army, and 79 of the crew and passengers were drowned. The following were of the 51st P.V.:

> Sgt. Maj. C. Jones Iredell
> Prv. John M. Young, Co. F
> Prv. James Gummo, Co. G
> Prv. George W. Meyers, Co. I

Iredell was universally liked by the whole regiment, and had he had lived, promotion would have followed him. He rendered important service to Lieut. Col. Schall at Camden N.C. None of the bodies were ever recovered. A lot of goverment property was also on board, which was all lost, I myself having eight sergents swords and six muskets.

Aug 14—Left our bivouac about 6 o'clock A.M. and arrived at Bealton Station on the Orange and Alexandria Railroad about 10 o'clock A.M. pretty well worn out. Stacked arms, and cooked some dinner and at 1 o'clock P.M. embarked on the cars, arriving at Telegraph Station at 3 o'clock P.M. and at Culpepper Court House at 4 o'clock P.M. Disembarked and marched a short distance back of the town and bivouacked as we thought for the night but only remained one hour, when we again took up the line of march, and marched some four miles, and at sundown went into bivouac in a meadow for the night in a very heavy rain, but with it all, we all slept soundly, as we were pretty well used up. We may say now that the detachment of the 9th A. C. under Genl. Jesse L. Reno has joined Pope's army and that we are now a part of the Army of Virginia.

Aug 15—Received marching orders early this morning, and at 2 o'clock P.M. took up our line of march in a drenching rain that lasted all day. The marching was most wretched. After a march of five miles, at sundown we reached Raccoon Ford on the Rapidan River. We immediately took up a position on the Raccoon Ford Road, and Somerville Ford Road, with our right resting on Cedar Creek, with instructions to repair the road leading from our camp to Mitchell's Station on the Orange and Alexandria railroad.[8] The whole of Company A was sent out on picket to-night, and a dreary cheerless night it is.

Aug 16—Detail made from the regiment for a foraging expedition to a Mr. Somerville's Mill, and the wagons came back well loaded down, and the boys looked pretty well after his garden, as they too came in pretty well loaded down. Company A remained on picket all day, but after dark were relieved and returned to camp.

Aug 17—Company A resting all day, other companies on picket duty and repairing the roads. Another foraging party sent out to-day to the same place for corn and coming in sight of the corn-crib discovered the enemy loading from the same crib. The teams came back at a double-quick. We can plainly see Stonewall Jackson to-day pitching his tents on a high hill on Slaughter Mountain. Can see them signal with flags from Cedar Mountain in day light, and with lights at night.[9] Attended a meeting of the Council of Administration. Wrote a letter to my brother.

The following named persons all belonging to the regimental band were mustered out to-day, and left for home the same day:

---

8. *O.R.*, vol. 12, part 3, 572.

9. Parker, *51st PA*, 202.

Samuel G. Arnold	John Earp	Jeremiah W. Buck
Joseph C. Millhouse	Jessie M. Bucks	Benjamin Rowland
James S. Baird	Charles Thompson	Charles Day
William Workizer	Alexander Earls	Simon Britton
George Y. Hansell	Benjamin Witkins	Philip Jacobs
	Williams Williams	

Gen. Buford's cavalry arrived in camp to-day having been temporally loaned to Reno, who is to guard and protect our front on the other side of the Rapidan, and the approaches from Louisa Court House and Hanover Junction.[10]

Aug 18—Regiment mustered for pay. Received marching orders. We left our bivouac at 12 o'clock midnight. A general movement all along the line. The corps of Banks, McDowell, Sigel, as well as our own, left their camps about the same hour. Reno has sent back his trains by the way of Stevensburg, with instructions to cross at Kelly's Ford and Barnett's Ford, and we following the trains with orders to take position behind the Rappahannock.[11] The 51st P.V. is covering our movement in the rear. Moved rapidly, pass Ford's Church near Raccoon Ford during the night. We marched all night, forded several rivers and streams and and did not make one stop for rest, as Jackson was at our heels and captured some few of our stragglers.

Aug 19—We reached Stevensburg at 7 o'clock A.M. made a short halt for a meal, the first halt made. Moved on very rapidly, Jackson still following close behind us, forded many streams, no halts made for rest. Reached the Rappahannock River at 4 o'clock P.M. and crossed it at Kelly's Ford, selected a field and went into bivouac for the night. Incredible as it may seem, the regiment marched 29 miles to-day, in eight hours, through a scorching hot sun, blinded with dust, with no halts for rest, and hardly time to stop to get a drink. Rude sheltering was put up with branches of trees, to protect us from the sun and a good rest enjoyed. Prvs. Wm. Percy Schall and Philip Whitehead Co. D captured.

Aug 20—Was detailed as Brigade Officer of the Day. Reno received orders from Pope that he intended to make a stand at this point, and that all things not necessary for camp use, ordered by Pope to be burned, and letters forbidden to be written.[12] More ammunition issued to the men. Went along the brigade picket line at midnight, along the banks of the Rappahannock. Got through with my visit, and on returning, lost my way in the underbrush, and it was near morning before I reached camp, and then pretty well used up.

At sunrise this morning the enemy became very uneasy, and began to fire at our pickets. The whole camp was aroused and stood by their arms. Durell's battery[13] fired a few shots, and the whole of Co. D sent out on picket on our front to prevent surprise. [Pvt. James Whitehead of Co. D captured.]

Aug 21—Hostilities opened this morning in dead earnest at 10 1/2 o'clock A.M. near the Rappahannock Station, by the enemy driving in our pickets, and about one hour later it began

---

10. *O.R.*, vol. 12, part 3, 589. Brigadier General John Buford commanded the cavalry brigade attached to Banks's Second Corps.

11. *O.R.*, vol. 12, part 3, 598.

12. *O.R.*, vol. 12, part 3, 604.

13. Captain George W. Durell commanded Independent Battery D, Pennsylvania Light Artillery, which had been assigned to Reno on August 12. I have used the correct spelling of Durell's name; Bolton consistently spelled it "Durrell."

in our immediate front. The 51st P.V. ordered to repel the attack, and was about to move off, when the cavalry was ordered instead. Reno ordered to send three regiments of cavalry under Buford, and two pieces of artillery, to make a strong reconnaissance towards Stevensburg, and to advance three regiments of infantry and a battery three miles south of the Rappahannock to support him.[14]

The fighting continued all day. The 51st was in support of Durell's battery. The fighting ended for the day at 6 o'clock P.M. favorable to the Union cause, Sigel having captured 19 guns. The 51st lay on their arms all night in the usual rain and without shelter.[15]

Aug 22—Hostilities commenced at 5 1/2 o'clock A.M. and continued incessantly all day. Regiment received marching orders, and left their bivouac at 6 o'clock A.M. and immediately crossed at Kelly's Ford and marched in the direction of Rappahannock Station, and after a tedious march all day reached that point at 10 o'clock P.M. in a drenching rain, and bivouacked for the night in an open field and without any shelter of any kind. We had been in support of Durell's battery all day. Some twenty cannon was captured by our forces during the day. The Union loss in killed and wounded was small. A good number of the 51st P. V. gave out during this march and as we had not an ambulance or wagons, and the men were compelled to straggle. Anticipating this, the men were ordered to destroy their guns if there was any fear of capture, and follow on the best they could. They all reached camp before morning but without their guns or knapsacks, pretty well worn out. The heavy rain that had set in had rendered the fords of all the streams impassable for twenty-four hours.

Aug 23—Hostilities commenced about 5 o'clock A.M. on both sides in good earnest. At 6 o'clock A.M. the regiment was again in motion not having taken time to get a mouthfull to eat. Made a halt at 12 o'clock M. near a large cornfield captured some corn, and made some corndogers. Had no salt to season them, made us all half sick. During the whole morning we had marched through a violent rain storm, the thunder and lightening it seemed to us far outdoing the roar of artillery. It was simply fearful. A negro sitting on his mule near his team, and near the regiment was struck by lightening and instantly killed, and about the same time a caisson loaded with ammunition was struck and blown up. It seemed that the whole heavens were torn loose.

The butchers of the regiment had killed several cows that wandered around loose near our bivouac, by the consent of Hartranft, and the boys were soon roasting it on the ends of their ramrods, but before it had time to cook, orders came for us to move on, and off we went leaving our meat in the fires. Marched all night, the rain still continuing in all of its fury. The men were almost famished for some time to eat, as they had had not more than a half dozen crackers for the past four days, and not an ounce of salt in the whole regiment.[16]

Aug 24—Bivouacked near Warrenton Junction at 1 o'clock A.M. in the rain. Soon after daylight the regiment again resumed their march, and continued it all day. A few crackers and a little tea was issued to men on the march, and it was all they had until next day. During the day Sigel corps crossed Great Run, with Reno and Banks following rapidly in support, under a heavy artillery fire, from batteries which the enemy had established all along the south side of the Rappahannock. The bridge which had been built at Sulphur Springs upon which the enemy crossed the day previous in escaping from Sigel advance was destroyed by the enemy,

14. *O.R.*, vol. 12, part 3, 609.

15. Parker, *51st PA*, 203.

16. Parker, *51st PA*, 204-5.

but Sigel pushed forward with his corps, his support following him, in the direction of Waterloo Bridge. This bridge was afterwards destroyed by Buford. We arrived at Sulphur Springs at 9 o'clock P.M. and bivouacked for the night.

Aug 25—Left our bivouac at daylight, taking the Warrenton Turnpike, reaching Warrenton at 12 o'clock M. foot sore, amd otherwise used up and almost famished for food, and in not the best of humor. Here we were expected to resist a charge of Stuart's cavalry, who had an eye on our wagon train. Hunger, and the want of sleep was beginning to tell very plainly on the men. The officers fared no better. From the 12th of August we had been on the constant march, day and night, with less than half rations, and very little sleep. At 4 o'clock P.M. we were again in motion, Stuart not making his attack on our train. Marched until 10 o'clock P.M. and bivouacked for the night in a meadow about one mile from the junction, where we lay on our arms all night. The nights are very cold and chilly, with heavy dews, no time to wash our clothing, and consequently we are becoming very dirty, and there is no help for it, and worse still the amount of rations are not improving.[17]

Aug 26—Left our bivouac at 7 o'clock A.M. and marching, counter-marching, and floundering around with some little skirmishing, reached Warrenton Junction about 9 o'clock P.M. and bivouacked for the night.

Aug 27—Left our bivouac at daylight, passed through Greenwich at 8 o'clock A.M. Regiment under fire all day and was marching and counter-marching all day. Reno ordered to take the road from Catlett's Station to Greenwich, followed by Heintzelman.[18] We marched late into the night and bivouacked near Warrenton.

Aug 28—Left our bivouac at daylight, and passed through Manassas Junction at 12 o'clock M. Here all was confusion. The rebels had reached this place ahead of us, captured seven trains of cars loaded with ammunition and provisions and army supplies generally. Ten locomotives were also destroyed. The enemy had supplied themselves with what they wanted and destroyed the balance. The ruins are still burning and it is said the destroyed property is worth $500,000. The 51st is covering the rear. McDowell is now engaging the enemy on the Plains of Manassas. The guns can be distinctly heard. We have had more or less skirmishing all day. Prv. Francis Stiver Co. I wounded at Pope's Hd.-Qeurs. The regiment marched late into the night, and bivouacked among the fortifications some four miles north of the Junction. It was here that we saw the quaker guns still in the fortifications that kept McClellan at bay for so long.[19] Darkness ended the fighting and we lay on our arms all night.

Aug 29—Regiment left their bivouac at daylight, after calling the four companies A, D, F, and I who had been on picket all night. Soon crossed Bull Run Creek, and passed through Centreville, and at 12 o'clock M. arrived on the old battle ground of Manassas, amid the roar of artillery, flying shells, solid shot and railroad iron, bolts and nuts. Immediately formed in line, devesting ourselves of our knapsacks, and lay down in line of battle in support of Durell's battery.

By this time the battle was raging in all of its fury, the air was simply filled with shrieking and exploding shells, and the dying and wounded men were being carried to the rear by the hundreds. Durell was sending forth shot and shell incessantly, and must have done terrible

---

17. Parker, *51st PA*, 208.

18. Major General Samuel P. Heintzelman commanded the Third Army Corps, Army of the Potomac.

19. Quaker guns were logs painted to resemble cannon at a distance. Outnumbered Southern troops had used these guns to deceive McClellan.

work within the enemies lines. The battle raged all day until after dark, when the darkness put an end to the conflict. Companies A, D, F, and I were again sent out on picket under the command of Lieut. Col. Bell. The balance of the regiment remained in the rear under Col. Hartranft in support of the battery. It was a fearful night, for the cries and groans of the wounded in the still hours of the night was simply heartrending. The woods was full of the wounded of both sides. We spent a sleepless night, and no pickets were relieved for rest as the two picket lines were in close proximity.

Privates Henry Derr and Thomas Troy of Co. I captured, and John Geddes, Co. K deserted.

Aug 30—A short time before daylight I ordered my brother Lieut. Jos. K. Bolton to advance in front of our pickets to endeavor to find out the position of the enemy in our immediate front. Everything seemed to be quiet. Not a sound could be heard on our right or left, so much so that we thought the Union army had possession of the field, and that the enemy had quietly stolen away during the night, but he had only proceeded from forty to fifty yards when he was discovered by the enemies pickets, who at once opened a volley of musketry at him, which very fortunately passed over his head, and our own. To him belongs the credit of opening the battle of the second day, for before that, not a sound had been heard. From that moment until 8 o'clock P.M. that battle raged in all its fury, the roar of artillery and musketry was some thing terrible and far beyond discription and those of us who were on that field of carnage that day will never forget it.

After some time, the four companies were relieved from picket duty, and fell back and rejoined the rest of the regiment, who were still supporting Durell's battery. The regiment lay in this position until sundown when we, with the rest of Ferrero's brigade was ordered to the left. The whole of the 51st P.V. were put in support of Graham's Regular U.S. Battery.[20]

While we were engaged in taking up our new position, our army was on the retreat, which at that time we were perfectly ignorant of. In going from our former position, we left all our knapsacks in a pile just where we had left them at noon the 29th. We of course left a guard with them, and with one of the guards Prv. Jesse Johnson, I left my field glasses, not wishing to have them with me in action. Also left a well filled haver sack of cooked chicken that my cook Kitty had prepared, and which we expected to enjoy after our return, but we never returned. The enemy had got possession of that part of the field, and all was lost to us.

From the moment we took up our new position the battle raged furiously in our front. At 10 o'clock P.M. orders came for us to withdraw, our brigade, the 2d, the last to leave the field, and covering the rear. It was suspected that we were to be sacrificed to save the rest of the army, but we succeeded in getting off, not losing a man, a piece of artillery or a wagon, and reached Bull Run Creek late during the night, plunged into it neck deep and reached the opposite bank in safety. It had been raining during the night, and the clay bank became very slippery, which made it very difficult to reach the top. You would think that you were up, then down you would go again. Everything was in confusion along the road that night, artillery and wagons blocking up the road and making it almost impassible for the infantry, but the men took it very cool, as there was no attempt made by the enemy to follow us.

The regiment lost as follows:

Wounded:

Cpl. William W. Smith, Co. D	Pvt. Dennis O'Neil, Co. D
Pvt. Thomas Deiner, Co. F	Pvt. John Miller, Co. G

---

20. Captain William M. Graham, Battery K, 1st United States, attached to the First Division, Third Army Corps.

Pvt. William Moore, Co. G   Pvt. Jewett S. Harding, Co. H (also captured)

Captured:

Pvt. Lindley R. Franklin, Co. A   Pvt. Jesse Johnson, Co. A
Pvt. Lewis F. Keyser, Co. A   Pvt. Harvey Pinch, Co. A
Pvt. Henry J. Warner, Co. H   Pvt. James C. Gallagher, Co. K
Pvt. Alfred Kuntz, Co. K

Deserted:

Pvt. Davis Campbell, Co. A

Aug 31—Regiment reached Centreville before day light, wet to the skin, and in a cold piercing rain and without any shelter. Lay down for a little rest. Hungry as we were, had we had had anything to cook, there was not a stick of wood or a chip to be found in our camp to build a fire, even a few little beans that I had picked up on the ground I could not cook for myself. Officers and men fared the same. Mus. John W. Shillich, Co. A, who had been missing turned up this morning. Remained here all day.

Sept 1—Regiment left their bivouac about 3 o'clock P.M. and marched to Fairfax Court House, and expecting to remain there, the men began to erect for themselves rude shelters, but after an hour's work, orders again came to move, and about 6 o'clock P.M. a rebel brigade was discovered, coming out of a woods into the Fairfax Road at a point called Chantilly or Ox Hill. Our brigade was on the advance, the 21st Mass. leading, with the 51st Penna. and the 51st N. Y. following a half mile in the rear with Durell's battery.

The battle opened as if by magic, and to us, very unexpectedly. The 51st P.V. was very hurriedly ordered up and took up a position in support of Durrell's battery. Very soon each side was hotly engaged and continued until 9 o'clock P.M. During the engagement a cold drenching rain set in. The grass in the field was very high, and in this we had to lay, right in rear of the battery, so close that the blood run out of our ears and noses until one of the gunners told us to place a chip between our teeth, and it would stop, and it had that result. During the engagement Generals Stevens and Kearney were killed and late at night their lifeless bodies were carried through the lines of the 51st P.V. to the rear.[21]

At 9 o'clock P.M. the engagement closed and the regiment was put out on picket and laid under arms all night, the rain still continuing and it was cold and chilling, and as we could not have any fires it was indeed cheerless, and worse still, we had nothing to eat all night. The pickets of Company B captured the adjutant of the 3d Louisiana and brought him into camp, much to his chagrin. This engagement was known as The Battle of Chantilly, Va. or Ox Hill, September 1st, 1862.

Sept 2—The enemy left our front during the night. Our whole army is now massed behind Difficult Creek, between Flint Hill and the Warrenton Turnpike, with the advance under Hooker in front of Germantown.[22] The regiment left their bivouac about 4 o'clock A.M. and marched in the direction of Fairfax, arriving there about 9 o'clock A.M. and then took up a position on a high hill overlooking the surrounding country, drew some rations and had a good cooked meal for once.

---

21. Major General Philip Kearny commanded the First Division, Third Army Corps.

22. Major General Joseph Hooker led the Second Division, Third Army Corps.

At 12 o'clock M. we again took up the line of march and moved in the direction of Clouds Mills and during the night reached Alexandria Va. and bivouacked under the guns of Fort Ellsworth.

Sept 3—Regiment remained in bivouac near Alexandria all day. I being the senior officer in camp, was placed in command. Rations are a little more plentiful, and the boys are making up for lost time and are resting after their long campaign.

Sept 4—Regiment still occupying the same bivouac, and near the same ground occupied by the old 4th Regiment in the three months service, strange but here we are. Many of us who had served in the three months service were again on the same spot and had gone through pretty much the same ordeal in 1861. Poor deluded McDowell, to find a cause for his defeat at Bull Run, endeavored to cast odium on the old 4th Penna. who only did what other regiments did through the war, but he wanted a cause, and he found it, but there are men still living who later on came to know that his loyalty to his country was under a cloud. During the day some new clothing was issued to the men in the place of that which was lost at Bull Run.

Towards evening received orders to prepare to march, and at 8 o'clock P.M. we left our bivouac and marched through Alexandria, crossed the Long Bridge during the night after many halts. Before leaving Alexandria we received a large number of new recruits from Camp Curtin.

Chapter 5

The Maryland Campaign

September 5–November 8, 1862

Following the defeat at Second Manassas, the Union armies were reorganized and General McClellan placed in command of the Army of the Potomac, to which the Ninth Corps was attached. McClellan moved against General Lee's Army of Northern Virginia, which had entered Maryland. The 51st participated in the fighting at South Mountain (September 14), and then charged across Burnside's bridge at Antietam (September 17), where it suffered a heavy loss. Here, Captain Bolton was wounded in the jaw and sent home to recover.

Sept 5—Regiment arrived in Washington D.C. about 2 o'clock A.M. and marched out Seventh St. and about 4 o'clock A.M. came to a halt and went into bivouac in a woods in sight of the Capital. I being the senior officer in camp, was placed in command. By an official order from the War Department, the Army of the Potomac and the Army of Virginia was to-day consolidated and placed under the command of McClellan, and Pope ordered to report to the Secretary of War. Received a letter from my sister.

Sept 6—Still in bivouac in the woods on Seventh St. and taking all the rest we can. To our great surprise, Mrs. Cadwalader Evans and Dr. Holstein of Bridgeport Pa. and during the day Burnside paid us a visit and of course received a heavy cheer from his old boys.[1]

Sept 7—Regiment left their bivouac about 9 o'clock A.M. and after a march of fifteen miles reached Leesborough after dark and went into bivouac for the night. During the night the following regiments arrived and were assigned to the Ninth Corps and was assigned to the brigades later:

15th Connecticut	17th Michigan
16th Connecticut	20th Michigan
35th Massachusetts	9th New Hampshire

Also thirty more regiments arrived and were assigned to the different corps.[2] Burnside was

---

1. Cadwalader Evans was a Bridgeport businessman. His wife Rachel and her sisters Mrs. Dr. George W. Holstein (Abby) and Miss Lizzie Brower, worked to provide comfort and supplies for local soldiers.

2. *O.R.*, vol. 19, part 2, 197.

to-day placed in command of the right wing of the army, composed of the First and Ninth Corps, commanded respectively by Hooker and Reno.[3]

Sept 8—Regiment left their bivouac at 6 o'clock A.M. marched a few miles, and came to a halt, and went into bivouac in an open field for the day and night. Here I received official notice of the discharge Priv. Ashbery M. Johnson of Co. A at Beaufort N.C. Burnside's headquarters are now at Brookville. Two of our divisions (Reno's) is now in position at Cracklinton and Goshen, with instructions to picket Triadelphia and Cooksville, and a squadron of cavalry is now moving across the pike and railroad in the direction of Franklinville and Liberty. Burnside is now between the rebel army and Baltimore.[4]

Sept 9—Regiment left their bivouac at 6 o'clock A.M. passed through Mechanicsville and arrived at Brookville Md. about noon, making fifteen miles in less than six hours. Our march through this section of country was indeed very pleasant. We were received by the people in great kindness, distributing fruit cakes and pies to the troops very freely. The regiment went into bivouac near a fine stream of water which gave us a royal chance to bathe and to wash our clothing. Here we also received an abundance of rations the first for many days.

At this date the position of our army is as follows: A portion of Burnside's troops are at Cracklinton, Sumner's and Bank's corps at Middlebrooke, Franklin at Darnestown, Couch at the mouth of Seneca Creek, and Sigel is on the other side of the Potomac, opposite Chain Bridge. Our cavalry are having some skirmishing to-day and have killed and taken a number of prisoners. Burnside has ordered out scouts to ascertain of the enemy's pickets are at Lisbon, and to push them in the direction of Franklinville, Unionville and Liberty. Our pickets are also doing duty on the National Road, and the scouts of the 9th A.C. are now at Ridgeville and within three miles of New Market. The rebel Gen. Jackson is said to have his headquarters there.[5]

---

3. The reorganized Ninth Corps included the following:
   First Division, Brig. Gen. Orlando B. Wilcox
       First Brigade, Col. Benjamin C. Christ: 28th MA, 17th MI, 79th NY, 50th PA
       Second Brigade, Col. Thomas Welsh: 8th MI, 46th NY, 45th, 100th PA
       Artillery: 8th MA Bty; Bty E, 2nd US
   Second Division, Brig. Gen. Samuel D. Sturgis
       First Brigade, Brig. Gen. James Nagle: 2nd MD, 6th, 9th NH, 48th PA
       Second Brigade, Brig. Gen. Edward Ferrero: 21st, 35th MA, 51st NY, 51st PA
       Artillery: PA Bty D; Bty E, 4th US
   Third Division, Brig. Gen. Isaac P. Rodman
       First Brigade, Col. Harrison S. Fairchild: 9th, 89th, 103rd NY
       Second Brigade, Col. Edward Harland: 8th, 11th, 16th CT, 4th RI
       Artillery: Bty A, 5th US
   Kanawha Division, Brig. Gen. Jacob D. Cox
       First Brigade, Col. Eliakim P. Scammon: 12th, 23rd, 30th OH, two companies
           WV cav, 1st OH Bty
       Second Brigade, Col. George Crook: 11th, 28th, 36th OH, one company IL cav,
           Simmonds's KY Bty
   Unattached
       6th NY Cav (8 cos), 3rd Ind Co OH Cav, Btys L&M, 3rd US

4. *O.R.*, vol. 19, part 2, 213.

5. McClellan's army included the First Corps (Maj. Gen. Joseph Hooker), Second Corps (Maj. Gen. Edwin V. Sumner), First Division, Fourth Corps (Maj. Gen. Darius N. Couch), Fifth Corps

Sept 10—Regiment still in bivouac at Brookville. Received and wrote several letters. Fruit is very plenty here, and as it is cheap the boys are making free use of it. Burnside sent to-day a strong reconnoitering force to the mountain pass at Ridgeville, and his advance guard is at Damascus.

Sept 11—Regiment left their bivouac at 6 o'clock A.M. passed through the little town of Unity and went into bivouac after dark near the town of Damascus. Burnside has pushed a strong reconnaissance across the National Road and the Baltimore and Ohio Railroad towards New Market. A corresponding movement of all the troops in the centre and on the left moved in the direction of Urbana and Poolesville.

Sept 12—Regiment left their bivouac at 12 o'clock in the morning in a heavy rain storm. Passed through Hampton, crossed the Baltimore and Ohio Railroad at Monroeville, passed through New Market, crossed the Monocacy on a stone bridge, after some little skirmishing on the outskirts of Frederick and in the streets, and a portion of Burnside's troops entered the city. The 51st bivouacked for the night on the outskirts of the city. Burnside has sent cavalry in pursuit of Fitzhuh Lee towards Westminster.[6]

Sept 13—Left our bivouac near the Monocacy about 3 o'clock P.M. and with the main body of the right wing passed through the City of Frederick. As Burnside entered the city, he and his troops were cheered by the inhabitants old and young, who waved Union flags and shouted "Hurrah for Burnside, Frederick is once more redeemed." This demonstration on the part of the people was very cheering to the troops as we passed through. Crossed Sugar Loaf Mountains at 11 o'clock at night and went into bivouac in a rough ploughed field near Middletown. Here the Rebels set fire to the mills and houses of the town before leaving it and then took up a position on South Mountain. Up to this date the 9th A.C. had been an independant command, but was to-day assigned to the Army of the Potomac.

Sept 14—We left our bivouac with the rest of our corps at 8 o'clock A.M.[7] We could hear heavy artillery firing at a distance. We passed through Middletown about 3 o'clock P.M. The buildings that the rebels had fired in leaving the town were still burning. About 4 o'clock P.M. our division commenced to ascend the mountain which was steep and very rugged. Passed many teams loaded with householdgoods coming down the mountain. The most of our corps had proceeded us and were engaged with the enemy. The 51st were soon put into position in front of Durell's battery as its support and ordered to lie down close to the ground, as the battery was bleaching forth its deadly missiles up the mountain gorge at a fearful and at aterrible rate over our heads, a regular artillery duel between the two contending armies. The enemy were well posted on the very top of the mountain. They had to depress their guns to reach us, and we had to elevate ours. The duel lasted until sundown, and Gen. Reno who commanded the old 9th Corps was near his old brigade, directing the artillery fire in person.

The artillery having cleared the mountain of the enemy, the 51st was soon ordered to advance towards the summit of the mountain, and on our march passed in one pile at least fifty dead rebels, and on reaching the top of the mountain witnessed the same thing, only there was at least one hundred and twenty-five dead rebels laying stretched acrossed each other

---

(Maj. Gen. Fitz John Porter), Sixth Corps (Maj. Gen. William B. Franklin), Ninth Corps (Maj. Gen. Jesse L. Reno), Twelfth Corps (Brig. Gen. Joseph K. F. Mansfield), and Brig. Gen. Alfred Pleasonton's Cavalry Division.

6. Brig. Gen. Fitzhugh Lee commanded a cavalry brigade in Lee's army.

7. General Sturgis, in his report (*O.R.*, vol. 19, part 1, 443) wrote that the division left its bivouac at 1:00 p.m.

along the stone wall. On the crest of the mountain ran a narrow lane protected by a stone fence on either side. The enemy had used the position as a sort of breastworks and all along this lane there was a sight to be seen. Along its whole length the rebels laid in piles up to the very top of the stone fence. Some were found in a kneeling position in the act of firing. Death to many of them must have been instantaneous. Their arms extended and in position as in the act of firing, and in some cases the bitten cartridges in their hands.

The 17th Michigan, a new regiment who had joined us on the march from Washington and had been assigned to our corps was on this immediate front, and it was its first engagement, but they fought like demons. About 7 o'clock P.M. our intrepid leader, and commander of the old 9th A.C. Gen. Jesse L. Reno, fell pierced with a ball, in what is known as Wise's field, about one hundred and fifty yards from the old brick barn. He lived but a few moments and expired in the arms of his class mate, and bosom friend Gen. Sam. Sturgis, our division commander.

About 10 o'clock P.M. the battle closed. After sundown Companies A, F, D and I were put out on picket for the night, and in moving to take our position on the right of the road and on nearing the spot designated for picket duty, not supposing for a moment that there was an enemy near, suddenly a murderous musketry fire was showered into the four companies in the darkness. We could see the flash, and fortunately for us, we all dropped to the ground and the volley passed over our heads. Recovering ourselves the four companies poured a stunning volley into them, which had the effect of clearing the woods, and we were masters of the situation, but through some mistake, a new regiment, the 35th Mass. which had just joined our brigade, gave us a volley from the rear, and for the time being we were between two fires.

After the enemy had been driven from their ambush, Company A was deployed as skirmishers in the dark and soon took possession of that part of the field that the enemy had been driven from. Pickets were soon established for the night, and from the groans and moaning of the wounded all night long, and lying right among the dead, we spent a cheerless, wretched, supperless night. The 35th Mass. who were on our right and rear, attempted to post their pickets by the aid of a lantern, which was no doubt the cause that drew the fire of the enemy on us, and this was the time that Reno was killed. Those of our regiment, and of course the wounded of other regiments were of a painful nature, as the rebels used explosive matallic cartridges, and were poisonous. We found many of the cartridges on the field and examined them. The balls were made in three sections, and a white poisonous paste placed between the sections.[8]

Late in the afternoon, Reno* coming on the field that his old brigade was occupying on the right of the Old Sharpsburg Road, his black piercing eyes flashing fire as it were, ordered Durell's battery to limber up and go in a gallop up the narrow road leading to the crest of the mountain, and noticing his old brigade now commanded by Ferrero exclaimed, "Look, see my old Iron Brigade, they are running like chickens, make for them." Reno thought the world of his old brigade, and why not, they had done honor for him as well as for themselves. It was this same brigade that won fame for him at Roanoke Island in turning the enemies position, which gave us the rebel fort. At Newbern the same brigade led the assault that gave him their works and the final capture of the city. At Camden or South Mills the same brigade led the assault that won us the day. At Bull Run it was they who opened and brought on the engagement on the morning of the 30th. It was they who were the very last to leave the field on the night of the 30th, and with the 9th A.C. covered the retreat of Pope's army. It was they who were among the first to meet the first shock of battle at Chantilly, and among the last to leave it.

As I have said before, Cox's division opened the engagement on the morning of the 14th. His division left its bivouac at or near Middletown at 6 o'clock A.M. and his first brigade reached the

---

8. Parker, *51st PA*, 227-8.

scene of action about 9 o'clock A.M. and was sent up the Old Sharpsburg Road by Pleasonton to feel the enemy, who were found holding the crest of the mountain in full force. Cox soon followed with his other brigade, when by the order of Reno, the whole division (Cox's) was ordered to assault the enemy's position with the information from Reno that the assaulting column would be supported by the whole 9th Corps. From that moment the battle raged until 10 o'clock P.M. The crest was soon taken by Scammon's brigade, which was kept by them until the last, although the enemy made several attempts to retake it, but were each time repulsed.[9]

About noon a lull occurred in the contest, lasting some two hours, during which the rest of the 9th Corps were coming up. Willcox's division being the first to arrive, and from an order from Reno, took up a position on the right of the Old Sharpsburg Road, overlooking the turnpike, two regiments being detached to support Cox. By this time Burnside and Reno had arrived at the base of the mountain, when Burnside ordered up the divisions of Sturgis and Rodman (this was about 4 o'clock P.M.) to the crest of the mountain held by Cox and Willcox, with orders to attack in full force as soon as Hooker made his attack on the right as ordered. Reno followed with the two divisions and assumed the direction of affairs. Sturgis' division took position in front of Willcox, occupying the new ground gained on the further side of the slope, and his artillery opened on the batteries across the gap. The enemy made an attempt to turn our left about dark, but were repulsed by Fairchild's brigade and Clark's battery. About 7 o'clock P.M. the enemy made another and a desperate effort to regain the lost ground, attacking along Sturgis' front and a part of Cox's. A lively fire was kept up, and several charges were made by the enemy but were repulsed with slaughter, and when the firing ceased, Sturgis' division occupied the highest part of the mountain. It was about this time that Reno was killed. Pleasonton says of Reno: "His clear judgment and determined courage rendered the triumphant results obtained by the operations of his corps, second to none of the brilliant deeds accomplished on that field. At his loss a mastermind has passed away."[10]

This engagement was known as the battle of South Mountain or Turner's Pass, Md., September 14th /62. The casualties in the regiment was as follows:

Killed:

Lieut. Samuel Fair, Co. D	Pvt. William J. Anderson, Co. I
Pvt. Samuel Kay, Co. D	Pvt. Zachariah Campbell, Co. I
Pvt. Nathaniel Snyder, Co. H	Sgt. Thomas T. Schock, Co. I

Wounded:

Cpl. John G. Coulston, Co. A	Pvt. William Munshower, Co. C (died Oct. 3)
Cpl. Isaac E. Filman, Co. A	Pvt. Charles Rodesbaugh, Co. C
Pvt. Charles Fix, Co. A	Pvt. Owen McConnell, Co. D
Pvt. Benjamin Goodwin, Co. A	Pvt. John Richards, Co. D (died Sept. 26)
Pvt. Benjamin D. Jones, Co. A	Sgt. Jacob W. Reed, Co. F
Cpl. Osman Ortlip, Co. A	Pvt. John E. Leamon, Co. H
Pvt. John Shade, Co. A	Pvt. Daniel S. Miller, Co. H
Pvt. Daniel Stout, Co. A	Pvt. Robert W. Passell, Co. H
Cpl. Joseph White, Co. A (died Sept. 15)	Pvt. Hugh C. Brown, Co. I
Pvt. John Hollowell, Co. C	Pvt. Clarkson R. Davis, Co. I
Pvt. George Mercer, Co. C	Pvt. Lewis E. Davis, Co. I (died Sept. 24)

9. This paragraph and the following one were generally taken from Cox's report in *O.R.*, vol. 19, part 1, 458-60; and from Burnside's report in *Ibid.*, 417.

10. Quoted from Pleasonton's report, *O.R.*, vol. 19, part 1, 210.

*Major Gen. Jesse L. Reno the intrepid and gallant soldier and noble Virginian, died as he wished to die, dauntless as became his heroic character, ever prompt, earnest, and soldierly, he was the model of an accomplished soldier, and a gallant gentleman, like others, namely, Farragut, Thomas, Sykes, Newton, Reynolds, Canby, Ord, Brannan, Wm. Nelson, Crittenden, Blair, R. W. Johnson, T. J. Wood, N. B. Buford, Terrill, Graham, Davidson, Cooke, Alexander, Getty, French, Fremont, Pope, and Hunter, all of Southern blood and lineage. Many of these were superb officers, and struck the South very many heavy blows.

Brig. Gen. Jacob D. Cox, commanding the Kanawha Division, on the death of Reno, succeeded to the command of the 9th A.C. but remained in command but a short time. The First and Ninth Corps composed Burnside's command in this battle. The Ninth were never in a better fighting condition than they were on this occasion. It was composed of four divisions commanded respectively by Generals Cox (afterwards Scammon), Willcox, Sturgis, and Rodman. Cox's division had been assigned to the 9th A.C. temporally and was known as the Kanawha Division, and had won distinction in West Virginia, and was composed entirely of Ohio troops. It was this division that first engaged the enemy, on the morning of the 14th. Lieut. Col. Rutherford B. Hayes of the 23d Ohio, afterwards Governor of Ohio and President of the United States, belonged to this division and was wounded.

The old 9th A.C. did noble work in this engagement, but strange to say, McClellan came on the field late in the night, and in his dispatch to the War Department announcing our victory, the name of Burnside or his troops were not mentioned. Up to this date, this was the most continuous musketry firing we had ever heard. It rolled from right to left with irresistible fury, and cannot well be discribed, but will be remembered by all who were engaged there.

Note: About midnight, after all firing had ceased on both sides, Gen. Ferrero passed along the line of his brigade and asked for a person who would volunteer to reconnoiter the enemys position, but holding out no hope for the person to safely return. The man was found in the person of Sergt. E. G. Maize of Company E. He received his instruction and started on his dangerous mission, returning and joining his command about 4 o'clock next morning reporting to Gen. Ferrero that the enemy was in full retreat, and getting so near their hospitals as to hear their conversation. Maize was complimented by Ferrero.

Sept 15—We were all up bright and early this morning going over the field to see what could be seen. In the narrow road which run through a deep cut near where we had been on picket all night we found that the road itself and the banks on either side of it was literally filled with dead and dying. We had heard their moanings the whole night long. The sight was pitiful in the extream. These were the wounded we had lifted to the either side of the roadway out of the road late on the previous afternoon soon after we had commenced driving the enemy from the summit of the mountain when Reno ordered Durell's battery to limber up and go in a gallop up the narrow road to the cress of the mountain and with all our care in removing them, many were run over by the battery in their hast to reach the crest. We found that the dead and wounded that still remained on the field had well filled haversacks and must to have done some very good foraging in their march through Maryland. Very many of the dead had turned black in the face during the night and were as a general thing well dressed and clean. In our ramble we came upon a dry well that was literally filled to the top with their dead.

After administering to the wants of the wounded of both armies, we were ordered about 8 o'clock A.M. to advance and were soon in motion down the mountain, and in our advance we found very many wounded who had hid away in the underbrush and made very many captured along our whole rout.

About the same time that the 9th A.C. advanced, Hooker's corps on our right was temporarily detached and ordered in pursuit of the enemy by the way of Boonsborough, the 9th A.C. following the Old Sharpsburg Road.[11] Why this pursuit was not ordered sooner was a mistery. It certainly showed overcautiousness or timidity or both. That was certainly the opinion shared in by very many of the 9th A.C.

11. *O.R.*, vol. 19, part 1, 418 (Burnside).

The regiment went into bivouac four different times during our march to-day. We finally passed through Keedysville and at sundown reached the neighborhood of Sharpsburg where the enemy was found in position and the 9th A.C. was ordered to take up a position on the extreme left under the crest of the mountain opposit Antietam Bridge. Company A was sent out on picket on the right of the road about one mile from the regiment. During the night received word that Corpl. Joseph White of Company A had died from the wound received yesterday.

Sept 16—The regiment remained in bivouac until 4 o'clock P.M. In the meantime very heavy firing was going on all day. Gen. Cox is in command of the 9th A.C. Continued our march until sometime in the night, and then came to a sudden halt in a miserable stubble field about one and a half mile from Antietam Bridge. During our whole march from South Mountain our whole pathway was strewn with the carcasses of dead horses and mules. We succeeded in getting something to eat, and a pretty fair sleep, as we knew by the surroundings that there would be a terrible racket in the early morning.

During the night Benjamin's Battery of six 20-pounders, with the remaining batteries was put in position on the crest of the hill immediately in front of the bridge.[12] In rear of Benjamin's Battery on the extreme right, joining Sykes division was Crook's Brigade with Sturgis' division in his rear; on the left, and in the rear of Benjamin's battery was Rodman's division, with Scammon's brigade in support, and Willcox's division in reserve.[13] Thus the 9th A.C. lay in bivouac in these positions in three lines on the night of the 16th, dreading the coming morrow. This place is known as Porterstown.

Sept 17—Before daybreak heavy cannonading commenced, and the roar of musketry soon followed. I arose from my slumbers with a terrible jumping toothache, and felt miserable and no doctor near at hand to give me any relief. A mail has arrived which has somewhat cheered us all up. I received a letter from my sister, and after reading it, destroyed it, and placed the envelope in my pocket, thinking if anything happened to me it might be of use to me.

Well orders have arrived for the regiment to move, and slinging our knapsacks we took up our line of march through a cornfield and came to a halt near a large log barn near Antietam Bridge. Here we found a fine spring of water. Burnside's corps consisting of Willcox's, Sturgis, and Rodman's divisions, and Cox's Kanawha Division was instructed with the difficult task of carrying the bridge across the Antietam near Rohrbach's farm, and assaulting the enemy's right, the order having been communicated to him (Burnside) about 10 o'clock A.M. The valley of the Antietam at or near this bridge is narrow, with high banks. On the right of the stream the bank is wooded, and commands the approaches both to the bridge and the ford. The steep slopes of the bank were lined with rifle-pits and breastworks of rails and stones. These, together with the woods, were filled with the enemy's infantry, while their batteries completely commanded, and enfiladed, the bridge and ford and their approaches.[14]

Cox's division consisting of six regiments, has been assaulting the bridge since 10 A.M. He has made three repeated assaults and each time were repulsed. The road leading to the bridge was strewn with his dead and wounded. It is a sickening sight. We of Reno's old Iron Brigade had on arriving at the old log barn divested ourselves of our knapsacks, blankets &c. and filling our canteens with good cold water, awaited orders, which we knew must soon come, as the bridge was still in the hands of the enemy.

---

12. Lieutenant Samuel N. Benjamin commanded Battery E, 2nd U.S.

13. Following Burnside's report in *O.R.,* vol. 19, part 1, 418-9.

14. Burnside's report in *O.R.*, vol. 19, part 1, 419.

Finally at 11 o'clock A.M. the dreaded order came from Burnside to Ferrero to take the 51st P.V. and the 51st N.Y. holding the 21st Mass. in reserve, and storm and take the bridge at all hazzards. Ferrero in a loud clear voice called for Hartranft and in a voice we all could hear, commanded "Burnside orders you to take the 51st P.V. and storm the bridge." Everyone of us knew full well the meaning of that order. Burnside always had the most explicit confidence in the old 51st and of the old Iron Brigade, who never yet had failed him.

The order for us to move was soon given, and the 51st P.V. marching to the assault in the advance by the flank leaving the road leading to the bridge to our left marching as if on regimental drill a sight never to be forgotten by those in that charge, gained the top of the hill overlooking the bridge and in full view. From that moment the regiment received volley after volley of grape, musketry, shot and shell, filling our faces and eyes with sand and dirt, all this time reserving our fire. Hartranft placing himself by my side, and after the regiment had cleared the fence that intervened between us and the bridge, the order to charge was given by Hartranft, certain death, as it were staring us in the face. We made the dash for the bridge through a perfect hell of shot and shell. A gate impeded our way quite near the Bridge, but it was soon torn from its fastenings by Corp. Levi Bolton of Company A and while thus engaged received a brick-shot in his shoulder which he still carries in his person. This obstacle removed the 51st plunged through and leaped the fence, all this time the men falling all around, but in a few moments we commanded the entrance to the bridge, and the stone wall running parallel with the stream, with only the creek and a road between us and the enemy.

After some delay, and about 1 o'clock P.M. the order was again given by Hartranft to charge the bridge, and in less than nine minutes the bridge and the heights beyond were in our possession and beyond dispute. During all this time the regiment stood the incessant rain of shot, shell, canister, grape and musketry, but with a loss to the regiment alone of one hundred and thirty-five men in killed, wounded and missing. Capt. Wm. H. Blair Company G with his company were the first to cross the bridge.[15]

Within a few feet of the bridge a minie ball came crashing through my right lower jaw bone carrying away all the teeth on the right side of my face, both upper and lower jaw, passed through my mouth, and came out on the other side of my face about one-fourth of an inch below the lower part of the ear. Finding myself wounded, and speechless, I succeeded in sheathing my sword, and attempted to go to the rear, but had not proceeded far, when from the loss of blood I fainted and fell to the ground, and attempted to crawl over the brow of the hill, but gave out through exhaustion, and while I lay there was between two fires, the shot, shell and minie balls were striking all around me, and troops passing over me. I was finally found by members of my own company, placed in a blanket and carried to the log barn, where I had but a few moments before left, with a bad case of tooth ache, but I lost it in that battle, and have never had it since.

The log barn soon began to fill up with our dead and wounded, and later in the day Lieut. Col. Bell was brought in a dying condition, and soon expired at my side. While here someone had the kindness to steal my sword and pistol, both having been presented to me by the citizens of Norristown. After we had possession of the field and all was quiet for the time being, Hartranft came over to the Log Hospital to look after us. I was of course speechless. During our stay, the rebels fired shot and shell at the Hospital, some of which went crashing through the barn, although there was a flag on the building warning them that it was a Hospital. Fortunately no one was injured from that cause.

Later in the day an ambulance was provided, and another officer and myself were lifted into it, and were driven to the Big Springs Hospital, where we arrived towards evening, after a

15. Parker, *51st PA*, 234, wrote that Capt. Allebaugh and Co. C crossed first.

pretty good shaking up in driving over the rough roads and fields. I received very kind attention from an Ohio doctor. There was twelve of us in a very small room in a private house. Here
the envelope I had retained was of some service to me, from that the doctor learned my name.
Bad as my wound appeared to be, it fortunately gave me no pain.

At about 3 o'clock P.M. the 9th A.C. advanced, and with success, the right driving the
enemy before it and pushing on nearly to Sharpsburg, while the left, after a hard encounter,
also compelled the enemy to retire before it. The enemy, here, however, were speedily re-enforced,
both by infantry and artillery, in consequent of which our troops were ordered to retire to the
cover of the hill which was taken from the enemy earlier in the afternoon. This position our
troops maintained until the enemy finally retreated from the field. Burnside in order to follow
up his success in this movement of his corps asked McClellan late in the afternoon for
re-enforcements, but they were refused, hence he was compelled to fall back to the hill.[16]

The following is the list of killed, wounded, missing, deserters & promotions that occurred
to-day in the 51st Regt. P.V.:

Killed:

Lieut. Col. Thomas S. Bell
Pvt. James Coulston, Co. A
Pvt. William Somerlot, Co. A
Cpl. George W. Bird, Co. B
Pvt. David S. Hutman, Co. B
Pvt. Henry C. Moore, Co. B
Sgt. Richard J. Williams, Co. B
Lieut. Davis Hunsicker, Co. C
Cpl. David Kane, Co. C
Pvt. Michael Mooney, Co. D
Pvt. William Comer, Co. F
Pvt. Henry Shultz, Co. F
Pvt. Henry D. Lentz, Co. F

Pvt. Miles Dillon, Co. G
Cpl. James Dowling, Co. G
Pvt. William Wenrick, Co. G
Pvt. Wallace Wiggins, Co. G
Lieut. Jacob G. Beaver, Co. H
Pvt. Isaac Beck, Co. H
Pvt. Edward Bear, Co. H
Pvt. Levi Marks, Co. H
Sgt. Matthew M. Vandine, Co. H
Pvt. Isaac Wittes, Co. H
Sgt. J. Clark Davis, Co. I
Cpl. Thomas P. Davis, Co. I
Pvt. William Scott, Co. K

Wounded:

Quartermaster Sgt. John J. Freedley
Adjutant George W. Shorkley
Sgt. Major Curtin B. Stonerod
Pvt. Levi Bolton, Co. A
Capt. William J. Bolton, Co. A
Pvt. James M. Bolton, Co. A
Pvt. George S. Buzzard, Co. A
Pvt. Charles Keyser, Co. A (died September 30)
Pvt. Harry C. Wood, Co. A
Pvt. Andrew Widger, Co. A
Sgt. George Bobler, Co. B
Cpl. Valentine Stocker, Co. B
Pvt. Aaron Thatcher, Co. B
Pvt. Lewis Young, Co. B
Pvt. Thomas Allen, Co. C

Pvt. Levi Baum, Co. C
Pvt. Henry Davis, Co. C
Pvt. Reuben DeHaven, Co. C
Cpl. Samuel Egolf, Co. C
Cpl. Simon P. Emery, Co. C (died September 29)
Pvt. Charles R. Fox, Co. C
Pvt. William H. R. Fox, Co. C
Pvt. William Gunn, Co. C
Pvt. John Hollowell, Co. C (died November 14)
Lieut. Davis Hunsicker, Co. C
Pvt. Henry Jago, Co. C
Pvt. Benjamin Johnson, Co. C
Pvt. George Kevin, Co. C
Pvt. William Lath, Co. C

---

16. Burnside in *O.R.*, vol. 19, part 1, 420-1.

Lieut. Thomas J. Lynch, Co. C
Pvt. George Mercer, Co. C (died October 3)
Sgt. Benjamin F. Miller, Co. C
Pvt. Henry Lightcap, Co. C
Pvt. Patrick Rogan, Co. C
Pvt. Levi W. Shingle, Co. C
Pvt. David R. Spare, Co. C
Pvt. John M. Springer, Co. C
Cpl. James Sullivan, Co. C (died February 23, 1863)
Pvt. James Sullivan, Co. C
Pvt. John C. Umstead, Co. C
Pvt. Abraham Walt, Co. C
Sgt. Edwin Bennett, Co. D
Pvt. John Earls, Co. D
Pvt. William Essick, Co. D
Pvt. William Faulkner, Co. D
Pvt. Hector Gillian, Co. D
Cpl. John Gilligan, Co. D
Pvt. William Hamburger, Co. D
Pvt. George Haybeery, Co. D (died October 18)
Sgt. William D. Jenkins, Co. D
Pvt. Samuel McDade, Co. D
Pvt. William McManamy, Co. D
Pvt. William Mogee, Co. D
Pvt. Isaac Sloan, Co. D
Cpl. Isaac Tolan, Co. D
Pvt. Abraham Benfer, Co. E
Sgt. James P. Cornelius, Co. E
Cpl. George W. Foote, Co. E
Sgt. George C. Gutilius, Co. E
Pvt. Lewis Klines, Co. E
Pvt. James Marson, Co. E
Pvt. Jackson McFadden, Co. E
Pvt. Martin G. Reed, Co. E
Pvt. C. W. Woodward, Co. E
Sgt. Howard Bruce, Co. F
Pvt. James Dolan, Co. F
Sgt. Allen H. Fillman, Co. F
Pvt. Daniel Freas, Co. F
Capt. Lane S. Hart, Co. F

Pvt. Robert McGee, Co. F
Cpl. William Montgomery, Co. F
Cpl. George Armstrong, Co. G
Pvt. Jacob Casher, Co. G
Pvt. George Dutott, Co. G
Pvt. Houston Heichel, Co. G
Pvt. Robert Hinton, Co. G
Pvt. Jesse Lucas, Co. G
Pvt. William Maurer, Co. G
Pvt. William Wilson, Co. G
Pvt. William Young, Co. G
Sgt. William F. Campbell, Co. H
Pvt. John W. Erdley, Co. H
Sgt. Hugh McClure, Co. H
Cpl. H. C. McCormick, Co. H
Pvt. John Rain, Co. H
Sgt. Jacob H. Santo, Co. H
Cpl. James M. Schooley, Co. H
Pvt. Henry B. Wetzel, Co. H
Sgt. Daniel M. Wetzell, Co. H
Pvt. Anthony Wiesenback, Co. H
Pvt. Charles Buley, Co. I
Pvt. Jacob Emrich, Co. I
Pvt. Jacob H. Meyers, Co. I
Pvt. John Murphy, Co. I
Sgt. Thomas H. Parker, Co. I
Sgt. George W. S. Pennell, Co. I
Sgt. Daniel W. Eichman, Co. K
Pvt. Jacob Fortner, Co. K
Cpl. Thomas Foster, Co. K
Pvt. Paul McBride, Co. K
Pvt. Irwin Richards, Co. K
Pvt. Samuel Royer, Co. K
Pvt. Joseph Sarba, Co. K
Sgt. Albert Snyder, Co. K
Pvt. Joseph Snyder, Co. K
Pvt. William Yates, Co. K

Captured:

Pvt. William Allen, Co. G
Pvt. John J. Fisher, Co. G

Pvt. Joseph J. Peters, Co. G

Deserted:
Pvt. Calvin Dougherty, Co. H
Pvt. Jacob H. Meyers, Co. I (also wounded)

Promotions:
Major Edwin Schall to Lieut. Col.
Capt. William J. Bolton to Major
1st Lieut. Joseph K. Bolton to Captain, Co. A
2d Lieut. Abraham I. Ortlip to 1st Lieut., Co. A
Orderly Sergt. John S. Moore to 2d Lieut., Co. A

Sept 18—I remained in the hospital all day. Late in the afternoon my brother Joe found me, but expected to find me dead, as it had been so reported in camp. Still later in the day, Quartermaster Samuel P. Stephens found me, and in the kindness of his heart, brought me a new outfit of clothing, and as I was covered from head to foot in blood, it was a God send. He also brought me a small flask of whiskey. My brother Joe after looking after my comforts, started out to hunt up a team to take me to Hagerstown, so that I could take a train for home. He told me that the regiment had been relieved by an Ohio regiment, and that the 51st had fell back across the bridge, and had gone into bivouac in an orchard a mile from the bridge. My wound is painless, and thus far gives me no trouble. The only trouble was in taking nourishment, as my jaw was broken.*

---

* Everyone on our end of the line (the left) expected another assault on the enemy in the early morning, and in fact if McClellan had given Burnside the re-enforcements he asked for on the afternoon of the 17th, the result of that day would have been far different, but no, he had Fitz John Porter, commanding the 5th A.C. massed idly by with 15,000 troops who had not been in action at all or scarcely so, yet he (McClellan) sent word to Burnside that he had no infantry to send him, although he had on the evening of the 17th received re-enforcements equal in number to what he had lost, and Burnside to his credit was willing to renew the battle if McClellan would give him 5,000 fresh troops to place in advance of his worn out troops, but no, this was war on the enemy, for whom he had a careful consideration, and poor pet Porter might get hurt.

McClellan had already lost two valuable days in not following up his foe in the early morning of the 15th after the South Mountain battle, a distance of only seven miles to Antietam, yet his army made it in two days. And here again, he adds two more days by his timidity, and allows Lee during the night of the 19th to steal away in the night, leaving nothing behind but a few stragglers, his unburied dead and a few thousand wounded. But he takes with him all his artillery, ammunition, wagon train, all the supplies he collected in Maryland, and the valuable spoils of Harper's Ferry, which he captured through the cowardice and imbecility of Cols. Ford and Miles, the latter a regular army officer, all through the tardy advance of McClellan through Maryland, which was characteristic of him from the time he was placed in command of the Army of the Potomac up to the very moment he was relieved from its command Nov. 5th 1862. And then again he does great injustice to the 51st P.V. in his official report, and again reiterate it in his Memoirs that the Bridge was carried by a brilliant charge of the 51st N.Y. and the 51st P.V. This is not so, the bridge was carried singaly and alone by the 51st P.V. and it was fully fifteen minutes before the 51st N.Y. or any other regiment came upon the bridge, and at that time the bridge, as well as the road on the other side, was in full possession of the 51st P.V. and there are men still living who will corroborate me in what I here say, and furthermore, as we marched to the assault, there was no regiment following us, and after I was wounded and coming to the rear, and as long as I could see, there was no regiment in sight. Sometime after I fell, a regiment (11th Conn.) marched over me and on in the direction of the bridge.

McClellan by his masterly inactivity, indecision, imbecility and painful vacillation, cost the government thousands of lives and millions of money, invarable overestimating his foe, and underestimating his own, as the records will prove. The "Young Napoleon," good God what a burlesque on such a good name.

Sept 19—My wound gives me very little pain, could not eat, or drink anything, and am very weak. My fellow wounded comrades are very kind to me. My Ohio doctor is all attention to me. Drink a great deal of water, and what runs through the two bullet holes keeps my wound clear. Joe succeeded in getting a team to take me to Hagerstown. He also procured a feather bed and put it in the bottom of the wagon, and after my wound was dressed by my own regimental surgeon (Duffell) and with Sergt. John S. Moore and my servant Kitty, in the afternoon started for Hagerstown, fifteen miles, arriving there about 9 o'clock P.M. pretty well used up as I had to set up all through the journey. Slept on the entry floor of the hotel all night. The town was full troops called out for the emergency. Came very near being tramped to death.

Sept 20—I left Hagerstown about 10 o'clock A.M. accompanied by Sergt. Moore and Kitty, my servant. All the wounded in town were put in box cars and we all laid on a litter of straw. I had a whole car to my self. On stoping at the stations along the road, the ladies would bring us refreshments, but poor me, I could not eat anything. Water was the only thing that I could take. The people were all very kind to us all along the road. I gave the ladies some shells that I had in my pockets, that I had picked up on the beach at Hatteras Inlet. Arrived at Harrisburg about 7 o'clock P.M. and found a large number of surgeons in waiting to attend to our wounds. I took up my quarters at the United States Hotel, with a lounge for a bed, a surgeon was with me until midnight.

The regiment left their bivouac in the orchard and marched to the mouth of Antietam Creek. Their line of march was over the field of carnage, and the field was strewn with the carcasses of horses and mules. Passing on, the regiment went into bivouac about one mile from the Antietam Iron Furnace, and two full companies put out on picket. To-day Gen. Burnside announced the death of Gen. Reno in the following orders.

General Orders   Headquarters Ninth Army Corps
No. 17.   Mouth of Antietam, Md., September 20, 1862.
The commanding general announces to the corps the loss of their late leader, Maj. Gen. Jesse L. Reno.

By the death of this distinguished officer the country loses one of its most devoted patriots, the army one of its most thorough soldiers. In the long list of battles in which General Reno has fought in his country's service, his name always appears with the brightest luster, and he has now bravely met a soldier's death while gallantly leading his men at the battle of South Mountain.

For his high character and the kindly qualities of his heart in private life, as well as for the military genius and personal daring which marked him as a soldier, his loss will be deplored by all who knew him, and the commanding general desires to add the tribute of a friend to the mourning for the death of one of the country's best defenders.

By command of Maj. Gen. Burnside.
Lewis Richmond, Assistant
Adjutant-General.[17]

---

17. *O.R.*, vol. 19, part 1, 423.

Sept 21—I left Harrisburg about 1.20 A.M. in the morning, and reached Philadelphia about 6 o'clock A.M. at the Penna. Railroad Depot at 11th and Market, and from there to 9th and Green, leaning on the arms of my orderly and Kitty, as the train for Norristown would not leave until 9 o'clock. They tried to secure a bed for me to lie down on at the hotel, but a bed was refused me, so I sat up on a chair until the train started at 9 A.M. On the train on my way home a lady on the train kindly offered me some grapes to eat, but of course I could not eat them.

I reached Norristown about 10 o'clock and met a great crowd assembled at the station. Mr. David Schall offered to get a carriage for me, but I declined the kind offer, preferring to walk, reached my home on Penn Street in a few moments, and found the whole street blocaded with people in front of the house. My mother was absent from home, being at church in Bridge-port, she not knowing of my being wounded. Mr. Charles Cauffman[18] went for her, and in the meantime I sent my servant Kitty for Dr. Dunlap[19] to have my jaw bone set. I had plenty of visitors to call, but it was impossible for me to talk to them. Up to this time my wound gave me no pain, and I passed a very good night, although Dunlap had failed to set my jaw.

The boys have learned that the 3d Georgia, who had confronted the old 51st at Camden and later at Bull Run, confronted us here. At Bull Run it was they who captured our knapsacks and blankets. Our boys found some of the deguerreotyp likenesses of sweet-hearts, bibles and nic-nacs &c in the re-captured knapsacks. Such are the little incidents of war.

The beautiful flag presented by the ladies of Norristown to the old 4th regiment in April 1861 now carried by the 51st, and also the state flag was torn into fragments. The staff of the former was shot in two, but it was immediately spliced by the aid of strips of cracker box lids, and remains in the same condition to this day. The boys relate the following of Private Henry Shultz, a gallant youth of only eighteen, a member of Company F. He met with a most hor-rible death. He had just about finished his forty rounds, as all of his comrads had already done, and was in a kneeling position, when a shell struck him in his head, cutting it off to the ears, and scattering his brains upon those around him.

Sept 22—My wound not at all painful. Am having plenty of visitors. Dunlap sent me word that he would leave for the battle field and that he would send Dr. Pawling to attend to me, which he did during the day, and succeeded in setting my jaw, making it the sixth day after I was wounded.

Regiment received orders, in fact the whole corps ordered to be ready to move to Harpers' Ferry to-morrow.[20]

Sept 23—My wound not very painful. Received plenty of visitors. Regiment marched to the Aqueduct of the Ohio and Chesapeake Canal and were sent out on picket to the Potomac.

Sept 24—My wound somewhat painful, and had bery little sleep. The regiment left their bivouac about 4 o'clock P.M. and again crossed Antietam Creek and again went into bivouac.

Sept 25—My wound very painful. Dunlap has returned, and is again in charge. Regiment received marching orders, but later in the day the order was countermanded.

Sept 26—Wound very painful. Regiment left their bivouac about 8 o'clock A.M. and again crossed Antietam Creek near the Furnace, marched about one mile along the creek, and re-joined the balance of the 9th A.C. and went into bivouac for the night.

---

18. Charles Cauffman was a grocer with a store near Main and Swede Streets.

19. Dr. Joseph B. Dunlap was a physician with an office on the west side of Swede Street below Marshall.

20. *O.R.*, vol. 19, part 2, 344.

Sept 27—Wound very painful. The troops of the corps to-day commenced company and regimental drills. Sgt. Robert Supplee of Company A died in camp to-day.

Sept 28—My wound still continues very painful. A delegation from Norristown consisting of B. E. Chain, S. E. Hartranft, and Abraham Markley arrived to-day, bringing with them a stand of colors to be presented to the regiment.[21]

Sept 29—My wound not so painful to-day. The stand of colors were presented to the regiment on dress parade by Benj. E. Chain. To-day the 10th & 11th New Hampshire, 21st Connecticut, and 7th Rhode Island regiments were assigned to the 9th A.C.[22] Regiment received orders to move, but towards evening the order was countermanded.

Sept 30—Wound behaving very well. The flag presentation committee took their departure for home, taking with them the old flags, which are pretty well used up. Quite a number of convalescents arrived from the hospital. Prv. Charles Keyser Co. A died from wounds received at Antietam.

Oct 1—Wound behaving very well, sleeping very good, have plenty of callers. Received a number of letters from the regiment. Prv. Wm. Barr and Abraham Custer of Company A deserted.

Oct 2—Feeling pretty well. Received a number of letters from the regiment.

Oct 3—Wound gives me no trouble. A great many visitors call to see me to-day. The army was reviewed to-day by Generals McClellan and Burnside, also by President Lincoln. This has been the first review the division has had since we left North Carolina. Lincoln and his escort, after the review passed up the road towards Sharpsburg, where other troops were waiting to be reviewed. The booming of cannon can be plainly heard in honor of the visitors. The troops marched to their quarters and rested for the balance of the day under the cool shade of their shelter tents.

Oct 4—Wound gives me but very little trouble. Wrote a number of letters to friends in the regiment. A number of ladies from old Montgomery visited the camp of the regiment to-day.

Oct 5—Feeling pretty well and sleeping very well. The men are now sleeping under tents for the first time since August 12th, nearly two months.[23] Yesterday the following order was issued.

> Head Quarters 9th Army Corps
> Mouth of Antietam Md. Oct. 4. 1862.
> Special Orders No. 53
>
> x x x x x x x x x x
> Private Wm. H. Griffith Co. F 51st Rgt. Penna. Vols. will proceed to Washington D. C. in charge of Private Samuel Hart Co. C 51st Pa. Vols. a prisoner under sentence of General Court Martial, and deliver him up to the Provost Marshal at that point & will then return to his Regiment.
> x x x x x x x x x x

---

21. Samuel E. Hartranft was the colonel's father, while Abraham Markley was superintendent of the Norristown Insurance and Water Company.

22. *O.R.* vol. 19, part 2, 373, has the date as September 30 that these regiments joined the corps. Page 368 includes a list of units which will be sent to the army.

23. Parker, *51st PA*, 250, wrote that these tents were shelter halves, and that the regiment for the first time used this type of tent.

By command of Major General Burnside
Louis Richmond Asst. Adjt. Genl.

Griffith left the camp this morning with his charge. To-day was also issued Special Orders No. 54, ordering Lieut. Jno. A. Morris 51st Pa. Vols. A.D.C. on the staff of the late Major Genl. Reno to report without delay to the commanding officer of his regiment for duty, who was then immediately appointed an aide-de-camp on the Staff of Major Genl. Burnside.

Oct 6—My wound has given me very little trouble to-day. Received quite a large number of visitors to-day.

Two days full rations were issued to the regiment to-day with orders to be ready to move at a moments notice and consequently struck tents. The camp rumor is that McClellan has received orders by telegraph direct from the President directing him to cross the Potomac and give battle to the enemy or to drive him south.

Oct 7—My wound is not giving me any trouble. Took a walk in the yard for the first time since being home. Received and wrote several letters to the regiment.

At sunrise the regiment left camp and march over a spur of South Mountain. Our line of march was through a bridle path and was laborious and tortuous, and after a march of some twelve miles, we reach Pleasant Valley Md. about 3 o'clock P.M. and went into bivouac, all hands pretty well used up. The First Brigade was ordered to Frederick Md. and the Second to guard the fords between Knoxville and the mouth of the Monocacy River. Other troops were ordered to march to and to guard Mock's Ford and Noland's Ferry.

Oct 8—Feeling very well, so much so that Dunlap took me out riding. To-day the regiment was again visited by friends from old Montgomery among whom were Alex Supplee, David Adams, and John Pywell. They remained in camp all night.

A Board of Survey has been appointed for Sturgis Division and met at Lt. Col. Schall's quarters for the purpose of ascertaining the amount of clothing charged to the troops of this command, and lost in action, with a view to have it replaced. Detail for the Board:

Lt.Col. Schall, 51st P.V.	Lt. Foster, 51st P.V.
Capt. Hovey, 21st Mass.	Lt. Wheeler, 21st Mass.
Capt. Wright, 51st N.Y.	Lt. Whitman, 51st N.Y.
Capt. Gibson, 35th Mass.	Lt. Hudson, 35th Mass.

Oct 9—Feeling very well and spent the day downstairs. Received quite a number of letters from the regiment.

Oct 10—Feeling very well. Received a letter from Col. Hartranft, informing me of my appointment as major of the 51st Pa. Vols., also informing me that he had found my sword. The regiment has now got down to hard drilling.

Oct 11—Feeling pretty well during the day, but in the evening taken with a very bad sore throat, rested very little all night.

Oct 12—Sore throat continues, and did not rest very well all night. Our brigade reviewed and inspected by Gen. Ferrero. In accordance with Special Orders No. 42 C.S. Headquarters 9th A.C. Capt. George W. Durell, Battery D, was detailed to proceed to Alexandria, Va. for the purpose of bringing up the stragglers and others now there belonging to this brigade. The sergeants detailed for this duty from the various regiments are ordered to report to Capt. Durell at his quarters at 6 o'clock this P.M.

Oct 13—Sore throat continues and am not at all well. In accordance with Special Orders No. 280 C.S. Gen. Burnside was assigned to the general charge of the defenses at Harpers' Ferry, and the Second and Twelfth Army Corps are placed under his orders for the present.[24]

Oct 14—Sore throat continues, and very little rest. Received a number of letters from the regiment.

Burnside received orders to-day to send a force to guard the fords between Knoxville and the mouth of the Monocacy River. Camp rumor has it that the rebels are concentrating near Leesburg.[25]

Oct 15—My throat and wound very bad.

Oct 16—My throat and wound still continues bad. Heavy cannonading is now being heard in camp from the direction of Maryland Heights and the regiment is under orders to move. Rations issued and are now being cooked. Col. Hartranft is now in temporary command of the brigade, and Lt. Col. Schall is in command of the regiment.

Oct 17—Wound and throat much better. Orders countermanded about moving. In accordance with General Orders No. 21 C.S. the following is the allowance of transportation for the several regiments of our brigade:

51st Penna. Vols.	5 wagons	1 for Regt. Hd Qs	6
21st Mass. Vols.	4 wagons	"	5
51st N.Y. Vols.	4 wagons	"	5
35th Mass. Vols.	5 wagons	"	6
11th N.H. Vols.	6 wagons	"	7

Oct 18—Feeling much better. Received a large number of letters from the regiment.

Oct 19—Feeling a great deal better and took a ride in the afternoon. Congratulatory orders were issued to-day by McClellan and Burnside complimenting the 51st P.V. for taking Antietam Bridge. They were read in front of the regiment on dress parade. During the night a terrible hurricane with rain paid the regiment a visit, scattering the tents in all directions and drenching the men to the skin.

Oct 20—Feeling quite well, took a walk in the morning and afternoon. Twenty men (five of whom were carpenters) were detached under the command of a sergeant armed with shovels, axes and picks, with two days cooked rations to report at 7 o'clock A.M. to-morrow to Dr. Von Beust at the hotel in Weaverton.

Oct 21—Feeling very well and took a ride to the State Fair Grounds. Orders from the Secretary of War reach camp to-day to the effect that all volunteers enlisting in the regular army for three years, the time served already would be deducted. The order has raised some commotion among the boys. By a Special Order No. 290 C.S. issued from Army Headquarters Lieut. A. L. Ortlip, Co. A, 51st Penna. Vols. commanding Ambulance Train, 2d Division, 9th Army Corps will proceed to Washington for the purpose of procuring the ambulances for the 9th Corps. On the completion of this duty he will rejoin his station.[26]

---

24. Order is in *O.R.* vol. 19, part 2, 420.

25. *O.R.*, vol. 19, part 2, 424.

26. Special Orders #290 is in *O.R.* vol. 19, part 2, 460. The printed order contains only the section dealing with the formation of a cavalry brigade and omits this section.

Oct 22—Wound gives me no trouble. Regiment still keeps up their drilling.

Oct 23—Feeling very well. Col. Hartranft left for Norristown on a short leave of absence. Lt. Col. Schall is in command of the regiment.

Oct 24—Feeling very well and took a ride to Bridgeport. In accordance with Special Orders No. 68 C.S. the commanding officer of the 51st P.V. commenced to organize a Pioneer Corps consisting of one lieut. one sergeant and thirty-one men to fully equip at once. They are to be excused from all guard duty and will remain with the regiment, but when separated from them will be under the command of Lt. Myrick 35th Regt. Mass. Vols.

Oct 25—Feeling very well. In accordance with Special Orders No. 21 the regiment was ordered to hold themselves in readiness to march to-morrow morning, the men to carry constantly (60) sixty rounds of ammunition and (2) two days rations. The camp was again visited by a terrible rain storm ripping the tents up generally.

Oct 26—Feeling very well, but remained in the house all day. The order to march was countermanded. The camp again visited by another violent storm. Two divisions of the Ninth Corps and Pleasonton's brigade of cavalry crossed at Berlin and occupied Lovettsville during the day.

Oct 27—Feeling very well. The regiment struck tents this morning and left camp at Pleasant Valley, Montgomery County, Md. about 9 o'clock A.M. crossed the Baltimore and Ohio Railroad at Weaverton, passed through Knoxville and under the Ohio and Chesapeake Canal, and crossed the Potomac at Berlin on a pontoon bridge into Virginia, and came to a halt a few miles from the river on the Lovettsville road about 4 o'clock P.M. Gen. Burnside in command.

Oct 28—Feeling very well, and out all day. Regiment remained in bivouac all day.

Oct 29—Feeling very well, spent the day in Philada. Regiment struck tents at 1 o'clock P.M. and at 3 P.M. left Lovettsville, and after marching some seven or eight miles, halted and went into bivouac for the night.

Oct 30—My wound is giving me no trouble, and am feeling very well. Regiment struck their tents at daylight, and after marching some three miles over the Leesburg Pike, about 11 o'clock A.M. went into bivouac on a rebel farm. On our march we passed Wheatland Mills. Strong picket line have been thrown out, and later in the night, plenty of rebels were found in the vicinity of the camp, and the whole of Company I was sent out to reinforce the picket line. During the night our pickets made a few captures of rebels.

Oct 31—Wound all right. Regiment remained in bivouac all day.

Nov 1—Wound all right. Wrote several letters to the regiment. Regiment remains in bivouac. The regimental sutlers has arrived. The men are without money, not having been paid for over four months. The sutlers are asking exorbitant prices.–$1.50 per plug of tobacco and all other things in proportion. Their indignation has no bounds.

Nov 2—Feeling very well, and took a ride to the Trappe. Regiment struck tents and left their camp near Wheatland Mills about 8 o'clock A.M., passed through Peshalville and came to a halt at Mountain Mills. The whole of Company A thrown out as pickets.

Nov 3—Wound gives me no trouble. Regiment struck tents and left Mountain Mills about 3 o'clock P.M. leaving Snicker's Gap to their right, passed Bloomfield, and late in the day went into bivouac in a field for the night.

Nov 4—Spent the day pleasantly. Regiment again struck tents and left their camp about 7 o'clock A.M. and at night reached Upperville and went into bivouac.

Nov 5—Feeling very well. Regiment again struck tents at 6 o'clock A.M. and left Upperville, crossed the Louden and Manassas Railroad at Piedmont Station, and went into bivouac about one mile from the railroad. The Ninth Corps is now between Piedmont and Salem, with a brigade at Manassas Gap. The following orders were read in front of the regiment to-day. [The orders relieved General McClellan from command and placed Burnside in charge of the Army of the Potomac. See *O.R.* vol. 19, part 2, 545, for these orders.]

Nov 6—Feeling very well, went out to dine with some friends. Regiment broke camp and left about 2 o'clock P.M., passed Oak Hill, came to a halt in the evening and went into bivouac. It is all the talk in the army as to the cause of McClellan's removal, and very many thought that the President had good cause for his removal.

Nov 7—Spent the day at home. Regiment broke camp and left about 4 o'clock P.M. The march was through a terrible snow storm, and hail to make matters worse. It became evident that the division (and it was then 11 o'clock) had lost its way as it found themselves in an ugly gorge and in a dense forest. The division was compelled to retrace its steps, marching back a few miles, then taking a new road on the left leading to another ford. The regiment renewed their march, but they were twelve miles out of their road. In our march, passed Orleans, Burnside's headquarters, and after midnight went into bivouac near the Rappahannock River on beds of snow, but before doing so, every panel fence in sight disappeared, fires were kindled, a hasty cup of coffee was made, and disposed of, and with wet clothes, and shoes full of snow, the men soon fell asleep.

Nov 8—Spent the day at home. Regiment broke camp at 7 o'clock A.M. crossed the Rappahannock at Waterloo and after marching some time came to a halt at a little village called Amissville and went into bivouac, the rebels having vacated the place only a few hours before our arrival, leaving behind plenty of cattle, hogs and sheep, which we of course took charge of and made use of. Before leaving, the rebels had placarded all the doors "small-pox" but the boys didn't scare worth a cent. Gen. Burnside to-day received the order relieving Gen. McClellan of the command of the Army of the Potomac, through Gen. Buckingham, and McClellan at once turned over the command to Burnside.

Chapter 6

Fredericksburg

November 9, 1862–February 4, 1863

Following the Maryland campaign, McClellan was relieved of command and replaced by Burnside, who devised a good plan but was foiled by miscommunication with Washington. The result was a defeat at Fredericksburg (December 13). Burnside was replaced by Hooker and the Ninth Corps was detached from the Army of the Potomac. Major Bolton missed this entire campaign owing to his severe Antietam wound.

Nov 9—Spent the day in the house. Regiment broke camp at Amissville about 7 o'clock and marched to Jefferson, crossing at Miller's Ford, arriving at 11 o'clock at night and bivouacked. Burnside in G.O. No. 1 assumed command of the Army of the Potomac.[1]

Nov 10—Spent the day at home in reading and writing letters to friends in the regiment. Regiment still in camp at Jefferson.

Nov 11—Received a number of letters from the regiment. Regiment still encamped at Jefferson.

Nov 12—Regiment broke camp at Jefferson about 2 o'clock A.M. crossed the Rappahannock river at Sulphur Springs. Had just reached the other side when the rebels made their appearance. Went into bivouac near the Springs Mansion House. Rations very scarce.

Nov 13—Paid a visit to Bridgeport. Quartermaster Saml. Stephens has succeeded in getting some little grub for the regiment. Two privates of Co. B were captured to-day by the rebel cavalry.

Nov 14—Received a letter from my friend Lieut. W. A. H. Lewis of the 93d regiment.[2] Regiment struck tents this morning and left their bivouac at White Sulphur Springs, proceeded about one mile when the rebels opened fire on them with artillery from the other side of the river. Regiment formed in line of battle and opened fire. The engagement lasted until 2 o'clock, when the regiment resumed their march, and after marching some seven miles, bivouacked for the night in a large field near the Rappahannock River.

　　To-day Gen. Burnside issued G.O. 184 from his headquarters Near Warrenton, Va. as follows: The Second and Ninth Corps formed the Right Grand Division commanded by Genl.

---

1. *O.R.*, vol. 19, part 2, 557.

2. Lieutenant William A. H. Lewis was adjutant of the 93rd Pennsylvania. He was discharged from service on August 15, 1862.

E. V. Sumner; The First and Sixth Corps formed the Left Grand Division commanded by Gen. Wm. B. Franklin; The Third and Fifth Corps formed the Center Grand Division commanded by Maj. Gen. Joseph Hooker; The Eleventh Corps with such other troops as may hereafter be assigned to it, constituted a reserve force, under the command of Maj. Gen. F. Sigel. Sumner at once announced in G.O. his assuming command and announced his staff.[3]

Nov 15—Wrote several letters to friends in the regiment. Regiment broke camp about 8 o'clock A.M. crossed the Alexandria and Orange Railroad a few miles below Warrenton Junction, and after a march over one of the most miserable roads of some nineteen miles, went into bivouac in the night in a rain storm along the railroad some sixteen miles from Fredericksburg. The men suffered from sore feet and very empty stomachs, but very late in the night rations were drawn, and all eaten up in one meal.

Nov 16—Wrote a letter to my brother Joe, and Lieut. Lewis. Regiment broke camp this morning and about dark reached the "Yellow House" situated on the road leading to Falmouth and some seven or eight miles from that place.

Nov 17—Wrote several letters to friends in the regiment. Regiment broke camp at 9 o'clock A.M. and left the Yellow House, and about noon reached Falmouth, opposite Fredericksburg, and bivouacked.

Nov 18—Received a number of letters from the regiment. Regiment broke camp about 6 o'clock A.M. marched until 12 o'clock M. and went into bivouac.[4]

Nov 19—Spent the day pleasantly. Regiment broke camp at 6 o'clock A.M. marched through Falmouth and arrived opposite Fredericksburg about 4 o'clock P.M. and pitched our tents about one mile from the old camping ground we had occupied the August before, but with sadness, I must state, with our ranks very much reduced—one half at least, of the number that we left here with three months before. The bloodstained fields of Manassas, Chantilly, South Mountain, Antietam, and Sulphur Springs, and the many skirmishes we had passed through with in those three months, has been the cause.

Nov 20—Spent the afternoon and evening with a friend. Heavy details made from the regiment for picket duty. Looks as if we are to remain here, as we have been ordered to fix up our camp to our own liking.

Nov 21—Received a number of letters from the regiment. To-day Burnside sent over the river a flag of truce to the civil authorities of Fredericksburg, demanding the surrender of the city, stating terms &c. giving them until 8 o'clock of the morning of the 24th to decide on the demand with a threat if not complied with, he would open on the town with his guns &c.[5]

Nov 22—Regiment is now receiving a plentiful supply of rations of all kinds, and are having plenty of rest, and are beginning to feel like themselves again. The regular camp routine duty has resumed and company and regimental drills and dress parade are the order of the day.

Nov 23—Spent the day at home. Regiment received orders to be ready to move at a moments notice.

Nov 24—Regiment struck tents at daylight and packed up every thing, expecting that the city would be shelled. Our whole division was moved back about one mile and went into camp

---

3. Burnside's order can be found in *O.R.*, vol. 19, part 2, 583-84. Sumner's follows on 584.

4. This entry seems unlikely, since the regiment had already reached Falmouth the previous day. Parker's regimental history provides no help here.

5. Burnside's surrender demand was sent through General Sumner. See *O.R.*, vol. 21, 783.

again, as the city was not surrendered nor was it shelled. Our brigade (Ferrero's) have a most beautiful camp, formed in the shape of a hollow square, the square being used as a drill ground, our only need now is clothing and shoes.[6]

Nov 25—Company, regimental drills and dress parade.

Nov 26—Company, regimental drills. Brigade review and dress parade.

Nov 27—Company, regimental drills. Division review and dress parade.

Nov 28—Company, regimental drills and dress parade.

Nov 29—Company and regimental drills.

Nov 30—Company, regimental drills. Brigade review and dress parade. During the time we were lying here in camp, pontoons, siege and field pieces and fresh troops were arriving daily and heavy picket details were made daily, and a careful watch was always kept on the movements of the enemy.

Dec 1—Company, regimental drills and dress parade.

Dec 2—Company, regimental and brigade drills and dress parade. Regiment settled up their clothing account for the last fourteen months.

Dec 3—Company, regimental drills and dress parade. Brigade review.

Dec 4—Company, regimental drills and dress parade.

Dec 5—Company, regimental drills and dress parade.

Dec 6—Company, regimental drills, division review and dress parade.

Dec 7—Company, regimental drills and dress parade. To-day a circular was issued from Brigade Headquarters relieving it from all drills for two days so as to enable the men to make their huts more comfortable. Three teams will be furnished to each regiment to have wood for that purpose.

Dec 8—[No entry]

Dec 9—Regiment engaged on their huts and are putting the camp in good shape.

Dec 10—Whole regiment detailed for picket duty and at 8 o'clock A.M. marched out from camp and were posted at the railroad bridge on the Rappahannock, opposite the city.

---

6. The Ninth Army Corps was now under the command of General Willcox, and was organized as follows:

First Division, Brig. Gen. William W. Burns
    First Brigade, Col. Orlando M. Poe: 2nd, 17th, 20th MI, 79th NY
    Second Brigade, Col. Benjamin C. Christ: 29th MA, 8th MI, 27th NJ, 46th NY, 50th PA
    Third Brigade, Col. Daniel Leasure: 36th MA, 45th, 100th PA
    Artillery: Bty D, 1st NY; Btys L&M, 3rd US
Second Division, Brig. Gen. Samuel D. Sturgis
    First Brigade, Brig. Gen. James Nagle: 2nd MD, 6th, 9th NH, 48th PA, 7th, 12th RI
    Second Brigade, Brig. Gen. Edward Ferrero: 21st, 35th MA, 11th NH, 51st NY, 51st PA
    Artillery: Bty D, 2nd NY; PA Bty D; Bty D, 1st RI; Bty E, 4th US
Third Division, Brig. Gen. George W. Getty
    First Brigade, Col. Rush C. Hawkins: 10th, 13th NH, 25th NJ, 9th, 89th, 103rd NY
    Second Brigade, Col. Edward Harland: 8th, 11th, 15th, 16th, 21st CT, 4th RI
    Artillery: Bty E, 2nd US; Bty A, 5th US

Dec 11—Regiment was put in motion about 8 o'clock A.M. and marched about one mile and laid on the ground all day. At 5 o'clock P.M. marched back to camp. Remained there a short time and moved again. During all this time Fredericksburg was being bombarded by one hundred and eight guns in order to cover the laying of the pontoon bridges for our troops to enter the city. The bridges were laid successfully but under a terrible fire from the enemy.

Later in the day our regiment was cautiously withdrawn from the river and returned to camp. All this time the guns were bleching forth their deadly fire on the doomed city and the troops were lying on their arms ready at a moments call to march to the bridges for the attack, but the 51st was not called up, but remained in their camp all night dreading the coming morning.

Dec 12—About 4 o'clock A.M. a terrific cannonade commenced. Regiment broke camp at 5 o'clock A.M. and marched across the Rappahannock River on the pontoon bridge and entered the city of Fredericksburg, and were placed in position and laid on the ground all night, doing picket duty.

The very earth trembled. All day the shot and shell could be heard crashing through the houses. By noon nearly all the troops had gained a crossing by bridge and swimming, but every inch was hotly contested by the rebels. The engineer corps of our army suffered terribly from the rebel sharpshooters hid in houses in the city. The 51st P.V. took up a position near the Phillips House, making that position about 8 o'clock A.M. It was an elevated position and the rebel lines could be distinctly seen. Very little sleeping is being had and all are wondering what the coming morrow will bring forth.

To-night Q.M. Sergt. Wm. Jones committed suicide by shooting himself. Having been for several days in a depressed state of mind he was left back in camp when the regiment was ordered to cross the river. The act was done in rear of his tent. He was buried near the hospital tent and later his remains were sent to Norristown.

Dec 13—Regiment remained in their bivouac until near 10 o'clock A.M. when it formed line and marched up a street in the lower end of the city, when it came very suddenly upon a brick-kiln that extended across the street. Here we became exposed and the rebels opened with their batteries on us without stint, but Hartranft was equal to the emergency. By a sudden dash the regiment succeeded in reaching the railroad cut without much loss, but all this time the regiment was under a severe fire of musketry and artillery. The air was full of ball and shell, but the regiment finally reached the position that had been assigned to them. Our course of march was very much impeded by a number of high board fences and of course could not advance by a regimental front, but they very soon put themselves on the other side of the fences in a very short time. But the men of the 51st P.V. were falling at every step and men were laying weltering in their gore all around, some killed outright, some with legs and arms torn off, and many with headless bodies. The sight was terrible in the extreme. Each regiment went into the engagement with one hundred rounds of ammunition on the person of each man, and it was all expended, was taken from the boxes of the dead and wounded.

The regiment was in action from 10 o'clock A.M. until after dark. Then it was withdrawn and quartered in houses in the city, and what was left of us was pretty well used up. In coming off the field, many a poor fellow was trodden on, and it was truly heartrendering to hear their groans and cries for water. The night was spent by all in cooking and sleeping, for it had been seven or eight days since the regiment had an hour of unbroken rest, and a great deal of that time without food. The regiment took into action some two hundred and eight men[7] and our loss was during the engagement from all causes ninety-one, and are as follows:

---

7. Parker, *51st PA*, wrote that the regiment entered battle with 270 effectives.

Killed:

Pvt. William Heard, Co. A
Pvt. Washington McDade, Co. A
Pvt. James McGuire, Co. A
Pvt. David McMicken, Co. A
Capt. Ferdinand W. Bell, Co. B
Pvt. William F. Strattford, Co. B
Pvt. Michael McMullen, Co. C

Pvt. George H. Sweeney, Co. C
Pvt. Benjamin Kremmer, Co. D
Pvt. J. Wesley Lonsdale, Co. D
Pvt. John Mogee, Co. D
Pvt. Manassas Reininger, Co. F
Sgt. William Allison, Co. H
Pvt. George Krieble, Co. I

Wounded:

Pvt. Abraham Custer, Co. A (died December 14)
Pvt. Edward Kellichner, Co. A
Pvt. Albanas Lare, Co. A
Sgt. John S. Moore, Co. A
Sgt. Jacob H. Moyer, Co. A
Pvt. Charles Toy, Co. A
Sgt. George W. Arnett, Co. B
Pvt. Allen J. Clifton, Co. B
Pvt. Charles Sharp, Co. B
Pvt. Thomas Unangst, Co. B
Pvt. James W. Detwiler, Co. C
Pvt. Charles R. Fox, Co. C
Pvt. Andrew Grim, Co. C
Pvt. James Gunn, Co. C
Pvt. David R. Spare, Co. C
Pvt. George Stout, Co. C
Pvt. Peter Undercoffer, Co. C
Cpl. John Beal, Co. D
Sgt. Freeman S. Davis, Co. D
Sgt. William Dignan, Co. D
Sgt. Isaac Fitzone, Co. D
Pvt. Alfred R. Grey, Co. D
Pvt. John G. Guyer, Co. D
Lieut. Lewis Hallman, Co. D
Cpl. Albert List, Co. D
Pvt. Elwood Lukens, Co. D
Cpl. John L. McCoy, Co. D
Pvt. James McKenna, Co. D
Sgt. John McNulty, Co. D
Pvt. Henry C. Moore, Co. D
Pvt. John Powell, Co. D
Pvt. Owen Rex, Co. D
Pvt. Samuel Sharp, Co. D
Pvt. Thomas D. Smith, Co. D
Pvt. Henry Sutch, Co. D
Lieut. Jonathan Swallow, Co. D
Pvt. Thomas Vanfossen, Co. D

Pvt. George W. Yarnell, Co. D
Pvt. Cyrus A, Eaton, Co. E
Pvt. James J. Kelly, Co. E
Pvt. Charles Lydle, Co. E
Sgt. Lewis G. Titus, Co. E (died January 17, 1863)
Pvt. Henry K. Adleman, Co. F
Pvt. Manassa Boyer, Co. F
Sgt. Howard Bruce, Co. F
Sgt. William B. Hart, Co. F
Pvt. Nathaniel Kulp, Co. F
Pvt. Willaughby Kulp, Co. F
Pvt. Christian McCormick, Co. F
Pvt. William McSparren, Co. F
Pvt. David Munsick, Co. F
Pvt. Albert Teany, Co. Fv
Pvt. Henry White, Co. F
Sgt. William Hichel, Co. G
Pvt. James Beightol, Co. G
Pvt. George Meisse, Co. G
Pvt. William Recides, Co. G
Sgt. David C. Brown, Co. H
Sgt. Jacob H. Santo, Co. H
Sgt. George Breon, Co. H
Pvt. Daniel Boone, Co. H
Pvt. Levi Brensinger, Co. H
Pvt. David Clark, Co. H
Pvt. John Doughterty, Co. H
Pvt. Henry Hain, Co. H
Pvt. John Moore, Co. H
Pvt. Robert W. Passell, Co. H
Pvt. Charles W. A. Tempel, Co. H
Sgt. George Carney, Co. I
Pvt. George W. Fulton, Co. I
Pvt. John R. Herd, Co. I
Sgt. Andrew S. Leedom, Co. I
Pvt. Thomas McGolrich, Co. I (died January 1, 1863)

Pvt. Antrim Meister, Co. I
Pvt. George Peters, Co. I
Cpl. James Shainline, Co. I

Lieut. Mark R. Supplee, Co. I
Pvt. Thomas Delp, Co. K

Missing:

Pvt. Christian Lock, Co. F

Pvt. Levi Brensinger, Co. H

Deserted:

Pvt. Thomas Selch, Co. A

Promotions:

Corp. Christopher Wyckoff Co. F promoted to Quarter-Master Sergeant

The death of Capt. Ferdinand W. Bell was a very serious loss to the regiment. Very unassuming, and a grand disciplinarian, and as fearless as a lion.

"Oh! smother the damp hair over his brow;
It is pale and white, and gastly now;
And hide the wound in his gory breast,
For his soul has fled to its final rest."

Dec 14—The whole regiment were sent out on picket at 7 o'clock P.M. relieving the picket of General Griffin along the Rappahannock River.[8]

Dec 15—Regiment remained on picket until 11 o'clock P.M. when it was relieved by Col. Zook's brigade and ordered to across the river. Our picketing was about equal to the fighting of the day before.[9]

Dec 16—Regiment recrossed the Rappahannock without any mishap and reached our old campground about 2 o'clock A.M. and at daylight began to fix up our camp. Early in the morning a detail of thirty men were sent across the river to bury the Union dead and to care for our wounded.

Dec 17—Our detail with many others still over the river burying the dead and caring for the wounded.

Dec 18—All of the details returned to their respective camps this morning, and they report that they found that nearly all of our dead had been stripped of their clothing and robbed of their money, as the most of them had four months pay on their persons. The dead were all buried in the trenches that had been thrown up during the battle.

Dec 19—I received a letter this morning from camp at Fredericksburg from my brother informing me that it has been discovered that very many of the shell used by our artillery had been filled with sand, sawdust, beans, &c. To-day Captain Wm. H. Blair Company G was discharged to enable him to be promoted to Col. of the 179th Regiment Penna. Vols. I received a letter to-day from Col. Hartranft requesting me to go to Harrisburg Pa. and hunt up all the commissions that are due the regiment. He also says that he expects to have command

8. Brigadier General Charles Griffin commanded the First Division, Fifth Army Corps.

9. Colonel Samuel K. Zook commanded the Third Brigade, First Division, Second Army Corps.

of the Third Brigade which is about organizing and ends his letter as follows "The 51st again behaved nobly and well. Can all be proud who are fortunate enough to be connected with it." The following address was issued to-day and read on dress parade:

Headquarters 2d Brigade
2d Division 9th Corps
Near Falmouth Va. Dec 19th,1862.

To the soldiers of the Second Brigade, the General commanding extends his congratulations and thanks for their gallant conduct and faithful service while under his command.

The patience, steadiness and courage displayed in desperate battle and wearisome marches, exhibit a spirit that never can fail, a determination that will in the end triumph over all foes.

The hardships endured, the difficulties overcome, the perils faced by this our valiant Brigade will live in history, long after you the heroes have gone down to the grave.

Your career will be pointed to by those who follow you, with admiration and praise, and a greatful country will bless ancestory that could endure such toils, that could perform such noble deeds, and so cheerfully sacrifice all that is dear on earth, for the sake of their country and their saced cause.

To the new troops who fought so nobly on the 13th on their first battle field, thanks are especially due, they have every way proved themselves worthy to stand side by side with the veterans of the Second Brigade. That in the coming campaign of 1863 we may stand by each other as faithfully as heretofore, that we may fight as bravely and successfully for our loved country, and that God's blessing may always rest on you and your exertions, is the earnest prayers of

Your General
Edward Ferrero
Brig. Gen. Comdg. 2d Brig.

Dec 20—Company and regimental inspection.

Dec 21—Company and regimental drills and dress parade.

Dec 22—Received a letter from Col. Hartranft and a number of others from the regiment.

Dec 23—The whole of Company A sent out on picket along the Rappahannock River.

Dec 24—Company A relieved at daylight from picket duty and returned to camp. Regimental drill and dress parade.

Dec 25—Company and regimental drills and dress parade in the evening. Details from the regiment for picket duty along the river.

Dec 26—Company and regimental drills and dress parade. Our usual picket from the regiment along the river.

Dec 27—Company and brigade drills and dress parade.

Dec 28—Company and regimental drills. Dress parade.

Dec 29—Whole of Co. A went out on picket along the river. Col. Hartranft has been detailed as a member of a Court Martial and are now in session at Brigade Headquarters.

Dec 30—Company A returned from picket duty early this morning. Received my commission this morning as major. The usual drills.

Dec 31—Wrote several letters to the regiment.

<h1 style="text-align:center">1863</h1>

Jan 1—Regimental and company drills and dress parade.

Jan 2—Company and brigade drills and dress parade. Sgt. Richard Martin Co. I died at Camp Nelson Ky. from wounds received at Camden N.C. Winter has set in in good earnest. Large details are sent out from the regiment every day to do picket duty along the river.

Jan 3—The usual drills. Received a number of letters from the regiment.

Jan 4—The usual drills and picket details.

Jan 5—The whole regiment went out on picket along the Rappahannock River.

Jan 6—Regiment relieved from picket duty at daylight, and in the afternoon with the rest of the brigade marched to the parade ground to be reviewed by Gen. Burnside, but as a storm came up, the troops were dismissed and returned to camp.

Jan 7—The usual drills, picket duty &c.

Jan 8—The usual drills, picket duty &c.

Jan 9—Paid a visit to Pennsburg in company with Capt. Hart and Saml. M. Markley to visit Lieut. Lynch of Co. C as we were all making ready to rejoin the regiment.[10]

Jan 10—The usual drills and picket duty &c.

Jan 11—The usual Sunday morning inspection and dress parade in the evening.

Jan 12—Whole regiment out on picket.

Jan 13—Regiment relieved from picket duty at daylight. Company drills.

Jan 14—The usual drills and dress parade.

Jan 15—The usual drills and picket duty.

Jan 16—Received orders to be in readiness to move to-morrow morning at an early hour with three days cooked rations in haversacks and sixty rounds of ammunition distributed to each man.

Jan 17—Company drills. No movement to-day as was expected.

Jan 18—Regular Sunday morning inspection and dress parade in the evening.

Jan 19—The whole regiment went out on picket along the river.

Jan 20—Regiment relieved from picket duty at daylight. On their way back to camp, Bob Bob a nickname for Robert Roberts, a member of Co. A discovered several wagons stuck in the snow and mud on the Falmouth and Bell Plain road. It was soon discovered that they were sutlers wagons, and the owners and mules had gone, and left the wagons and contents in charge of a negro. Bob and his few companions were equal to the emergency. With his gun in hand and bayonet fixed, he advanced towards the darkey, and asked him if he was on guard, and on receiving an affirmative reply, Bob told him he had come to relieve him. The poor darkey was only too glad to get off, as it was very cold and the snow knee deep. The darkey once out of sight, Bob and his companions began to unload the goods, and to carry them into camp informing some more of the men of the rich prize, and with his reenforcements proceeded to the place and in less than an hour every dollars worth of goods were carried into

---

10. Captain Lane S. Hart of Company F and Lieutenant Thomas J. Lynch of Company C both had been wounded at Antietam.

camp. Of course the owners soon returned but found their wagons empty, but of course the tracks through the snow led them to the camp of the 51st. An order from Gen. Ferrero for permission to search the camp was the next thing in order. The search was made but not an article found although each company's quarters were searched, but the boys covered up their tracks pretty well.

Orders again issued to be ready to move at 4 o'clock A.M. to-morrow, but the tents to be left standing, and all knapsacks to be left in the officers tents under guard of convalescents, with the instructions should it continue raining, not to have the troops under arms at the hour designated.

Jan 21—The morning was ushered in by a circular from brigade headquarters to hold ourselves in readiness to move at an hours notice. The whole army appears to be on the move, and part of it is stuck fast in the mud, artillery, wagons and caissons are in the same fix. Troops are returning to their camps.

Jan 22—Company drills and dress parade.

Jan 23—Received a letter from Col. Hartranft.

Jan 24—Regimental drill and dress parade.

Jan 25—Whole regiment on picket duty along the river. By G.O. No. 20 War Department, the President has directed as follows: First, That Major General A. E. Burnside, at his own request, be relieved from the command of the Army of the Potomac. Second, That Major General E. V. Sumner, at his own request, be relieved from duty in the Army of the Potomac. Third, That Major General W. B. Franklin be relieved from duty in the Army of the Potomac. Fourth, That Major General J. Hooker be assigned to the command of the Army of the Potomac.[11]

Jan 26—To-day General Burnside in G.O. No. 9 transferred the command of the army to Gen. Hooker. In winding up his address he thus speaks of the 9th Corps: "In taking an affectionate leave of the entire army, from which he separates with so much regret, he may be pardoned if he bids an especial farewell to his long-tried associates of the Ninth Corps." Gen. Hooker in General Orders No. 1 assumed command of the army to-day.[12]

Jan 27—Wrote a letter to Col. Hartranft. Company drills and dress parade.

Jan 28—Regiment went out on picket along the Rappahannock in a terrible rain and snow storm. Prv. Adam Yeager of Company A got loss in a snow drift.

Jan 29—Received letters from Capt. Hart and Lieut. Moore. Regiment relieved from picket duty. Camp rumor has it that Burnside has been ordered to the Department of Ohio.

Jan 30—Company drills and Brigade review.

Jan 31—Company and regimental drills and dress parade. For sometime the men have been using gunpowder for splitting their wood. To-day a circular was issued to the men forbidding them to use powder and if caught at it, to be charged for them at Government price.

Feb 1—I attened the funeral of Private Abraham Custer Co. A who died from wounds received at Fredericksburg Va. Usual Sunday morning inspection. 9th A.C. orders to report to Gen. Dicks Fort Monroe.[13]

---

11. See *O.R.*, vol. 19, 1004-5, for the text of this order.

12. *O.R.*, vol. 19, 1005.

13. Major General John A. Dix commanded the Department of Virginia.

Feb 2—Regiment went out on picket duty along the Rappahannock.

Feb 3—Regiment relieved at sunrise and returned to camp in a blinding snow storm.

Feb 4—All drilling dispensed with, as a terrible snow storm has been prevailing for some time, and the men who are not on duty are keeping within their huts. The following orders were received in camp to-day, which set the boys of the old 9th Corps all thinking what next.

Special Orders   Hdqrs. Army of the Potomac
No. 35   February 4, 1863

x x x x x x x x x

II. The Ninth Corps, under Maj. Gen. William F. Smith, will embark for Fort Monroe without delay. Major-General Sedgwick will relieve Major-General Smith of the command of the Sixth Corps, and will enter upon this duty on the receipt of this order. Staff officers on duty with these corps will be governed by the provisions of General Orders No. 212, War Department, December 23, 1862. On arriving at Fort Monroe, Major-General Smith will report to Major-General Dix for further orders. The troops will embark with three day's rations, sending all invalids of a serious type to Washington City, and those of a slight character will accompany the commands to which they belong. The chief quartermaster will furnish the necessary transportation.

x x x x x x x x x

By command of Major-General Hooker.

        Jos. Dickinson,
        Assistant Adjutant-General.[14]

---

14. Major General John Sedgwick had assumed command of the Ninth Corps on January 16, 1863, and was transferred to the Sixth Corps by this order.

Chapter 7

The Department of the Ohio

February 5–June 5, 1863

After leaving the Army of the Potomac, the Ninth Corps at first went to the Yorktown Peninsula as part of the Department of Virginia. Then, two divisions of the corps were transferred to the Department of the Ohio, of which Burnside had assumed command on March 25. The 51st spent most of this time in Mount Sterling and Lancaster, Kentucky, on garrison duty. Major Bolton rejoined the regiment just prior to the transfer.

Feb 5—All drilling suspended on account of the snow.

Feb 6—All drilling still suspended on account of the snow. Third Div. 9th A. C. struck tents and left for Newport News.

Feb 7—Nothing doing on account of the snow, which is very deep. Gen. Sturgis being absent, Gen. Ferrero assumed command of the 2d Division, and Col. Hartranft assumed the command of the 2d Brigade, 2d Division, and announced the following staff:

Capt. Lane S. Hart	A.A.A. Genl.
Lieut. Jno. H. Genthier	A.C.S.
Lieut. H. S. Hitchcock	Aides-de-camp
Lieut. D. C. Harriman	Aides-de-camp
Surg. J. P. Hossack	Brigade Surgeon

Hartranft also issued orders to-day that the brigade should be in readiness to move at an hours notice, and for each man to keep constantly on hand three days cooked rations. Orders was also issued to-day relieving Brig. Gen. Wm. W. Burns from serving in the Ninth Corps and ordering him to report to Gen. Rosecrans. The same order directs Gen. O. B. Willcox to report to Gen. Smith commanding Ninth Army Corps, who was assigned to the command of the First Division. Lt. Col. Schall in command of the regiment.

Feb 8—Regiment making all preparations for moving but ignorant of their destination. To-wards evening received orders to strike tents and to be ready to march at daylight with three days rations in haversacks, and two in wagons, and canteens filled before starting, wagons to report at daylight.

Feb 9—Regiment struck tents before daylight and 8 o'clock A.M. marched to Falmouth and at once embarked on board of the cars and started for Aquia Creek, arriving there in the afternoon, and at once embarked on board of the steamer *Louisiana,* which, along with other vessels, were in waiting along the wharves awaiting the arrival of the Ninth Corps.

Capt. Hart, Samuel M. Markley, and myself left home to rejoin the regiment at 6 o'clock P.M. leaving Philadelphia at 12 o'clock midnight for Washington, and before reaching there, our train ran off of the track three times.

Feb 10—Our party arrived in Washington about noon, all putting up at the Dorsey House. The fleet of steamers and transports with the whole of the Ninth Corps on board casted away their lines about 3 o'clock A.M. and all steamed down the Potomac and soon passed into Chesapeake Bay. Passed Point Lookout and came to anchor about midnight opposite Fortress Monroe near the Rip-Raps. Sewalls Point and Hampton in plain sight. The First Division struck tents and left for Newport News.

Feb 11—Our party remained in Washington all day. Our fleet hoisted anchor at 10 o'clock A.M. and steamed up the James River to Newport News, arriving there about noon and immediately disembarked and went into camp near its former camping ground.

Feb 12—Our party left Washington at 8 o'clock A.M. and took passage in a barge loaded with mules and hay. In accordance with G.O. No. 5 General George W. Getty took command of the Post at Newport News.

Feb 13—Our party left Aquia Creek at daylight for Newport News.

Feb 14—Our party arrived at Newport News about 9 o'clock A.M. and reached camp 5 o'clock P.M. The boys all very glad to see us.

Feb 15—Our camp is very well situated with plenty of water and wood. Usual Sunday morning inspection and the Articles of War read in front of the regiment.

Feb 16—Company and regimental drills and dress parade.

Feb 17—Company drills and Brigade review.

Feb 18—Company and regimental drills and dress parade. To-day the regiment received new tents.

Feb 19—Company and regimental drills and dress parade. Wrote several letters home.

Feb 20—Company drills, and regimental and brigade review.

Feb 21—Company and regimental drills. Received a lot of papers from Rob Iredell.

Feb 22—Rain and snow all day, men kept well in their tents all day.

Feb 23—Company and regimental drills and dress parade. Corpl. Andrew McKain Co. A who had been detailed on recruiting service, deserted.

Feb 24—Company and regimental drills and dress parade. Brigade review in the afternoon.

Feb 25—Company and regimental drills and dress parade. Brigade reviewed by Maj. Gen's. Smith and Dix. Commanded dress parade for the first time.

Feb 26—In command of the regiment. Company and regimental drills and dress parade. Received a number of papers from Rob Iredell.

Feb 27—Company and regimental drills. Had command of dress parade.

Feb 28—I was mustered out of United States service as Captain of Company A and immediately re-mustered as Major. Detailed as Brigade Officer of the Day. The troops of our brigade was inspected and mustered for payment as follows:

51st Penna. Vols. by Col. Hartranft
21st Mass. Vols. by Col. Clark
51st N.Y. Vols. by Lt. Col. LeGender [LeGendre]
35th Mass. Vols. by Lt. Col. Carrudh [Carruth]
11th N.H. Vols. by Col. Harriman

Mar 1—The usual Sunday morning inspection and the Articles of War read in front of each company. The 9th A.C. is now in the Department of Virginia commanded by Gen. John A. Dix with Headquarters at Fort Monroe.

Mar 2—Company and regimental drills. All officers attended brigade school for the instruction of officers. I was in command of dress parade.

Mar 3—Company and brigade drills and dress parade.

Mar 4—Company and regimental drills.

Mar 5—All the field officers of the brigade attended brigade school for theoretical instruction in evolution of the line at brigade headquarters at 10 o'clock this morning. Brigade drill in the afternoon. Dress parade. Lieut. S. N. Benjamin 2d U.S. Arty was appointed to-day Acting Asst. Inspector General of the 9th A.C. Capt. J. Merrill Linn of Co. H was to-day appointed a member of a Court Martial which is to meet at the Headquarters of Col. Sigfried 48th Penna. Vols. on March 7th.

Mar 6—Company and regimental drills.

Mar 7—Wrote several letters home and attended brigade school. Company and regimental drills.

Mar 8—Detailed as Brigade Officer of the Day. Company and regimental drills and dress parade.

Mar 9—Regiment inspected by Capt. Wright Asst. Insp. Genl. of the brigade. Commanded dress parade.

Mar 10—Company and regimental drills and dress parade. Major E. Jardine 9th N.Y. Vols. was to-day appointed Provost Marshall of the Corps.

Mar 11—Company and regimental drills. Commanded dress parade. Wrote a letter to my sister.

Mar 12—Company and regimental drills. Receievd a lot of papers from Mr. Iredell. Brigade Surgeon C. C. Cutter having been ordered to report for duty to his regiment, Surgeon J. P. Hossack of our regiment has been appointed to fill the vacancy.

Mar 13—Company and regimental drills and dress parade. In accordance with S.O. No. 25 the 51st Penna. Vols. and the 51st New York Vols. were detailed to occupy the Post of Newport News and will strike tents and move inside the intrenchments, folding tents neatly and store them in the unoccupied barracks.

Mar 14—The regiment struck tents early this morning and moved inside of the intrenchments. To-day being the anniversary of the Battle of New Berne, Gen. Ferrero issued a circular, directed the commandants of regiments to issue one ration of whiskey to each man in his command. Gen. Ferrero was to-day appointed commandant of the Post of Newport News.

Mar 15—Company inspection and the Army Regulations read in front of each company. Major R. C. Mitchell 51st N.Y. Vols. was to-day appointed Provost-Marshall of this Post.

Mar 16—Company and regimental drills and dress parade. 1st Lieut. John A. Morris Co. E appointed Assistant Quartermaster and transferred to Gen. Burnside's staff.

Mar 17—Company, regimental drills and review. Officers of the corps mostly attended a ball and supper on board of the steamer *City of Hudson*, now lying at the wharf, and all hands spent an enjoyable evening. Col. Hartranft to-day was appointed a member of the Post Council of Administration, the council to meet at his Headquarters to-morrow.

In pursuance to G.O. No. 1 issued at Washington by the Secretary of War, General Burnside assumed command of the Ninth Army Corps to-day. The same order gives to make preparations at once for the moving of two divisions--Sturgis and Getty's--leaving Willcox's division for the present, detached and remain in the command of Maj. Gen. Dix, and ordering Gen. Parke to proceed to Newport News to take command of the two divisions, and to make all the necessary preparations and arrangements for their removal.

Mar 18—Detailed as Brigade Officer of the Day. Company and regimental drills.

Mar 19—A severe rain and snow storm set in this morning and continued all day. The monitor *Keskese* arrived in the river and is anchored off our camp.[1]

Mar 20—Storm continues and is of great severity. Impossible to do anything of an out of door nature.

Mar 21—Storm continues with four inches of snow on the ground. Circular issued to-day to commandants of regiments to have their commands constantly in readiness to embark on transports with five days cooked rations, three days rations in haversacks, and two days packed securely, and so stored on board of vessel, as to be easily distributed when necessary. Private horses will be embarked when possible on the transports containing the troops. Officers will only be allowed to carry their baggage and tents; no furniture of any discription allowed on the transports. Regimental commanders to see that all men detailed on extra duty "at the post" accompany the regiment to which they belong. All common or A. tents and all surplus tents of all kinds when camp is broken up will be turned over to the Post Quartermaster. Every man to be provided with at least forty rounds of ammunition. Capt. J. G. Wright Act'g. Asst. Insp. General ordered to inspect the baggage and camp equipage of each regiment on embarking.

Mar 22—Company drills and dress parade. Received a letter from my sister.

Mar 23—Company and regimental drills and dress parade.

Mar 24—Company and regimental drills and dress parade.

Mar 25—Company and regimental drills and dress parade. Received orders to be ready to move to-morrow afternoon. Gen. Burnside assumed command of the Department of the Ohio to-day, relieving Maj. Gen. H. G. Wright.

Mar 26—Received marching orders, and at once struck tents and at sunrise marched to the wharf at Newport News and embarked on board of the steamer *Kennebec* and soon steamed down the James River to Fortress Monroe and dropped anchor.[2] Weighed anchor and left the Fortress about 3 o'clock P.M. and steamed into Chesapeake Bay, passed Fort McHenry and Fort Carroll. The men enjoyed themselves in playing cards and dancing.

Mar 27—The regiment arrived in Baltimore about 3 o'clock P.M., disembarked about 8 o'clock P.M. While waiting for the regiment to land, I with some other officers took a stroll leaving a brand new overcoat, the material of which was given me by Mr. George Bullock, in my state

---

1. It is not known what ship Bolton meant here.

2. Parker, *51st PA*, wrote that the steamer's name was *Louisiana*.

room. On my return to the regiment, I found that they had landed, went on board to get my traps, but found that my overcoat was missing and could not be found, and left Baltimore without it. Some of the crew had gone through the state rooms, as very many things were missing, but the master of the steamer promised me to hunt it up and forward it to me if found.

After unloading the baggage, the regiment marched to the Northern Central Railroad, arriving there about 11 o'clock P.M. There being no cars for us ready, we lay in the street until morning. The citizens were very hospitable. The 2d Maryland being in our brigade, made them more so. Things very lively during the night, and some of them landed in Fort McHenry.

Mar 28—Sometime after midnight cars arrived and the regiment embarked and left Baltimore about 3 o'clock A.M. leaving some of the boys behind. We arrived at Little York about 10 o'clock A.M. and the kind citizens came out and gave us a good breakfast, and here again some of the boys got left behind, but overtook us by jumping passing trains, meeting us at Marysville, near Harrisburg. About sundown we arrived at Bridgeport opposite Harrisburg but only remained there only a short time. Some of the men took advantage of the place, and to their shame, deserted.

Mar 29—About midnight we arrived at Altoona on the Pennsylvania Central Railroad, where we stopped for about an hour and got a good breakfast. Everything here was served up in abundance. We were soon again in motion crossing the Alleghany Mountains, and arriving in Pittsburg about 10 o'clock A.M. Here we were treated to a good collation in the City Hall, and were warmly received by Mayor McCook, in a very spirited speech which was well received by our boys. After the spread was over, the citizens took us in charge and for the time being, things were very lively. At 8 o'clock P.M. we marched to the Pittsburg and Cincinnati Railroad depot, and embarked on the cars, and were soon in rout to Columbus, Ohio.

Mar 30—Traveled all night and arrived in Columbus, Ohio, about 3 o'clock P.M. Here again the citizens furnished us with a splendid repast of coffee, bread and butter, boiled eggs, and ham, and every thing else a man could desire. Some of the men took a short stroll while waiting for the train to start, but it was not long before they came in contact with the Provost Guard. Words soon followed, then came shots from the guard, which resulted in the wounding of Prv. Edward Quinland of Co. A and others of the regiment. Fearing trouble the train pulled out of the depot at 6 o'clock P.M. for Cincinnati.

Mar 31—Traveled all night and arrived in Cincinnati about 3 o'clock A.M. and here again were entertained very kindly by the citizens. At 11 o'clock A.M. the regiment marched to the banks of the Ohio River and embarked on board of the steamer *Queen City*, crossed the river to Covington, Ky. On our way to the river we marched pass the Burnet House, where Gen. Burnside had his headquarters. He appeared on the balcony and made a splendid speech to the troops. Regiment embarked on the cars of the Kentucky Central Railroad about 6 o'clock P.M. in rout to Paris, Ky., which is some eighty miles from Cincinnati. Traveled all night.

Apr 1—We arrived in Paris, Ky. about one o'clock A.M., disembarked at daylight and marched to the county Fair Grounds about one mile from the town and took up our quarters in the cattle sheds. Having been on a constant move since the 26th of March, all hands felt pretty well used up, and very little was done in fixing up our quarters, the men preferring to sleep and rest for the day. During the day received word that Prv. Edward Quinlan Co. A died from the wound he had received in Columbus Ohio.

By virtue of S.O. No. 114 Headquarters Dept. of the Ohio, Col. W. S. Clark 21st Mass. Vols. assumed command of this Post and announced Capt. J. Merrill Linn Co. H 51st P.V. as A.A.A. Gen. and Lieut. B. F. Fuller 21st Mass. Vols. as A.A.Q.M. Genl. Ferrero has his Headquarters at Lexington Ky.[3] This afternoon we received orders to hold ourselves in readiness to move at a moments notice, with three days cooked rations in haversacks, fresh beef to be issued in the morning. It looks as if we are not to have any rest.

Apr 2—A very heavy detail was made from the regiment to go on picket to relieve the pickets of the 45th Penna. The detail left camp at 9 o'clock A.M. Notwithstanding the order to be ready to move, the men are spending some time in fixing up their quarters, and resting all they can. Quite a number of the officers and men of the brigade took a stroll to Paris this evening and they were not very long in finding out that the town was full of secesh and it was not long before a row was in progress. Capt. Nicholas Co. B received swollen eye, but the secesh was soon put to flight, and the soldiers returned to their camp at a late hour.

Apr 3—Regiment struck tents at daylight and left Paris at 7 o'clock A.M. passed through North Middletown and arrived at Mount Sterling Ky. at 8 o'clock P.M. having marched during the day twenty-three miles in a blinding snow storm and over a hard turnpike. We were completely worn out with fatigue. During the day a number of teams were pressed into service to haul our knapsacks and every thing else that was cumbersome. The regiment went into bivouac along the road side for the night completely used up. Pickets were thrown out around our camp and the rest fall into a sound sleep.

Apr 4—Regiment left their bivouac about 9 o'clock A.M., marched about two miles to the outskirts of the town and went into camp. I was detailed as brigade Officer of the Day. On reaching our new camp and immediately after receiving instruction from headquarters, rode out to take a survey of the country and station the pickets. Learned from a citizen who appears to be a Union man that it was here that the rebel Gen. Breckinridge made a speech of a violent nature before accepting a commission in the rebel army.

Apr 5—Regimental inspection and muster for pay. Dress parade in the evening. This morning our pickets brought into camp five guerillas and a more God forsaken set of humanity I never saw.

Apr 6—Company and regimental drills. I spent the day in Mount Sterling. To-day in accordance with G.O. No. 14 Gen. Ferrero assumed command of the forces at this place, and to-day appointed Capt. J. Merrill Linn Co. H 51st P.V. Provost Marshal of the Post. He also detailed Co. H 51st P.V. as Provost Guard. Linn relieved Capt. Anderson of the 24th Ky. Vols. who was ordered to report to his regiment.

In accordance with S.O. No. 29, Dr. Calvin Cutter, Surgeon 21st Mass. Regt. was to-day appointed Brigade Surgeon, relieving Dr. J. P. Hossack 51st P.V. who was ordered to report to his regiment. Also by. S.O. No.29, all horses captured on the road are to be immediately turned over to Lieut. Fuller, Acting Brigade Quartermaster.

Apr 7—Company and regimental drills and dress parade. Col. Hartranft, who had been home on a leave of absence, rejoined the regiment to-day. Several other officers and men of the regiment accompanied him. They brought with them a handsome sword and belt to be presented to Capt. G. W. Bisbing of Co. I. Our pickets captured and brought into camp seven more guerillas this morning.

Apr 8—Company and regimental drills and dress parade. To-day I made my maiden attempt in drilling the regiment in field movements. In accordance to G.O. No. 15, a Board of Survey was appointed to appriase all horses and mules taken from citizens for the use of the forces of the U.S. The Board are as follows: Capt. J. G. Wright, 51st N.Y. Vols.; Capt. L. S. Hart, 51st Penna. Vols.;

---

3. See *O.R.*, vol. 23, part 2, 196.

Capt. C. F. Walcott, 21st Mass. Vols.; to meet at Capt. G. W. Durell's headquarters.

Apr 9—Company and regimental drills and dress parade. Wrote a letter to Joseph Garton, master of the steamer *Kennebec* at Baltimore in regard to my stolen overcoat. Good news reached camp to-day, by an order from the War Department. A General Muster of all troops in the service of the United States, and in accordance with that order our brigade will be mustered to-morrow at 10 o'clock A.M. for pay.

Apr 10—Regiment inspected and mustered for pay. Dress parade in the evening.

Apr 11—Regimental and company drills and review. Brig. Gen. O. B. Willcox has been ordered to assume command of all the troops in the vicinity of Lexington Ky., relieving Gen. Gillmore. Willcox has also been ordered to send a brigade from Camp Dick Robinson to report to Gen. [Samuel P.] Carter at Stanford and to concentrate all of Walker's cavalry at Winchester, also the two battalions of the Second Ohio, which has reached Mount Sterling by the way of Maysville. He is also authorized to employ any number of scouts and to send them in the direction of Jackson, Prestonburg, and Paintville. We are all ordered to be ready to move at short notice. By G.O. No. 37 all troops serving in the Department of the Ohio will hereafter be known as the Army of the Ohio and general headquarters will at once be removed to the field.[4]

Apr 12—Company inspection and dress parade. In accordance with circular order, one-fourth of each command have the privilege to attend divine service at Mount Sterling, to be under the charge of a commissioned officer and must carry their arms with them.

Apr 13—Company and regimental drills and dress parade. I was detailed as brigade Officer of the Day. I received notice of my appointment as a member of a General Court Martial to meet at Lancaster Ky. at 10 o'clock A. M. to-morrow. Detail for the Court:

Col. Chas. W. LeGendre	51st N.Y .V.	Lt.Col. James Shaw	12th R.I. V.
Major Wm. J. Bolton	51st Penn. V.	Major Thos. F. Tobey	7th R.I. V.
Capt. Saml. H. Sims	51st N.Y. V.	Capt. Wm. Gibson	35th Mass. V.
Capt. Nat Sow, Jr.	11th N.H. V.		

Apr 14—Company and regimental drills and dress parade. I attended a meeting of the Court Martial at Lancaster. The following Special Order was received and read on dress parade to-night:

Headquarters District of Central Kentucky
Lexington, Ky. April 14, 1863.
Special Orders
No. 68.

I. The following named officer having tendered his resignation is herby discharged the Military service of the United States.
Captain Edward Schall Co.D 51st P. Vols.

By command of
Brig. Genl. Willcox
Rob. A. Hutchins,
A. A. Genl.

---

4. See *O.R.*, vol. 23, part 2, 231-32, for this order.

1st Lieut. Lewis Hallman Co. D commissioned Captain of Company D.

Apr 15—Company drills and dress parade. Regiment paid off.[5] I received $965.28. Attended a meeting of the Court Martial in Lancaster.

Apr 16—Company and regimental drills and dress parade. Wrote a letter to my mother and brother. Sent home $750.00. The men having plenty of money and are living grand. The following address was read on dress parade this evening:

> Headquarters Mount Sterling
> Ky. April 16th 1863.
>
> Soldiers.
>
> In accordance with Orders from the Government of the United States, I resign my command of this Brigade that has so long been identified with me and that has so long marched with me only to victory.
>
> In saying farewell to you, let me tell you how earnestly I have loved you, how eagerly I have ever striven for your comfort and happiness, and how dearly I have prized your esteem and affection.
>
> I can only hope that your devotion to me will be shown and memorialized by your faith and trustfulness in those who may succeed me.
>
> For you who have been with me so long and under such trying ordeal I have nothing but expression of esteem and affection to leave. For the Officers who may follow me, I can desire nothing more than that they shall be obeyed and followed as bravely and faithfully as I have been.
>
> I bid you all adieu, trusting that you may be preserved to see the end of this wicked rebellion, and the restoration of universal peace and liberty throughout this now desolated land.
>
> Your General,
> Edward Ferrero.

Col. Hartranft at once assumed command of the division and issued orders for the brigade to be ready to move to-morrow morning at 10 o'clock with two days rations in haversacks, and baggage and stores that cannot be carried into wagons, to be sent to Mount Sterling to be stored. Early this morning our division trains, numbering over one hundred and fifty-six mules teams and about fifty ambulances, started from Covington Ky., the train being in command Capt. Plate, A.Q.M. 1st Brigade team under Capt. Zimmerman A.A.Q.M., the 2d Brigade trains under Capt. Rapelgi A.Q.M., and the Ambulance Corps under Capt. March of Gen. Willcox's Staff. Lieut. Ortlip, 51st P.V., Lieut. George, 35th Mass., and Lieut. Fisher, 48th P.V., to join their respective commands in the field. After marching some ten miles they parked their teams about one mile from Florence, videttes being thrown out for the protection of the camp, some three miles in advance, and the advance guard one mile from the train. The next morning started at six o'clock passed through Williamstown, the county seat of Grant. Here the ladies appeared very patriotic, and waved their handkerchiefs and the Union flag. At three o'clock the trains were parked at Big Eagle.

Apr 17—Our brigade struck tents and left their camp near Mount Sterling about 3 o'clock

---

5. Parker, *51st PA*, wrote that the regiment was paid on April 14.

A.M., marched until 9 o'clock A.M., when we all halted for breakfast, and after enjoying a hearty meal, proceeded on our march, and at sundown reached Winchester Ky., making the march of thirty-two miles that day, but very many of the men were left along the road being unable to keep up. We went into bivouac about two miles on the outskirts of the town, all the stragglers reaching the camp during the night.

Col. Hartranft, now commanding the brigade, issued S.O. No. 42, detailing Capt. J. Merrill Linn, 51st P.V., as Provost Marshal of the town of Winchester, relieving officers of the 10th Ky. Cavalry. The same order detailed Companies G, H and K of the 51st P.V. for Provost Guard, to report to Capt. Linn to-morrow.[6] To-day Company I, 51st P.V. was detailed to guard and take care of the ferry at Boonsboro, on the Kentucky River some ten miles from this place.

Our division train has reached Georgetown, the county seat of Scott, and is a very pretty town and the people are loyal, but we are informed that the county has furnished more soldiers for the rebel army, and fewer for the Union army, than any other county in the state, with the one exception of Owens.

Apr 18—Company drills and dress parade. Received a very welcome letter from my sister.

Apr 19—Find myself in command of the regiment this morning. As to-day is the first anniversary of the Battle of Camden, company drills and dress parade was indulged in, and the men in their way celebrated it.

Apr 20—Still in command of the regiment. Detailed as brigade Officer of the Day. Company drills and dress parade.

Apr 21—Still in command of the regiment. Company and regimental drills and dress parade. I spent a part of the day in Winchester. S.O. No. 4 issued to-day, announces the following officers as members of a General Court Martial to convene at the quarters of Col. LeGendre, 51st N.Y.V.:

Col. Walter Harriman	11th N.H.V.
Lt.Col. Edwin Schall	51st Pa. V.
Major S. Smith	14th Ky. V.
Capt. Wm. Allebaugh	51st Pa. V.
Capt. Henry W. Francis	51st N.Y.V.
Capt. Lane S. Hart	51st Pa. V.
Capt. Wm. Gibson	35th Mass. V.

with Capt. Horace C. Bacon 11th N.H.V. Judge Advocate.

Our division train arrived in Lexington Ky. yesterday. It is the county seat of Fayette and contains a population of about 8,000 people, and is a very pretty place. Gen. Willcox, who commands the Ninth Army Corps, has his headquarters there, and Col. Sigfried of the 48th P.V. is the Military Governor, and his regiment is doing the provost duty.

Apr 22—Still in command of the regiment. Company and regimental drills and dress parade. I again received a letter from the master of the Steamer *Kennebec* in regard to my overcoat stolen in Baltimore. Our brigade train arrived about seven o'clock this evening. Our regiment is somewhat scattered. Only Companies A, B, D, and E are in camp as all the rest are on special detail.

As many of the citizens have been violating an order prohibiting the sale of liquors to soldiers, it has become necessary to confiscate all the liquor found in the neighborhood. Accordingly Lieut. Jacob P. Brooke Co. F with a detachment of cavalry has been sent out to hunt

6. Parker, *51st PA*, 298, wrote that Companies C and H were detailed for provost guards.

it up. Brooke succeeded in capturing some sixty barrels of whiskey and brandy, some of which is from six to eight years old. It was hauled to town in wagons and stored in the basement of the Court House. Another party that was sent out captured a few rebels and a lot of horses and mules.

Apr 23—Still in command of the regiment. Company drills and dress parade.

Apr 24—Still in command of the regiment. Company and regimental drills and dress parade.

Apr 25—Still in command of the regiment. The usual drills and dress parade. Spent the evening in Winchester. Corpl. Jacob Backenhamer Co. H was detailed as printer in the Government Printing Office by order of Gen. Willcox and has been ordered to report to his headquarters at once.

Apr 26—Still in command of the regiment. Company inspection and the Articles of War read in front of each company. Dress parade in the evening.

Apr 27—Still in command of the regiment. Company and regimental drills and dress parade. Received a number of newspapers from my friend Mr. Iredell.

Apr 28—Still in command of the regiment. The usual drills and dress parade. Received from Paymaster Yard an additional pay of $172.62 as major.

Apr 29—Still in command of the regiment. The usual drills. Was somewhat surprised on receiving my long lost overcoat from Baltimore through the master of the Steamer *Kennebec*. Our division marched to Winchester and marched in review before Brig. Gen. Saml. D. Sturgis. In accordance with G.O. No. 22, Capt. J. Merrill Linn 51st P.V. was to-day appointed Acting Asst. Inspector General for our brigade.

Apr 30—Still in command of the regiment. In accordance with a proclamation of the President of the United States and by G.O. No. 7 in pursuance of a Resolution of the Senate, appointed to-day as a day of National Humiliation fasting and prayer: all drills and all labor not necessary for the safety or the police of the camp will be suspended, and at 11 o'clock A.M. Divine Service will be held throughout the entire command. In accordance with G.O. No. 24, the troops of this brigade were inspected and mustered for pay at 2 o'clock P.M. I was detailed as Brigade Officer of the Day.

May 1—Still in command of the regiment. Drills and dress parade. All companies that were on special duty ordered to return to camp and the regiment ordered to prepare to move at a moments notice. Received a letter from my mother.

May 2—Still in command of the regiment. Drills and dress parade.

May 3—Still in command of the regiment. Company inspection and Articles of War read. Dress parade.

May 4—The regiment broke camp at daylight and moved at 8 o'clock A.M. marched all day through a terrible rain storm and at dark went into bivouac along the road side about 8 miles from Lexington Ky. The ground was under water several inches and we passed a most disagreeable night.

May 5—Left our bivouac about 8 o'clock A.M. passed through Lexington about 11 o'clock and after marching about six miles beyond went into bivouac for the night in a drenching rain storm. Sent home to my mother $150.00.

May 6—Left our bivouac at 8 o'clock A.M. passed through Nicholasville, crossed the Kentucky River at Hickmans Bridge, and went into bivouac about one mile beyond on the side of a very rocky hill near the turnpike. The rain, together with the darkness, was beyond discription. Shelter tents were of no use and all hands were wet through and through, and our wagon train did not get into park until late into the night. Our camping ground happened to belong to a violent rebel, and the boys found a lot of guns buried on the place. He of course denied all knowledge of them, but a slave declared that he and his son had buried them on the approach of the regiment. The men were not in a very good humor, wet and hungry, and they consequently did not spare his fences and built huge fires to dry themselves.

May 7—Left our bivouac about 9 o'clock A.M. marched through the rain and mud and during the day passed through Bryantsville, Camp Dick Robinson and Lancaster, and halted and went into bivouac about one mile beyond the latter place, for what we supposed for a long rest, but orders came for us to move on, but after marching some distance, we again went into bivouac for the night pretty well used up.

May 8—Was detailed as Brigade Officer of the Day. Regiment broke camp at 8 o'clock A.M. marched through Paint Lick, arrived at Lovetts' late in the evening and went into bivouac for the night.

May 9—Regiment remained in bivouac all day. Dress parade in the evening.

May 10—Regiment left their bivouac at 8 o'clock A.M. as they were ordered to return to Lancaster immediately, arrived there about 11 o'clock A.M. and again went into bivouac. Some of our 1st Division have had a racket with Morgan on Greasy Creek.[7]

May 11—Company drills and dress parade. I spent the evening in Lancaster. Quartermaster John J. Freedley resigned his commission, as he has received the appointment of Provost Marshal for the 6th District of Penna.

May 12—I was detailed as Brigade Officer of the Day. Received a number of letters from home, and some papers from Robert Iredell. The 1st Division of the Ninth Corps is now in and about Middleburg. Ours, the 2d Division, are in and about Lancaster, and Gen. Carter's entire force is at Somerset.

May 13—Company, regimental drills and dress parade. Com'ry Sgt. Samuel P. Stephens was to-day promoted to 1st Lieut. and Regimental Quartermaster.

May 14—Was detailed as a member of a division Court Martial, to meet in Lancaster. During the day, regiment received orders to be ready to move at a moments notice, with three days cooked rations and sixty rounds of ammunition, to move to Somerset to head off Gen. Morgan's contemplated raid on Lexington Ky.

May 15—Attended a meeting of the Court Martial at Lancaster. Commanded dress parade. Took a ride around the country. A good number of the men to-day received furloughs to return home for a few days.

May 16—Attended a meeting of the Court Martial at Lancaster. Company and regimental drills.

May 17—Company and regimental inspection and Articles of War read. Spent part of the day in Lancaster.

May 18—Attended a meeting of the Court Martial. During the day moved our camp to a better location. Had no sooner got our tents pitched when orders were again received to move to another location, and to be at all times ready to move at a moments notice. The rebel General Morgan's whole force is on the opposite side of the river at Horse Shoe Bend, and is

---

7. This action was officially known as Horseshoe Bottom, on the Cumberland River in southeastern Kentucky. See the reports of the First Brigade, First Division, Ninth Corps, in *O.R.*, vol. 23, part 1, 303-9. Brigadier General John Hunt Morgan attacked the 20th Michigan here and compelled it to recross the river in the face of Morgan's entire force.

estimated at from 8,000 to 12,000. This is the news from the 1st Division, now in camp about Middleburg Ky. and it is thought that he will make a desperate attempt to advance into Central Kentucky.

May 19—Not feeling very well, did not attend the meeting of the Court Martial. The usual drills and dress parade.

May 20—Not feeling very well and did not attend Court Martial. The usual drills and dress parade.

May 21—Attended the meeting of the Court Martial. The usual drills and dress parade.

May 22—Attended the meeting of the Court Martial at Lancaster. Our whole division received orders to be ready to move on short notice. By direction of the President, the troops in Kentucky not belonging to the Ninth Army Corps are to be organized into the 23d Army Corps, to be commanded by Maj. Gen. G. L. Hartsuff.[8]

Late in the day Col. Hartranft received the following:

[Confidential]   Colonel Hartranft, Lancaster:
You will please start the Second Division for Somerset to-morrow morning. As the road from Stanford to Somerset is already crowded with trains for the troops now at Somerset, you had better move at least part of the division by the Crab Orchard road, if you think it will facilitate the movement. Acknowledge receipt of this dispatch, and let me know what regiments will be ready to start to-morrow morning.
    O. B. Willcox,
    Brigadier-General Commanding.[9]

May 23—Our whole division broke camp at Lancaster about 5 o'clock A.M. and soon after left. Passed through Preachersville and after an hours march, Col. Hartranft received the following dispatch:
          May 23, 1863–6 A.M.
Colonel Hartranft, Lancaster:

Please halt your command at Crab Orchard and wait for further orders.

        O. B. Willcox.[10]

Late in the afternoon we went into bivouac near Crab Orchard Springs along Dick's River. It was only a nine mile march but the heat was intense and the dust terrible, the springs and creeks all dried up and water scarce, and the suffering of the men for water was beyond discription.

May 24—Remained in bivouac all day, and towards evening again received marching orders.

May 25—Whole division left their bivouac about 8 o'clock A.M. Marched through Crab Or-

---

8. *O.R.*, vol. 23, part 2, 357.

9. *O.R.*, vol. 23, part 2, 356.

10. *O.R.*, vol. 23, part 2, 360.

chard, and after marching some distance again went into bivouac. But there was to be no rest for us, for at 7 o'clock P.M. we again broke camp, crossed the Dick River and arrived at Stanford Ky. after midnight, and went into bivouac. The rebel General Morgan was threatening a raid on the town, and hence our hasty march. Lieuts. Supplee and Campbell had command of the rear-guard and reached Stanford about daybreak. The night was clear and cool; and water was plenty and of good quality.

The 51st New York of our brigade has been ordered to Hustonville and Hartranft has his division headquarters at Stanford.[11] I with the rest of the members of the Court Martial remained at Crab Orchard to hold sessions of the Court, which will meet at the Spring Hotel.

May 26—Attended a session of the Court.

May 27—Attended a session of the Court. All the officers and men who had been absent on furloughs returned to camp to-day.

May 28—There being no business before the Court, it adjourned for the day. Spent the day in Crab Orchard.

May 29—There being no business before the Court, it adjourned for the day.

May 30—All the members of the Court left Crab Orchard this morning in an ambulance, arriving in Stanford about noon.

May 31—Company inspection and dress parade. Sent home my check for $1,000 towards purchasing a house for my father and mother.

Jun 1—Attended a meeting of the Court Martial, which convened in the court house at Stanford, Ky. Regimental drill and dress parade.

Jun 2—Attended a meeting of the Court Martial at the court house. Company, regimental drills and dress parade. Our camp is again in a "bustle and a hurry" officers and men are busy in packing up all surplus baggage, to be sent to Hickman's Bridge on the Kentucky River. We have also sent some fifty rebel prisoners who have been captured at Cumberland Gap to Lexington. There is to be another important move certain but are ignorant of the destination.

Jun 3—Attended a session of the Court Martial. Company drills and dress parade. The 11th N.H. and 35th Mass. of our brigade struck tents about sundown and left immediately for Lexington. Now, we have received orders to be in readiness to move to-morrow. Gen. Ferrero has returned after an absence of six weeks and has assumed command of the 2d Division and Hartranft is now in command of the brigade.

Jun 4—Regiment struck tents about 6 o'clock A.M. and after a march of seventeen miles, reached Camp Dick Robinson about 4 o'clock P.M. and went into bivouac for the night, all hands pretty well used up, and very many sore feet. The day was quite warm. In passing through Lancaster the town was in full possession of the loyal young ladies making ready to give a concert for the benefit of the sick soldiers. We found the 8th East Tennessee encamped, and they enjoyed our dress parade very much. It is in this camp that most all the Kentucky troops assemble.

Jun 5—Reveille was beatin at 2 o'clock A.M. and at 3 o'clock A.M. struck tents and moved soon after, passed through the town of Bryantsville, crossed the Kentucky River at Hickman's Bridge at sunrise and here the scenery is very romantic, the rocks are fully two hundred fifty feet high. The Lexington Pike winds around one of these high bluffs. After a march of some fifteen miles we reached Nicholasville at 10 o'clock A.M. and no transportation being in readiness, the regiment filed into an adjoining woods and enjoyed a good sleep for several hours.

---

11. *O.R.*, vol. 23, part 2, 363-4.

At 2 o'clock P.M. cars were in readiness and we were not long in embarking on them, and in a short time left Nicholasville for Lexington, arriving there about 3 o'clock P.M. and an hour later left for Covington, reaching there during the night, sleeping in the cars until daylight. The few hours we had to spare was spent by many of us in visiting the cemetery, which is near the depot. Here we saw the monument of Henry Clay and is built of native marble. In passing Paris, Prv. Mat. Delany of Company B fell from the top of the cars he was riding on, and everyone supposed that he had been killed, but he turned up all right, and with but slight injury.

Chapter 8

Vicksburg and Jackson

June 6–August 17, 1863

Two divisions of the Ninth Corps, led by Major General John G. Parke, were detached from the Department of the Ohio and sent to join Major General Ulysses S. Grant's troops at Vicksburg, Mississippi. Parke's men joined Major General William T. Sherman's divisions in protecting the rear of the besiegers against a threatened attack from Confederate General Joseph E. Johnston's troops. Once Vicksburg surrendered, Sherman moved his command east to Jackson (the state capital) and after a short siege, forced Johnston to evacuate the city.

Jun 6—Regiment disembarked from the cars about 7 o'clock A.M. marched through the city to the wharf on the Ohio River and embarked on board of the steamer *Queen City*, crossed the river to Cincinnati and marched through the city the depot of the Ohio and Mississippi Railroad, and at once embarked on the cars, and after procuring some refreshments from the citizens such as our purses would permit. But the people were very kind and charged us reasonable prices. At 9 o'clock A.M. the train pulled out from the depot with the usual cheering and the waving of flags and handkerchiefs. At 4 o'clock in the afternoon we received some coffee and other refreshments at Seymour and at midnight we had bread and coffee at Vincinnes [Ind]. We traveled all day and all night, and it was tiresome, as the cars were very much crowded.

Jun 7—Arrived at Sandoval [Ind.] about 9 1/2 o'clock and immediately changed cars for those of the Illinois Central Railroad and at once steamed away for Cairo Ill. Passed through the entire breath of Indiana. On reaching the town of DeSoto Illinois, we received a good cup of coffee, bread and butter, &c. Arrived in Cairo about 10 o'clock P.M. hunted up something to eat, and then made our beds on the platform of the depot, and all hands enjoyed a good sleep. We were also supplied with refreshments at Centralia.

Jun 8—About 8 o'clock A.M. the regiment moved up along the river a mile and went into camp. Towards evening the Paymaster came around to pay us, and was about to commense when orders came for us to embark on board of the steamer *Hope* and left Cairo about 6 o'clock P.M. and steamed down the Ohio River. The steamer is a very fine boat and there is ample room for all, and the officers of the boat are very kind. Wrote a letter to my mother. Five steamer-loads left here to-day.

Jun 9—Our fleet of steamers during the night passed Island No. 10 and New Madrid on the Missouri shore, and Columbus on the Kentucky shore. On our passage down the river the regiment was paid by Paymaster Major McCook. I received $317.70. We stopped twice to-day along the river bank to take in wood, and lay over part of the night on account of the darkness. Our steamer was made fast to trees on the Arkansas shore, at the same time the rain was coming down in torrents.

Jun 10—Passed Fort Pillow before daylight, arriving at Memphis Tenn. about 6 o'clock A.M. During the day went to Adams Express Office and sent home to my mother $300.00. Very many thousand dollars was sent home by the men of the regiment, and a good amount that was not, as many of the men had their pockets picked while in the city. I with a number of other officers went to the theatre in the evening and spent a pleasant evening. Met several friends now residing here whom I had known in Norristown: Allen Lindsey, who has a brother in the regiment, Mr. Leidy, who formally kept a hat store on Main Street near DeKalb and his son Monroe, with whom I had gone to school with. They all treated us very kindly. Returned to our steamer in the wee hours of the night and had a good rest. Gen. Parke left Cairo this morning for Vicksburg. Our brigade was the first to arrive at Memphis.

Jun 11—We laid here all day moored to the wharf, which gave us all a good chance to visit the city. The city of Memphis is a grand place, streets well laid out, and run at right angles. All the large buildings are in use of the military and are mostly used for hospitals and store houses. Provisions are very high, eggs 40 cts. per doz. bread 12 1/2 cts. per loaf, cigars 10 cts. per piece, plug tobacco 25 and 30 cts., cakes three for a quarter &c. Received a letter from my sister. During the day, we disembarked from the Steamer *Hope* and immediately embarked on board of the Steamer *Commercial.* Durell's battery was also with us on the same steamer.

Jun 12—We left Memphis on the *Commercial* about 4 o'clock A.M. and steamed down the Mississippi River. Our pilot house being protected from the guerillas that infested either shore, by boiler plates and cotton bails, but we were not molested on our way down, as we were escorted by several gunboats past the most dangerous points. We learn that all the towns on both shores from Memphis to Vicksburg have been burned, as they afforded shelter for the guerillas to fire at our pilots. All the Mississippi boats we have seen bear the marks of cannon shot, and the wheel-houses are pretty well battered.

About 10 o'clock A.M. we touched at Helena, Arkansas. The short time we lay there at the wharf, many of Gen. [Benjamin M.] Prentiss troops who soon began to line the river bank, began to tease our men, wanting to know among other things what we had come from the East for. Our men retorted by saying that we had come to show them how to fight. This appeared to raise their ire, and there came very near a clash of arms between us. Prentiss, who was on the ground all the time and had heard all the conversation, finally interfered, but taking sides with his own troops. After some more war of words, we cast loose our hawser and proceeded on our way, reminding them that they would hear tell of us in our new field of action.

Jun 13—Steaming very carefully down the river and enjoyed ourselves as best we could.

Jun 14—About daylight we passed Milliken's Bend, and later on, the mouth of the Yazoo River, and at 8 o'clock A.M. landed on the Louisiana shore, at Sherman's Landing, in sight of Vicksburg, most of the regiment bivouacking in Sherman's celebrated canal for the day and night. Long lines of mortar boats are laying under the cover of the high banks, and long lines of mortars on the river banks in front of the beleaguered city, and we are told, keep up an incessant fire on the city day and night. By the aid of glasses we can see objects moving in the streets. This evening we received orders to be ready to move in the morning.

Jun 15—Regiment left their bivouac at 4 o'clock A.M. in our march crossed the Memphis and Charleston Railroad and early in the day halted at Carthage and stacked arms. Here we met hundreds of negroes, men, women and children who had fled from their masters. Most of them where almost white. Later in the day, we embarked on board of the Steamer *Silver Wave*, crossed the Mississippi River, and landed at Warrenton, Miss., about one mile below Vicksburg. Ordered to pitch our tents, which we did expecting to remain, but in a short time, again ordered to strike tents, and immediately recrossed the river on the *Silver Wave* and again landed at Carthage, marched up along the banks of the river, and again went into camp, but again, about dark, we received marching orders, and in a short time we were on the move again for Sherman's Landing, reaching there in the night, and again went into bivouac in the canal for the night.

Jun 16—No rest for us. At 2 o'clock P.M. to-day we again formed line, and marched to the landing, and embarked on board of the Steamer *John H. Dickey*, and immediately steamed up the Mississippi River, and soon entered the mouth of the Yazoo River and steamed up to Snyder's Bluff, and in sight of Haines Bluff, and cast anchor for the night. During our passage up the river, a terrific hail-storm visited us, and we had to keep under shelter. We also saw on our trip, many huge alligators. Regiment remained on board all night.

Jun 17—Disembarked at daylight, and marched to Milldale Church, and went into camp and made up our minds after fourteen days and nights constant traveling and marching to have a little rest.

The advance of the Ninth Army Corps has reached Young's Point. We learn from some of the Illinois troops that we are here to hold in check Gen. Joe. Johnston[1] from getting in rear of Grant while the siege continues. We of the Ninth Corps are holding the extreme left of the line. Gen. Parke, who is now in command of the Ninth Corps, has also the command of Gen. Lauman's and Herron's forces. The boys are enjoying themselves in picking fruit and there is plenty of it.[2]

Jun 18—A general inspection of the whole regiment.

Jun 19—Company drills. Very heavy cannonading heard to-day in our camp, from the direction of Vicksburg. Col. Hartranft is again back in command of the regiment the first time for many months.

Jun 20—Regiment struck tents, moved a few miles to Haines Bluff. Cannonading and musketry distinctly heard in camp from the direction of Vicksburg. Snyder's and Haine's Bluffs are connected by a ridge, though flanks on the river side are separated by two ravines and a bayou

---

1. Although he used the correct spelling here, Bolton usually misspelled Johnston's name by omitting the "t." I have used the correct spelling throughout this edition.

2. General Parke's detachment of the Ninth Corps was as follows:
  First Division, Brig. Gen. Thomas Welsh
    First Brigade, Col. Henry Bowman: 36th MA, 17th, 27th MI, 45th PA
    Third Brigade, Col. Daniel Leasure: 2nd, 8th, 20th MI, 79th NY, 100th PA
    Artillery: PA Bty D
  Second Division, Brig. Gen. Robert B. Potter
    First Brigade, Col. Simon G. Griffin: 6th, 9th NH, 7th RI
    Second Brigade, Brig. Gen. Edward Ferrero: 35th MA, 11th NH, 51st NY, 51st PA
    Third Brigade, Col. Benjamin C. Christ: 29th MA, 46th NY, 50th PA
    Artillery: Bty L, 2nd NY
  Artillery Reserve: Bty E, 2nd US

slope. Snyder's commands the lower, Haine's the upper bend of the Yazoo. The days are very hot, but the nights are very cool. We get our water from the springs in the ravines but this source is running out. Many of the regiments are digging wells; others are hauling water from a distance. The health of the troops is excellent. The thermometer sometimes rising to ninety at noon. The bluffs are covered with cane-brakes, blackberry bushes and any amount of underbrush and filled with all kinds of venomous reptiles. We are about nine miles from Vicksburg.

Jun 21—Detailed as Brigade Officer of the Day. The regular Sunday morning inspection and dress parade in the evening.

Jun 22—Company drills and dress parade. About one-half of the regiment detailed this morning to fell trees and dig entrenchments for the first time in its history. We have found out this is a great country for mosquitoes, in fact all kinds of insects, such as ticks, sand-flies, beetles, ants, and all kinds of worms. At night we cannot sleep for them.

Jun 23—This morning the whole regiment was detailed to fell trees and to throw up intrenchments. Just before dark, heavy cannonading commenced and continued all night.

Jun 24—One-half of the regiment detailed to fell trees and throw up intrenchments. Heavy cannonading continued all day at Vicksburg. Gen. Parke has issued orders detailing Lieut. Saml. P. Stephens for duty at the Quarter-Masters Department as Actg. Asst. Q.M.

Jun 25—One-half of the regiment felling trees and throwing up intrenchments. The cannonading was again resumed. Blackberries are found here in abundance, and we are to enjoy fresh baked bread in a few days. Men are now building the oven.

Jun 26—Regiment still felling trees and entrenching. Dress parade in the evening.

Jun 27—Was detailed as Brigade Officer of the Day. Regiment still felling trees and entrenching. Gen. Parke has sent four brigades of our corps to occupy the line extending from A. Green's on the Benton Road, by way of McCall's to Tiffin's on the Bridgeport Road. Grant has also ordered Parke to send a force of infantry to support his cavalry and to obstruct the advance of the rebel Gen. Loring, who has crossed his troops below Vernon, who is supposed to be advancing towards the Big Black River, by the way of Bear Creek. The troops are ordered to travel with as little baggage as possible and to use all his teams as an ordnance and supply train.[3]

Jun 28—Regular Sunday morning inspection and dress parade in the evening. Orders were issued to-day by Gen. Grant, forbidding news boys selling newspapers at a price exceeding fifteen cents per paper. A detail of a working party of one-hundred and sixty-five men without arms, is ordered to report at Milldale Church to-morrow.

Jun 29—The whole of the Ninth Corps struck tents this morning and left their camp at 9 o'clock A.M. leaving a small guard at Milldale and Templeton's to hold those points. By the orders of Sherman, whom we are now under, we are to march to the east side of Clear Creek, connecting our forces at a place called Brant's, with Gen. McArthur's, his center near Wixon's and his guard connecting with Gen. W. S. Smith near Mrs. Neighly's. Gen. Tuttle is holding the spur leading from McCall's to Markham's and Young's, and is intrenching his position back of Tribte's. Smith is in position at Oak Ridge Post Office, with pickets on the two Benton roads, his right connecting with Parke at Mrs. Neily's. All the roads are being effectually blockaded, also all by-paths coming from the north and lying between the ridge road and Yazoo Valley Road.[4]

---

3. Major General William W. Loring commanded one of Johnston's divisions.

4. The officers mentioned are Brig. Gen. John McArthur (commanding the Sixth Division, Seventeenth Army Corps), Brig. Gen. William Sooy Smith (First Division, Sixteenth Army Corps), and Brig. Gen. James M. Tuttle (Third Division, Fifteenth Army Corps).

We left our camp in light marching orders, carrying only shelter tents and knapsacks, and one days cooked rations. The headquarter guards and teamsters of our corps arrived to-day from Kentucky on board of the steamer *Prima Donna*. She had some fifty cannon shots and several vollies of musketry fired into her while coming down the Mississippi River below Helena Ark. Some horses and mules were killed. Our regiment after a very tedious march arrived at McCall's cross-roads at 5 o'clock P.M. and went into bivouac.

Jun 30—Remained here in bivouac at McCall's, was mustered and inspected for pay.

Jul 1—Remained in bivouac at McCall's all day. Heavy detail from the regiment to throw up intrenchments. A long pontoon train is now passing along the road in the direction of the Big Black.

Jul 2—Detailed as Brigade Officer of the Day. Regiment remained in bivouac at McCall's all day. The whole regiment detailed to throw up intrenchments and felling trees. Col. Hartranft was ordered to-day to detail one Corpl. and three privates for guard duty at the house of Dr. Scott, one mile from camp on the Vicksburg road.

Jul 3—Regiment still in bivouac at McCall's and engaged in throwing up intrenchments and felling trees. Very heavy firing to-night in the direction of Vicksburg. Sherman has ordered troops to secure the three crossing places–Jones' Ford below Birdsong, Messinger's, where he intends to build a good bridge by means of the log houses and materials of Messinger's planta- tion, and at the railroad crossing. In the event of Vicksburg surrenders, as is expected, he intends to put two corps in motion, his own corps to cross the bridge at Messinger's, the artillery and wagons of one corps at the same place, the cavalry and infantry of the Ninth at Jone's, thus giving three roads, all of which converges at a point not far beyond Big Black River, near Jeff Davis' plantation. his movement is intended to interpose between Johnston's scattered forces, the troops to move light and rapid. Each regiment is to carry five days rations and ammunition, and a train to carry bread, salt, sugar and coffee for ten more, depending on the country for forage and beef.[5]

Jul 4—Vicksburg surrendered to Gen. Grant to-day at 10 o'clock A.M. Parke immediately sent the following to Grant:

> Oak Ridge, July 4, 1863.
> General Grant:
> General Sherman desires me to tender his warmest congratulations. Please accept my own. General Sherman will hold the railroad bridge for Ord, Messinger's for the Fifteenth Corps and Birdsong for the Ninth. Orders are issued for the movement.
> John G. Parke.[6]

Orders received to be ready to move at a moments notice, with 150 cartridge per man. Re- ceived a number of letters and papers from home.

Jul 5—Regiment left their bivouac at McCall's at daylight and we are now in hot pursuit of the rebel Gen. Joe. Johnston. By the orders of Sherman, the First Division, Sixteenth Corps, Brig. Gen. Wm. Sooy Smith, has been temporarily attached to our corps. It is supposed that Johnston is falling back from the Big Black, and that his cattle and wagon train is going by the way of Canton, then east to the Mobile & Ohio Railroad, and designs to put his army behind his

---

5. For Sherman's directives, see O.R., vol. 24, part 3, 461-63.

6. *O.R.*, vol. 24, part 3, 471.

intrenchments at Jackson, Miss. Our corps is advancing by the way of Birdsong Ferry, the whole to converge on Bolton, Miss. After a long tedious march, we came to a halt late in the night, and bivouacked at Oak Ridge.

Jul 6—Laid in bivouac all day at Oak Ridge. Very heavy skirmishing on our front all day and night. The heat and dust is terrible. This evening Gen. Ord crossed the Big Black at the railroad bridge and Gen. Steele, with the Fifteenth, crossed at Messinger's.[7] To-day a ferry-boat was found three miles below the ferry that had been scuttled and sunk. This was raised, and brought up to the crossing during the day and night.

Jul 7—Regiment left their bivouac at 12 M. and after a short march crossed the Big Black at Birdsong Ferry in a violent rain storm, the water running over the top of the floor of the bridge. The frail bridge giving away, our First Brigade with Roemer's battery were obliged to pass around by Messinger's. This bridge was temporary one, constructed from the old buildings along the banks of the river. The immense weight of the heavy guns, horses and caissons full of ammunition, was too much for it. The consequences was, they all went down but some of the horses were cut loose,, and a few drowned. The river is very narrow, but deep and sluggish.

Gen. Ord, with the 13th Corps, is now holding the ground to the south of the railroad, and Gen. Steele, with the 15th Corps, the ground to the north, connecting at the bridge at Bolton. The day is excessively hot, and the troops are suffering exceedingly from the heat and dust. Johnston is rapidly falling back as we advance. After a long tedious march, we halted at Manuel's and bivouacked for the balance of the night.

Jul 8—Regiment left their bivouac at 4 o'clock A.M. The First Brigade and Roemer's battery is covering the rear and guarding our trains. All the corps commanders and division commanders have been ordered to report to Sherman at the Porter House, at Bolton Depot, at 10 A.M.[8] Orders issued for each company to capture a mule to carry water to the regiment, and in a short space of time, there were plenty of mules in camp, and their use proved to be a success, as water had to be carried some distance. Last night, the advance bivouacked at Robertson's, adjoining Jeff Davis' plantation, near Bolton. Sometime after midnight, we came to a halt at Hall's Cross-Roads, and bivouacked for the balance of the night. A terrible rain storm set in at 9 o'clock P.M. and continued all night Made my bed on two rails, with my canteen for a pillow, and a gum blanket for a covering, and I think I never slept better.

Jul 9—Regiment left our bivouac at 9 o'clock A.M. and proceeded on the Clinton Road. Passed through Clinton on our march. Had considerable skirmishing during the day. We are marching on a parallel road to Gen. Steele, and are keeping up communication with him. There appears to be but one main road, and we of the Ninth Corps are compelled to cut through timber, but are succeeding in opening a road through the plantations, nearly or quite parallel with the main road.

Near sundown we came upon the enemy's cavalry with some skirmishing ensueing and artillery was used on both sides. About 9 o'clock P.M. we went into bivouac not far from Jackson. Prv. James Milton Co. I was to-day accidently killed by the discharge of a gun in the hands of one of the guards of the wagon train.

Jul 10—Regiment left their bivouac at 9 o'clock A.M. moved forward, crossing the roads to Brownsville and Pearl River, and taking a plantation road that brought us out on the Livingston

---

7. Major General Frederick Steele led the Fifteenth Army Corps (Sherman's) and Major General Edward O. C. Ord had command of the Thirteenth Army Corps.

8. See *O.R.*, vol. 24, part 3, 490.

and Canton Road, five miles north of Jackson. As we advanced on Jackson, the enemy's vedettes and pickets were driven in, until we approached the insane asylum ridge. The enemy retired as our steady and determined line advanced, and about dark we occupied a line at right angles to the Canton Road, and extending from the Pearl River over to the Livingston Road, crossing the railroad. Sherman has now got Johnston closely invested, from the Pearl River on the north to the river on the south. by this move we have an immense amount of rolling stock separated from the Confederacy, both north and south of Jackson, and the roads completely destroyed and rendered worthless.

Col. Hartranft is in command of our brigade. Knapsack and shelter tents have been left in camp under a small guard. Pickets are being thrown out. We are now quite in front of the city, and are ordered to lie on our arms all night, but to secure all the sleep we can. The disposition of the troops are as follows: Sherman is holding the center; Ord with the 13th Army Corps along the Raymond Road; Steele with the 15th Corps along the Clinton Road, and Parke with the 9th Corps along the Livingston Road, all connecting by pickets. Ordered to dig wells near our positions. We are sleeping and doing picket duty on the plantation of the rebel Col. O. J. Stuart, and very near his mansion. Water very scarce.

Jul 11—Early this morning we advanced our line and in range of the enemy's breastworks. Had no sooner done so when the rebels commenced to throw shot and shell in a very careless manner at us, and in turn commenced to throw the same kind of stuff into the city from all along our line. We are supporting skirmishers. Christ's First Brigade is supporting Edwards' and Benjamin's batteries. The 51st New York are doing skirmishing on the left of the line. It has been raining all day and all night, and we are all wet to the skin. Griffin's brigade is now destroying the railroads north of Jackson. We are all employed. By the order of Parke, all the telegraph wires have been destroyed, and the railroads have been made useless for miles around.

The enemy is posted behind a continuous line of riflepits, with batteries at intervals, raking the road and approaches. To-day the enemy has made several attempts to drive in our skirmishers but have always failed. By an order from Sherman, a general cannonading will commence at 7 o'clock A.M. to-morrow lasting not to exceed one hour. Each gun will fire not to exceed thirty rounds, solid shot and shell in proper proportions, to be directed at the enemy's troops, or in the direction of the town of Jackson, which lies northwest and south of the State House, which is seen from all points of our line.[9] In consequence of this order we are working like beavers with spades and picks to have everything ready before daylight, to resist any attack that may be made against us.

Jul 12—Regiment still in support of skirmishers on the left of our line. This has by far been the hottest day of the fighting. The colors of the 45th Penna. Vols. floated from the cupola of the insane asylum since the 10th. Agreeable to promise, Sherman has given Johnston one hour's shelling. Our troops are in good health and spirits and our army is in possession of all avenues out of Jackson this side of Pearl River, and we are at this moment threatening the rear. By order of Sherman all corps commanders have been directed to send guards to the rear, at least three miles out, to prevent and warn all parole prisoners coming from Vicksburg from coming within the lines of this army or attempting to get into Jackson.[10]

Jul 13—Regiment still in support of skirmishers. Both of our flanks now rests on the Pearl River. Deserters report that our shells yesterday reached all parts of the city. To-day the enemy tried to drive back our line, but were repulsed. During yesterday and to-day we have thrown

---

9. *O.R.*, vol. 24, part 3, 502-3.

10. *O.R.*, vol. 24, part 3, 507.

into Jackson about 3,000 rounds, mostly from 10 and 20 pounder Parrotts and 12-pounder Napoleons. Jackson is now completely invested and we are in undisputed possession of all the roads leading to the place on the west bank of Pearl River, and our artillery is within easy range of every part of the city, with the State House in plain view. Water still scarce.

Jul 14—Our whole division was relieved from the skirmish line at daylight, having been on the front for ninety-six hours. Fell back about one mile near the insane asylum and went into bivouac in a woods near at hand for a short rest.

During the day, Johnston sent out a flag of truce, asking for three hours to bury our dead as well as his own. The request was granted by Sherman and by his orders all firing ceased all along the lines until 4 o'clock P.M. at which hour the pickets will resume their places and firing resumed.[11]

By the orders of Sherman, a shot from our artillery was fired every five minutes baring the time of course occupied by the flag of truce. The shots from Parke's were ordered to be aimed in the general direction of the State House, enfilading the town of Jackson, to be fired every five minutes, day and night. The guns on Steele's front also to be directed at the State House, so as to enfilade the general line of works in front of Parke. The guns of Ord's front directed at the road or line of communication from Jackson across Pearl River towards the east, chiefly at the bridge, to prevent the passage either way of wagons, horses, or men.[12]

Wrote a letter to my mother.

Jul 15—A heavy detail was made from the regiment to go on a reconnaissance to the left, and the Pearl River in the rear of Jackson. The detail was under the command of Capt. Lane S. Hart Co. F and it proved to be successful. During the day the regiment moved their camp to a better location. The object of the party sent out was to try and locate a ford or a suitable place to build a bridge. Their movements was discovered by the rebel cavalry. On their return to camp they captured about twenty-five head of fine cattle. Segt. Wm. Pope Co. I wounded.

Jul 16—Regiment left their bivouac at 3 o'clock A.M. marched to the front and relieved the 1st Division, who had been on duty 48 hours. Was again put in support of skirmishers. Laid on our arms all night and ordered to be very vigilant. Had a sharp engagement with the enemy during the day in trying to advance our line. The advance was made in gallant style by the whole of Parke's corps, but with severe loss, particularly in General Smith division. The advance developed the fact that the enemy was well intrenched with formidable batteries which made free use of shrapnel, canister, and shell. There has been very heavy cannonading to-night on our part. There seems to be some commotion among the rebs and we think that there will be some kind of a racket before morning. A wagon load of spades and shovels was sent to the regiment to-day. Lt. Henry Jacobs, Sergt. Benj. White, of Co. F, and Capt. Geo. W. Bisbing and Sergt. Thomas H. Parker, Co. I wounded. Our great trouble is the want of water.

Jul 17—Regiment was ordered into the rifle pits at daylight, and we were not very long in discovering that the enemy had evacuated the city. Our brigade at once marched into the city. The 35th Mass. of our brigade being the first regiment to place their flag on the dome of the state Capitol and the 51st P.V. the first regiment to plant its colors in the yard of the Capitol. The regiment with the rest of the brigade reached the city at 6.30 A.M. and in their own way for over an hour. During the day the regiment was ordered to the outskirts of the city, and at once began to clean up, as all hands had left Haines' Bluff in light marching order, and without any change of clothing.

---

11. *O.R.*, vol. 24, part 3, 509-10.

12. *O.R.*, vol. 24, part 3, 510.

I made my headquarters in a large frame mansion while the men occupied the rebel works and thinking that I would have time to have my under clothing washed, proceeded to have it done, but to my dismay, orders came for me to report to Gen. Sherman, in the city of Jackson, for orders. Mounting my horse, off I started to report to Sherman, minus all under clothing or with shirt of any kind, and blouse buttoned up to the chin. After a short ride, I found Sherman in his tent in the lawn in front of the governors mansion, surrounded by his staff. He received me very kindly, and gave me orders to organize a patrole of two hundred men, and patrole the city from one end to the other, hunt up all stragglers, and have them all returned to their respective regiments, giving me full control in the matter. I found that I had the most trouble with the Western troops. It was an all night job for me, but I had the satisfaction of riding the city of the stragglers.

At 8 P.M. Sherman telegraphed to Grant that he had made a circuit of Jackson, for which I well know, as I met him on my rout during the night. He informed him that he was in full possession and that Johnston was retreating east, with 30,000 men. The place is well fortified. He also informed Grant that he proposed to break railroads 10 miles south, east, and north, and out for 40 or 60 miles in spots, and is in possession of 50 cars which will be burned. At 9 P.M. he telegraphed Grant that all his cavalry was off breaking railroads at and beyond Canton to the north, and as far as Brookhaven south.[13]

Parke, by the order of Sherman, has sent Gen. Welsh, commanding the 1st Division of our corps, to march north along Pearl River to Grant's Mills, to entercept the enemy's cavalry now west of the river and prevent them from crossing and to keep on destroying the railroad from Jackson north.[14] By the orders of Sherman, Gen. Steele will occupy Jackson with one division, the line of pickets will occupy the parapets. And Parke by the same order is to group his corps convenient to the Lunatic Asylum.[15] By the order of Gen. Sherman, all of the regiments of our corps were directed to inscribe on their flags: Siege of Jackson, Miss. July 10/17/63. On entering the city, the 51st halted in front of the Capitol and stacked arms. All hands began to roam all over the city in search of tobacco, sugar, or what might by chance come in their way. Some of the boys of the regiment came upon a large quantity of sugar, and at once commenced to fill their canteens. Sometime later they came upon some whiskey. Their canteens were filled up to the top with sugar, and now how to get it out was the question, as the whiskey was now more important. But they succeeded in filling them with hot water, and soon they were filled with the whiskey. We found tobacco in abundance. We found the streets and yards pretty well dug up to make bombproof for themselves. Late in the afternoon the regiment was ordered to take up their position in a large fort extending across the main street on the out skirts of the city. They made a very grotesque appearance, clad in female attire, sun-bonnets, frocks, skirts, shawls, band-boxes, and brooms in their hands. It was indeed ludicrous. Sherman in passing the regiment could not help but smile. The fort is principally built of cotton bales and is well constructed and mounts many guns. I have my headquarters in a large frame mansion near the fort. About one hour after the 51st had stacked arms in front of the Capitol, regiments of Western troops came marching down the street playing "My bold soldier boy." This soon created a laugh among our boys, and commenced to tease them. The 9. A.C. have been here over an hour and we have all the spoils. You have been asleep.

13. *O.R.*, vol. 24, part 2, 528.

14. *O.R.*, vol. 24, part 3, 523.

15. *O.R.*, vol. 24, part 3, 524-25.

Jul 18—Regiment laid in bivouac all day cleaning up and resting. Sherman has given the people of Jackson 200 barrels of flour and 100 barrels of pork. To-night Sherman entertained at supper at the Governor's mansion the generals of this army. By orders from division head-quarters all calls and drills are resumed, and roll-calls will be four times each day, and absentees punished. Also by orders from the Headquarters Army of the Tenn., Gen. Potter is instructed to send in the names of such officers recommended for promotion.

Jul 19—Remained in bivouac all day. Regimental inspection and dress parade in the evening. Parke has been given the necessary orders to make all preparations to move his two divisions back to Milldale or Vicksburg, and to report by letter to Gen. Grant.[16]

Jul 20—Regiment left their bivouac about 4 o'clock A.M. Passed through Clinton during the day, came to a halt about 11 o'clock at night and went into bivouac in a large field some twenty-eight miles from Jackson. Out of the whole regiment, there was not more than forty muskets stacked so hard was the march and so intense was the heat, water scarce, and rations short. Amid the great darkness, the men found some water to make some coffee, and to their surprise next morning found that they had got the water from a filty stagnant pond, but this has been our lot all throught this campaign and had got used to it.

Jul 21—Regiment left their bivouac at 3 o'clock A.M. and without any breakfast, had the right or advance of the whole column. Passed through Brownsville, halted to get some breakfast, marched until 10 o'clock P.M. and went into bivouac in a large field. Killed some cattle during the day. Being on the advance, we had the first pick. Found plenty of good fruit of all kind, and the very best of green corn. Our camp is near Messinger's.

Jul 22—Early this morning we moved into a large cornfield a few miles from the Big Black. Remained here until 4 o'clock P.M. to give the stragglers time to catch up. The time spent here was used in bathing, swimming and washing clothes. Large fires was built, and we had roasted corn to our satisfaction. The field was an immense one, our whole column marched through it. At the hour mentioned we marched to the river and crossed it in a fearful rain storm, and it was as dark as pitch. The road of the thunder and the vivid lightning was beyond discription, men and horses fairly shuddered, and what a few moments before had been dust was now liquid mud over boot top, and before the whole column got over, there was two feet of water on the floor of the bridge. Regiment reached McCall's about 10 o'clock P.M. and went into bivouac, drenched in rain to the skin and covered with mud from head to foot. Rumor in camp that we are to be sent to Rosecrans.[17]

Jul 23—Left our bivouac at 4 o'clock A.M. after partaking of a good morning meal of green corn and a good cup of coffee. Arrived at Milldale Church after a ten mile march about 9 o'clock A.M. and again went into camp on our old camp ground at Haines Bluff. On reaching this place Chaplain Daniel G. Mallory tendered his resignation and was forward to headquarters for action.

Jul 24—Find myself in command of the regiment. Men engaged in cleaning up and resting after their evenful campaign. Dress parade in the evening. The following order was read on dress parade to-night:

Special Orders	Headquarters Dept. of the Tennessee.
No. 200	Vicksburg, Miss. July 24. 1863.

---

16. *O.R.*, vol. 24, part 3, 533.

17. Major General William S. Rosecrans commanded the Department of the Cumberland.

x   x   x

V. Maj. Gen. John G. Parke, commanding Ninth Army Corps, will proceed with his command to Cincinnati, Ohio, and report to Maj. Gen. A. E. Burnside, commanding Department of the Ohio. The quartermaster department will furnish the necessary transportation.

x   x   x

By order of Maj. Gen. U. S. Grant.
T. S. Bowers,
Major and Acting Assistant Adjutant-General.[18]

In accordance with the above, a circular order was issued to-day and read on dress parade, ordering us to hold ourselves in readiness to embark on transports at short notice, and to draw (10) days rations & forage.

Jul 25—Company drills and dress parade. One hundred men detailed from the regiment to dig rifle pits and to fell trees in front of the earthworks.

Jul 26—Regimental inspection, and dress parade in the evening. Camp was visited by a terrific rain storm, blowing down the tents and making things very lively generally.

Jul 27—Company drills and dress parade. Some detail made again to-day for the same kind of work. One gill of whiskey issued to each man. Prv. James Brady Co. I killed at Milldale by lightning while on picket.

Jul 28—Heavy detail again made to-day to dig and fell trees. A Court Martial appointed to meet at division headquarters to-morrow. Capt. J. M. Linn, 51st P.V., appointed Judge Advocate.

Jul 29—Regiment still at work on the trenches. Dress parade in the evening.

Jul 30—Still working on the trenches. The following order was read on dress parade:

July 30. 1863.

General Parke:

I was in hopes to meet you at Vicksburg, but you left the day before I got in. My corps is encamped on beautiful ground about 2 miles back of the railroad and Messinger's bridges, with fine shade and plenty of water.

I want to recruit and reorganize here, ready for the fall campaign. I trust we may meet again about Atlanta in October; we by way of the Alabama River, and you by Chattanooga. I may not have done justice in my oral and written expressions to my feelings towards you and your corps. Be kind enough to assure all of my hearty respects. When you see Burnside give him my love. Tell him for me that we are armed against all the enemies to law and Government; that we fire upon the Secessionist of the South, the autocrat of the North, and the anarchist everywhere. If another Vallandigham arise, let him be banished to that land from which there is no appeal on earth.

Our Government must govern, and not be ruled by every agitator of the hour.

W. T. Sherman.[19]

---

18. *O.R.*, vol. 24, part 3, 548.

19. *O.R.*, vol. 24, part 3, 563.

By order of Gen. Parke one ration of whiskey per day will be issued to each man of this command until it arrives at its destination. Surg. John A. Hosack and Chaplin Daniel G. Mallory of the 51st P.V. having tendered their resignation have this day been honorably discharge the service of the United States by the order of Gen. Parke.

Jul 31—Still working on the trenches. The following order was read on dress parade this evening:

> Headquarters Department of the Tennessee.
> Vicksburg Miss. July 31st 1863.
> In returning the 9th Corps to its former command, it is with pleasure that the General commanding acknowledges its valuable services in the campaign just closed. Arriving at Vicksburg opportunely, taking position to hold at bay Johnston's army, then threatening the forces investing the city, it was ready and eager to assume the aggressive at any moment.
> After the fall of Vicksburg it formed part of the army which drove Johnston from his position near the Big Black River into his intrenchments at Jackson, and after a siege of eight days, compelled him to fly in disorder from the Mississippi Valley.
> The endurance, valor and general conduct of the 9th Corps are admired by all, and its valuable co-operation in achieving the final triumph of the campaign, is gratefully acknowledged by the Army of the Tennessee. Major General Parke will cause the different regiments and batteries of his command to inscribe upon their banners and guidons "Vicksburg and Jackson."
> By order of,
> Maj. Gen. U. S. Grant.
> T. S. Bowers, A.A.A.Gen.[20]

Col. Hartranft received a leave of absence for (20) days on Surgeons Certificate. In accordance with Special Orders No. 207, Headquarters Department of the Tennessee, dated at Vicksburg Miss. this date, the Ninth Army Corps, Maj. Gen. J. G. Parke commanding, is ordered to return to the Department of the Ohio as rapidly as transportation can be provided. And on arriving at Cairo, Gen. Parke will telegraph to the General-in-Chief of the army and to Major-General Burnside for further instructions.

Aug 1—Regiment still digging and intrenching. Received and wrote several letters. Corporal Daniel Wetzel Co. H was detailed as clerk at division headquarters. Gen. Parke sent the following to General Sherman to-day:

> Headquarters Ninth Army Corps
> Milldale, Miss. Aug. 1, 1863.
> Major-General Sherman:
>
> General: My report is ready and will be forwarded to you to-day. I was very sorry not to meet you in Vicksburg.
> We are now at our old camp (Milldale) under orders for the Department of the Ohio, but waiting for transportation.

---

20. *O.R.*, vol. 24, part 3, 565-66.

Be assured that we fully appreciate the kind feelings expressed towards the Ninth Corps. They fully reciprocate.

I sincerely hope that the small part borne by us in the recent campaign met your approbation. I need hardly tell you that the campaign has been very severe upon both my officers and men. Still, I hope after we are all recruited, that we may again meet, and the proposed rendezvous, Atlanta, would meet with a cheerful response. I will convey your messages to General Burnside.

John G. Parke.[21]

Aug 2—Regimental inspection and dress parade.

Aug 3—Regiment still digging and intrenching. In accordance with G.O. No. 122 Headquarters Department of the Ohio, Cincinnati, August 3d, 1863, all officers and enlisted men belonging to this army found absent from their commands 7 days after the date of this order, without proper leave from these headquarters, will be considered as deserters.

2d Lieut. Wm. W. Owens left to-day on a leave of absence for 20 days, also Lieut. Tho. J. Lynch for 30 days. There is a great deal of sickness in our corps, but the old 51st seems to keep in good health, the best of any in the whole corps. We are now enjoying fresh bread every day, have built our own ovens in the banks and have our own bakers. Large quantities of fine peaches and plums are near at hand and we have fresh pies every day.

Aug 4—Regiment still digging and intrenching.

Aug 5—Regiment still digging and intrenching. Dress parade in the evening.

Aug 6—In accordance with the Proclamation of the President, Burnside directs that the day be kept sacred, and abstaining so far as is practicable from all military business or movements, and to observe the day in a manner worthy of the victories that have been granted us, and the cause we have espoused. Lt. Col. Schall has been detailed as Division Officer of the Day. Capt. Jos. K. Bolton received a leave of absence for 30 days. Our First Division are sending all of their sick to Keokuk Iowa and they have quite a number of them. We received orders this afternoon to be ready to move at a moments notice.

Aug 7—Regiment still engaged in digging and intrenching. Dress parade in the evening.

Aug 8—Digging and intrenching as usual. Everything is being packed up and is being sent down to the Yazoo River to the landing.

Aug 9—Struck tents early this morning and sent them to the wharf at Haines's Bluff. At noon the regiment formed on the color line and under the command of Lt. Col. Schall, left Milldale Church and marched to the wharf, a distance of some three miles, but it was a tortures march. The heat was intense and it took us three hours to make the march, and at least twenty-five men fell prostrated by the scorching rays of the sun.

The Steamer *Emerald* was not ready to receive us as Durell was loading his guns, caissons, horses and men, and we were compelled to stand in the hot sun until he was done. Finally we embarked on board and selected our quarters, and made ourselves as comfortable as we could. Late in the afternoon everything was in readiness to leave, the hawser was casted off and the proud steamer with her living freight glided down the sluggish Yazoo, amid the cheering of the men on board and on land, and the many brass bands as we passed along the river. We run all night.

Aug 10—The *Emerald* reached the Mississippi River about sunrise, and "laid to" for a few hours, and them steamed up the river, very often striking the bottom. A man was kept busy

21. *O.R.*, vol. 24, part 3, 569.

taking the soundings. Stopped several times during the day for the purpose of "wooding up." Passed Lake Providence during the day. Run all night. During the night we hauled in along the Arkansas shore to "wood up. "The rain came down in torrents and it was as dark as pitch. Pickets were thrown out to protect the deck hands from guerillas. The shore was lit up by huge woven wire baskets which we hung on long poles from the bow of the steamer. These baskets were filled with large balls of tow, saturated with turpentine.

Aug 11—We arrived at Helena, Arkansas, about 5 o'clock P.M. and laid under a high bluff all night. Pickets were thrown out for protection against guerillas and to guard the deck hands while "wooding up" the steamer.

Aug 12—We left Helena at daylight and arrived at Memphis Tenn. about one o'clock P.M. Laid over there until 10 o'clock P.M. when we again dropped our hawser and proceeded on our way running all night.

Aug 13—Passed Fort Pillow and Island No. 10 during the day.

Aug 14—We arrived at Cairo Ill. about 4 o'clock P.M. and held our quarters on board all night. The following order was issued to-day by Gen. Burnside:

> Headquarters Army of the Ohio
> In the Field.
> Camp Nelson, Kentucky, Aug. 14, 1863.
>
> General Field Orders
>   No. 3
>   The Commanding General welcomes back to the Department the veterans of the 9th Corps. The inscriptions "Vicksburg" and "Jackson" they bring with them on their banners bear testimony to their valor, and to the faithfulness with which they have fullfilled their mission, and sustained the high reputation of a name already prominent in the annals of Patriotism.
>
>   By command of Major General Burnside.
>   Lewis Richmond
>   Assistant Adjutant General.[22]

He also issued General Field Orders No. 2, calling attention to the fact that the coming campaign will take the army through a friendly territory, and that humanity and the best interests of the service require that the peaceable inhabitants be treated with kindness, and that every protection be given by the soldiers to them, and to their property and enjoins on all officers to enforce the strictest discipline to prevent straggling, and ill-treatment to citizens, depradations, or wilful distruction of private property, holding the officers strictly responsible. Prisoners of war, particularly the wounded, will be treated with every consideration. And whenever evening regimental dress parades are held, it shall be the duty of the commanding officer to see that the Chaplain, or some proper person in his absence, holds some short religious service, such as the reading of a portion of the Scripture, with appropriate prayer for the protection and assistance of Divine Providence.[23]

---

22. *O.R.*, vol. 30, part 3, 31.

23. *O.R.*, vol. 30, part 3, 30-31.

Aug 15—Regiment disembarked from the steamer about 5 o'clock A.M. and about noon, embarked on board of the cars of the Illinois Central Railroad, for Sandoval Ill. some sixty miles east of St. Louis. Brig. Gen. Thomas Welsh commanding the 1st Division 9th A.C. having died at Cincinnati Ohio yesterday, Burnside issued the following orders:

> Headquarters Army of the Ohio
> In the Field.
> Camp Nelson, Kentucky, August 15, 1863.
>
> General Field Orders
> No. 4
>
> This Department has received, with the deepest regret, the intelligence of the death of Brigadier General Thomas Welsh, Commanding 1st Division 9th Army Corps; this sad event closes a life marked by the purest patriotism, and deprives the Army of the services and example of a brave and efficient officer whose sole aim in his military history was his country's good.
>
> The colors of the 9th Army Corps will be draped in mourning, and the officers at General Headquarters and the 9th Corps will wear the customary badge for thirty days.
>
> By Order of Major General Burnside,
> Lewis Richmond,
> Assistant Adjutant-General.[24]

Aug 16—Early this morning we changed cars at Sandoval Ill. for those of the Ohio and Mississippi Railroad, and were soon on our way to Cincinnati. We were very heartily greeted all along the road by the populous, by the waving of handkerchiefs, hot coffee, cakes and sandwiches were furnished us at each stopping place.

About 8 o'clock in the evening our train consisting of some twelve cars containing the regiment, all our horses and baggage, ran off the track about two miles from a small hamlet, called Shoals' Indiana, and about one hundred and fifty miles from Cincinnati. The train had just crossed a bridge that spanned a very deep stream. The fourth car from the engine left the track on account of a broken flange. The car containing our baggage rolled down the embankment, and another containing the horses followed soon, falling on the top of the other crushing it to pieces. Four or five men had to be cut out of the cars, as likewise the horses, and with it all only one man was killed. My horse was the only one hurt. Ten of the cars went down the embankment, which was some thirty feet, and they were piled up on their ends like the roof of a house, and strange to say, many of the men were asleep on top of the cars when the accident happened.

A telegraph operator soon appeared on the ground and the wires were cut and word sent each way. A Dr. Martin and son, and a Dr. Peck arrived about midnight, but by that time we had straighened up things and they found many of us cooly sleeping. The greatest trouble was in relieving the horses, but the men were very cool, and seemed to know what to do, and when to do it. Their work and coolness rather surprised the old railroad men. Later in the night another soldier was discovered belonging to the 11th N.H. lying by the roadside dead, making two deaths and some eight or nine wounded. Prv. Thomas McQuerin of Co. D was the victim of this accident. When this accident happened, nearly all hands were asleep.

---

24. *O.R.*, vol. 30, part 3, 45.

Aug 17—At daylight, all hands set to work again to clear away the wreck and by noon the track was clear for the passing of trains. Company D placed the body of Thomas McQuerin in the hands of an undertaker to be buried, and at 1 o'clock P.M. the regiment again boarded the train and proceeded on their way.

In passing through Seymour the train made a stop for a few moments. An ale wagon stopped near the train to deliver ale to a hotel. This was too much of a temptation for the boys and a keg was of course captured from the wagon and was as hastily disposed of, the head knocked in and afterwards used as a water tub. The original intention was to leave the Ohio and Mississippi Railroad at this place and take the cars on another road for the Ohio River, and proceed to Louisville, Ky., but the order was countermanded and we proceeded on to Cincinnati, traveling all night.

Chapter 9

The Department of the Ohio

August 18–November 3, 1863

Upon arriving back in Kentucky, the Ninth Corps detachment was dispersed throughout central Kentucky. The 51st Pennsylvania moved at first to Nicholasville, then marched to Crab Orchard. In early October, the regiment marched all the way to Knoxville, Tennessee, to join Burnside's main force.

Aug 18—Regiment arrived in Cincinnati at 5 o'clock A.M. Formed in line and marched through the city and came to a halt in front of the Burnet House, the headquarters of Gen. Burnside, who soon appeared on the balcony and made us a short speech, and he in turn was loudly cheered by the men. We then took up our line of march and on reaching the Ohio River, embarked on board of the Steamer *Covington*, crossed the river, and went into camp one mile from the city.

Col. Hartranft, Captains J. K. Bolton and Allebaugh left us at Cincinnati on a short leave of absence. The regiment was paid to-day two months pay. I received $297.80 and sent home by my brother $225.00. We are now back again in the Army of the Ohio. Orders were received yesterday to division commanders to at once recommend and forward through Corps Headquarters the names of three commissioned officers and six enlisted men from each of the three-year regiments of their commands, from the following States: N.H., Mass., R.I., N.Y., Penna., Md. & Ohio, to be detailed to proceed to the rendezvous for drafted men for the states that their regiments are from, for the purpose of receiving and conducting to their several regiments the men of the draft assigned to fill them up.

Aug 19—The men remained in camp all day, fixing up their camp, resting and writing letters.

Aug 20—Company and regimental drills and dress parade. Received a number of letters from home. Lt. Col. Schall is now in command of the Brigade and myself in command of the regiment. Six roll calls has been ordered each day until further notice. Since the death of Brig. Gen. Welsh, Gen. Ferrero is in command of the division.

Aug 21—Company and regimental drills and dress parade. Received a letter from my brother Joe. Prv. Rob. H. Erwin Co. E was detailed on extra duty, detached service as Orderly at Burnside's headquarters at Cincinnati.

Aug 22—Company and regimental drills and dress parade. Received marching orders.

Aug 23—Company and regimental inspection.

Aug 24—Company and regimental drills and dress parade. Drum Major John N. Johnson left camp for Norristown on account of ill health. A great deal of sickness prevails throughout the 9th A.C., mostly chills and fever, but very little sickness in our regiment.

Aug 25—Company and regimental drills and dress parade.

Aug 26—Regiment struck tents about 1 o'clock P.M. and marched to Covington, and took the cars of the Kentucky Central Railroad and left there at 8 o'clock P.M. traveling all night.

Aug 27—Regiment arrived at Nicholasville Ky. about 6 o'clock A.M. immediately disembarked and marched about four miles and went into camp in a beautiful woods. Our new home of canvas tents was named "Camp Parke." Nicholasville is in Jessamine County about seven miles south of Lexington.

Aug 28—Company drills and dress parade. Received and wrote several letters. Parke has gone home on a sick leave. Our 1st Division is now at Crab Orchard. There are fourteen men of Company A on the sick list. There are but two line officers in the 35th Mass. the Adj. and Q.M., all the rest are home on sick leave. Official notice received of the sentence of Prv. Samuel Slingluff of Co. A for desertion, time not fixed. He is to be shot, and is now in the hands of the Provost Marshal.

Aug 29—Company and regimental drills and dress parade.

Aug 30—Company and regimental drills and dress parade.

Aug 31—Regimental inspection and muster for pay. Dress parade in the evening. In accordance with G.O. No. 34, Assistant Surgeon J. B. Reinholdt has been announced as Acting Brigade Surgeon of our brigade, and by S.O. No. 90 Prv. Charles M. Jones Co. K 11th N.H.V. has been detailed for duty as Brigade Post Master.[1]

Sep 1—Engaged in signing the muster and pay rolls. Also made out pension papers for Prv. A. M. Johnson Co. A. Received a letter from the Provost Marshal of Philada. Gen. Potter is in command of the corps and his headquarters is at Lexington, Ky. and Col. Griffin is in command of the 2d Division with headquarters at Camp Nelson.

Sep 2—Company and regimental drills and dress parade. News reached camp that Burnside in conjunction with Rosecrans has taken Kingston Tenn.

Sep 3—Company and regimental drills and dress parade. A number of ladies visited our camp to see our dress parade. After it was over they very kindly invited the officers to take tea with them.

Sep 4—Company and regimental drills and dress parade. In accordance with S.O. No. 43, Department of the Ohio, Capt. Daniel Nicholas, First Lieut. Geo. Schall, Second Lieut. Wm.

---

1. On August 31, the Ninth Corps, under Brig. Gen. Robert B. Potter's command, was organized as follows:

    First Division, Brig. Gen. Edward Ferrero
        First Brigade, Col. David Morrison: 36th MA, 8th MI, 79th NY, 45th PA
        Second Brigade, Col. Ebenezer W. Peirce: 29th MA, 27th MI, 46th NY, 50th PA
        Third Brigade, Major Cornelius Byington: 3rd, 17th, 20th MI, 100th PA
        Artillery: Btys L&M, 3rd US
    Second Division, Colonel Simon G. Griffin
        First Brigade, Col. Zenas R. Bliss: 6th, 9th NH, 7th RI
        Second Brigade, Lt. Col. Edwin Schall: 35th MA, 11th NH, 51st NY, 51st PA
        Artillery: Bty L, 2nd NY; PA Bty D
    Unattached: Bty E, 2nd US

R. Foster, with six enlisted men, will at once proceed to Carlisle Penna. the rendezvous for drafted men of that state, and there report to the commanding officer for the purpose of receiving and conducting to their regiment the drafted men assigned to fill it up. Burnside occupied Knoxville yesterday with his forces, and appointed Brig. Gen. S. P. Carter Provost Marshal General of East Tennessee.

Sep 5—Company and regimental drills and dress parade. Regimental Court Martial convened in camp to-day for the trial of Prv. John Smith Co. A and others. Musician Samuel G. Doud Co. A having wickedly destroyed his drum at Cairo Ill. his company commander was directed to enter upon the pay-roll the stopping of six dollars.

Sep 6—Company and regimental inspection and dress parade.

Sep 7—Company and regimental drills and dress parade. Regiment was paid two months pay. I received $297.40. Received orders to be in readiness to move at short notice with three days cooked rations in haversacks. Towards night the order was countermanded. I received orders to-day to detail six (6) privates from the regiment for temporary service with Lt. Benjamin's Battery at Lexington to report with blankets and shelter tents.

Sep 8—Company and regimental drills and dress parade. Sent home to my mother $225.00. Received and wrote several letters. Capt. Lane S. Hart was to-day announced as Acting Assistant Adjutant General of the 2d Brigade 2d Division. 1st Lieut. Geo. Schall having been detailed to proceed to Penna., Lieut. J. P. Brooke was to-day announced as Acting Adjutant. Also Sergt. Major Curtin B. Stonerod being absent for the same purpose, 1st Sergt. Isaac Fitzone was to-day announced as Acting Sergent Major.

Sep 9—Early this morning I received orders to be in readiness to move at short notice. During the day we struck tents at Camp Parke. Left camp at 12 o'clock M. during the day crossed the Kentucky River at Hickman's Bridge and towards night went into bivouac at Camp Dick Robinson. Was invited to take tea with Col. Dick Robinson. During the evening, received the news that Burnside's forces under [Brig.] Gen. [James M.] Shackelford had captured Cumberland Gap with 2,000 men and 14 pieces of artillery. Capt. Lane S. Hart received a leave of absence for 20 days.

Sep 10—Left our bivouac at 6 o'clock A.M. reaching Lancaster about 11 o'clock A.M. and went into bivouac one mile beyond. Was invited and took dinner with a Judge Lusk, and very strong Union man.

Sep 11—Left our bivouac at 6 o'clock A.M. and marched one mile beyond Crab Orchard and went into camp about 12 o'clock M.

Sep 12—Laid in camp all day. Received and wrote several letters.

Sep 13—Company and regimental inspection and dress parade. There is a large encampment of invalids near our camp.

Sep 14—Company drills and dress parade. Received orders to be in readiness to report to Gen. Burnside at Knoxville.

Sep 15—Company and regimental drills and dress parade. Received and wrote several letters. In G.O. No. 38 Capt. Laird 17th Mich. Vols., Provost Marshal of the town of Crab Orchard is relieved, and Capt. Wm. Gibson 35th Mass. is announced in his stead. Capt. Geo. P. Carman received a leave of absence for 20 days on Surgeon's certificate.

Sep 16—Company and regimental drills and dress parade. The order to reenforce Gen. Burnside countermanded. Our brigade is stationed as follows: the 51st P.V. and 35th Mass. are stationed at this place, the 51st N.Y. at Hickmans' Bridge, the 11th N.H. at London, some forty miles from here, to do duty at Post Pitman, and the 21st Mass. has been transferred to the 1st Brigade.

On this date the regiment has only four officers with them, and the companies are now commanded as follows:

Co.A under command of a 2d sergeant
Co.B under command of a 1st sergeant
Co.C under command of 2d Lt. Wm. F. Thomas
Co.D under command of a 5th sergeant
Co.E under command of a 1st sergeant
Co.F under command of a 1st sergeant
Co.G under command of a 3d sergeant
Co.H under command of Capt. J. Merrill Linn
Co.I under command of a 1st sergeant
Co.K under command of a 1st sergeant[2]

Sep 17—Struck tents this morning and moved our camp to a better location. The officers of the regiment by the invitation of the clerks of the 2d Brigade Headquarters attended an oyster supper given in camp in honor of the Battle of "Antietam." Captain George H. Laird 17th Mich. Vols. was to-day announced as Acting Quarter-Master of Convalescent camp at Crab Orchard Ky. From this point all the stores for the army of Burnside at Knoxville are shipped, and immense trains numbering into the hundreds leave here daily for the front. The government is now constructing a large store house here capable of holding 500,000 rations.

Sep 18—Company and regimental drills and dress parade.

Sep 19—Company and regimental drills and dress parade. A regimental Court Martial consisting of Linn, Bisbing, and Owen meets in session to-day in camp.

Sep 20—Left camp this morning in company with Captains Hart and Hallman for Norristown on a 20 day leave of absence, leaving Capt. Bisbing in command of the regiment.

Sep 21—Company drills and dress parade. Our party arrived in Cincinnati about 11 o'clock A.M. and left there at 10 o'clock P.M. for Pittsburg.

Sep 22—Our party left Christline at 1 o'clock and arrived in Pittsburg at 9 o'clock and stopped at the St. Charles Hotel. Missed the train and had to lay over.

Capt. Linn in command of the regiment. By the order of Col. Schall commanding the brigade, one Captain, two Lieut. ten Sergts. thirty-five corpls. and one hundred men are ordered for fatigue duty to be employed in repairing the road from this place to Mount Vernon some fifteen miles on the Cumberland Gap road. The detail is ordered to report at 12 o'clock M. to-day to Capt. Bisbing, commanding the working party. 35 men has also been detailed, who are competent to drive mules to report to Capt. Rapelji at the train now encamped at Sick's River.

Sep 23—Our party left Pittsburg at 3.40 A.M. Very few men in camp. Bisbing busy in building corduroy roads, and otherwise improving the almost impassable road.

Sep 24—Our party arrived in Philadelphia at 6 o'clock A.M. and in Norristown at 10 A.M. Here I first heard of my nomination as Clerk of the Courts of Montgomery County. Made up my mind at once to decline the honor, but was persuaded not to do so, as I could not be elected in any event. Bisbing still at work on the road.

---

2. Parker, *51st PA*, 390.

Sep 25—Spent the day pleasantly at home among my friends. Regiment still at work on the corduroy road, but finished during the day and returned to their camp late in the evening pretty well fagged out. Capt. Linn received a leave of absence for 20 days.

Sep 26—Spent the day very pleasantly among my friends. Drills resumed.

Sep 27—Spent the day pleasantly, and went to church in the evening. Regimental inspection and dress parade.

Sep 28—Spent the day pleasantly in Philada. Company and regimental drills and dress parade. The 51st Pa. and 35th Mass. were inspected to-day by Capt. Wm. Allebaugh, Act. Asst. Adj. Genl. on brigade staff.

Sep 29—Attended state fair. Company drills.

Sep 30—Attended state fair. Regiment received orders to hold themselves in readiness to march at an early hour to-morrow morning with eight days rations. Our orders are to report to Burnside at Knoxville Tenn.

Oct 1—With a number of friends I attended the state fair then being held in Norristown Pa. Circular issued by Lt Col. Schall to strike tents and to be ready to march to-morrow morning at 6 o'clock. Lt. Jacob P. Brooke received a leave of absence to-day. A Board of Survey consisting of Capt. Gaulin 51st P.V. and Lt. Ingalls 35th Mass. was appointed by Lt. Col. Schall commanding the brigade to estimate and report the amount of damage done to the land of Morris Harris, on which the 35th Mass. Vols. were encamped, the board to meet at the house of said Harris. Sixteen men detailed from the regiment to report to the Commissary Department.

Oct 2—Regiment struck tents at 8 o'clock A.M. at Crab Orchard and left camp at 4 o'clock P.M. under the command of Capt. Bisbing. Capt. Gaulin, Lieuts. Thomas and Owen were the only line officers present. The other seven companies were under the command of their sergeants. Benjamin's six-gun battery of 20 pound Parrotts and Edwards's six-gun battery of 12 pound Parrotts accompany us on our march. After a march of sixteen miles over a very rough road, the regiment went into bivouac at Mount Vernon.[3]

Oct 3—Regiment left their bivouac at 10 o'clock A.M. and after a good days march went into bivouac at a place called the Two Caves.

Oct 4—Regiment left their bivouac at 7 o'clock A.M. during the march, forded the Big Rockcastle River, crossed Wild Cat Mountain, marched over the field where Zollicoffer had been encamped a few days before, and where he had met his death. At 2 o'clock P.M. came to a halt and went into bivouac at Little Rockcastle. The night was cold and frosty.

Oct 5—Regiment left their bivouac at 7 o'clock A.M. and after a march of some ten miles halted at Pitman's Tavern and went into bivouac.

Oct 6—Regiment in bivouac at Pitman's Tavern and rations very short, but fortunately the country abounds in plenty of game, and there are plenty of hogs and sheep roaming around and the boys will not suffer. Quartermaster Stephens is acting brigade quartermaster and Lieut. Owen is acting regimental quartermaster, Allebaugh is acting A.A.Genl. to Lt.Col. Schall commanding brigade.

Oct 7—Regiment still in bivouac at Pitman's. It has rained all day and all night, and everything is disagreeable and uncomfortable.

Oct 8—Captains Hart, Hallman and myself left Norristown this evening at 10.40 P.M. to rejoin the regiment now on its way to Knoxville.

---

3. Captain John Edwards, Jr., commanded Batteries L&M, 3rd US. Lieutenant Samuel N. Benjamin was still in command of Battery E, 2nd US.

The regiment still in bivouac at Pitman's. A very large train of wagons parked here to-day between our camp and London. Also a railroad train passed here to-day loaded with 300 or 400 bales of cotton, captured by Burnside. He is sending it to Lexington on account of Uncle Sam. The lot is reported to be worth from $50,000 to $60,000.

Oct 9—Hart, Hallman and myself arrived in Pittsburgh at 12 o'clock M. and left there at 1 o'clock P.M. Regiment still in bivouac at Pitman's. The wagon train has been loaded up with coal, which is abundant here. It is to be delivered at Crab Orchard.

Oct 10—Hart, Hallman and myself arrived at Dayton, Ohio, at 5 o'clock A.M. and at Cincinnati at 1 o'clock P.M. proceeded to Covington Ky. and left there at 2 P.M. arriving at Nicholasville Ky. at 7 P.M.

Regiment left their bivouac at Pitman's at 12 o'clock M. passed through London. After a march of some ten miles came to a halt, and went into bivouac at Laurel Bridge. Here again the boys found a large number of hogs, and of course appropriated them.

Oct 11—Hart, Hallman and myself, left Nicholasville early this morning by stage, arriving at Crab Orchard in the evening.

Regiment left their bivouac at 7 A.M. and after a march of 20 miles over a very mountainous road, and passing through Barboursville, about 6 P.M. went into bivouac on the banks of the Cumberland River.

Oct 12—Hart, Hallman and myself spent the day in Crab Orchard. Regiment left their bivouac at 7 A.M. forded the Cumberland River, and after a march of fifteen miles went into bivouac among the mountains at dark.

Oct 13—Hart, Hallman and myself spent the day in Crab Orchard. Regiment left their bivouac at 8 A.M. during the day crossed three very steep mountains. Rained all day, and mud over shoe top, and after a march of fifteen miles, bivouacked at Cumberland Gap.

Oct 14—Hart, Hallman and myself left Crab Orchard at 7 A.M. with our horses and an ambulance, for Knoxville. Rode 23 miles and stopped for the night at a point called "Roberts."

Regiment left their bivouac at 8 A.M. crossed Cumberland Gap. Parson Brownlow and his daughter in a carriage with baggage and a font of type passed the regiment during the day on their way to Knoxville.[4] Rained all day. After a march of sixteen miles, they went into bivouac at 5 P.M. at Tazewell Tenn.

Oct 15—Hart, Hallman and myself left "Roberts" at 6 A.M. and after a drive of 28 miles stopped for the night at the house of the "Widow Colver's."

The regiment remained in camp all day, having run out of supplies and forage. Our supply train reached camp about 5 P.M.

Oct 16—Hart, Hallman and myself left the "Widow Colver's" at 7 A.M. and after a drive of 35 miles stopped for the night eight miles beyond Cumberland Ford.

Regiment left their bivouac at 8 o'clock A.M. in a drenching rain. During the day forded Clinch River, which was very deep, and the waters cold, with a very swift current. After a march of 14 miles went into camp on the roadside.

Oct 17—Hart, Hallman and myself left at 7 A.M. and after a drive of 34 miles stopped at the "Widow Haines" for the night.

---

4. William G. Brownlow (1805-1877) was a Methodist minister and strong Unionist who edited the Knoxville Whig until that paper was suppressed in October 1861. Brownlow fled, was captured, then banished to Federal territory. He returned to Knoxville after Burnside recaptured the city and opened a new paper, the *Whig and Rebel Ventilator*.

Regiment left their camp at 8 A.M.. During the day passed through Maynardsville and at 3 P.M. after a march of 15 miles went into camp in a large field some 21 miles from Knoxville. On this march there was no stint for water for a stream of water ran over the road bed for at least six miles.

Oct 18—Hart, Hallman and myself left the "Widow Haines" at 7 A.M. Rained all day. Regiment left their camp at 8 A.M. crossed Coffer Ridge, passed Gravestown, and after a march of 17 miles went into bivouac about one mile of Knoxville. We caught up with the boys about 5 P.M. just as they were pitching their tents for the night.

Oct 19—Regiment left their bivouac at 8 A.M. in the rain and mud, and marched into Knoxville and went into camp on the outskirts of the town. By an order from Gen. [Col.] Griffin, commanding the 2d Division, Privates Theo. MoserCo.K and Frederick Smith, teamsters in the Q.M. Dept. each of the 51st Penna., having been apprehended in the act of killing a pig belonging to a citizen of Knoxville, it is hereby ordered that they be fined one-half months pay for two months ending Oct 31, 1863, and I am ordered to see that the above is executed. Orders received for the 9th A.C. to be prepared to march at a moments notice with two days rations, hard bread, sugar, coffee, and beef on the hoof, with the usual amount of ammunition, all wagons baggage to go with the troops, those who cannot march to go by rail. The sick to be left in hospital in Knoxville.

Oct 20—Col. Hartranft being absent on leave, and Lt. Col. Schall in command of the 2d Brigade, I again assumed command of the regiment. Wrote a letter to my mother, also one to Col. Ripley, Ordnance Officer at Washington.[5] First Division, Ferrero commanding left to-day for Loudon Bridge, a distance of 30 miles from here.

During the day I received orders to be in readiness to move to-morrow morning at 6 o'clock A.M. with three days rations in haversacks. In accordance with S.O. No. 103, 2d Brigade headquarters, Privates Owen McBride Co. C, Conley McCormick Co.H, Barnard O'Donnell Co.D and Michael Harrington Co.I all of the 51st P.V., having voluntarily returned to their companies and regiment after and absence without leave, at the request of their company commanders, returned to duty.

Oct 21—For some reason, we did not move, and remained in camp all day. Regimental inspection.

Oct 22—Regiment struck tents at 8 A.M., formed on the color line, and marched to Knoxville, to the depot of the East Tennessee and Virginia Railroad. Laid on the streets and around the depot all night.

Oct 23—After remaining in the street nearly all day, the regiment at 3 P.M. embarked on the cars and were soon on their way to Loudon, arriving there at 8 P.M. and bivouacked on the banks of the Tennessee River. The day was very cold, and we had a very heavy rain. Our train got stuck very often during our trip and we were compelled to get off and push the train along. Burnside, who was on our train, helping along with the rest of us. The First Division has also arrived here and has crossed over the river to Loudon. It is on the west side of the Tennessee River and is entirely surrounded by very high bluffs and is well fortified, and commands the surrounding country for many miles. On our approach, the enemy fled in a hurry, leaving behind a fine pontoon bridge, but they destroyed a fine railroad bridge that spanned the river at this point. Nothing remains now but the ten well built piers.

---

5. Brig. Gen. James W. Ripley had been the army's Chief Ordnance Officer. On September 15, 1863, Colonel George D. Ramsay replaced the aged Ripley.

We were unloaded in a narrow ditch, and we are in mud up to our knees, and raining like thunder, and our troops are all mixed up, and daylight is the only thing that can remedy the matter.

Oct 24—Selected a camp ground and moved the regiment to it early this morning. Had no sooner entered the field when we discovered that it was swarming with rabbits. The boys made a charge without orders, and they had good living at least for a while. Soon had our tents pitched and we were at home again.

Oct 25—Regiment remained in camp all day, companies all inspected, and dress parade in the evening.

Oct 26—Regiment remained in camp all day. Dress parade in the evening. Received notice that Private Charles Younger Co. A a deserter had been captured in the 8th District of Penna. and that $3,000 had been paid for his apprehension. Capt. Bisbing and Lt. George B. Campbell appointed as members of a General Court Martial, to meet at the headquarters of the 21st Mass. to-morrow, near Loudon.

Oct 27—Received orders from brigade headquarters to break camp to-morrow morning at 4 o'clock A.M. and to have the regiment in readiness to move at a moments notice. Wagons to be in camp at 4 1/2 A.M.

Burnside has asked the President to be relieved on account of of the state of his health. Has been suffering more or less since the Mexican War, with chronic diarrhea, but does not wish to be relieved during the present emergency. Ferrero, commanding the 1st Division 9th A.C. and White, commanding the 2d Division 9th A.C. have received orders to be in readiness to re-cross the river to-morrow at 5 A.M. sending their trains and batteries in advance, all to be over by 6 A.M., Ferrero to move out on the road leading to Lenoir's halting at 1 1/2 miles. Locomotives and cars be thrown into the river and the pontoon bridge to be swung to the north side entire.[6]

The following letter dated October 7th 1863 reached our camp to-day, and was read on dress parade in front of the regiment:

October 7, 1863.
To the officers and men of the 51st Regiment Penna. Volunteers:

Gentlemen you will not, I hope, deem us presumptuous when we assure you with what intense interest your movements have been viewed by an appreciative community. True there are those in our midst who most mysteriously sympathize with the enemies of our common country. But let that not discourage you.

The patriotic wise, & good, look with gratitude and admiration upon your intrepid bravery and unflinching devotion in our glorious cause, the defense of that freedom so dearly bought, and bequeathed to us by our noble and venerated fathers of revolutionary memory. We truly mourn the loss of the many brave spirits who have fallen by your side, and are devoutly thankful to our Heavenly Father for the preservation of so large a number who have willing hearts and strong hands to carry through this important work. We sincerely and most fervently hope the day is not far distant when we shall have our country to its former peace and prosperity, and founded upon firmer basis than before, universal freedom to the great human family. We shall hail with exceeding joy the period that

6. *O.R.*, vol. 31, part 1, 757-8.

will enable you to stack your arms, and return to the bosom of your anxious families, leaving to the historians to record your many valiant deeds such as the memorable pass at the Bridge of Antietam.

The many glorious victories gained by the noble 51st.

From the Women's Loyal League of Montgomery County. With their highest regards and best wishes for your success.

> Annie C. Yerkes,
> Sec. of the League,
> Norristown, Pa.

Oct 28—Regiment left their camp at 4 o'clock A.M., marched to the banks of the Tennessee River, remained there sometime, and then ordered to the railroad to load the pontoon boats and planks, which took us until dark. Remained by them all night. There was 52 of them, and they weighed over a ton each.

The First Division and a part of the 23d A.C. evacuated Loudon early this morning, and before doing so run all of the locomotives and cars over the abutment into the river, some one hundred feet, cut loose the pontoon bridge, which swung over to our side of the river which was the one we loaded on the cars. The bridge was taken up out of the water by Capt. Orlando M. Poe, U.S. Corps of Engineers, Chief Engineer, Department of the Ohio, and dragged to the railroad by mules. The bridge and anchorage was taken to Knoxville. These boats were constructed by the confederates and fell into our possession at the first occupation of Loudon. They were very heavy, built of 2 1/2 inch southern pine plank, the main body of each boat being rectangular in form, and finished at the upstream, and by an addition which was an equilateral triangle in plan. There was material enough for three boats in each one of these. And to get them out of the stream, twelve mules were hitched to each boat and they were dragged on the ground for about half a mile to the railway cut. The chess-plank were carried the same distance on the backs of men.

While the transfer of the bridge from the river to the railroad was in progress, two squadrons of confederate cavalry appeared on the south bank. We fully expected them to open fire upon us, as we were within easy range, and could have stopped our work, but they looked quietly on, and did not molest us, and towards night disappeared.

Oct 29—Regiment formed line in the morning and marched to Lenoir Station, six miles from Loudon, arriving there at 11 A.M. and went into camp, all hands pretty well used up. Gen. White of the 23d A.C. informs Burnside that from appearances the enemy intend to occupy Loudon and suggests that the trains intended to carry away the balance of the bridge be sent down as speedily as possible, otherwise there will be trouble, should the enemy open fire from across the river.

Oct 30—Regiment remained in camp all day. At 8 P.M. received orders to march and laid on our arms all night in a cold drenching rain. Received orders to have all the carpenters in the regiment to report to corps head quarters without delay.

Oct 31—Regiment inspected and mustered for pay at 2 A.M. Our camp is on the banks of the Holston River some 22 miles from Knoxville. 9th A.C. headquarters and troops of the same are now stationed at Lenoir's Station, with the exception of the 3d Brigade, 2d Division, which is on detached service at Cumberland Gap, Ky., and Battery D on detached service at Covington, Ky. Wrote a reply to the Ladies Loyal League of Montgomery County.

Nov 1—Detailed as Division Officer of the Day. Wrote a letter to Brig. Genl. Ripley, Washington D.C. Company drills and dress parade. A detail of fifty men from the regiment under the command of Captain Gaulin sent up the Holston River some seven miles to Leiper's Ferry to do picket duty. The pontoon bridge that the regiment has worked so hard to load and save, after working day and night, was successfully relaid and finished about 1 P.M. to-day, and Sanders' division of cavalry commenced crossing it to the south side of the Holston, and moved out in the direction of Marysville. The bridge has proved to be simply invaluable.

Nov 2—Changed our camp this morning to a much better location. Very little drilling, no men to drill, nearly all detailed for some duty. At the muster for pay on the 31st, Company A had no officers and only four men. The other companies are on about the same footing. Lt. J. R. Gilliland is now Acting Adjutant.

Nov 3—Foraging parties sent out from the regiments to collect corn and hay, and have succeeded in coming in with well filled wagons. Our pickets now connect with Thomas' near Cotton Port.[7] Burnside has started wagons to Crossville to meet the clothing that is to be started from McMinnville. Bisbing and Owen have been appointed members of a General Court Martial to meet at the headquarters of the 21st Mass. to-morrow. Prvs. Albert List Co. D and Edwin R. Wirth Co. F has ben detailed as bakers to report at the brick house near railroad station. Lt. John H. Genther Co.B has been announced on division staff as A.C.S.

---

7. Major General George H. Thomas was in command of the Department of the Cumberland.

Chapter 10

Knoxville

November 4, 1863–February 9, 1864

In early November 1863, the 51st PA was part of the force Burnside assembled to defend Knoxville from a Confederate army led by Lieutenant General James Longstreet. The Southern general placed the city under a short siege, then retired when Union reinforcements neared. Burnside's men followed Longstreet toward Virginia, then went into winter quarters at Blaine's Crossroads. Here, the majority of the 51st reenlisted as veteran volunteers and went home on furlough.

Nov 4—Company drills and dress parade. All the carpenters detailed from the regiment reported to Lt.Col. [Orville E.] Babcock, assistant inspector-general, 9.A.C. at the old saw-mill of Mr. Lenoir's, near the railroad station, to work on pontoon boats. A heavy detail from all the regiments was sent to dig away the embankment near the mouth of the Little Tenn. River for the pontoon bridge, and a road to reach it.

Nov 5—Company drills and dress parade, but a very few men to attend them. All the recruiting parties sent out by the 9.A.C. in East Tenn. is by S.O. No. 172, broken up, and officers in command are ordered to close up their business and report to their respective regiments.

Nov 6—Company drills and dress parade. Srgt. Um. B. Hart, one corporal and seven men, ordered to report to Capt. Blanchard, Provost Marshal.

In accordance with S.O. No. 173 9.A.C. and G.O. No. 173 War Department, the following named enlisted men of the 51st Penna. Vols. are hereby transferred to the Invalid Corps and their names will be dropped from the rolls of the regiment:

Prv. Daniel M. Gugan, Co.A	Prv. John Felter, Co.E	Prv. Sol. Sensendefer, Co.A
Prv. Henry Fry, Co.E	Mus. Samuel G. Doud, Co.A	Prv. Jackson McFadden, Co.E
Prv. Irwin Barndt, Co.A	Prv. Lewis S. Kline, Co.E	Corp. Silas C. Beers, Co.B
Prv. Henry L. Gerhard, Co.F	Prv. Josiah Diety, Co.B	Prv. Nathan Kulp, Co.F
Prv. Edward L. Buck, Co.B	Prv. Robert McGee, Co.F	Prv. Levi Baumn, Co.C
Prv. Francis McFadden, Co.F	Prv. Abraham Kile, Co.C	Prv. Samuel G. Doub, Co.F
Prv. Patrick McDade, Co.C	Wag. Ferdinand Evans, Co.F	Prv. William Hamberger, Co.D
Prv. William Mackey, Co.G	Prv. Irwin Creighton, Co.D	Corp. Wm. H. Calhoun,Co.G
Prv. Denis Oneal, Co.D	Corp. Jesse G. Lucus, Co.G	Prv. Samuel Sharp, Co.D
Prv. Andrew Hall, Co.G	Prv. James G. Katen, Co.G	Prv. Henry Hain, Co.H
Prv. Thomas Irwin, Co.G	Prv. Daniel B. Moyer, Co.H	Prv. John Allart, Co.G
Corp. Hugh McGill, Co.I	Corp. John Q. Adams, Co.H	Prv. Jacob Emerich,Co.I
Prv. Charles Merrill, Co.H	Prv. Jacob Climer, Co.K	Prv. Peter Bastain, Co.H

| Prv. John L. Singer, Co.K | Prv. Samuel S. Miller, Co.H | Prv. John Kimmel, Co.K |
| Prv. John Dougherty, Co.G | Corp. Edward Held, Co.K | Prv. John Hain, Co.H |

Nov 7—Company, regimental drills and dress parade. Received notice about three deserters from the regiment.

Babcock reports to Parke, Chief of Staff, that he has thirty pontoon boats ready for the water. He had many obstacles to overcome, not a log was cut at the mill when he commenced, had nothing but mules to haul with, and no chains, made cables of telegraph-wire for anchoring. Work has been delayed for the want of carpenters and blacksmith tools. There are a sufficient number of oxen in the country, but the owners have safeguards and will not allow their cattle to work. He made his nails from old scraps of iron picked up wherever he could find it. Is running the cotton mill here at the station, spinning the cotton and making his own ropes. Thirty men has just been detailed, armed with picks, axes, and shovels, to report to Lt. Col. Babcock.

Nov 8—Detailed as Division Officer of the Day. During the day visited the pickets at Leiper's Ferry. The enemy's pickets extend from Loudon to Davis' Ford, four miles up the Little Tenn.

Nov 9—Company drills and dress parade. By G.O. No. 64, coffee and sugar is issued only on alternate days, and only in half rations. Lt. J. P. Brooke and Lt. Wm. F. Campbell have been detailed to take charge of a detachment of convalescents to be forwarded from Camp Nelson to Knoxville Tenn.

Nov 10—Company drills and dress parade. Received orders to have the regiment under arms and in line at 6 o'clock to-morrow morning, camps will be left standing. [Pvt. William Albert, Co. B, captured at Leiper's Ferry.]

Nov 11—Pontoon boats hauled to the banks of the Little Tenn. River. Received orders to form on the color line, and later to detail 100 men fully armed to cross the river to protect the engineers and workmen in laying the pontoon bridge. The detail was placed under the command of Capt. Bisbing. It took eight days to prepare the bank for the use of this bridge. The bank was about 16 feet above the level of the water. The cut was 15 ft. deep, 22 ft. wide at the top, and 15 feet at the bottom, and over four hundred feet long. This digging was all done by the 51st. The bridge was successfully laid, and the regiment returned to their camp late in the evening. Another one was put down on the Clinch River at Kingston.

Nov 12—Detailed as Division Officer of the Day. Paid a visit to the pickets on the other side of the Little Tenn. River, crossing over the pontoon at 12 o'clock at night. The night was pitch dark and it rain in torrents.

Nov 13—Took a good rest to-day. By the way things look, there will be a rumpus soon. Camp rumor has it that Longstreet is approaching from Chattanooga with from 20,000 to 40,000 troops and is building pontoons on Pond Creek and elsewhere.[1] Gen. White reports to Parke that the enemy are crossing in some sort of flat boats six miles below Huff's Ferry.[2]

Nov 14—Shortly after midnight, received orders to be in readiness to move at a moments notice. At 5 A.M. regiment struck tents and formed on the color line. The morning is anything but pleasant, cold and cheerless and very little to eat, as the men had been on quarter rations for several days. The men stood and laid aroundin the rain all day, without shelter, until dark, and then pitched tents again. The pontoon bridge over the Little Tennessee, which had cost us

---

1. *O.R.*, vol. 31, part 1, 258 (from Charles A. Dana's report).

2. *O.R.*, vol. 31, part 2, 139. Brigadier General Julius White commanded the Second Division, Twenty-third Corps.

so much labor, and which was built under much difficulty, has been ordered to be destroyed, after the withdrawal of our pickets from the other side.

Longstreet has made his appearance near Loudon, and a portion of Burnside's troops, the 1st Division 9.A.C. and 23d A.C. are now pouring into Lenoir. Burnside arrived at Lenoir at 10 P.M. from Knoxville in a special car. All the troops that had fallen back were faced about, and sent back to the front, and a number of batteries dashing down the road after them. The rain was falling in torrents. We of the 2d Division remained in our old camp ground wrapped in our blankets, but wet to the skin. Camp rumor is that Longstreet commenced at midnight to throw two pontoon bridges across the Tennessee River near Loudon.[3] Shackelford reports to Parke that heavy cannonading is heard on the Poor Valley road in the direction of Tazeville, and thinks that the enemy's cavalry are trying to occupy Blain's Cross- Roads.[4]

Nov 15—Regiment were aroused from their slumber at 2 A.M., formed on the color line, and in the mud and rain marched in direction of Loudon, reaching there about daylight, and ordered to the front, but on the way, the order was countermanded and we fell back to the heights opposite Loudon, stacked arms and awaited orders. We soon learned that Longstreet had crossed his whole army estimated from 30,000 to 40,000, at Huff's Ferry, six miles below Loudon, and is now attacting Burnside in force.[5] The 1st Brigade of the 2d Division sent forward and deployed as skirmishers our brigade the 2d following in support. Our army gradually falling back on Lenoir, the scene very exciting and we are keeping the rebel advance in check. We reached Lenoir at 5 P.M., a running fight the whole distance some six miles, still have the enemy in check. Drew five days rations here, but did not have the time to cook them. Near dark, a train from Knoxville reached the station and off stepped Col. Hartranft, who had just arrived from home. We were all glad to see him. He at once assumed command of the 2d Division, Lt. Col. Schall retaining command of the 2d Brigade and myself the regiment.[6]

After destroying the pontoon bridge, saw-mills, factories, one hundred wagons which had been corralled there loaded with provisions, a division of the 23d A.C. cut the spokes of the wheels, burnt the harness, tents and officers baggage. Barrels of bacon, coffee, and sugar were broken open and distributed to the men, and what could not be used was destroyed. The mules were needed for our artillery. The distruction of all this property was a military necessity, as it would certainly have fallen into the hands of the enemy.

---

3. *O.R.*, vol. 31, part 1, 259 (Dana).

4. Brigadier General James M. Shackelford commanded Burnside's Cavalry Corps.

5. Lieutenant General James Longstreet led a force of some 25,000 troops, including infantry divisions of Lafayette McLaws, Micah Jenkins, Bushrod R. Johnson, and Robert Ransom, Jr. Major General Joseph A. Wheeler commanded the Confederate Cavalry Corps sent to cooperate with Longstreet.

6. The depleted Ninth Corps was now organized as follows:
    First Division, Brig. Gen. Edward Ferrero
        First Brigade, Col. David Morrison: 36th MA, 8th MI, 79th NY, 45th PA
        Second Brigade, Col. Benjamin C. Christ: 29th MA, 27th MI, 46th NY, 50th PA
        Third Brigade, Col. William Humphrey: 2nd, 17th, 20th MI, 100th PA
        Artillery: Bty L, 2nd NY (34th NY Bty); Bty D, 1st RI
    Second Division, Col. John F. Hartranft
        First Brigade, Col. Joshua K. Sigfried: 2nd MD, 21st MA, 48th PA
        Second Brigade, Lt. Col. Edwin Schall: 35th MA, 11th NH, 51st PA
        Unattached Artillery: Bty E, 2nd US

Our brigade left here about dusk, taking the road leading to Knoxville, following Benjamin's battery of six 20 pounders. We marched all night through the rain and mud, and it was a severe and a laborious one. Men and horses were completely fagged out. The enemy were on our flank, and there was more or less musketry firing through the entire night. In fact it was a race with the contending forces for Knoxville, and Campbell Station was the key to the situation. The horses and mules gave out, and the men were compelled to drag the artillery over the deep gullies and steep hills, or abandon them, but with it all some of the ammunition had to be thrown away to lighten up the caissons. When daylight appeared, we found after our hard march that we had only made three miles in twelve hours from Lenoir. Our division has the advance in this movement. During this nights march, Buckley, commanding Battery D, and Benjamin, 2d U.S. Artillery, asked Burnside for mules or horses. Burnside promptly turned over ten mule teams to each of them, burning the wagons for that purpose, and ordered them to abandon the rear part of their caissons if they could not get along, but with it all, they were compelled to abandon their battery wagons, bodies and contents and the rear part of some of the caissons. But they were destroyed and rendered useless.[7] Longstreet is now advancing in two columns, McLaws' division taking the left hand road leading to Campbell's station and Hood's division (commanded by Jenkins) the one to the right, following the line of the railroad to Lenoir's. The road upon which Burnside was moving followed by Jenkins intersects that along which McLaws was advancing about a mile southwest of Campbell's Station. It was therefore essential to the safety of his trains, if not of his entire command, that Burnside should reach the junction point before McLaws.

Nov 16—After partaking of something to eat, we moved off again about daylight, and we were more able to pick our road. We arrived at Campbell station which is on the Knoxville & East Tenn. Railroad, and near the point the Kingston Road joins the Loudon Road about 9 A.M. and not a moment too soon, as their advance skirmishers were on our heels, and fired into our rear. Hartranft had scarcely made his dispositions when McLaws appeared and at once attacked, but we steadfastly held our ground until the remainder of our troops and all our trains had safely passed. The trains continued on the road to Knoxville under the guard of the 79th New York (Highlanders). The troops formed in line of battle about half mile beyond the junction with Ferrero's division on the right and White in prolongation to the left, whereupon Hartranft withdrew from his advance position and took his place in line on the left of White.

About noon, Longstreet unsuccessfully attacked our right, and afterwards our left centre. A white horse battery made its appearance on the outskirts of the woods in full view of us. Our artillery turned upon it at once and the very hills trembled under the reverberation. Almost immediately an attempt was made to turn our left, the enemy coming up evidently to strike Hartranft's left and rear. Again our artillery opened, and the enemy's broken ranks sought shelter in the woods. Burnside determined to retire to a new position about two-thirds of a mile to his rear. The difficult and hazardous undertaking was successfully accomplished in the face of the enemy. It was a grand sight. The troops moved with the greatest coolness, deliberation and precision under a heavy and continuous fire, and resembled a drill rather than an actual battle.

McLaws' Division promptly advanced to attack the new position whilst Jenkin's continued his turning movement, but the difficulties of the ground delayed him until nightfall stopped his further progress. McLaws failed in his attack, and at the close of the action Burnside remained in possession of his own ground. Burnside's object was to fight long enough to give his trains time to reach Knoxville, and to gain cover of night under which to

---

7. *O.R.*, vol. 31, part 1, 347 (Captain William W. Buckley's report).

complete his withdrawal to that place, and therefore can fairly claim a victory. Seldom during the war had there been given so unobstructed a view of the whole field, as spread itself out before our position. Great gaps were made in their ranks by our firing. They would immediately "close up" and again advance. The artillery at every discharge would make great gaps again. Boomer's battery alone fired 429 rounds.[8] Under the cover of night the troops began falling back. 17 long muddy miles lay between us and Knoxville. Seventeen of the longest, weariest miles that it has ever been our misfortune to travel, and many fell asleep along the roadside during the retreat. The 1st Division reach Knoxville about midnight our Division the 2d arrived at daylight next morning.

The following were wounded:

> Sgt. Frank B. Sterner, Co. B
> Pvt. Joshua Raub, Co. B (died November 28)
> Pvt. Benjamin J. Reily, Co. B (died November 28)
> Cpl. William Robinson, Co. C
> Pvt. George E. Peters, Co. I
> Sgt. William S. Mellick, Co. K
> Pvt. Absalom Baldum, Co. K

Nov 17—After marching all night over rough roads and fording many streams, we reached the outskirts of Knoxville at daybreak, halted for about two hours, made coffee. I myself roasted some corn on a shovel and that constituted my breakfast. During the retreat, I fell asleep on my horse and lost my hat. At 9 o'clock A.M. received orders to move my regiment into Knoxville, and took position in the center of line of battle and commenced immediately to throw up rifle pits, useing many cotton bales. Having no means of transportation, we were compelled to leave all of our killed and wounded numbering 242 on the field who of course fell into the hands of the rebels. By the aid of the "contrabands" we succeeded by midnight in having a pretty good line of works and the regiment was moved into it, the very first time in its history that they were ever placed behind anything that afforded any protection to themselves. The balance of the troops were also engaged in the same work, and by midnight we had the city completely encircled with a line of earthworks.

We occupy four prominent hills which command the city as well as the open country to the south of it. Ferrero's division occupies the line from the Holston River to Second Creek, Hartranft's part of the line between First and Second Creeks, [Col. Marshal W.] Chapin's brigade extends from Second Creek over Temperance Hill to near Bell's house, and the brigades of Colonel's [William A.] Hoskins and [John S.] Casement extends to this point to the river and the interior line is occupied by some regiments of loyal Tennesseans. The position on the south side of the river is occupied by Shackelford's cavalry and [Col. Daniel] Cameron's brigade of Brig. Gen. Milo S.] Hascall's division, [Col. James W.] Reilly's brigade in reserve. Our force at this time in Knoxville is about 12,000 effective men. The enemy is estimated at 20,000 to 23,000.

The immediate position of the 51st is on the north side of Gay Street, and the right of the brigade resting near First Creek and connecting with White's line. Fort Sanders is garrisoned by Battery E, Second U.S.A. and Battery D, First R.I.A. supported by the 79th N.Y.V.I. Battery L, Second N.Y.A. occupies the ground of the seminary, supported by four companies of

---

8. Bolton meant Captain Jacob Roemer's Battery L, 2nd NY, which became the 34th NY Battery after November 19.

infantry. Batteries L and M, Third U.S.A. are posted on the bluff overlooking the railroad depot about the center of the line held by the Second Division. The 15th Indiana Battery (3) guns [Captain John C. H.] von Sehlen's, occupy the field works of the 51st. The Powell's house to the left of the Kingston Road has been barricaded and loopholed for musketry, and the house of Mr. Barnes, on the extreme right of the line of the First Division, is occupied by a company of infantry. The skirmish line of our division the 2d is 1 1/8 mile long from flank to flank. This is our position at midnight.[9] What it will be in the morrow is hard to tell.

Nov 18—The day opened with considerable skirmishing between our forces under [Brig.] Gen. [William P.] Sanders and Longstreet advance of dismounted cavalry. The men of the 51st engaged in barricading Gay Street with old carts, wagons, barrels, lumber, and cotton bes. In fact all streets leading into the city are being barricaded, and everything movable is in demand for that purpose. This looks as if we are going to be surrounded. Burnside issued orders to-day that no men must be excused from duty who are able to handle a musket, holding the surgeons strictly responsible.

Nov 19—This morning revealed the stuborne fact that the enemy had thrown up during the night, a parallel line of works to our own. Very heavy firing all day, and some shell thrown into the city. [Pvt. Michael Dillon, Co. C, wounded.]

The whole regiment detailed to build a dam in our immediate front, at First and Second Creeks. The dam across the former was made at the Vine Street bridge. The dam across Second Creek was made at the tunnel by which the creek passes under the railroad and they can only be crossed by bridges. Our position has been very much strengthened, and begin to feel secure and confident. The citizens of the town and all the contrabands within reach have been pressed into the service and relieve the almost exhausted soldiers who have had no rest for more than a hundred hours. But many of the citizens were rebels and worked with a very poor grace, which blistered hands did not tend to improve. Our dams have dammed up the water for several miles and is from five to eight feet deep.[10]

Burnside telegraphed to the commanding officer at Camp Nelson, Ky. directing all stores &c. en route to him, to be turned back, as we are completely surrounded. Prv. John McCoy Co. D was to-day detailed as orderly at 2d Division headquarters. By G.O. 85 Headquarters 9.A.C. no colors except the national colors and battery guidons will be shown on our lines. Night is at hand, and it reveals the fact that we are in a state of siege and there is no communications between our main line and the skirmish pits during the day time. The regular "relief" marches out at 9 P.M. and the men posted at that time remain on duty 24 hours. The enemy to-day from a battery on the Tazewell Road situated about a mile and a half from our main line, threw quite a number of shells into the city.

Nov 20—Was detailed as Division Officer of the Day. Visited the outer lines six times during the night. Regiments still intrenching, and protecting their works by abattis and sheval-de-frise. A selected detail of 15 men from the 51st was sent out as sharpshooters to occupy the vacant houses and mills bordering on the dam. The enemy's offensive lines are beginning to show up, his right approaching the river near Armstrong's house just west of Third Creek. Earthworks on each side seem to grow like magic, but we are doing the most digging. General Field Order No. 30 Army of the Ohio, announces Captain John A. Morris A.Q.M. formerly 1st Lt. Co. E 51st P.V. as Chief Quartermaster of the Army of the Ohio in the field.

---

9. O.R., vol. 31, part 1, 336-7 (Potter).

10. *O.R.*, vol. 31, part 1, 297 (Poe).

Nov 21—The enemy commenced to shell the works the 51st occupied, directing their fire at Von Sehlen's three guns. The gun embracers were lined with cotton bales, and resisted their shots very well. The men behaved splendidly, being the first time in their history of being behind works when fired upon. Not a man left his post.

To-day our lines were made continuous except the gorge between Temperance Hill and Mabry's Hill. Began work on a third line of rifle-pits between Temperance Hill and the river, and commenced the construction of a battery on Flint Hill. It has been raining all day and well into the night, and fears are entertained for the safety of our dam.[11]

Lieut. Geo. Shorkley, 51st P.V. has been announced as Actg. Insp. Genl. on the staff of the Second Division.

Nov 22—Rather quiet to-day, very little firing. A good number of houses are standing in the way for the range of our guns, and a detail of 35 men to be known as houseburners were sent out to-night to destroy them. During the night the pickets of the 2d Maryland were driven in but Hartranft sent out a force and soon retook them without any loss.

As we all feared, our dam gave way and a heavy detail was sent out to rebuild it. Burnside received information that the enemy was constructing a raft at Boyd's Ferry, which they intend to set adrift in the river with the hope that it would carry away our pontoon bridge and break our communications with the south side of the river. Poe, his chief engineer at 5 P.M. commenced the construction of a boom, made by stretching an iron cable across the river above the bridge. The cable was 1,000 feet in length. He used all the chains he could get from the wagons. The boom was borne by wooden floats. Rebels floating trees down the river to destroy our bridge.[12]

Nov 23—Regiment still working on the dam. At 8 1/2 o'clock P.M. it being quite dark and hazy, the enemy suddenly advanced in force on our front near the Clinton Road, poured in a heavy fire, driving our men in and following them up closely. The house burners barely had time to fire the buildings and some of them were taken before they could make their escape. The machine shop and round-house on the railroad occupied by the ordnance department, which contained a good deal of explosive material and prevented any farther advance of the enemy. Our line of skirmishers on the right fell back just far enough to protect their flank. Hartranft advanced his skirmishers through the burning buildings and held his position until morning. Prv. David Clark Co. H was captured to-day. Camp rumor has it that Sherman with some 13,000 troops is at Loudon, on his way to reinforce us and to raise the siege.

When Burnside first occupied Knoxville he captured with it the arsenal which had been established by the rebel government, and was under the command of a rebel Major Reynolds. It consisted of a fine brick building with storehouse, blacksmiths and carriage-makers shops. The engine and stores had been removed by the rebels, but in their hurry to get away they abandoned about 2,000 pikes or spears and some 2,500 pounds of crude niter. This was placed in charge of the ordnance department, as well as the fine machine-shops and foundry of Messers. Shepard, Maxwell & Hoyt, car manufacturers and machinists. The arsenal was under the immediate superintendence of Mr. Charles E. Mallam, and furnished employment to about 50 loyal citizens besides the regular employees of the department. Unserviceable arms was repaired and cleaned, cooking utensils for the troops were cast and finished, gun-carriages and their spare parts were made and repaired; castings made of machinery and tools for the use of the engineer, ordnance, quartermasters and commissary departments,

11. *O.R.*, vol. 31, part 1, 297 (Poe).

12. *O.R.*, vol. 31, part 1, 297 (Poe).

and coffins, arm-chests, packing boxes, &c. The expense to the government was but slight, but the whole thing went up in smoke and fire to-night, and it was a grand sight. The troops were under arms all night.

Nov 24—Not much firing during the day, but during the night the rebels drove in our picket line to the main line in the city. Rumor is that the enemy have thrown a pontoon bridge across the Holston below their line, and are crossing a considerable body of troops. S.O. No. 109 issued to-day, directs that all animals designated as unserviceable will be driven over the pontoon bridge and outside the pickets line and there turned loose.

Nov 25—Detailed as Division Officer of the Day. At 10 o'clock this morning the enemy drove in the 2d Maryland, and our brigade under the command of Lt. Col. Schall ordered to retake the line. Formed on the color line at 2 o'clock A.M. and moved to the front with orders to retake the line before daylight. The night was as dark as pitch. We passed to the rear of the railroad depot, marching through the ruins of the late fires and formed the brigade in line of battle. It was yet too dark, and after a long delay, the order was given when it was quite daylight, and over wrecked buildings, cellars, fallen trees, and stumps and withholding our fire, and with a yell, the line was retaking without the loss of a man. After establishing the line, the brigade withdrew and marched back to their camp.[13]

During the day, this part of the line was strongly reinforced by a detachment of the 23d A.C. To-day the enemy made a desperate attempt to seize the heights commanding the town, but was severely repulsed by Gen. Shackleford's forces. More rumors about a raft being sent down the river to destroy our pontoon bridge, in consequence of which, Poe constructed another boom made of long timbers fastened together at the ends by fifth-chains taken from the wagon trains. This boom was 1500 feet long, and floated in the river above the other and was fastened on each side of the river. By the orders of Burnside regimental commanders are ordered to make a rigid personal inspection of the quarters of their commands and of their wagon trains, and every axe, pick and shovel that is not absolutely necessary for collecting fuel will be immediately turned over to division headquarters.[14]

Nov 26—To-day everything is quiet along the whole line, very little firing. In accordance with the proclamation of the President, to-day will, so far as military operations will permit, be observed by this army as a day of thanksgiving for the countless blessings vouchsafed the country and the fruitful successes granted to our arms during the passed year.[15]

But for all this we are busy strengthening our whole front, and all of our intrenching tools are in use. A cheval-de-frise of pikes has been put in front of Col. Hoskin's position, fastening the pikes in place with telegraph wire. Rumor has it again that Sherman is at Loudon with 20,000 men. G.O. No. 46 from brigade headquarters directs that at least one half of the men not on duty on the skirmish line, are at all times to be in the rifle pits, also that the pits are so enlarged that all the men can remain in them constantly if necessary, and to be in readiness to move at a moments notice, until further orders, and division commanders areinstructed to have a staff officer always on duty in the trenches.

Nov 27—Very quiet to-day all along the line. A large number of men on picket. The enemy continue to be very active on both sides of the river. Some additional artillery fire endulged in

---

13. Parker, *51st PA*, 496-98, wrote that this episode took place on November 24.

14. *O.R.*, vol. 31, part 1, 298 (Poe).

15. *O.R.*, vol. 31, part 3, 248.

by the enemy, but our men are silent. They [the enemy] are vigorously at work on the ridge north of Fort Sanders, and appear to be connecting their works, or rather batteries by a line of rifle-pits.[16] During the night, a great deal of cheering within the enemy's line, and bands playing. Burnside informs Potter, from indications in the movements of the enemy, that some important movement is on foot to-night, and desires that unusual vigilance be displayed to-night by both officers and men in the trenches. Prv's. Robert Hinton, Co.G, and Geo. Buss, Co. K, wounded to-day on the picket line.

Nov 28—Both armies hard at work. The enemy displayed six guns at their position on the south side of river, and opened upon Roemer's battery, throwing an occasional shot at Fort Sanders. In the afternoon we could hear them distinctly chopping trees. At 10 o'clock P.M. the enemy made a furious attack on our pickets in the center of Gen. Ferrero's line, capturing many of them and establishing his line on the crest of the ridge about 80 yards in front of the fort (Sanders). The skirmishing was continued all night, with a slow cannonade from all the guns upon the enemy's right, principally directed upon Fort Sanders. The whole army lay on their arms all night, as it was evident that this was the real point of attack.[17]

The day and night was wet and foggy and generally disagreeable. Lieut. Geo. Shorkley, Co.H, was detailed Actg. Asst. Insp. Genl. and ordered to report to Col. Hartranft, commanding 2d Division.

Nov 29—Detailed as Division Officer of the Day. At 6 A.M. under cover of a fog, the enemy assaulted Fort Sanders (called by the rebels Fort Loudon) moving along the capital of the northwestern bastion. It was a gallant and persistent attack, but it was handsomely repulsed. Prv. James Dunne of Co.D, for the time had been detailed for Benjamin's battery also displayed daring bravery, seizing a worm screw, reached through an embrasure, screwed it into his man, and dragged him into the fort. During the day a flag of truce was sent to Longstreet for permission for him to bury his dead, which ended towards night. Prv. Wm. H. Dougherty Co.H was killed to-day in Knoxville. [Pvt. Robert Hinton, Co. G, wounded.] I made frequent reports to Gen. Burnside during the day and night, as Division Officer of the Day.

Nov 30—All quiet along the whole line. The regiment engaged in building a fort on the hill overlooking the depot. Cotton bales and sandbags are being used. The street is being barricaded with old wagons and carts. A line of rifle-trenches from Sevierville Road to the central hill has been staked out and men are at work on it.

Dec 1—All very quiet, very little firing. All hands except the pickets at work on the sand-bag and cotton fort, which was finished at sundown. We have a great many contrabands at work on the fortification. A line of rifle-pits has been run along the gorge between Temperance Hill and Mabry's Hill, and the troops are hard at work on the south side of the river. During the afternoon large trains belonging to the enemy were seen to move towards the eastward, and we think that the siege will be raised soon.[18] This is the fourteenth day of the siege, and the rations are getting shorter and shorter every day. We learn by courier that Granger[19] has crossed the Hiwassee River in boats at Kincannon's Ferry, working day and night. Corp. Ed. H. Patterson, Co.K, was killed to-day.

---

16. *O.R.*, vol. 31, part 1, 298 (Poe).

17. *O.R.*, vol. 31, part 1, 298 (Poe).

18. *O.R.*, vol. 31, part 1, 300 (Poe).

19. Major General Gordon Granger commanded the Fourth Corps, Army of the Cumberland.

The following order was issued and read on dress parade to-day:

Head-Quarters Ninth Army Corps
Knoxville, Tenn. Dec. 1.1863.
General Order
No. 72

The Commanding General desires particularly to congratulate the officers and soldiers composing the garrison of Fort Sanders, on their gallant conduct during the assault on that Work on the morning of the 29th ult. To Benjamin's Battery, with such portion's of Buckley's and Roemer's as were with them in the Fort, the 79th Regt., New York Vols., the 2d Mich. Vols., and a detachment of the 29th Regt. Mass. Vols. is due the credit of repulsing a picked column of the enemy, killing, wounding, and taking prisoners there from treble their own numbers, beside capturing three stand of colors.

To all the officers and soldiers of the Corps, too much praise cannot be awarded, for the heroism, patience and valor displayed by them, on all occassions for the past three weeks. Whenever you have met the enemy in battle or skirmish you have shown your superiority. The enemy can no longer afford to remain inactive; already large forces are pressing forward to our relief from different points. Should he hazard an assault on our lines before retreating, he will find that his reception at Fort Sanders was a foretaste of what he will receive at every point of our works.

By command of Brig. Gen. R. B. Potter, Nicholas Bowen A.A.G.

The following S. O. was also issued to-day:

Head-Quarters Ninth Army Corps
Knoxville, Tenn. Dec. 1st. 1863.
Special Order
No. 187

The accompanying orders will be distributed promptly. The General commanding the Army recommends Nine cheers be given by the troops in honor of the victory.

By command of Brig. Gen. R. B. Potter
(signed) Saml. Wright, A.A.G.

Official
(signed) G. H. McKibbin. A.A.G.
Official   Lane S. Hart   A.A.A. Genl.

Dec 2—The enemy very quiet. The sand-bag and cotton fort the regiment has been so industriously working on was finished to-day, and von Sehlen's 15th Indiana Battery, which formally occupied the works of the 51st, moved into the new works. The Engineer Battalion and contrabands are still engaged in the rifle-trenches between Temperance Hill and Mabry's Hill, and an epaulement for two guns in the gorge. These were all finished by midnight. We are still at work on the large fort at Bell's house and on the rifle-trenches on the south side of the river.

This is the fifteenth day of the siege. Orders issued to-day to regimental commanders that their forage is used at half rations only. Capt. Jos. K. Bolton is now in command of the Post of Crab Orchard, Ky. Capt. J. M. Linn is ordered by S.O. No. 1 to report to Capt. Geo. H. Laird, commanding Convalescent Camp, for duty at the Post of Crab Orchard. Prv. Daniel Lane, Co. A, was wounded to-day.

Dec 3—Detailed as Division Officer of the Day. Made frequent visits along the line during the day and night. On our rounds, Sergt. John W. Fair, who was my orderly, captured a chicken, and we made sure of one good meal, but it was a wonder to us how it escaped so long. Late in the afternoon, the enemy appear to be moving their trains to the eastward. Hopes are entertained that the siege will soon be raised. We are still at work on both sides of the river.

Dec 4—Our artillery commenced early this morning with some heavy cannonading. The enemy do not reply either with artillery or infantry. Our troops still working a little, but the news of approaching re-enforcements and the movements of the enemy's trains lead us to believe that he will soon abandon the siege. This morning I sent the following report to Col. Hartranft, commanding 2d Division:

> Knoxville Tenn.,
> December 4. 1863.
> Col. John F. Hartranft
> Commanding 2d Division, Ninth Army Corps:
>
> Colonel: I have the honor to make the following report as division officer of the day for the 3d instant: Capt. Joseph H. Haskins, Forty-eight Pennsylvania, commanding pickets of First Brigade, reports to me where had been previously seen the enemy's camp from the top of the Suck flour-mill, has now disappeared; he also reports at 10.30 o'clock P.M. a move of artillery or heavy wagons and trains were heard distinctly moving towards the right; also 1 prisoner captured by a vedette of the Twenty-first Massachusetts, who was sent to headquarters; also at 1.30 o'clock this morning two rockets were seen on the hills opposite his center, and one blank shot fired. Teams and artillery moving on our right and left. Capt. Gaulin, of the Fifty-first Pennsylvania Volunteers, commanding picket-line of the Second Brigade, also reports, as he supposed, the moving of artillery or wagons, between 9 and 10 o'clock A.M. Considerable firing by the enemy in front of the Second Brigade early this morning; more quiet at 8.30.
>
> I am, colonel, your obedient servant.
> Wm. J. Bolton.
> Major and Division Officer of the Day for the 3d instant.

Dec 5—The siege raised at 4 o'clock A.M. by the enemy retreating in the direction of Strawberry Plains. Troops were immediately put in pursuit, the 51st among the number. Quite a number of their pickets were captured, but Longstreet had made good his escape, and the troops returned to their camps.

Surgeon W. H. Church, Medical Director on Burnside's staff, resigned to-day on account of impaired health. Burnside issued the following order to-day:

General Field Orders   Hdqrs. Army of the Ohio.
No. 34   In the Field, December 5. 1863.
   The commanding general congratulates the troops on the raising of the siege. With unsurpassed fortitude and patient watchfulness they have sustained the wearing duties of the defence, and, with unyielding courage, they have repulsed the most desperate assaults. The Army of the Ohio has nobly guarded the loyal region it redeemed from its oppressors, and has rendered the heroic defence of Knoxville memorable in the annals of the war. Strengthened by the experience and the successes of the past, they now, with the powerful support of the gallant army which has come to their relief, and with undoubting faith in the divine protection, enter with the brightest prospects upon the closing scenes of a most brilliant campaign.

By command of Major-General Burnside:
Lewis Richmond,
Assistant Adjutant-General.[20]

Burnside also issued the following:

                              Headquarters Army of the Ohio
                              Knoxville, Tenn. Dec. 5. 1863.
General Field Orders
     No. 36.
   The Army of the Ohio will commemorate the series of victories, all culminating in the redemption of a loyal district, by inscribing on their Colors and Guidons the comprehensive words, expressive of the grand result "East Tennessee"

          By command of Major-General Burnside,
          Lewis Richmond, A.A.G.

Dec 6—This is Sunday morning, and the good news came to camp that the Paymaster, who had all along been in Knoxville during the siege, notified me that he would pay the regiment. I received $297.69.

   During the siege we were pretty hard up for rations for both man and beast. This is a sample of what was issued to each man: one quart of corn-meal for five days; four ounces of sugar and two ounces of coffee; bean-bread, hard, one loaf, weighing forty-two ounces, for four men for one day; two spoonsfull of salt for five days per man; a little fresh beef sometimes, at times about ten inches of pork for five days; two spoonsfull of molasses per man; one-half plug of tobacco every five days, and at times corn issued to the men on the cob. And if a horse or a mule would by chance drop a grain of corn from their feed boxes, it would be eagerly picked up by the soldiers, and the very manure would be searched for corn, and pounded into meal. The horses and mules fared no better. Have seen them eat the ropes, and knaw into the collars for the straw they contained. Their feed boxes and tail-boards of the wagons were not spared. The trees on the streets were cut down for firewood. Horses and mules half-starved were driven to the Holston River, their throats cut and thrown into the river.

---

20. *O.R.*, vol. 31, part 1, 280.

Burnside, as was his custom, had thrown his headquarters flag out of one of the upper windows. This was obnoxious to some of the women of the city. They much preferred to walk in the road in the mud. But he soon stopped that, and had his guard to compell them to walk under it. And it was no uncommon thing for them to spurt their tobacco juice in our faces. They all more or less used the weed, but that was soon stopped.

Our ammunition got very short before the siege was over, and projectiles for our rifle guns were made here. All of us from Burnside down to the last private were in good spirits during the entire siege, and no man thought of retreat or surrender. We were determined to defend the place and many novel plans were devised for the purpose. Skirmishers were supplied with cotton balls saturated with turpentine that in case of an attack at night, were to be lighted and thrown out to uncover an attacking column. Rockets were placed along the lines to be fired for the same purpose. In some places locomotive tracks and driving-wheels were fastened with ropes to stakes within our works, so that in the event of an assault, the ropes could be cut, and the trucks and wheels would roll down the hill. Creeks were dammed up and the flats in our front converted into ponds. Cotton bales were freely used in the construction of our works, and nearly one-half of the troops had two guns each.

Dec 7—The 9th A.C. under Potter and 23d A.C. under [Brig. Gen.] Mahlon D.] Manson, the whole under Gen. Parke, left Knoxville this morning at 9 A.M. in pursuit of Longstreet. Orders were for three days rations in their haversacks, which the 51st did not have, and much less in their stomachs. But off we started leaving our tents standing, marching in the direction of Morristown, Tenn. After a march of 14 miles the regiment went into bivouac some distance from Rutledge. Quartermaster Stephens issued about a pint of corn-meal to each man. Before leaving Knoxville, our division, the 2d, stored all of their baggage at Fort Comstock.

By S.O. No. 96 Asst. Surgeon Charles S. Duffell was detailed to remain at Knoxville in charge of convalescents in camp of Second Division.

Dec 8—Regiment left their bivouac about 10 A.M. marched seven or eight miles, and at 2 P.M. came to a halt near a small creek, and took up quarters in some empty houses near at hand. Here Quartermaster Stephens issued per man, six ounces of flour & two crackers. In the evening, the whole regiment sent out on picket. Parke's headquarters is at or near Flat Creek Bridge.

Dec 9—Detailed as Division Officer of the Day. Regiment left their bivouac at 9 A.M. and after a march of eight miles halted about one mile from Rutledge, some 22 miles from Knoxville. Made shelter for overselves out of fence rails, covered with pines and cedars. Quartermaster Stephens issued to the men one-half pound of corn-meal, and one-fourth pound of beef, for two days per man. Our cavalry has halted at Bean's Station, and the enemy has halted at or near Red Bridge, between Bean's Station and Rogersville. Heavy detail made from regiment for picket duty.

Dec 10—Regiment remained in bivouac at this point all day. The weather very inclement and our shelter very poor. Burnside relieved from command of the Army of the Ohio by Gen. John G. Foster. Potter has men at work here at the mills grinding corn and grain. Enemy trying to capture the working party but have been driven off. Some 400 prisoners from Longstreet army was brought into Knoxville yesterday having been picked up in squads on the French Broad.

Dec 11—Regiment laid here in bivouac all day. Wrote a letter to my mother and sent her $225.00. Foster assumed command of the Army of the Ohio.

Dec 12—Regiment still remaining in bivouac, and doing the usual picketing. One-half pound of flour issued to each man. Received a large mail, the first for six weeks. Lieut. Col. Schall was granted a leave of absence for 30 day and left for home to-day, taking with him a large sum of money the men are sending home. Burnside also left for Cincinnati via Lexington by the Jacksborough and Somerset road. Foster in G.F.O. forbids the troops taking fences for fuel. The order is intended to protect the farmers with their crops.[21]

Dec 13—Regimental inspection. One-half pound of flour issued to each man. The men managed to find some damaged wheat in an out-building, and with the aid of an old coffee mill succeeded in reducing it into some kind of flour.

Dec 14—Regiment received marching orders. A very small amount of sugar and coffee issued to each man, the first for three weeks. Rumor reached our camp that a Union wagon train was captured at or near Clinch Mountain Gap. Prvs. Geo. Crawford and Courtland Dult of Co. B. captured.

Dec 15—Regiment still under orders. Received some letters from home. Left our camp at 9 P.M. in a big hurry, leaving all grub on the fires cooking. Moved through a gorge in the Clinch Mountains. Marched until 2 o'clock next morning and came to a halt in a large cornfield near Blains' Cross-Roads, some 22 miles from Knoxville. Had some skirmishing during the night. The marching was terrible as the mud was knee-deep. Learned that four men of the regiment was captured with the wagon train at Clinch Mountain yesterday. They were as follows: Pvt. Samuel Jones, Co.A, Prv. Abraham Jones, Co. A, Cpl. Chas. M. Henniss, Co.A, Prv. Wm. McIntyre, Co.F. [Also, Pvt. Henry Derr, Co. I, captured at Cumberland Gap.]

Dec 16—Regiment left their bivouac at 9 o'clock A.M. Marched some five miles, formed in line of battle, constructed some crude breastworks out of fence rails, and laid on our arms all night in a drenching rain. It is now learned that the enemy on the 15th captured sixty-eight of our wagons at Clinch Mountain, about forty loaded with sugar and coffee and other stores.

Dec 17—Regiment still occupy their rude breastworks along the road side, lying on their arms all day and night. During the day the rebels succeeded in driving in Wolford's and Sturgis's cavalry. The 51st thrown out as skirmishers and there was considerable of it done during the day, but the regiment stubbornly held their ground, and towards nightfall all was quietness, the enemy's cavalry having withdrawn from our front. Prv. Geo. Meisse Co.G wounded.

Dec 18—Regiment still occupy the same rude breastworks. Skirmishers under Lt. Foster advanced some three miles without much opposition, the enemy falling back, and we are posting out infantry pickets and establishing our troops in camp.

Dec 19—Regiment still occupy the same rude breastworks. During the day Companies D, E, G, H, and I were sent out over the mountains towards Indian Bridge to do vidette duty. Co.I was sent to White's Cross roads leading to Buffalo Creek and Chanfrau's Bridge. Two crackers issued to each man. G.O. No. 46 Headquarters 9.A.C. informs us that the whole corps are to hold themselves in readiness to march at a moments notice, with ten days rations, hard bread, sugar, coffee and beef on the hoof, with the usual amount of ammunition.

Dec 20—Our tents and camp equippage having been sent out to us from Knoxville, the regiment was moved into an adjorning woods where they pitched their tents and are making themselves as comfortable as the surroundings will admit. Two crackers and nothing else was issued to each man to-day.

Longstreet is at Rutledge with a force equal to our own, but shows no disposition to attack us in our position. The high water from rains and the state of the roads impede operations very much, and the men are suffering for want of shoes and clothing. Ammunition is also becoming scarce, and some kinds entirely expended.

---

21. *O.R.*, vol. 31, part 1, 394.

Dec 21—All quiet to-day. My brother Joe, Lt. Brooke and others of the regiment arrived in camp, direct from Crab Orchard. The five companies detailed on picket duty on the 19th returned to their camp this morning, having been relieved by the 35th Mass. They brought in some few prisoners. Corpl. Chas. M. Henniss who was captured at Clinch Mountain made his escape and rejoined his regiment. Dr. Calvin Cutter, surgeon 21st Mass. regiment, was to-day appointed Acting Chief Surgeon of our division by Col. Hartranft.

Dec 22—Regiment remained in camp all day. Wrote several letters home. It has been learned by scouts that the enemy, under cover of the night, retreated to the south side of the Holston River. Prv. Geo. W. Rogers Co.G was to-day detailed to run a mill at Lenoirs.

Dec 23—The whole regiment left camp on a reconnaissance, and returned to camp after dark. Foster's horse fell upon a ledge of rocks and contused his wounded leg, and has confined him to his quarters. Parke is now, and has been in command of the forces in the field. Our demonstration this morning was eight or nine miles up the valley, and the citizens report Powder Spring Gap evacuated, and deserters report that the cavalry has crossed the river.[22]

Dec 24—All very quiet to-day, and regiment remained in camp all day. Wrote some letters. Sturgis engaged the enemy early this morning at Mossy Creek and drove them.[23]

Dec 25—Company drills and dress parade, the first for some time. Sent out this morning for picket duty, four companies to relieve the same number of companies of the 11th N.H. now on picket.

Dec 26—Company drills and dress parade. Parke ordered to send 5,000 men to Strawberry Plains, and to make his headquarters there. The fords to be guarded as far down as Armstrong's Ford. And all the mills on the river road to be kept running, infantry guards to be placed at each mill, with cavalry scouts to give timely warning of the approach of the enemy.[24] Adjt. Geo. Shorkley, having been appointed A.A.I.G. of the 2d Division, 9th A.C., 1st Lt. Wm. F. Campbell Co.H was to-day appointed Adjutant of the regiment.

Dec 27—Regular Sunday morning inspection and dress parade in the evening. In accordance with G.O. No. 190 Department of the Ohio, 1st Lieut. Wm. R. Foster Co.E was detailed recruiting officer for the 51st Penna. Vols. for Veteran Volunteers.

Dec 28—Company drills and dress parade. Very little said in the regiment about re-enlisting for three years.

Dec 29—Was detailed as a member of a Court Martial. Company drills and dress parade.

Dec 30—Attended a meeting of the Court Martial at division headquarters. Dress parade in the evening.

Dec 31—Attended a meeting of the Court Martial. Company drills and dress parade. The situation of the army to-day is: the Fourth and Ninth Corps are at Blain's Cross-roads, and Twenty-third at Strawberry Plains, with one brigade of Sturgis' cavalry at Mossy Creek and Talbott's Station. Longstreet is at Morristown. Regimental inspection and muster for pay.

In accordance with S.O. No. 103, Prv. John A. Halstead, 51st Regt. Vols. {9 month conscrip} arrested as a deserter, and sent to the regiment, is ordered to duty in the regiment to serve out his term of enlistment {9 months} the term to commence on the day he joined the regiment.

---

22. *O.R.*, vol. 31, part 3, 477.

23. Brigadier General Samuel D. Sturgis was in command of the cavalry in East Tennessee.

24. *O.R.*, vol. 31, part 3, 504.

The expenses of arrest and transportation amounting to thirty-nine 60/100 dollars will be charged against him on his pay roll. Captains J. M. Linn, Jos. K. Bolton, Lieut. Brooke, and Orderly Sgts. O. Ortlip Co.A, John Gunsoless Co.G and Harrison Hause Co.H, and Privates Thomas Morton and Isaac Fillman Co.A, Harmon Fisher and John Powell Co.D, and Philip Hates, James Hilbert and Thomas Fay Co.I having made satisfactory explanation before a military commission of absence without leave, have been returned to duty.

1864

Jan 1—All the officers engaged in re-enlisting men for the regiment. Prv. John Sibert Co. B was the first to re-enlist. The headquarters of the corps and troops are at Blain's Cross-Roads, a distance of 18 miles northeast of Knoxville. And our troops are now distributed from Buffalo Creek to Strawberry Plains, and no more forage or subsistence is to be had in the country, and the roads are now almost impassable.

The following named Privates of the 51st Regt. Penna. Vols. temporarily attached to Battery E, 2d U.S. Arty. since Sept. 9, 1863, were relieved from duty with said battery and ordered to report to the commanding officer of this regiment:

Benjamin F. Bolton, Co.A	George M. Aurand, Co.E
Robert Inglis, Co.C	William Achenbach, Co.H
John Dunn, Co.D	Daniel Eichemen, Co.K

The other nine companies to-day were marched to the headquarters of Lt. Bartlett, U.S.A. and acting Commissary of muster and mustered into the U.S. service for three years:

Company A—21 Men

John H. Coulston	Benj. R. Thompson	Jacob H. Moyer
Osman Ortlip	Edward L. Evans	Frank H. Mills
George Ubele	Charles M. Henniss	Levi Bolton
Jesse Herbster	John W. Shillich	William Hoffman
George Bodey	William Barr	George S. Buzzard
Henry Dickinson	Isaac E. Filman	Charles Hansell
James O'Neil	Jacob Oster	Washington Smith

Company B—33 Men

Valentine Stocker	Milton Ackerman	John W. Brunner
John W. Mecker	Enos Schock	William Coltrath
Samuel A. Apple	Samuel F. Knapp	Edward Hill
John W. Beam	Henry Schooly	Thomas P. Miller
Alson Stocker	Matthew Delaney	Christian B.Myers
Conrad Swazer	Edward Bullman	Jno.Obeholzer
Charles S. Knauss	George W. Moser	John Seibert
John M. Wein	Josiah Ackerman	Charles Sharp
Philip A. Barndt	Harrison Ackerman	Thos. Unangst
George Johnson	Adam Buzzard	Daniel W. Vannatta
Nicholas Wooring	Cyrus Werkeiser	Lewis H. Young

Company C—47 Men

George H. Smith	William Bean	George Stout
John W. Fair	Andrew J. Grim	Henry Undercofler
Nathan H. Ramsey	William Kocker	A. Walt

Benjamin F. Miller
Montgomery Smith
Peter Undercofler
William R. Gilbert
Levi W. Shingle
Patrick Kevin
John C. Umstead
Henry Lightcap
A. J. Reed
Hugh Lynch
Benjamin R. Sill
High McLairn

Isaac Fisone
David Long
John Powell
Henry Foreman
William Dignan
William D. Jenkins
John McNulty
John R. Gray
Wm. W. Smith
Isaac Tolan

Francis R. Frey
James L. Seibold
George C. Gutelius
Jno. M. Wierman
Thomas D. Reed
E. G. Maize
Charles Mills
C. Edelman
George Diehl

Howard Bruce
Henry Jacobs
A. H. Fillman
Benj. F. White
Um. B. Hart
J. W. Reed
J. G. Guder
Wm. H. Fil
Geo. W. Hiltner
Silas Kelley
Wm. H. Yerger
A. Casselbeery

Joseph Cornog
Michael Dillon
Samuel Dean
H. D. Espenship
James W. Elliott
David Espenship
Charles R. Fox
George McGinley
Andrew J. O'Neil
George Pickup
Jacob B. Rinker
James Sullivan

Company D—39 Men

Albert Wood
Joseph Anderson
Noble Creighton
William Essick
John R. Fleck
Alfred R. Gray
John Johnson
Elwood Lukens
Charles Lysinger
Samuel McDade

Company E—27 Men

Jno. H. Sortman
Cyrus A. Easton
Frank S. Shaffle
Jno. W. Sheckler
Tho. S. Alauck
George M. Aurand
George H. Beers
James P. Cornelius
Thomas H. Claphan

Company F—36 Men

Jno. J. Scholl
Jos. Fizone
M. Hiltner
J. W. Truscott
Thomas B. Yerger
Rob. B. Lindsay
E. R. Worth
J. Wood
Wm. C. Hansell
W. Allen
H. K. Adleman
M. Boyer

H. P. Wood
Mark L. Yerger
Wm. H. R. Fox
William Gunn
Frank Grubb
Ellwood Hamilton
Henry Jago
Benjamin Johnson
Jacob Keely
Benjamin Kooker
George W. Lightcap

Dennis O'Neil
Barney O'Donnell
Thomas D. Smith
William P. Schall
Hiram Vanfossen
John L. McCoy
Andrew Fair
John Dunn
Albert List

Isaac Dobby
Jas. McDunkle
Jacob Miller
S. M. Gregor
S. Searless
P. Strubble
D. High
E. Sprowles
Levi H. Ammons

J. Callender
E. Charles
M. H. Dunn
E. M. Johns
W. Kulp
R. Mckevin
E. W. Reed
A. Wentzel
J. Wisler
G. D. Williams
S. D. Weidner
J. C. Young

Company G—22 Men

J. Gunsalles	L. Cartingval C.	B.Stonerod
J. J. Peters	S. Moore	George Decker
J. Ammerman	T. McCafferty	W. Heichel
J. Casker	B. McHarney	E. Shannon
R. Hinton	P. Powers	G. Dumont
J. E. Wilt	N. Rolley	D. Youts
L. Bowers	G. Wertz	D. C. Ammerman
J. Heinel		

Company H—20 Men

H. McClure	B. Dietrick	J. Hartz
D. G. Brown	R. Baker	T. P. Mars
G. Breon	J. Moore	J. Philiger
H. Hause	A. Bernade	P. Smith
H. J. Lingerman	G. W. Carey	J. H. Smith
A. Durst	J. Pike	F. Smith
H. Fogleman	A. Henry	

Company I—30 Men

Thomas H. Parker	Geo. W. S. Pennell	Sam. E. Bradbury
George W. Patterson	Lewis Patterson	Charles Baley
John R. Davis	John M. Engle	Thomas Cornog
George Carney	James Tinney	Edward Doyle
Stephen S. Davis	J. J. Tomkins	Henry Clay Davis
James Cameron	James Chase	Charles V. Evans
William Pope	Albert H. Bisbing	George W. Fulton
Philip Hattel	Frederick Holbine	Thomas Rinehart
Michael Harrington	Francis R. Keating	Thomas Troy
James R. Hibbert	John Murphy	Abraham Wampole

Company K—30 Men

J. Frayburger	J. Gibson	M. S. Adams
J. Hawk	S. Odenwilder	W. D. Ritter
F. B. Sterner	J. Barnhart	J. Babcock
J. Vanlew	C. E. Cole	S. Crossgrove
D. W. Eichman	F. Truxell	A. Frey
J. C. Diller	J. P. Huber	H. Gangwer
Theo. Moses	J. Sutton	W. R. Logan
Uriah Dean	D. Shingle	F. Schep
F. S. Moyer	J. Truxell	W. H. Vogel
T. C. Pierce	T. Foster	J.Winegarden

A-21, B-33, C-47, D-39, E-27, F-36, G-22, H-20, I-30, K-30, Total-305. From this date the regiment became a Veteran organization, with recruiting going on.[25]

Jan 2—Detailed a member of a general Court Martial to meet at 2d Division headquartes 9th A.C. at 10 o'clock A.M. on the 4th inst. A few more men enlisting.

Jan 3—Recruiting still going on. Two (2) ears of corn on the cob issued to each man to-day. Seven men detailed from the regiment to go to Strawberry Plains as guard to supply train, also two masons detailed to report at division headquarters.

25. List follows Parker, *51st PA*, 511-13.

Jan 4—Attended a meeting of the general Court Martial. A few men re-enlisted to-day. Notice received that men who have served less than two (2) years are not entitled to the hundred ($100) dollars bounty authorized by Act of Congress. They can however be re-enlisted as veteran volunteers, and will receive ($300) dollars bounty and (30) days furlough. Those who do not re-enlist will be required to serve out their term of service in some other regiment of their own state and of their own selection. Parke, commanding forces in the field, has been authorized to furlough one regiment from each brigade who have re-enlisted as veteran volunteers after the sixth inst.

Jan 5—Attended a meeting of the general Court Martial. Still a few more men re-enlisting.

Jan 6—Attended a meeting of the general court-martial. A very heavy snow storm has set in. Lt. Bartlett, Commissary of Muster, issued the following:

Circular.

In consequence of the impossibility of procuring blanks, for the Muster of Veteran Volunteers the necessary rolls will not be made out until the regt's. arrive at some station across the mountains where they can be obtained; meanwhile, Commanders of regiments will cause the men, (remustered), of their commands to sign the following on a sheet of paper.

We the undersigned, "to have been mustered into the United States' service to serve for three years or during the war," to date from January 1st 1864, that though the muster rolls have not been made out we do not, on the account consider our obligations any the less binding, and that we will serve the United States honestly and faithfully during the term for which we have re-enlisted. The Regt's can, after signing to the above be sent home at such times as the General Commanding shall select and their papers will be made out as soon as practicable. After crossing for the East, these tests will be immediately forward to this office.

This was immediately complied with by the men signing their names, town or ward in which they lived, county, and state.

Jan 7—Snow still continues. The one coffee mill is going night and day grinding corn. Asst. Surg. J. B. Rineholdt announced the senior asst. surgeon of our brigade. Was ordered to detail one corpl. and three men for guard to prisoners of war in General Hospital.

Jan 8—The general Court Martial adjourned to meet on the 11th inst. Burnside has been assigned to duty by the Secretary of War to recruit and fill up the old regiments of the Ninth Corps, to increase said corps to a strength of 50,000 men for such services as the War Department may specially designate. The recruitment to be conducted in the New England States and New York, also in Michigan and Pennsylvania. Burnsides headquarters is now in New York. I received the following just as I was about to retire for the night:

Hd Qrs. 2d Brig. 2d Div. 9th Army Corps.

Major.–From the best information (and upon good authority) I can get, the Regt. will be ordered off before many days elapse. There will be no shoes drawn whatever as there are none in the Dept. and Col. H. suggests that the men who are almost shoeless, get raw hide and fix them so as to wear to Camp Nelson, where an outfit will be drawn in full.

Very Respectfully,
Lane S. Hart.

Jan 9—Was very busy all day and well into the night in signing the discharge papers of the men. Very cold and still snowing.

Jan 10—Still busy signing discharge papers and making ready for our homeward march. Men busy in making raw hide shoes.

Jan 11—Court Martial adjourned to meet at the call of the President. Men are quite shoeless, the hides that come off the cattle in the morning, by night are manufactured into moccasins. Still busy making out and signing discharge papers, muster rolls, inspection and requisition, ordnance and quartermaster returns &c.

Jan 12—Still busy signing papers, and the men busy at their moccasins. The weather very cold and the rivers all very high. Everything is eaten out north of the Holston River and up to Mossy Creek, and we are destitute of bread, coffee, and sugar.

S.O.No.12 Head Quarters Department of the Ohio, directs Parke to order home for furlough one-third of those regiments yet remaining in his command that have re-enlisted as veteran volunteers. All of our men who have been detailed on special duty are being returned to the regiment.

Jan 13—Still busy on regimental papers. About 12 o'clock at night I received the orders to prepare to leave Blain's Crossroads for home, which order was immediately communicated to the men, who were all at that time asleep in their tents, and they of course made the woods merry with their yelling.

During the day forty men from the 48th Penna. Vols. was assigned to the regiment until further orders, they not having re-enlisted, and the 48th was ready to start for home. I immediately assigned them to companies E, H, D and K. Their names are as follows with the letter of their companies to which they belonged:

A	**F**	Crawford Bennie
Charles Goodman	Charles W. Haines	John M. Howell
Oliver Williams	Cyrus Hains	William Davis
B	Edward G. Pugh	Marlin Acorn
Philip D. Hughes	John Philips	Wm. V. B. Kimmel
Samuel Stouck	**G**	Peter Smith
George Evans	James C. Meiss	John H. C. Heffner
Joseph Johnson	Mathusalem Bergen	J. F. Wildermouth
Jacob Fuskly	Thomas Clark	Allen Reock
Joseph Brooks	John S. Clemons	Samuel F. Rehl
Philip Carlon	John Wonders	Alfred Forney
Matchen Hume	Robert Reid	Michael Scott
John Howels	John Hutton	**I**
Frederick Knittler	**H**	John Moyer
E	Jacob Weise	**K**
John Breeman	John Bam	Philip M. Kever

Jan 14—Attended a meeting of the General Court Martial at division headquarters, finished up all the business and adjourned sine die.

S.O.No.14 from division headquarters received this morning directs that the commanding officers of the 45th and 51st Penna. regiments make suitable preparations and proceed with their respective commands as soon as possible to the State of Penna., there to report through the Governor of the State to the Superintendent of the recruiting service for furlough and reorganization. The regiments will march with six days' rations, and forty rounds of ammunition per man. All animals belonging to the U.S. will be turned over to the Q.M. Dept. excepting a sufficient number for the transportation of officers baggage. Those to be turned over to the Quartermaster at Camp Nelson, Ky. on arrival at the nearest point where Rail Road transportation can be procured. The regiments will march via Cumberland Gap, Barboursville, Loudon, and Camp Nelson. The Quartermasters Dept. will furnish the necessary transportation. All men of the regiments not re-enlisting as Veteran Volunteers together with all men of other re-enlisted regiments transferred by Special Order No.10 and 11 from these Hd.-Qrs. will be assigned to duty in such other regiments as division commanders may direct. Division Head-Quarters to be informed when the regiments are ready to move. We have plenty of ammunition to comply with this order but where the six days rations are to come from God only knows.

A detail of (30) men for picket duty made from the regiment, to report at 2d Brigade Hd.Qrs. to-morrow morning. Later in the day the order was countermanded and the detail will come from the 2d Md.

Jan 15—Capt. Bisbing who had been in command of the regiment during my attendance on the Court Martial was relieved to-day by myself assuming command. Worked all day and well into the night on the official papers, which must be done before leaving for home. Took time to write a letter to my mother. The men are jubilent at the prospect of getting home.

S.O. No.12 from 2d Div. Hd.-Qrs. and S.O. No.6 from 2d Brg. Hd.-Qrs. relieved from detached duty from the several departments seventy-four (74) men, who are ordered to report to the regiment for duty. The same S.O. No.12 that the forty (40) men from the 48th Penna. Vols. who were assigned to the 51st on the 13th with the following named members of the 51st Pa. Vols. who did not re-enlist, be assigned to the 11th New Hampshire regiment for duty:

A

Thomas B. Doud
Thomas Merton
Joseph N. Lewis
Edwin Kellischner
Charles Fix
Theodore H. Gilbert
Adam W. Yeager
Benjamin F. Bolton
Jesse Johnson
Jacob Rittenhouse
Patrick Hammel

B

Samuel Moore
Allan Clifton
William H. Deihl
Jacob H. Sweeney
John Weidnecht
Samuel Weidnecht
Israel Crocket
Jackson Bullman
Michael Henning

John H. Deihl
Charles Sheets
Thomas Moser
William A. Smith
Henry Poff
Charles Ricker
Aaron Thatcher
Henry Thompson
John A. Halstead
Aaron Lattig
Hiram Woodring

C

George W. Breish

D

Walter M. Thompson
John Sutch
Charles Widger
Harman G. Fisher
Francis Yeager
Hunter Smedley
Mifflin Smedley
Isaiah Smedley

Henry C. Moore
Hiram C. Fisher

E

Lewis J. Benner
James T. Kelley
Isaiah Henitsman
William S. Sholley
Joseph A. Moll

F

Isaac Detwiller
William Gerhart
Frederick Kremer
Samuel L. Tarrence

G

George Cox
George W. Roodgers
George Meisse
John F. Deistine
James Elder

H

R.A.M. Harmer
Henry C.McCormick

Henry B. Wetzell	Samuel S. McEwen	Samuel Moyer
Wm. Aauchbaugh	**I**	William Buoy
David Yoder	Chas. Powers	Thos. J. Arbuckle
Robert W. Passell	Henry Derr	Samuel Stidinger
John C. Leaman	Josh. Wharton	Philip Richards
John Moore	Edward R. Wilfong	Daniel Sheets
Thomas Weaver	**K**	Mike Shires
Thomas Hollen	David Mills	Phil. Bratton
Wm. F. Christie	Christian Sheets	

I received late this evening from div. headquarters orders to turn over all surplus arms and equipment of the regiment to the division ordnance officer and ordered to see that the teams are loaded as lightly as possible, surplus baggage and mess chests cannot be taken.

Jan 16—Finished up all my official papers. All the blank leaves in our regimental books and all the foolscap and letter paper of all the officers were collected to print our blanks, as we were not in a position to get them from the government. S.O. No.7 directs Capt. Lane S. Hart, Act. Asst. Adj. Genl. of the 2d Brig. 2d Div.; Capt. Wm. Allebaugh, Act. Asst. Insp. Genl. 2d Brig. 2d Div.; Asst. Surg. J. B. Rineholdt of the 2d Brig. 2d Div.; to report to their respective regiments.

Jan 17—Wrote several official communications to the Chief of Ordnance Gen. Balch[26] at Washington. The men are all engaged in washing all their underclothing and patching up all rips, and making all preparations for leaving for home to-morrow morning. Towards night two ears of corn on the cob was issued to the men and the old coffee mill was in operation from that time until morning grinding up the corn. Snow is falling and is now four or five inches deep, and bitter cold is the air and the bleak winds are blowing a hurricane through the leafless trees in the woods, and the smoke and fire is blowing in all directions.

Jan 18—The regiment broke camp at 6 o'clock A.M. loaded up baggage &c, at 7 A.M. bade farewell to Blains' Cross-roads and through the mud, rain and snow, started on our long march of 191 miles, with two ears of corn in our haversacks, partly ground, with very little sugar, coffee or hard bread, but with it all the men are cheerful and happy at the thoughts of home.

The morning opened up cold and bitter, and as the sun became stronger, the snow melted, and made the marching in the raw hide moccasins anything but pleasant, and finally rain set in which made it more disagreeable. After a march of some 18 miles we came to a halt about 3 P.M. pitched our tents and went into bivouac in a woods on the road leading to Tazewell, Tenn., built fires, dried our clothing, cooked something to eat, and went to bed early for a good rest for an early start in the morning.

S.O. No.18 directs the C.O. at Loudon to arrest Prv. George Rogers Co.G 51st Regt. Penna. Vols. and deliver him under guard to the C.O. of 9th A.C. for trial.

Jan 19—We left our bivouac in a blinding snow storm at 6 1/2 A.M. during the march crossed Clinch River, and after a march of 18 miles, came to a halt at 4 P.M. and went into bivouac in a pine woods surrounded by the Clinch Mountains, and within three miles of Tazewell. During this days march, our baggage train broke down, but reached camp at nightfall. Posted a line of pickets around the camp and had a good nights rest. In the night I was awakened by a courier from Cumberland Gap with a message as follows:

---

26. Brigadier General George D. Ramsey was Chief of Ordnance at this time.

Cumberland Gap, Jan. 19. 1864.

Major Bolton--The Post Commander Lt. J. R. Maher has promised me to issue a little coffee & sugar. I think that after you are away from Cumberland Gap 2 days that you will be able to take all the rations that are left, divide them to the men, take with you forage for your horses, and have the teams, that is if the teams' delay your marching. Beat the 45th if you can. I think they have stopped to grind flour. You may be able to get coffee &c at Barboursville, Ky.

I am yours &c

J. F. Hartranft.

Jan 20—We left our bivouac at 6 3/4 o'clock A.M. passed through Tazewell and came to a halt after a march of 16 miles at 3 P.M. within 2 miles of Cumberland Gap, and went into bivouac along the roadside for the night, throwing out pickets for the protection of our camp. Our trains late in reaching camp. "Stevie," our quartermaster, this evening issued a little corn to the men.

Jan 21—We left our bivouac at 6 1/2 o'clock A.M. crossed over Cumberland Gap and at night reached Cumberland Ford, and crossed it, and after a march of 18 miles went into bivouac at 5 o'clock P.M. Threw out pickets for the protection of the camp.

Jan 22—We left our bivouac at 7 o'clock A.M. and during the day passed through Barboursville, Ky., and after a march of 17 miles went into bivouac one mile beyond the village about 4 o'clock P.M. Posted pickets for the protection of our camp.

Jan 23—We left our bivouac at 6 o'clock A.M. and after a march of 18 miles came to a halt at 3 P.M. one mile beyond Laurel Bridge. Posted the usual pickets for the protection of our camp.

Jan 24—We left our bivouac at 6 o'clock A.M. During the day passed through Loudon and Pitman's Cross-roads, and after a march of 14 miles came to a halt three miles beyond about 2 P.M. and went into bivouac. Posted the usual pickets.

Jan 25—We left our bivouac at 5 o'clock A.M. crossed over the Little Rockcastle River over Log and Wild Cat Mountains, crossed over the Big Rockcastle River, passed the Two Caves, and after a march of 23 miles came to a halt at 4 o'clock P.M. and went into bivouac one mile beyond Mount Vernon. Several officers and myself took supper and breakfast, and occupied the parlor floor for the night, of a rebel Doctors, who was in the rebel army.

Jan 26—We left our bivouac at 6 o'clock A.M. passed through Crab Orchard and after a march of 16 miles went into bivouac about 1 o'clock P.M. some distance beyond Crab Orchard. The regiment has been on quarter rations from November 11/63 until to-day, and had only received one full days rations from October 2d/63 up to this date, nearly four months. We are now making up for it as we have reached a land of plenty.

Jan 27—We left our bivouac at 5 o'clock A.M. passed through the town of Lancaster and after a march of 22 miles came to a halt and went into bivouac at Camp Dick Robinson about 4 o'clock P.M. Being somewhat acquainted with Judge Lusk I stopped on the way and dined with him. He and his family were good Union people. The regiment had done some guard duty on his plantation when we previously held that part of the country. On my reaching our camp in the evening, Col. Dick Robinson invited me to dine with him, and spent a pleasant evening.

Jan 28—We left our bivouac at 6 o'clock A.M. During the day passed through Bryantsville, crossed the Kentucky River at Hickman's Bridge, and went into bivouac, having marched 15 miles during the day.[27]

27. Parker, *51st PA*, 519, wrote that these events occurred on January 29.

Jan 29—We left our bivouac at 6 o'clock A.M. and after a march of six miles came to a halt at Camp Nelson, and went into bivouac. During the day drew from the government a complete outfit for each man in the regiment, turned over to the quartermaster of the post our teams, such as they were. The poor mules could hardly stand on their feet. This march was accomplished in 12 days, a distance of 191 miles. Lt. Col. Schall, having reported for duty, assumed command of the regiment. The regiment took up their line of march to Nicholasville, and at 3 o'clock P.M. embarked on the cars of the Kentucky Central railroad and in the evening left for Covington traveling all night.[28]

Jan 30—We arrived in Covington, Ky. early in the morning, disembarked from the cars and marched to the Barracks, and at 12 o'clock M. marched through Covington to the wharf, embarked on board of the Steamer *Queen City*, crossed the Ohio River to Cincinnati and marched through the city to the Barracks, where the regiment took quarters while they remained in the city, while the officers made their headquarters at the hotels. Made my home at the Clifton House.[29]

Jan 31—To our utter dismay, we have just learned that all of our rolls that we had spent so much time on, are all wrong, and new ones will have to be made out, which will require some four days. The 21st and 29th Mass. Vols., 45th, 48th, 50th, 51st, and 100th Penna. Vols., 2d and 8th Mich. Vols., 46th and 51st N.Y. Vols., and 2d Md. have re-enlisted and are all on their way home for reorganization.

Feb 1—The field officers of the regiment paid, I receiving $299.00. All the companies engaged in making out new rolls and all the expert penmen in each company pressed into service.

Feb 2—Companies all hard at work on their rolls.

Feb 3—Companies still hard at work on their rolls. Regimental inspection and parade. And dress parade in front of the Clifton House in the evening.

Feb 4—Companies still hard at work on their rolls. Company drills, and dress parade in the evening.

Feb 5—The rolls are completed nine to each company, and we are now waiting for the paymaster. Company drills and dress parade.

Feb 6—The paymaster showed up early this morning and the men received their full pay, and all allowances and about 9 o'clock P.M. formed line and marched to the Little Miami Railroad Depot, and at midnight left Cincinnati for Pittsburg, in a heavy snow and rain storm. Traveled all night.

Feb 7—Changed cars at Crestline, took supper at Alliance and reached Pittsburg at 10 o'clock P.M. Disembarked from the cars, formed line and marched to the Union Refreshment Saloon and had our suppers, provided for by the citizens, and after satisfying the inner man, marched back to the depot and embarked again on the cars, and rested ourselves the best we could.

Feb 8—Left Pittsburg at 3 o'clock A.M. for Harrisburg arriving there after dark, the regiment taking up quarters in the Soldiers Refreshment Saloon where supper was supplied to them. The officers took up quarters at the hotels.

Feb 9—Left Harrisburg at 7 A.M. for Norristown with Companies A, C, D, F and I. The other companies at the same time proceeded to their individual homes. The Norristown companies

---

28. Parker, *51st PA*, 519, stated that the regiment arrived at Camp Nelson on January 30.

29. Parker, *51st PA*, 520, wrote that these events took place on January 31.

arrived at Bridgeport at 1 P.M. immediately formed line on DeKalb Street, and proceeded by the Chief Marshal, Capt. Rob. E. Taylor, with the following escort, to Norristown:

Burgess and Town Council of Norristown
Burgess and Town Council of Bridgeport
Carriages containing sick and wounded soldiers
Carriages containing 35 little girls singing patriotic and national airs
Citizens on horseback under the command of Capt. Haws
Kulpsville Brass Band
Norristown Hose Company
Norristown Cornet Band
Montgomery Hose Company
Liberty Cornet Band
Humane Engine Company
Co.E, 95th Regt. P.V., Capt. H. Oscar Roberts
Orginal band of the 51st, under the leadership of Lt. Col. Geo. W. Arnold
Discharged members of the 51st P.V.

The five companies of the 51st P.V.V. from Montgomery County, containing 188 men, rank and file, headed by Col. Hartranft and Lieut. Col. Schall

"Iron Workers" of Norristown and Conshohocken
Puples of Treemount Seminary, headed by Principal Mr. John W. Lock
Norristown Encampment I.O.O.F.
Martial Music
Union League of Norristown and L. Merion

The line moved across the upper bridge to Norristown; thence along DeKalb Street to Egypt, down Egypt to Franklin; countermarch up Egypt to Markley; countermarch down Egypt to Swede; up Swede to Oak; down Oak to DeKalb; down DeKalb to Reiff's market house, and after a speech of welcome by B. E. Chain Esq. the regiment set down to a splendid collation provided for them by the citizens of Norristown. Triumphal arches were erected in front of the Public Square, at the Humane Engine House, and in front of Gen. Schall's residence. Complimentary resolutions were adopted by the citizens in town meeting and the Union League, and a fine poem by Octavia, "Welcome Home!" dedicated to the regiment. The decorations were fine, and in fact everything was done to make things pleasant for us.

Major General Ambrose E. Burnside
(Source: author's collection)

Third State Color, issued to the regiment in July 1864
(Source: PA Capitol Preservation Committee)

Second State Color, captured at Spotsylvania, May 12, 1864
(Source: PA Capitol Preservation Committee)

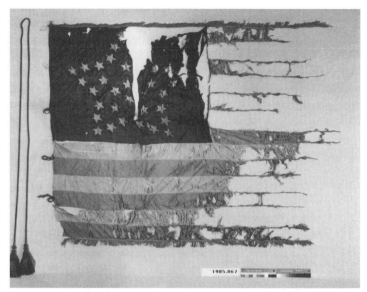

National Color, 1861 presentation to the 4th PA, then used by the
51st until September 1862
(Source: PA Capitol Preservation Committee)

Regimental Color, 1861 presentation to the 4th PA, badly damaged at Antietam
(Source: PA Capitol Preservation Committee)

National Color, March 1864 presentation, captured at Spotsylvania, May 12, 1864
(Source: PA Capitol Preservation Committee)

Surgeon William C. Shurlock

Captain Joseph K. Bolton
Company A

Captain John H. Coulston
Company A

Lieutenant John H. Genther
Company B

Sergeant Freeman Davis
Company D

Captain William R. Foster
Company E

Lieutenant John A. Morris
Company E

Captain Robert E. Taylor
Company F

Lieutenant Joseph C. Reed
Company F

Lieutenant Howard Bruce
Company F

Lieutenant Allen H. Fillman
Company F

Major Lane S. Hart

Corporal Thomas B. Berger
Company F

Lieutenant George B. Campbell
Company G

Captain James M. Linn
Company H

Captain George Shorkley
Company H

Captain George W. Bisbing
Company I

Lieutenant George Schall
Company I

Corporal John J. Schall
Company I

Private Edwin W. Reed
Company F

Corporal James Y. Shainline
Company I

Private Samuel Royer
Company K

Corporal Jacob F. Cole
Company K

Lieutenant William F. Campbell
Company H
(Source: Robert T. Lyon)

Brigadier General Jesse L. Reno
(Source: US Army Military History
Institute, MASS-MOLLUS Collection)

Colonel John F. Hartranft

Captain Peter A. Gaulin
Company G

Captain John R. Gilliland
Company G

Sergeant William B. Hart
Company F

Lieutenant Mark Supplee
Company I

Lieutenant Thomas J. Lynch
Company C

First State Color

Chapter 11

The Ninth Army Corps

February 10–May 3, 1864

The 51st remained at home recruiting and enjoying a furlough until it reassembled at Camp Curtin on March 10. Soon thereafter, the regiment was sent to Annapolis, where the newly reorganized Ninth Corps was forming. In late April, the corps marched from Annapolis to northern Virginia to support the Army of the Potomac in its spring offensive against General Robert E. Lee and the Army of Northern Virginia.

Feb 10 —From this date until the 9th day of March the companies were all engaged in recruiting and filling up their depleted ranks. On the 22d of February the regiment formed in line in front of the Montgomery House, and made a street parade. On the 27th of Feb. the companies had recruited as follows: Co. A 36 men; Co.F 25 men; Co.D 7 men; Co.C 20 men; Co.I 5 men; Total 93 men. On the 25 of Feb. Mr. Saml. Jamison[1] gave a supper to the officers of the regiment, and one to the privates at the Montgomery House by the citizens.

Feb 16—Col. Hartranft issued the following:

> Headquarters 51st P.V.V.
> Norristown, Pa. February 16/64.
> Special Order No. 30.
>
> Capt. Wm. Allebaugh Co.C 51st regt. P.V.V. is authorized to received from Brig. Gen. Gibbon[2] at Philadelphia all recruits for the 51st Regt. P.V.V.
> He will take charge of such recruits as may be turned over to him by Brig. Gen. Gibbon and proceed with them to Norristown, Pa. and there report them to the officer commanding the regiment.
> By command of
> Col. J. F. Hartranft
> Geo. Shorkley Adjt.

---

1. Samuel Jamison was an Irish native who came to Norristown in 1828 to superintend the city's first cotton factory. In 1837 he erected a spinning mill; several of his sons joined in this business.

2. Brigadier General John Gibbon, on detached service from the Second Corps, was at this time in command of the draft depot in Philadelphia.

Mar 3—In accordance with S.O.No.18 issued at Head-Quarters 9th A.C. New York, Capt. J. M. Linn Co.H, 51st P.V.V. was detailed on Special Recruiting Service for the 9th A.C. and ordered to report in person to Capt. J. A. Morris A.Q.M. chief of recruiting service for 9th A.C. in Penna. at Harrisburg for instructions by the order of Gen. Burnside.

Mar 8—By S.O. No.110, War Dept., the 1st Regiment Mich. Sharpshooters have been assigned to the 9th A.C. by S.O. No.55 and will be placed en route without delay, for the depot of the 9th A.C. at Annapolis, Md. The same order announces as a depot and rendezvous for such troops of the 9th A.C. Maj. Gen. Burnside, U.S. Volunteers, commanding, as have been, or may be, ordered to that point. New organizations in the respective states, now or hereafter to be assigned to the 9th A.C. will, so soon as their recruitment is completed, be placed en route to the depot in question.[3]

Mar 9—Surg. Wm. C. Shurlock was transferred from the 100th P.V. to the 51st P.V.

Mar 10—Agreeably to orders, the time of their furlough having expired, five companies A, C, D, F, and I of the regiment left Norristown this morning for Harrisburg. They were formed in line about half-past 7 o'clock in front of the Public Square by Lt. Col. Schall. An immense concourse of people were on hand. Having formed in line, they were marched down to the front of Col. James Boyd's office, where Major Wm. H. Yerkes, on behalf of the Committee of Resception, and the people of the Borough, addressed them, and presented, in a neat and appropriate speech, a beautiful stand of colors. They were received on behalf of the reg't. by Lt. Col. Schall, with a few brief and patriotic remarks. This stand consisted of a National and a state flag, with two "markers" with the number of the regiment upon them.

After the presentation was over, the regiment took up the line of march and moved across the river to Bridgeport, where the cars were in waiting for us. In a few minutes we were all on board, and off we started for Harrisburg, arriving there at 2 o'clock P.M. and immediately proceeded to Camp Curtin, where we found the other five companies awaiting us. Sibley and A. tents were issued to us. They were soon pitched and the old routine of camp life began with us again.[4]

Mar 11—Company drills and dress parade. Recruiting still going on in all the companies.

Mar 12—I received a leave of absence and went to Norristown on recruiting business for the regiment.

Mar 13—Company drills and dress parade.

Mar 14—My leave of absence having expired I returned to camp. Usual drills and dress parade. The following was issued to-day:

Nashville, Tenn., March 14.1864.

Major General Burnside.
New York:
I have ordered the Ninth Army Corps from Knoxville to Annapolis and requested the Secretary of War to direct the veterans to rendezvous at that place. Please send this order to all regiments of the corps about to return to the field.

U. S. Grant,
Lieutenant-General.

---

3. *O.R.*, vol. 33, 657.

4. Parker, *51st PA*, 531-2, wrote that the regiment left for Harrisburg on March 9.

This order ends all of our connection with the Army of the Ohio. [Major General John M.] Schofield has been ordered to hasten the movement of the corps.

Mar 15—Company, regimental drills and dress parade. Grant has ordered Burnside to leave the 20-pounder Parrotts of Benjamins' battery also the horses and harness of the same, as well as all the horses and harness of all the other batteries belonging to the Ninth Corps; as they can be replaced at Annapolis. The corps is also to leave without its transportation. By S.O. No. 118 War Department, on the expiration of their furloughs, all veteran troops of the Ninth Army Corps, Maj. Gen. Burnside U.S.V. commanding, will be sent to the depot of the Ninth Corps at Annapolis, Md.[5]

Mar 16—Company, regimental drills, and dress parade. Grant from his headquarters at Nashville, Tenn., has ordered Parke to report immediately in person to Burnside in New York and Brig. Gen. O. B. Willcox assumed command of the corps.[6]

Mar 17—Company drills. All the Penna. troops now here in Harrisburg was reviewed by Gen. Burnside. I received a leave of absence and went to Norristown on recruiting purposes.

Mar 18—Company, regimental drills and dress parade.

Mar 19—Company drills and regimental inspection. My leave of absence having expired I returned to Harrisburg. Regiment received orders to break camp to-morrow morning to leave for Annapolis. The 9th Corps has reached Knoxville and is waiting transportation. Col. Hartranft in G.O. No. 1 assumed command of the Depot for the concentration of the troops of the 9th A.C. at Annapolis, and announces his staff, Lane S. Hart and Geo. Shorkley of the 51st P.V.V. among the number.

Mar 20—Regiment broke camp and left at 10 o'clock A.M. marched through Harrisburg and crossed the Susquehanna River and took the cars of the Northern Central Railroad at Fort Washington for Baltimore, arriving there at 7 P.M. Disembarked and marched to the Washington Depot, and took supper at the Union Refreshment Saloon. There being no transportation ready for us, we remained there all night sleeping in the cars and depot.

Mar 21—Our baggage unloaded and taken to the Boston steamship wharf, put on board of the steamer *Georgiana*, the regiment following soon after and at 10 A.M. steamed down the river into Chesapeake Bay, arriving at Annapolis, Md. at 2 P.M. Disembarked and marched through the city to the barracks at Camp Parole, the same ground we had occupied in 1861.62.

The 48th Penna. arrived here on the 19th. Yesterday arrived the 21st Mass. 6th N.H. and 45th Penna. and to-day besides ourselves the 50th Penna. 1st Mich. Sharpshooters with one company of Indians.

Mar 22—A very heavy snow storm set in to-day and continued all day, very cold, men keeping within their tents.

Mar 23—Moved our quarters and pitched our tents on the old Camp Union drill and parade ground. Lt. Col. Schall has in orders named our new home Camp Bell, after Lt. Col. Bell and Capt. Bell, both of whom were killed in action. He also issued congratulatory orders to the regiment, which was read on dress parade.

Mar 24—Company drills and dress parade.

Mar 25—Camp overflowed with water and all hands had to seek quarters elsewhere. The camp looks dismal and everybody out of humor.

5. *O.R.*, vol.. 33, 681.

6. *O.R.*, vol. 33, 685.

Mar 26—Camp still underwater. 100 recruits reached the regiment to-day. We number some 700 men now. Of the 30 original line officers there is now only 10 left. The rest have been killed, resigned or have been transferred to the V.R.C. Struck our tents and moved our camp along the railroad on a more elevated piece of ground. This afternoon 400 parole prisoners arrived from Richmond. They looked very thin and pretty well used up.

Mar 27—Company, regimental drills and dress parade. Wrote a letter to my mother, and made out ordnance papers for the period covering the time I was captain of Co. A.

Mar 28—Forwarded my ordnance papers and receipts of arms turned over by me to my successor to Washington.

Mar 29—Company, regimental drills and dress parade. Lt. Col. Schall received a leave of absence for three days and left for home. Consequently it places me in command of the regiment.

29th Conn. [colored] 8th Mich. & 56th Mass. arrived in camp, also the 26th U.S. [colored]. There is quite a number of colored troops here and it is supposed that they will be attached to the 9th Corps. Maj. Gen. C. C. Washburn, U.S.V., is ordered to repare to Annapolis, Md. and report to Gen. Burnside, U.S.V., for assignment to duty to command a division of the 9th Corps.[7] The 100th Penna. has just arrived.

Mar 30—Company, regimental drills and dress parade. A few more recruits received and assigned to the various companies.

Mar 31—The usual drills and dress parade. S.O. No. 8 directs Capt. Wm. Allebaugh to proceed to Phila. and there report to Brig. Gen. Gibbon for the purpose of receiving all recruits and stragglers under his charge belonging to the 9th Army Corps.

The 9th Army Corps has reached Camp Nelson, Ky. Willcox, from Detroit, Mich. informs Burnside that the advance of the 9th Corps will reach Nicholasville, Ky. to-day, and that the baggage has all arrived at Covington, and that the 51st N.Y. and most of the convalescents have left for Annapolis, and that the batteries have started, and the paymaster will go to Annapolis and pay the troops there.

Apr 1—Company drills and dress parade.

Apr 2—Company drills and dress parade. Received a letter from my mother. Sixteen cars with 600 men and three cars with horses and baggage, all belonging to the 9th A.C. left Nicholasville, Ky. at 6 P.M. to join us at this place.

Apr 3—Regimental inspection and dress parade. Mrs. Col. Hartranft and son arrived in camp yesterday. They will remain several days.

Apr 4—Company, regimental drills and dress parade.

Apr 5—Company, regimental drills and dress parade.

Apr 6—The usual drills and dress parade.

Apr 7—The usual drills and dress parade. Mrs. Col. Hartranft paid our camp a visit to-day. Forwarded to the Chief of Ordnance my quarterly returns for the years of 1861 and 1862. One hundred men detailed from the regiment to report to Capt. [Gardner S.] Blodgett A.Q.M. for fatigue duty. Burnside is now in New York, and Hartranft is still in command of this post.

Apr 8—The usual drills and dress parade. I had the pleasure of receiving the portion of a box of good things, sent to the regiment by Miss Yerkes of Norristown. Asst. Surg. J. E. Rineholdt of our regiment is ordered to report at once to commanding officer 1st Mich. Vols. (colored)

---

7. *O.R.*, vol. 33, 757.

for duty. Grant has informed Burnside that he will pay his camp a visit about the middle of next week. Chaplain Danl. G. Mallory, who resigned last July, has been re-commissioned and has rejoined the regiment.

Apr 9—The usual drills and dress parade. Received a letter from my mother.

Apr 10—The usual drills and dress parade. This order was issued to-day:

> Headquarters 9th A.C.
> New York, Apl. 10th. 1864.
>
> General Orders No.6
>
> The following badge is announced as the badge of the Ninth Army Corps:
>
> A shield with the figure nine in the centre, crossed with a foul anchor and cannon, to be worn on the top of the cap or front of the hat.
>
> The 1st Division to be red, with gilt anchor, cannon and number. 2d Division to be white, with gilt anchor, cannon and number. 3d Division to be blue, with gilt anchor, cannon and number. 4th Division to be green, with gilt anchor, cannon and number. Corps Headquarters of red, white, and blue, with gilt anchor, cannon, and green number.
>
> Those who desire can also wear a medal of the same design, made of gold or gilt, silver or white metal, bronze or copper, to be attached to the left heart of the coat, as a pin, or suspended by a red, white, and blue ribbon. The designs for this badge are now in the hands of Messrs. Tiffany & Co., New York, and samples will be at Headquarters about the 27th.
>
> By command of
> Major Genl. A. E. Burnside
> Edward M. Neill, Ass't. Adj't. Gen'l.[8]

Col. Hartranft commanding 9th A.C. issued S.O. No. 18. The Quartermasters of each regiment in the corps to proceed to Washington D.C. without delay, for the purpose of procuring ordnance and ordnance stores for their respective commands. Q.M. Saml. P. Stephens left this morning.

Apr 11—The usual drills and dress parade.

Apr 12—The usual drills and dress parade. Burnside has arrived and has relieved Hartranft of the command of the corps. Lt. Col. Schall has detailed Prv. Geo. Body Co. A regimental shoe maker, and is ordered to provide himself with the necessary implements of the trade.

Apr 13—Generals Grant and Burnside arrived in camp this morning and this afternoon they with their staffs reviewed the 9th A.C. and it was a magnificent sight.[9] it looks very much like a movement soon, and we will have to give up our magnificent camp. Much pains have been taken both by officers and men in beautifying it. The streets are all laid out in military precision, and the quarters are bedecked with all kinds of evergreens, and arches thrown across he streets. The health of the regiment is generally good, but we have some chills and fever. The roads about here are hub-deep in mud.

Apr 14—Lieut. Col. Schall is absent, and I find myself in command of the regiment. The usual drills and dress parade. Chaplain Mallory rejoined the regiment to-day.

---

8. *O.R.*, vol. 33, 837.

9. Parker, *51st PA*, 539, wrote that Grant reviewed the regiment on April 12.

Apr 15—Am still in command of the regiment. Usual drills and dress parade. The 11th New Hampshire arrived in camp from East Tennessee, bringing with them all the men of the 51st who had not re-enlisted, and who had been assigned to that regiment while we were at home enjoying our thirty day furlough.

Apr 16—Still in command of the regiment, Lt. Col Schall being detailed as a member of a court martial. By a Circular Order issued by Burnside, Catholic service will be held in one of the barracks at Camp Parole every Sunday morning while the troops are encamped at this place, the men to be under the charge of a commissioned officer who will be responsible for the return of the men to camp. By the order of C. C. Gilbert, Superintendant Volunteer Recruiting Service, Eastern Division of Penna., Sergt. David Long was to-day relieved from recruiting service with Lieut. Wm. F. Thomas in Norristown, Pa., and ordered to rejoin the regiment without delay.

Apr 17—Regimental inspection, and new arms issued.

Apr 18—Company and regimental drills and dress parade. All the old men belonging to the regiment were transferred back to us from the 11th New Hampshire, which now makes us number with the recruits, about 900 men.

Apr 19—The usual drills and dress parade. Wrote a letter to my sister, and made some corrections in my ordnance papers and returned them to Washington.

Grant has ordered Burnside to divert all troops that are on the way to Annapolis or yet to start, to Alexandria, and is ordered to send a general there to take charge of them, and is also ordered to commence moving the 9th A.C. on the 23d inst. In accordance with G.O. No. 7 9th A.C. headquarters, the following is now the organization of the 9th A.C.:

1st Division	Major-General Crittenden
2d Division	Major-General Parke
3d Division	Brigadier Genl. Willcox
4th Division	Brigadier Genl. Ferrero (colored)[10]

Apr 20—The usual drills and dress parade. A great many colored regiments are arriving here, and are supposed to be for our corps. The 1st Mich. has just arrived, and have been assigned to our corps. Two of the companies are composed of Chippewa Indians, and they make a fine appearance. By S.O. No. 50 9th A.C. headquarters Lieut. John H. Genther o. B is ordered to report to Gen. Willcox, commanding 3d Division, for assignment to duty as Act. Commissary of Subsistence. By G.O. No. 1 headquarters 1st Brigade, 3d Division, 9th A.C. Col. Hartranft assumed command of the 1st Brigade, 3d Division.

Apr 21—The usual drills and dress parade. Wrote a letter to my mother. Col. Hartranft in G.O. No. 2 announces his staff as follows:

1st Lt. Geo. Shorkley	51st P.V.V.	A.A.A.G.
Capt. Lane S. Hart	51st P.V.V.	A.A.I.G.
Capt. C. W. Davis	21st Mass. Vols.	Pro.Mar.
Capt. R. D. Johnson	2d Mich. Vols.	A.C.S.
1st Lt. Geo. D. Martin	79th New York	A.A.QM.

Apr 22—The usual drills and dress parade. I was detailed a member of a General Court Martial, met in Annapolis and was made President of the court. The men of the regiment were

---

10. *O.R.*, vol. 33, 913.

paid their ration money, for the thirty days of furlough. Received marching orders and ordered to turn in our tents and quartermaster stores. Shelter-tents was immediately issued to the men in their stead. Three days rations issued to each man and cooked during the night. Wrote a letter to my mother. Over 1400 letters have been sent home from camp the pass week.

Brig. Gen. Willcox, having been temporarily assigned to the command of the corps, Col. Christ has assumed the temporary command of our division (3d). G.O. No. 13 9th A.C. headquarters, orders the corps to commence moving from this place at 6 o'clock A.M. to-morrow morning in the following order: First.–Two Battallions of the 3d New Jersey Cavalry then the four divisions in the order of the numbers each followed by its train, and lastly one Battallion of the 3d New Jersey Cavalry. Sufficient rearguards will be established by division and brigade to prevent all straggling and the Battallion of cavalry in the rear will act as the rearguard to the entire command, and the commanding officers will see that all stragglers will join their regiments. The line of march will be indicated by the advance cavalry.[11]

Apr 23—The corps struck tents at 6 o'clock A.M. and all baggage was put on board of a steamer at Annapolis and left her dock at 12 M. for Alexandria, Va. The corps left their camps at 10 o'clock A.M. and after a march of 15 miles went into bivouac at 8 o'clock P.M. about 4 miles from the Junction House. With half an hour after stacking arms, without waiting for wagons, every man had his shelter-tent up and all were housed. This was our first experience with the shelter-tents.

Burnside has for his corps 600 wagons and 180 ambulances. Of the wagons five go to 1,000 men for ammunition, three only for baggage; provisions and forage take up the rest. Grant's orders to Burnside is that he is to march his troops with as little delay as possible, and to take position from Bull Run to the Rappahannock, so as to protect and guard the road between the two streams. The men are to carry seven days' rations without meat in haversacks and knapsacks. Baggage to be reduced to nothing in wagons. One hundred and fifty rounds of ammunition per man will be the amount required to be carried on the person and in wagons together.[12]

Apr 24—We left our bivouac at 6 o'clock A.M. marched 20 miles and at 7 o'clock P.M. halted and went into bivouac within six miles of Bladensburg.

Apr 25—We left our bivouac at 6 o'clock A.M. After marching some distance Company A was detailed to build a bridge over the East Branch of the Potomac River at Blandensburg, where we all crossed. Passed Fort Lincoln at 1 o'clock P.M. Our column passed through Washington D.C. and were reviewed by the President and Genl. Burnside. Crossed the Long Bridge into Virginia and after marching 22 miles, went into bivouac at 7 o'clock P.M. along the roadside between Washington and Alexandria.

Apr 26—Troops remained in bivouac all day awaiting orders. Troops ordered to be supplied with six days rations and forage and ordered to leave here at 6 o'clock in the morning.

Apr 27—We left our bivouac at 6 o'clock A.M. marched through Alexandria, Va., and after a very tedious and provoking march of 19 miles, bivouacked at 12 o'clock midnight one mile beyond Fairfax Court House. All hands pretty well used up.

Apr 28—We left our bivouac at 6 o'clock A.M. passed over the old Chantilly battle ground, and through Centreville, saw the old Bull Run battle field at a distance, forded Bull Run passed through Manassas Junction and after a march of 18 miles went into bivouac along Broad River

11. *O.R.*, vol. 33, 946.

12. *O.R.*, vol. 33, 955.

near Bristow's Station on the Orange and Alexandria Railroad. There met my old friend Dr. L. W. Read.

Apr 29—We left our bivouac at 9 o'clock A.M. marched through Catlett Station and after a march of 16 miles at 5 o'clock P.M. reached Warrenton Junction and went into bivouac along the railroad.

Apr 30—Was detailed as Brigade Officer of the Day. Had a provoking time in posting the pickets. The night was dark and disagreeable. The ground to be covered was all underbrush, almost impassable for a horse. Succeeded in posting the pickets but lost my way, but finally reach camp late in the night hat-less and pretty well used up. Orders were received from corps headquarters to be prepared at all times to march at short notice.

May 1—The regiment accompanied by Capt. Cloke, Company B, 3d New Jersey Cavalry, left their bivouac at Warrenton Junction at 11 A.M. and went on a reconnaissance to the town of Warrenton, arriving there at 4 P.M. threw out pickets around the town and bivouacked for the night. After repeated inquiries made of citizens (both male and female) and contrabands, we could learn of no rebel force being or having been in that vicinity, but learned that small squads of guerrillas are in the habit of visiting Warrenton daily. We also made a reconnaissance in front and left of the town, but could see nothing of the enemy.

Burnside to-day issued a General Circular to the corps impressing the importance on those who are now to share with him the honor of a soldier's life; the order was more intended for those just entering the service. He admonished them not to quit the ranks, on any pretense whatever, that the army is about to move into the country of an active enemy, with no friendly force behind or near it, and every straggler runs the risk of Libby Prison or a bullet. Not to leave camp without his musket. Sleep with his arms within reach. Washing the feet at night, soaping the stockings, and greasing the shoes, will prevent foot-soreness. Cavalry and Artillery to husband their forage. Every soldier to endeavor to make his rations hold out longer than the time for which they were issued. Blankets and overcoats should never be thrown away. And lastly when on picket he must remember that the safety of the whole army depend upon his vigilance. That prisoners of war, wounded or not, should be treated with the soldierly kindness and consideration which the 9th Corps has always honorably shown, and which is due an open enemy.[13]

May 2—The cavalry escort and ourselves left our bivouac at 8 A.M. and after an easy march reached our old camp at 12 M. at Warrenton Junction, and was surprised to learn of the death of Prv. George Bodey of Company A, who had remained in camp. George was well known by everyone in the corps. He was of an unusual height and build. Gov. Curtin, on Bodey leaving Harrisburg in 1861, was compelled to have made for him extra large blankets and shoes and was given a good supply of each. He was very good among horses, and no one could put more on a wagon than he. At Blains-Cross-roads, Tenn. he proved to be invaluable, as he made all the raw hide moccasins for the men to wear over the mountains on their way home. He was buried at Warrenton Junction, Va., with military honors and his body was never brought home.

Gen. John G. Parke, from West Chester, Pa., informs Burnside that he is much better, and will leave home to rejoin the 9th A.C. on the 4th inst. Received a letter from my mother.

May 3—I attended a meeting of a General Court Martial setting at the headquarters of the 8th Mich. Col. Ely of the 8th Mich. President of the court.

S.O. No. 8 from 3d Div. headquarters directs that Prv. Chas. Yunker Co. A, who had been dropped from the rolls of his regiment as a deserter, is restored to duty on the recommendation

---

13. *O.R.*, vol. 36, part 2, 341.

of his regimental and brigade commanders with the loss of all pay and allowances from Sept. 1st/62 to Oct. 1st/63.

General Field Orders directs us to resume are march to-morrow morning at 7 o'clock, the 1st Brigade taking the advance, to be followed by the artillery, ambulances, baggage and supply trains in the order mentioned. The pickets will be relieved at 5 o'clock A.M. to-morrow. It is also ordered that hereafter commencing to-morrow the commanding officer of the brigade in advance, will make a detail of one commissioned officer and ten (10) pioneers who will march in advance of the baggage train.[14]

---

14. The Ninth Corps was now organized as follows:
Provost Guard: 8th US
First Division, Brig. Gen. Thomas G. Stevenson
    First Brigade, Col. Sumner Carruth: 35th, 56th, 57th, 59th MA, 4th, 10th US
    Second Brigade, Col. Daniel Leasure: 3rd MD, 21st MA, 100th PA
    Artillery: 2nd ME Bty, 14th MA Bty
Second Division, Brig. Gen. Robert Potter
    First Brigade, Col. Zenas R. Bliss: 36th, 58th MA, 51st NY, 45th, 48th PA, 7th RI
    Second Brigade, Col. Simon G. Griffin: 31st, 32nd ME, 6th, 9th, 11th, NH, 17th VT
    Artillery: 11th MA Bty, 19th NY Bty
Third Division, Brig. Gen. Orlando B. Willcox
    First Brigade, Col. John F. Hartranft: 2nd, 8th, 17th, 27th MI, 109th NY, 51st PA
    Second Brigade, Col. Benjamin C. Christ: 1st MI Sharpshooters, 20th MI, 79th NY, 60th OH, 50th PA
    Artillery: 7th ME Bty, 34th NY Bty
Fourth Division, Brig. Gen. Edward Ferrero
    First Brigade, Col. Joshua K. Sigfried: 27th, 30th, 39th, 43rd USCT
    Second Brigade, Col. Henry G. Thomas: 30th CT, 19th, 23rd USCT
    Artillery: 3rd VT Bty, PA Bty D
Cavalry: 3rd NJ, 22nd NY, 2nd OH, 13th PA
Reserve Artillery, Captain John Edwards, Jr.: 27th NY Bty; Btys D, H, 1st RI; Bty E, 2nd US; Btys G, L&M, 3rd US
Provisional Brigade, Col. Elisha G. Marshall: 24th NY Cav, 14th NY Hvy Art, 2nd PA Provisional Hvy Art

Chapter 12

The Overland Campaign

May 4–June 15, 1864

The Ninth Corps moved up to support the Army of the Potomac and was engaged in the heavy fighting in the Wilderness on May 6. The armies then moved to Spotsylvania; here the 51st suffered heavy casualties on May 12 when Hartranft's brigade was flanked by a North Carolina brigade. During the hand-to-hand encounter, the regiment lost two of its three colors. After participating in the combat along the North Anna River, the 51st charged the enemy works at Cold Harbor on June 3; among the casualties here was Lieutenant Colonel Schall, shot through the head and instantly killed at Major Bolton's side.

May 4—We left our bivouac at Warrenton Junction at 7 A.M. Hartranft left the 2d and 17th Mich. on the line of the railroad near Warrenton Junction with orders to remain until relieved and we moved with the balance of the command down the railroad passing Bealton Station, crossed the Rappahannock River at 2.20 P.M. on a pontoon bridge, marched a mile beyond and went into camp. At 5 P.M. formed line and moved one mile to the front, when the column was halted, and soon after ordered back to camp. Firing heard in the distance. Guards were placed on all the occupied houses on, or in the vicinity of the route of the army and in advance towards the Rapidan, so as to prevent any communication with the enemy by the inhabitants. At 1.15 P.M. Burnside received orders from Grant to make force marches until he reaches Germanna Ford.[1]

May 5—We left our bivouac at 5 A.M. after a very hasty breakfast, crossed Mountain Run at Paoli Mills, arriving at Germanna Ford on the Rapidan River at 11 A.M., crossed the river on pontoons and marched immediately to the front in the direction of the firing, which was now raging between Warren[2] and the rebels. The most of the 9th A.C. had marched 30 miles. Our brigade moved down the road nearly 2 miles, then filed into a woods on the right of the road, advanced about half a mile, and relieved part of Ricketts' division Sixth Corps,[3] forming line

---

1. *O.R.,* vol. 36, part 2, 380.

2. Major General Gouverneur K. Warren led the Fifth Corps.

3. Brigadier General James B. Ricketts had command of the Third Division, Sixth Corps.

in the edge of the woods. In front of our left was a large open field, where planely could be seen the cavalry videttes of both armies watching each other's movements.[4]

About dark part of the 1st Division of the 9th A.C. under command of Gen. Stevenson moved up, taking position in our rear, with his right resting on the Rapidan at the curve. During the afternoon, the 2d and 17th Mich. who had been left behind at Warrenton rejoined us, and was placed in reserve. Later in the day the 51st P.V.V. was moved to the right of our former position and after dark, the right wing, myself in command were placed on picket, and remained until 4 A.M. next morning. During the night some miscreant stole my overcoat and blanket off my saddle.

Gen. Parke, who had been absent sick, rejoined the corps, and is now chief of staff to Burnside. The wounded began to come in about 12 M. and 9 P.M. from all the corps. They were fed, dressed, and sheltered.

May 6—The battle of the Wilderness was renewed by us at 5 o'clock this morning, and continued with unabated fury until darkness set in, each army holding substantially the same position that they had on the evening of the 5th.

The 51st P.V.V. was relieved from the picket line at 4 o'clock A.M. and retired to the rear for a little rest and to get something to eat. At 6 o'clock A.M. our brigade (the First) was immediately pushed forward to the front, following the Second Brigade, Col. Christ commanding, to the left of the Fifth Corps.

The Second Corps was already engaged still further to the left. Our Second Division, commanded by Potter, 9th A.C. moved about one mile to the front, between Second and Fifth Corps. Our Division the 3d, commanded by Willcox followed. Our brigade formed line on the left of Potter's division facing southwest, about 7 A.M. Very soon Potter's division was ordered to the left, and we were ordered to his support. This movement was to the rear, and on account of the underbrush was not promptly made, but after moving back nearly a mile the lines wereagain formed. The advance was made with some difficulty on account of the woods and underbrush, which was on fire. Our brigade succeeded in finding the enemy. We formed our line. The enemy was in force in front of our left.

At this junction Col. Hartranft, who was in command of the First Brigade, received orders from Gen. Burnside to advance and carry the enemy's works. The order to advance was given at 10 o'clock A.M. by Hartranft. The Second Michigan was held in reserve, and the 17th Mich. was ordered to watch well the right flank. The line moved forward in grand style, and succeeded in carrying the enemy's works and held them, but only for a few moments. A panic seized the left, which brought the whole line back in confusion. Skirmishers were immediately advanced from the 2d and 17th Mich. and on these regiments the line was reformed. Many prisoners were taken from the enemy, but we lost perhaps an equal number.

At 4.30 P.M. the brigade again advanced, but found the enemy's fire very severe, and halted. Afterwards orders came from the division commander that no further advance would be made. Our brigade was relieved at dark by Bliss' brigade, and we moved to the right to cover the road leading south.

During the day a Circular Order was issued advising the importance in economizing the ammunition, and the ammunition of the killed and wounded be collected and distributed to the men and to use the bayonet where possible.[5]

---

4. Bolton used Hartranft's report for this entry and the following day. See *O.R.*, vol. 36, part 1, 947-48.

5. *O.R.*, vol. 36, part 2, 439.

At 2.20 P.M. Willcox's division was withdrawn from the road to Parker's Store, and the artillery regiments of the 9th A.C. were posted there on the road to hold it. It has been well said, "this was a battle which no man saw or could see." It was fought in the midst of dense thickets of second-growth underbrush, evergreens, pines, sweet-gums, scrub-oak, and ceder, rendering the use of artillery impossible, and compelling the opposing lines to approach very near each other in order to see their opponents. It was simply a series of fierce attacks and repulses on either side, and the contending lines swayed back and forth over a strip of ground from 300 yards to 2 miles in width, on which the wounded of both sides were scattered, and to add to the horror the woods was on fire in many places, and a great many of the wounded, who were unable to escape, were thus either suffocated or burned to death. The number is supposed to be about 200. Every effort was made to bring off the wounded between the two lines, especially at night, but with very light success. They were scattered throughout the dense thickets, and the enemy firing at every moving light, or at the slightest noise.

The loss in the regiment killed, wounded and missing in this engagement as follows:

Killed:

Lieut. John S. Moore, Co. A	Pvt. Aaron Thatcher, Co. G
Pvt. Philip Bond, Co. B	Cpl. John E. Wilt, Co. G
Cpl. Edward Bullman, Co. B	Pvt. Frederick Smith, Co. H (died May 7)
Color Sgt. Patrick Kevin, Co. C	Pvt. John Murphy, Co. I
Pvt. David H. Yerkes, Co. D	Pvt. Frederick Schwep, Co. K
Cpl. Levi H. Ammon, Co. E	

Wounded:

Pvt. James M. Baker, Co. A	Pvt. Levi W. Shingle, Co. C
Pvt. John Bare, Co. A (died May 10)	Pvt. Abraham Tochler, Co. C
Pvt. Levi Bolton, Co. A	Pvt. Noble Creighton, Co. D
Pvt.. Thomas J. Bolton, Co. A	Pvt. Hiram C. Fisher, Co. D
Pvt. Charles Fix, Co. A (died June 18)	Sgt. John Gilligan, Co. D
Pvt. Theodore Gilbert, Co. A	Pvt. John R. Grey, Co. D
Pvt. Amandas Garges, Co. A	Sgt. William D. Jenkins, Co. D
Pvt. Samuel Himes, Co. A	Pvt. John Sutch, Co. D
Pvt. Daniel Hood, Co. A	Sgt. Walter M. Thompson, Co. D
Pvt. Jesse Johnson, Co. A	Pvt. E. Barton Kennedy, Co. E
Pvt. John A. Jordan, Co. A	Pvt. Charles Kline, Co. E
Sgt. Osman Ortlip, Co. A	Pvt. John Millhouse, Co. E
Pvt. William Bowman, Co. B	Pvt. Francis Adelman, Co. F
Pvt. Adam Buzzard, Co. B	Pvt. Thomas G. Ashton, Co. F (died June 9)
Pvt. Reuben Dotter, Co. B	Pvt. John Bateman, Co. F
Pvt. George Paul, Co. B	Sgt. Howard Bruce, Co. F
Pvt. Conrad Schwoerer, Co. B	Cpl. George S. Castleberry, Co. F
Pvt. George W. Breisch, Co. C	Pvt. Elwood Charles, Co. F (died May 24)
Pvt. John E. Emery, Co. C	Pvt. James G. Guyder, Co. F
Pvt. Franklin R. Fox, Co. C	Lieut. William W. Owen, Co. F
Pvt. William Gunn, Co. C	Pvt. George M. Reed, Co. F
Pvt. Henry Jago, Co. C	Pvt. Jacob W. Reed, Co. F
Pvt. Andrew J. Reed, Co. C	Pvt. Allen Teany, Co. F

Pvt. Henry White, Co. F (died July 5)

Pvt. George Dutot, Co. G

Pvt. William Heichel, Co. G

Pvt. John Aldendorfer, Co. H

Pvt. Reuben Baker, Co. H

Pvt. Harrison Bower, Co. H

Pvt. George W. Carey, Co. H

Pvt. John C. Leamon, Co. H

Cpl. H. C. McCormick, Co. H

Pvt. Peter Smith, Co. H

Pvt. George Vangeeser, Co. H

Pvt. Thomas Weaver, Co. H

Pvt. Edward Doyle, Co. I

Pvt. John George, Co. I

Pvt. Francis M. Keating, Co. I

Lieut. Lewis Patterson, Co. I

Pvt. James W. Baten, Co. K

Pvt. John Betzer, Co. K

Pvt. John T. Cox, Co. K

Pvt. John Fangford, Co. K

Pvt. Daniel Fritz, Co. K

Lieut. Jacob Fryburger, Co. K

Pvt. Nathan Hanan, Co. K

Sgt. Jacob A. Hawk, Co. K

Pvt. John P. Huber, Co. K

Pvt. Daniel G. Oakes, Co. K

Pvt. John T. Ocker, Co. K

Cpl. Theodore Odenwelder, Co. K

Pvt. Joseph Poeth, Co. K

Pvt. David Rossman, Co. K

Pvt. Albert Schilling, Co. K

Cpl. John Sutton, Co. K

Pvt. Robert Wertz, Co. K

Captured:

Pvt. George Paul, Co. B

Pvt. Henry Meixell, Co. B

Pvt. Andrew J. O'Neil, Co. C (May 7)

Pvt. Franklin T. Grube, Co. K

Pvt. John Hoffman, Co. K

Deserted:

Pvt. James F. Baker, Co. F

Lieut. Moore, of Co. A, was hastily buried on the field, but was afterwards disintered and buried in the Wilderness Cemetery, Va., where it still remains.

May 7—At 4 o'clock A.M., the regiment partook of a hasty cup of coffee, formed in line and marched some distance, halted near a public road and commenced to throw up a rail and log breastworks. When about finished we were ordered to take up a new position. This occurred five times during the day. The enemy kept up a brisk fire all day. Laid on our arms all night. Reconnaissances sent out this morning demonstrated the fact that the enemy had fallen behind his intrenched lines, with pickets to the front, covering a part of the battle-field.

Soon after dark our 2d Division was moved on the high ground in rear of the Wilderness Tavern. Our division the 3d and the Provisional Brigade were withdrawn during the night, and concentrated in rear of the 2d Division, the 3d Division constituting the rear guard of the corps. The rear of the 6th Corps did not pass the Wilderness Tavern until nearly daybreak of the 8th. Our division bivouacked near the Perry's House, some 2 miles from Chancellorsville, and the remainder between the two places.

May 8—At 1 1/2 A.M. we moved off slowly towards Chancellorsville, leaving all of our wounded behind. We reached the old battle ground of Chancellorsville about 4 P.M. rested for a short time, and again moved off slowly and again came to a halt a few miles to the left of the old battle grounds. Water very scarce and hard to find. The day was hot and sultry, and the roads very dusty, with dense woods on fire in many places, covered the whole country with smoke, preventing the full circulation of air or the dissipation of the dense clouds of dust raised by the moving troops. The regiment as well as the rest of the division, received orders late to-night to be ready to move at one hour's notice.

May 9—Left our bivouac under orders from corps headquarters about 4 A.M. for a point called Gate, where the Fredericksburg and Spottsylvania road crosses the Ny River, to take position, without orders to cross the river. Our division found the enemy's pickets about one mile from the river, chased them back rapidly, seized the bridge, and crossed Christ's brigade, the 60th Ohio, a new regiment, deployed as skirmishers. Willcox ordered the two batteries, Roemer's and Twitchell's, on the north side to take position on the crest of a slope on the opposite side, some 300 yards from the river, with our left resting at one of the Beverly houses. The enemy opened immediately on us with a field battery, and followed it first with a charge of a brigade of dismounted cavalry, and afterwards with a brigade of Longstreet's corps.

In the meantime our brigade (Hartranft's) except the 2d Mich. was moved over. At this junction Willcox send back for the 1st Division, which Burnside had ordered up part way from Chancellorsville to support him, but by 12 M. and before the 1st Division arrived, the enemy's repeated assaults were effectually repulsed, and the enemy retired behind a narrow strip of woods towards Spottsylvania Court House, a distant of about a mile from our front, leaving 50 prisoners, including some wounded, in our hands.

During the rest of the day, Willcox crossed two brigades of the 1st Division, retaining one as a reserve and to guard the fords, and we held the position without further annoyance, except from skirmishers. The day was intensely hot and the roads and fields very dusty. At 4.20 P.M. Burnside informed Willcox that Potter was moving up to near Silver's on the plank road, where he will be in supporting distance. Burnside has placed a strong guard at Tabernacle Church. Willcox is directed to intrench, and to hold his position strongly, only falling back at the last extremity. Prv. Joseph Supplee Co. A was the only one in the regiment wounded. The regiment was principally engaged in throwing up rail and log works all day. We laid on our arms all night.

May 10—A very pleasant day. Very heavy firing. The regiment laid in support of the 20th Mich. until about 12 M. when it was ordered to move one mile to the right and ordered to erect works and immediately commencing felling trees. Those with the rails in a very short time had a strong line of works, but we had no sooner finished them, when we were ordered to throw out skirmishers and advance, which we did, gaining some nine hundred yards, and again making a sudden weal to the left, gained about one mile, which we held subject to a heavy fire all night. Brig. Gen. Stevenson, commanding our 1st Division, was killed by a sharpshooter. Burnside joined us this afternoon with the 2d Division. At 10.30 A.M. Grant informed Burnside that a general attack would be made on the enemy at 5 P.M. and that he is to reconnoiter the enemy's position, and if there is any possible chance of attacking the enemy's right, to do it with vigor, and with all the force he can bring to bear. In consequence of which Willcox received orders at 4 P.M. to open with his artillery promptly at 5 P.M. and to have our division ready to follow up the effect at once. Potter is now on his way to join us, and Burnside is now on his way to join us at the front.[6]

The enemy's lines are in rear of a strip of woods, and it looks as if he is throwing up some slight breastworks, and some indications of planting batteries. We have thrown up fence-rail breast-works along our whole line. For some cause or other the intended attack did not take place, and at 7.15 P.M. all is quiet. We are well intrenched, and feel perfectly easy.

May 11—The morning opened with a heavy disagreeable rain. At daylight we again commenced to throw up breast-works. As usual got them completed and ordered to take up a new

---

6. *O.R.*, vol. 36, part 2, 610, 613-14.

position, and again commenced to build a line of works. Finished them about 3 P.M. and again ordered to take up a new position. Commenced the same work again, when orders came for us to fall back across the Ny River. Built fires to cook rations, but before they were out on the fire, orders came for us to advance. Marched about one mile, ordered to about face at 10 P.M., and finally reached a very muddy field, and went into bivouac but without shelter of any kind.

May 12—Regiment roused from their slumbers at 2 A.M. partook of a hasty meal and at 3 A.M. our division moved to the front, crossed the Ny River and marched in reserve to the corps, and finally ordered up to attack on the left of the 1st Division. The division moved up in echelon, our brigade (Hartranft's) on the right and in advance. Found Gen. Crittenden,[7] commanding 1st Division, had refused his left, and Hartranft was moved up in line with his right. Willcox posted Twitchell's battery[8] on his right front and Roemer's battery in rear of Humphreys' brigade. At this juncture Willcox reported to Burnside that he expected an attempt of the enemy to attack and turn his left, now the extreme left of the Army of the Potomac.

The 51st P.V.V. was ordered to the left of the 27th Mich. A little later six companies (myself in command) was ordered to charge a crest in our immediate front, but before the order was put in execution, another order came countermanding the former, and four companies under Lt. Col. Schall were ordered to the support of Hancock, but shortly returned when a general charge was ordered by our division, and six companies of the 51st P.V.V. under the command of Capt. Jos. K. Bolton was immediately deployed as skirmishers, the other four companies supporting them. They succeeded in securing the crest in the woods, and compelled the enemy's skirmishers to burn a house, and fall back. At this juncture Hartranft was with his brigade and ordered to the support of Hancock, withdrew as quickly as possible and had moved about a half mile with his advance regiment, when the movement was countermanded. As we moved to and fro, the enemy opened his batteries on our lines.[9]

Our brigade again reformed about on the same ground, except extending a little more to the left, in the following order: 8th Mich. 109th N.Y. 27th Mich. four companies 51st P.V.V. and 17th Mich. During this time, our skirmishers had been driven in. They were immediately advanced again. The 2d Mich. was at this time supporting two guns of Wright's battery.[10] Immediately to the left of the line, on the left of the 51st P.V.V. skirmish line was a thicket of woods and underbrush. The woods were shelled by our batteries. It was now 2 P.M. and Hartranft was ordered to attack at once.

Capt. Jos. K. Bolton again advanced with his skirmishers, and attacked them in a field work made of fence rails in the form of the letter V and drove them from there into a log house some distance in the rear. He did not get beyond this point, but was so near the enemy's works that a stone could have been thrown into them.

As we moved up we soon discovered that the enemy were at the same time moving through the thicket in front of our left. The enemy's left and our left became entangled, which resulted in the loss and gain of some prisoners, and the loss of one stand of colors of the 17th Mich. and two stands of the 51st P.V.V. The enemy's artillery poured their shot through our lines from the

---

7. Major General Thomas L. Crittenden assumed command of the division on May 12.

8. Captain Albert B. Twitchell commanded the 7th Maine Battery.

9. This paragraph, as well as succeeding ones, were drawn from Hartranft's report in *O.R.*, vol. 36, part 1, 950.

10. Captain Joseph W. B. Wright commanded the 14th Massachusetts Battery.

front, and his infantry being in superior force on our left, our lines was compelled to retire. The enemy were within a few feet of Wright's two guns on the left. All the gunners were killed or wounded, but Capt. [James] Farrand of the 2d Mich. mended the guns from his regiment, but he too was killed. Six other guns further to the right and rear were also in danger and Burnside ordered men to be ready to spike them, but that contingency did not arise, and we saved our guns.

This was a repulse to our lines, but the enemy failed equally in his object. Lt. Col. [Frederick W.] Swift, 17th Mich. and Capt. Allebaugh, 51st P.V.V. were captured with their colors. After two color-bearers had been shot down, Allebaugh seized the colors of his regiment with the determination to rally his men, but the enemy appeared in overwhelming numbers, and he was forced to yield. Corp. James Cameron Co.I who was one of the color-bearers was captured here. He carried one of the colors that was presented to the regiment on the morning the regiment left Norristown. He was taken to Danville, Va., and was sent from there on the 28th of May 1864 to Andersonville, Ga. and from there to Florence, S.C. Oct. 5th 1864, and from there to Wilmington, N.C. Feb. 28th/65; when he was exchanged and entered our lines, after being in captivity about 9 months and 16 days.

We laid on our arms all night, in a very heavy rain storm. In fact, it rained more or less all day. Casualties sustained by the regiment to-day from all causes:

Killed:

Pvt. Jesse Frease, Co. A
Lieut. Thomas J. Lynch, Co. C
Pvt. Jefferson C. Clare, Co. D
Pvt. John Jefferson, Co. D
Cpl. Robert B. Lindsey, Co. F

Pvt. Samuel Moore, Co. G
Pvt. Abraham Wampole, Co. I
Lieut. Frank B. Sterner, Co. K
Pvt. Charles W. Willet, Co. K

Wounded:

Cpl. Levi Bolton, Co. A
Pvt. Jacob H. Derr, Co. A (died May 28)
Pvt. John B. Ellis, Co. A
Pvt. Thomas B. Farrell, Co. A
Pvt. Charles Fix, Co. A (died June 18)
Pvt. Samuel H. Frease, Co. A
Pvt. Jeremiah Gray, Co. A (died May 16)
Pvt. Edward Hallman, Co. A
Pvt. Charles H. Hansell, Co. A
Pvt. Jesse Johnson, Co. A
Pvt. John Jordan, Co. A
Pvt. Henry W. McLain, Co. A
Pvt. Ephraim Parvin, Co. A
Pvt. John Saylor, Co. A
Pvt. George Smith, Co. A (died May 30)
Pvt. Henry Smith, Co. A (died May 14)
Pvt. Charles Yunker, Co. A (also captured)
Pvt. Adam Buzzard, Co. B
Pvt. Charles Chambers, Co. B

Pvt. William Draher, Co. B

Pvt. Reuben Dutter, Co. B
Pvt. Edward Hardy, Co. B

Pvt. Patrick McDonald, Co. B

Cpl. George W. Moser, Co. B (died June 13)
Capt. D. L. Nicholas, Co. B
Pvt. Adam Ruff, Co. B
Pvt. Henry Scott, Co. B
Pvt. John H. Seiple, Co. B
Pvt. John Stone, Co. B
Pvt. Lewis Young, Co. B

Pvt. George W. Breish, Co. C
Pvt. John C. Emery, Co. C

Pvt. Enos D. Espenship, Co. C
Pvt. Pvt. Josiah M. Faringer, Co. C
Pvt. Patrick Fitzpatrick, Co. C
Pvt. Charles R. Fox, Co. C
Pvt. Franklin R. Fox, Co. C
Pvt. Andrew Grim, Co. C
Pvt. William Gunn, Co. C
Pvt. Henry Jago, Co. C
Cpl. Hugh McLain, Co. C
Sgt. Nathan H. Ramsey, Co. C
Pvt. Andrew J. Reed, Co. C
Pvt. Abraham Walt, Co. C
Pvt. Mark L. Yerger, Co. C
Pvt. Jeremiah Aikey, Co. D (also captured)
Pvt. Albert Aronimer, Co. D
Pvt. William Bodley, Co. D (died May 16)
Pvt. Noble Creighton, Co. D
Cpl. Andrew Fair, Co. D
Sgt. Henry Foreman, Co. D
Sgt. John Gilligan, Co. D
Pvt. William H. Hardy, Co. D
Pvt. John Kain, Co. D

Cpl. John L. McCoy, Co. D
Pvt. Daniel R. Yost, Co. D
Pvt. Charles Widger, Co. D
Pvt. Jacob Boop, Co. E
Pvt. Isaac Dobly, Co. E (also captured)
Pvt. Cornelius Edelman, Co. E
Pvt. Jacob Frederick, Co. E
Pvt. William H. Hackman, Co. E
Pvt. Barton Kennedy, Co. E
Pvt. Charles Kline, Co. E
Pvt. Charles Lloyd, Co. E
Pvt. James Miller, Co. E
Pvt. William Dresher, Co. F (died July 8)
Pvt. Albert Teany, Co. F
Pvt. Augustus Rolley, Co. G (also captured)
Capt. George W. Bisbing, Co. I (died June 7)
Sgt. John R. Davis, Co. I
Pvt. Thomas Henderstine, Co. I
Pvt. Michael Dillon, Co. K
Sgt. Franklin S. Moyer, Co. K (died June 16)
Pvt. John Rank, Co. K (died May 14)

Captured:

Pvt. George Boswell, Co. B
Cpl. Matthew Delaney, Co. B
Pvt. John Burns, Co. B
Capt. William Allebaugh, Co. C
Pvt. William Barry, Co. C
Pvt. Michael Dillon, Co. C
Pvt. Benjamin Kooker, Co. C
Pvt. Joshua A. Kevin, Co. C
Pvt. Hilary Sloop, Co. C
Pvt. Benjamin F. Smith, Co. C
Pvt. Philip Stofflet, Co. C
Pvt. John Hummell, Co. E
Pvt. John Rohback, Co. E
Pvt. M. C. Zachman, Co. E
Lieut. William F. Campbell, Co. H
Sgt. George Breon, Co. H
Sgt. David C. Brewer, Co. H

Sgt. John R. Davis, Co. H
Pvt. Simon Goss, Co. H
Pvt. John Hartz, Co. H
Sgt. Harrison Hause, Co. H
Pvt. William J. Lattimer, Co. H
Lieut. Hugh McClure, Co. H
Pvt. William A. Miller, Co. H
Pvt. Jacob Smith, Co. H
Pvt. Isaiah Smith, Co. H
Sgt. Daniel M. Wetzell, Co. H
Cpl. James Cameron, Co. I
Pvt. Philip Hattle, Co. I
Pvt. Thomas J. Arbuckle, Co. K
Pvt. Absalom Baldwin, Co. K
Pvt. John Fangford, Co. K
Pvt. James Ludwig, Co. K

Deserted:

Pvt. Peter Meyers, Co. C
Pvt. James Bangs, Co. I

Pvt. Robert Buggy, Co. I

There are reasons to believe that quite a number more were wounded in this engagement, and more captured, but there is no official count of them.

Some years after the close of the war, several ladies from Norristown, visiting Washington D.C. in going through the War Department saw the two captured flags of the 51st P.V.V. The fact was reported, and several years after, I made application for their return through Senator Don. Cameron. A special act was passed the Senate and the flags were returned by the then Sec. of War Rob. T. Lincoln to me. There is a singular coincident about one of our captured flags. On the lower stripe next to the staff appears the name of Lieut. O. A. Wiggins, Co.E 37th regiment North Carolina Volunteers, Lanes Brigade, Willcox's Division, A. P. Hill Corps, Army of Northern Virginia. This same regiment we fought at Newberne, N.C. March 14.1862, drove them out of their works, and planted the flag of the old 4th Regiment thereon.[11]

May 13—Still raining and very unpleasant and disagreeable. In fact it has been raining for the last 36 hours, which renders the roads very difficult for wagons and artillery. Regiment as well as our whole division engaged all day in throwing up works, with orders to hold our position as an attack is expected and ordered to be on the alert, and repel any attack that may be made against us.

The enemy in front of the 51st P.V.V. made a demonstration about 5 P.M. but they were kept at bay, our artillery playing an important part. At 6 P.M. Grant informed Burnside that there would be a night movement of two corps from the right to his {Burnside's} left, and that they will attack immediately on getting into position if the chance offers, and asks him to be ready to support them, if required.[12] Prv. Harrison Ackerman Co. B, killed.

May 14—Still raining and very disagreeable. In fact we have had rain for the last five days without any prospects yet of its clearing up. The roads are impassable. Very heavy and rapid firing on our left. Orders issued for a general advance along the whole line, but for some cause was not executed. A night attack expected, and ordered to use the utmost vigilance during the night, but all passed off quietly.

May 15—till raining. Regiment remained on the front all day, and ordered to be very vigilant. During the day the rebels commenced a rapid shelling. Dug a number of traverses to our works to better protect ourselves from their shells. Our works are very close. We can see each other's battle flags, and can hear the rebels singing religious hymns. The weather hot and mucky, and the stench coming from between the two lines from the dead bodies of the men of both armies, and dead horses is simply terrible. Took time during the day to write a letter to my mother, the first since crossing the Rapidan. The regiment heard camp rumors of the appointment of Col. Hartranft as a brigadier general. The roads are impassable.

May 16—Regiment still holding its old position, and for once we have a pleasant day. Our artillery opened a vigorous cannonading on the enemy this morning to cover the removals of some hospitals left by Hancock when he withdrew from the extreme right yesterday. Their fire is returned very feebly. Skirmishers sent out during the day to feel their lines. Can hear their bands playing quite plain. We have had five days of constant rain, no prospect clearing up.

May 17—Our supply trains ordered to Fredericksburg, and our wounded sent there. I was detailed as Corps Field Officer of the Day, and reported to Burnside for orders, who gave me the whole picket line of the 9th A.C. to look after. In the saddle all day and night, and made

11. Bolton was not entirely correct about this fact. The 37th North Carolina was indeed at the Battle of Newbern, but it was the 26th North Carolina that opposed the 51st and Reno's brigade.

12. *O.R.*, vol. 36, part 2, 731.

hourly reports to him the condition of things along the line. Always found him pleasant, and was always met with a cordial greeting and took refreshments with him during the evening.

The weather is splendid, and roads rapidly becoming dry. The bands of both armies trying to outdo the other in playing sweet music. The 9th Corps received orders this afternoon to get ready for a night march and Burnside was ordered to hold his command in readiness to move out of his present place at 3.30 in the morning, to move to the left flank, to follow up the two attacting corps and support them, our pickets to remain until driven in or recalled, as it is to be a night march. Burnside sent out staff officers to reconnoiter the roads over which his troops are to pass.[13]

On reaching Burnside's headquarters at 6.30 P.M. I was handed the following circular:

> Headquarters Ninth Army Corps.
> May 17. 1864--6.20 P.M.

Circular

The following is the order of march for the pending movement of the Ninth Army Corps: The entire picket-line will be kept out until driven off or relieved. The senior officer of the day of divisions, Major Wm. J. Bolton, Fifty-first Pennsylvania, will be in general command of the picket-line of all the divisions, and Major Colburn of Fifty-ninth Massachusetts, officer of the day of the First Division, and Maj. [John G.] Wright, Fifty-first New York, officer of the day of the Second Division, will report to Major Wm. J. Bolton for instructions. Major Wm. J. Bolton's headquarters will be with the Fifty-first Pennsylvania, or just in rear. Major Wright should see that his picket-line connects with that of General Birney's division, and co-operate with the officers in charge in case they are driven in or withdrawn.[14]

May 18—I was relieved as Field Officer of the Day at 7 A.M. by Major [Samuel] Moody of the 27th Mich. The day bids fare to be hot and sultry. Ordered to remain in our works. Later orders came for an attack. The 2d and 6th Corps, with the 2d Division of the 9th Corps and the 1st Brigade 3d Division to which the 51st P.V.V. were attached followed.

The battle opened with a most furious cannonading on both sides, shells and solid shot filled the air, many of ours falling short, killed and wounded many of our own men. It was truly deafening. In going to the point of attack we traversed over the same ground which we had fought so desperately on six days since, and as but a portion of the dead of that day's contest had been buried, the stench which arose from them was so sickening and terrible that many of the men and officers became deathly sick from it. The general appearance of the dead who had been exposed to the sun so long was horrible in the extreme as we marched past and over them—a sight never to be forgotten by those who witnessed it.

During the day two or three charges were made by the divisions of Crittenden and Potter of our corps which resulted in considerable loss. Some ground, however, was gained which commanded part of their lines. It was found that their works could not be carried by assault and at 9 A.M. Burnside received orders from Grant to assume a defensive position, holding himself in readiness for being withdrawn to his left at short notice. At 10 P.M. Burnside issued orders for our withdrawal at 2 A.M. to-morrow. Hancock withdraws to-night to Anderson's Mill. We of the 9th Corps withdraw to the Massaponax Church Road to the south side of the Ny by the Beverly House and are to take position on the left of the 6th Corps, our extreme left

---

13. *O.R.,* vol. 36, part 2, 849-50.

14. *O.R.,* vol. 36, part 2, 850-1.

resting near the Quesenbeery House, within a mile of the Po River. Wright returned to his former position at Myers'.[15] Our pickets remained on the line until 4 A.M. when they were withdrawn by the division officer of the day.

May 19—Agreeable to orders we abandoned our position at 4 A.M., our artillery proceeding us. About noon took up our new position immediately in rear of the 6th Corps. The enemy followed up our withdrawal very closely. The head of the column of the 9th Corps reached Myers House at 5.30 A.M., but cannot proceed as Wright's troops are in the way. Our whole corps is now massed here. Finally reached our new position. During our march we had to cut our way through a perfect wilderness, making our own roads at this point. Met quite a number of our old friends from Norristown in the 95th and 138th regiments. Burnside ordered to occupy the Quesenbeery House, and Gen. Ledlie's brigade has been sent for that purpose. He is to push out pickets to the Po River.

The regiment drew a full supply of rations to-day, the first for sometime. Very heavy cannonading in the evening on our right. Our regiment occupy the second line of battle, and we feel pretty well used up.

May 20—Under all the circumstances, a very pleasant day. The regiment on the front all day in support of troops in the works. In connection with Wright, Burnside pushed out a heavy line of skirmishers in the direction of Stanard's and Smith's Mills, and the Po, gained about one mile and are holding it. A great deal of music in both camps. Regiment received a very large mail this evening. By a general field order from Willcox, Surgeon Wm. C. Shurlock is temporarily detached from the regiment, and is to report for orders to the Surg.-in-chief 3d Division 9th A.C. as "operator" in field hospital.

May 21—Lt. Col. Schall detailed as Field Officer of the Day and I am in command. The whole regiment detailed for picket duty and sent to Stanard's Ford on the Po River. Started for the Ford at 3 A.M. Col. Hartranft is Corps Officer of the Day. About 2 P.M. the skirmish line of the 51st were driven in, but were soon rallied and retook the line and kept it, and all remained quiet as far as our front was concerned. [Pvt. J. A. Halsted, Co. G, captured.]

At 3 P.M., our division moved, the 51st was left on the picket line, and the 109th N.Y. in the field works. Potter is instructed to retain one brigade to watch the ford until the entire 9th and 6th Corps have passed over, when it will bring up the rear, take the advance with his other brigade and proceed to Downer's Bridge, on the Ta River, by the way of Smith's Mills, on the Ny, and Guiney's Station. The 1st and 3d Divisions were halted near general headquarters at Guiney's Station.

May 22—Our regiment withdrew from the picket line at 4 A.M. and immediately moved towards the left. The day very warm. The country looks well. Fences, fields, and houses on our line of march in fine condition. Neither army could have passed through this section of country before. The 9th A.C. marched all night, last night, and we are following them up. Before our leaving the picket line during the night a rumbling noise frequently heard within the enemy's lines, indicating the movement of wagons, trains and artillery.

The First and Third divisions of our corps were halted near general headquarters at Guiney's Station soon after sunrise this morning. After a march of some 18 miles the 109th N.Y. and 51st P.V.V. came up to the corps about 5 P.M., and went into bivouac. Prv. Wm. H. Showalter, Co. D, was killed to-day.

May 23—Regiment left their bivouac at 4 1/2 A.M. in advance of the corps. Crossed Pole Cat

---

15. *O.R.*, vol. 36, part 2, 881.

Creek at 12 M. moved towards Ox Ford on the North Anna River. Here we fell in with the 2d Corps. Our march during the day was through circuitous plantation roads which was frequently interrupted. At 2 P.M., the 2d Corps was ordered to procure a suitable camping grounds on the banks of the North Anna, near the New Bridge. The 9th Corps is ordered to take position to the right of the 2d Corps and will seize Ox Ford, a ford over the Anna next west of New Bridge. After a march of some 20 miles we came to a halt at Jericho Bridge on the North Anna River about 6 P.M., our brigade relieving [Brig. Gen. Gersham] Mott's brigade, 2d Corps, their pickets being relieved by the 27th Mich. Very heavy cannonading throughout the whole day.

At midnight commenced to throw up intrenchments. Could distinctly hear the whistles of the rebel locomotives all night. Heavy rain set in during the night. Four of our companies on picket. Our 1st Division assaulted the rebel works during the day but met with a repulse, with some loss. The 1st and 2d divisions of our corps are now in position immediately in rear of our division. During this movement 15 ambulances moved in the rear of each division. The banks of the river here is very high and precipitous and the roads on either side very rough, being partly new corduroy, and in part a series of rocky steps and shelves. The stream is 150 feet wide, the bluffs are from 50 to 75 feet high.

May 24—Was detailed as Brigade Field Officer of the Day. The regiment in line of battle all day in support of 12 guns. The pickets of our brigade advanced some distance, and got possession of an island. Found the enemy in force on the other side. The opposite banks and bluffs were in themselves natural fortifications being very rocky and abrup covered with heavy timber and thick underbrush. Any further advance was abandoned by the order of Burnside, as the enemy was there in force.[16]

Regiment received a small mail to-day. During the day the following S.O. was issued:

Hdqrs. Army of the United States.
Jericho Ford, Va., May 24, 1864.
Special Orders No.25
  To secure the greatest attainable unanimity in co-operative movements, and greater efficiency in the administration of the army, the Ninth Army Corps, Maj. Gen. A. E. Burnside commanding, is assigned to the Army of the Potomac, Maj. Gen. G. G. Meade commanding, and will report accordingly.

By command of Lieutenant-General Grant,
T. S. Bowers, Assistant Adjutant-General[17]

May 25—Was relieved as Brigade Officer of the Day by Maj. Lewis of the 8th Mich. at 5 A.M. Very heavy firing along the lines all day, a regular artillery duel. Very heavy rain storm. Our division {Willcox} is strongly entrenched in front of Ox Ford, with artillery well in position, and Maj. Morton[18] is laying out additional rifle-pits near the ford. We have less than 3,000 men for duty in our division. The weather very hot. Regiment captured some five or six rebels who said that they were after some beef.

16. Following Hartranft's report, *O.R.*, vol. 36, part 1, 951.

17. *O.R.*, vol. 36, part 3, 169.

18. Major James St. Clair A. Morton was an engineer officer attached to Burnside's staff.

May 26—The day very warm. The regiment in position near a fort on the North Anna River in a pine woods. 200 men detailed from the regiment for picket duty. Very heavy musketry firing on our left. Rebel bands playing. Received orders to be ready to move at 11 P.m. to-night. Afterwards countermanded. We have not been paid for five months.

May 27—Regiment left the Ford at 4 A.m. and moved towards the rear, leaving our pickets in the rifle pits. We marched some distance and halted. Remained until 11 A.m., when we again moved off, taking the ro by Moncure's Plantation. During our march, we passed Mount Carmel Church, crossed the Fredericksburg and Richmond Railroad, rested at St. Paul's or Reeder's Church a short time, and then pushed on, and at 12 o'clock midnight came to a halt and went into bivouac, all hands pretty well jaded out. It appears very much like a flank movement. The 51st lost in this movement as follows:

Killed:

Prv. John W. Erdley, Co. H

Captured:

Pvt. William Barr, Co. A	Pvt. Andrew Wherle, Co. D
Pvt. George W. Berliss, Co. A	Pvt. David Yoder, Co. H
Pvt. Andrew J. Bell, Jr., Co. C	Cpl. George B. Slough, Co. I
Pvt. Lemuel Moode, Co. D	Pvt. Alexander Deibler, Co. K
Pvt. Philip Wampole, Co. D	Cpl. James S. Garrett, Co. K

Deserted:

Pvt. William Andrews, Co. B

May 28—We left our bivouac at 6 1/2 A.m., Willcox's division in the advance of the 9th Corps, and the 51st leading the division. Potter's division follows us, and Crittenden's division bringing up the rear, with orders to force up all stragglers. The 35th Mass. under the direction of Maj. Morton, is ordered to repair the ford over Reedy Swamp, and build a foot bridge. During our march this morning we passed Brookville Church, and Enfield. At 12 M., we made a halt for dinner and rest.

At 1 P.M., again moved off marching very rapidly. We learned that our cavalry are pushing out on all the roads leading to Richmond. We crossed the Pamunkey River at 10:30 P.M. and marched one mile beyond, and went into bivouac after a march of 29 miles, and the men were all pretty well jaded out. At 10.30 P.M. Burnside received orders to move from his present position to Haw's Shop at early daylight and take position with his right on the left of Hancock, and extend so as to cover the road from Haw's Shop past Norman's.

May 29—Regiment aroused from their slumbers at 3 A.M., eat a very hasty breakfast, and at 4 A.M. left our bivouac. Marched about three miles, were halted and ordered to throw up a line of works, got them nearly completed and ordered to stop. Later on was moved one mile to the right, and 90 men detailed to report to Col. Humphrey[19] to be sent out on a reconnaissance to feel for the enemy's left. At 1 P.M., the regiment fell back a short distance, and were massed with other troops as an attack is expected, but did not take place. At 5 P.M. our brigade withdrew from the works, and were placed in reserve. Received several mails. A great deal of music heard in the rebel camps. The men held prayer meeting during the evening.

---

19. Colonel William Humphrey commanded the 2nd Michigan.

May 30—Regiment left their bivouac at 6 A.M. After marching some distance, came to a halt at Salem Church, for a short rest. The whole army ordered to draw three day rations from the general supply train now at the Hundley house. This is done so that the troops wll have five days rations on their persons from to-morrow morning. After a short rest, we again moved on, and had more or less skirmishing all day. Building breastworks and abandoning them, are moving slowly and are fighting over every foot of ground as we advance. Our artillery horses have not had their harness taken off for the last nine days, and the men has done no better. We have been cuting through our own roads through the dense woods we have encountered.

Our whole corps crossed the Totopotomoy Creek during the day. We reached our new position about 8 P.M., and occupy a position from Whitlock's House to the left of Warrens position, relieving a division of Gen. Griffin of the 5th Corps. Our position is a strong one, but have a very long line. It runs in advance of the Tate House and the Timberlake House. We intrenched in face of the enemy, on the left of the Second Division 9th Corps, and right of Griffin's division 5th Corps. We were engaged in throwing up works until after midnight, and are pretty well faged out. We are only seven miles from Richmond.

May 31—This morning Burnside ordered Potter and Willcox to at once take measures to advance their lines. Accordingly at 10 A.M., the two divisions advanced about one mile, and ordered to throw up works. Started with the work, and was then ordered to stop, and again ordered to advance, the enemys skirmishers falling back as we advanced. Commenced again to throw up works, again stopped, made another advance, this time gained 500 yards on the cress of a hill and threw up another line of works, within 200 yards of enemys main line of intrenchments. We laid on our arms all night, and received but little rest.

Jun 1—I was detailed as Division Officer of the Day, and reported to Burnside for orders. Our brigade left their bivouac at daylight and moved towards the right making connection with the lines of the 1st Division of our corps, and commenced to throw up a line of works, which occupied all day. The left of our brigade extends to the Shady Grove Road. Our whole line is in a woods, but there is a clearing in front of our right, and on our left. Across the road is an open field. The enemy made an attack up the Shady Grove Road about 5 P.M. Our First Division fell back without making any resistance which exposed our left very much. Our regiment the 51st P.V.V. was at this point. We held our position by strengthening the left by two companies from the right wing, Companies A and F. Part of the 60th Ohio was also moved up, facing to the left and forming a right angle. The firing was continued till long after dark, and there was more or less until midnight. Our rifle-pits and the enemy's are in some places not more than 30 yards apart.[20] Privates Abraham Walt, Co. C and Charles Prescott, Co. G, [died June 4] were wounded to-day. Wm. Lepley, Co. H also wounded.

Jun 2—I was detailed as Division Officer of the Day, and reported to Col. [John I.] Curtin, 45th Penna. for instructions. Later in the day was made Corps Officer of the Day by Burnside. During the morning our regiment as well as the brigade fell back half mile in the rear to works originally built and occupied on the 30th of May. At 12 M. the regiment moved to the left, and began throwing up works in a violent rain storm. A part of the 9th Corps this afternoon was moved to a new position on the right of the 5th Corps with their left not far from Bethesda Church, the main line running part of the way parallel to the Mechanicsville Road, then crosses it to a point near the Via House not far from the Totopotomoy. In moving to this position we were attacked by the enemy with vigor and suffered some loss in Crittendens division, which was bringing up the rear. The enemy got around the Via House and cut the telegraph line. At 4.30 P.M. Burnside had his whole corps (except the pickets which were left on

---

20. Following Hartranft in *O.R.*, vol. 36, part 1, 952.

the picket line, under my charge) massed near Bethesda Church, his right resting on the Totopotomoy, just beyond the Whitlock House, and his left connecting with Warren. By instructions from Burnside, I was ordered to withdraw the pickets of the 9th Corps after dark, and follow the main army, the course of march being designated by a number of markers being planted in the ground, and the trees being barked in the route taken. Soon after dark the pickets were withdrawn without any loss, and took up the line of march as directed in a violent rain-storm, and without halting for rest, rejoined our corps about 11 P.M. and just in time. The enemy had discovered our movement. Had I stopped for rest one moment, we would certainly have been engaged. As it was we had just reached the main column when our rear ws fired into. We took up the markers as we advanced. Hard fighting during the night. During the night a general attack was ordered to take place in the morning along the whole line of the army. The day was hot and sultry, and whenever troops or wagons were moving, the dust hung in dense clouds.

Jun 3—The regiment left their bivouac at 4.30 A.M., nearly every-one carrying a cup of coffee in his hands, as we were all at breakfast when the order came, and we had just received a mail, and time was not taken to distribute it. Our division was formed in three lines, the 51st P.V.V. occupying the third line. At 5 A.M., the order to charge was given. The two first lines soon gave way, but not so with the third line. It advanced steadily passing over everything, driving the enemy and taking their works. During the charge and at 5 1/2 A.M. Lt. Col. Schall was shot dead at my side, and the command of the regiment fell on me. Schall's body laid on the field until after dark, as it would have been certain death to have attempted to recover it in daylight. Potter's division advanced at the same time on our right.

Our brigade was formed in two lines, the first line in charge of Col. Fox,[21] containing the 27th Mich. in the centre, 109th N.Y. on the right, the 8th Mich. on the left; the second line in charge of Col. Humphrey, containing 2d Mich. on the right, 51st P.V.V. on the left. The line advanced in elegant style driving the enemy from the pits and occupying the same, which were within 200 yards of the enemy's main line, which formed re-entering angle, with four guns at the angle. The enemy fired but very few shots from any of these guns, as our sharpshooters watched the gunners closely. But their infantry had an enfilating fire on us from our left, and we had no cover, but our troops made a temporary cover by using their bayonets, tin cups, plates &c. Guns were placed in position by Captains Roemer and Twitchell.[22]

During the day orders were received to advance and dispositions were made for it, but fortunately the order was countermanded, and the troops remained in this position until dusk, when relieved by troops of Christ's brigade, when we withdrew to the lines occupied in the morning. Lt. Col. Schall's body had been laying in the broiling hot sun all day, but after dark his body, as well as the rest of the killed, were recovered. Schall was universally loved by the whole regiment, and his loss was severely felt.

> "Bury him where the brook shall sing
> His requiem, and returning Spring
> Shall deck his peaceful grove;
> And heaven shall watch, with starry eyes, The mound under the starry skies.
> Where sleeps the bravest brave."

The regiment lost as follows:

---

21. Colonel Dorus M. Fox, 27th Michigan.

22. Hartranft in *O.R.*, vol. 36, part 1, 952.

Killed:

Lt. Col. Edwin Schall

Cpl. Frank H. Mills, Co. A

Pvt. Cyrus Werkheiser, Co. B

Pvt. John Upright, Co. C

Lieut. Isaac Fizone, Co. D

Pvt. James M. Dunkle, Co. E

Pvt. Henry K. Adleman, Co. F

Pvt. Emil Held, Co. G

Pvt. Levi Brensinger, Co. H

Pvt. Aaron Williamson, Co. H

Cpl. David Shingle, Co. K

Wounded:

Lieut. Martin L. Schock, Adjutant

Pvt. George B. Baker, Co. A

Capt. Joseph K. Bolton, Co. A

Lieut. John H. Coulston, Co. A

Sgt. Jacob H. Moyer, Co. A (died July 12)

Pvt. Jacob Sterns, Co. A

Cpl. George Uebelli, Co. A (died June 18)

Pvt. William Draher, Co. B (died June 21)

Pvt. Peter Myers, Co. B

Pvt. Henry Warner, Co. B

Cpl. Andrew J. Grim, Co. C (died June 6)

Pvt. Mark L. Yerger, Co. C

Pvt. William F. Diehl, Co. D

Pvt. Reuben Kline, Co. D

Pvt. Robert Heckernell, Co. E

Pvt. Joel Kline, Co. E

Lieut. Jacob P. Brooke, Co. F

Pvt. Sylvanus H. Daub, Co. F (died June 27)

Pvt. William O'Reilly, Co. F

Pvt. William C. Rider, Co. F

Pvt. Joseph C. Young, Co. F

Pvt. Lewis Cartinwells, Co. G

Pvt. Reuben Hinet, Co. G

Pvt. Charles Prescott, Co. G

Pvt. Jacob Backenhamer, Co. H

Pvt. Elias Bradbury, Co. I

Pvt. Samuel E. Bradbury, Co. I

Sgt. William S. Mellick, Co. K

Cpl. William Buoy, Co. K

Pvt. Benjamin Rank, Co. K

Pvt. Benjamin Roush, Co. K

Pvt. John Widdell, Co. K (died October 26)

Jun 4—At 7.15 A.M., Burnside received orders to withdraw his corps, and move by the right of Old Church and Cold Harbor Road, and be prepared to move in support to any part of the line that may require it, and in accordance with those orders we moved to the neighborhood of the Woody House and took position between the 5th A.C. and the 18th A.C. Our division had the advance, and was followed by Potter's division. Crittenden's division remained until evening, when it was relieved by Warren. A very heavy rain during the day. Received and wrote several letters.

Jun 5—We left our line of works at daylight in a heavy rain storm, and took possession of the first line of works. Received orders to move at a moments notice. At 4 P.M. Burnside received orders to change his position, keeping his left united with Gen. Smith's[23] right and extend his lines along Roundabout Creek, and the Matadequin, past Allen's Mill, toward the forks of Old Church Road near the crossing of the Matadequin. Ferrero is ordered to hold his division ready to move to-morrow morning. Burnside afterwards threw back his right to the Boshor'sHouse and extended his line of skirmishers beyond. Willcox issued orders that until further orders all music from bands in the division be prohibited.[24]

23. Major General William F. Smith commanded the Eighteenth Corps, Army of the James.

24. *O.R.*, vol. 36, part 3, 603.

Capt. George W. Bisbing Co.I died in Washington to-day. He like Schall was universally loved by all in the regiment.

> "Green be his mossy grave,
> Immortal be his name,
> Above his banner proudly waves,
> While heaven records his fame."

Jun 6—A detail of 200 men from the regiment sent out to work on Redoubt Fletcher, being built near the widow Thompson's House. We are advancing our lines by boyaux and parallels. The enemy drove in the skirmishers in front of the 2d division this afternoon which gave them possession of the high ground near Tucker's and Bosher's House, at which point they planted artillery and opened a very heavy fire upon our lines, but without doing much damage to us. At 9 A.M., division commanders were ordered to place all their wagons, caissons, and artillery not in position, in some sheltered place near their commands and in such a position as to move readily when ordered, and if necessary, roads will be cut through the woods on the Cold Harbor Road, and staff officers are to make themselves acquainted with the roads over which trains will pass.[25]

At dark Willcox was ordered to push the construction of the redoubt in front of the Thompson House to-night with vigor.[26] The regiment on this date mustered only 388 men. This army has been marching and fighting 32 consecutive days, in which time no vegetable rations have been issued, and we have now reached a region of country notoriously unhealthy. The water used is entirely derived from surface drainage. The ground around many camps is strewn with dead and decomposed horses and mules, and with the hides and offial of slaughtered beef-cattle, and between the lines are many dead bodies of both armies partly unburied and decomposing in the burning sun. Fort Fletcher is named after Lt. Fletcher, 2d Infantry, killed at Spottsylvania.

I received a letter and papers from my sister. Prv. John Winegarden, Co. K, wounded.

Jun 7—Was detailed as Division Officer of the Day, and went on duty at 4 A.M., and relieved Capt. [C. B.] Grant of the 20th Mich. and later reported to Gen. Willcox for orders. Early in the day 100 men were detailed to work on Fort Fletcher, working day and night. Our 1st Division has taken up a line nearly at right angles with the main line, extending from near the Woody House in the direction of Allen's Mill. At 9.30 A.M. Burnside was directed to send a brigade to guard the crossing of the Matadequin at Allen's Mill, and the crossing between his right and Allen's Mill made by the road from Bosher's.

A flag of truce has been agreed upon to exist from 6 to 8 P.M., and corps commanders are directed to send out, under a white flag, medical officers with stretcher-bearers to bring in the dead and wounded, but no intercourse of any kind will be held with the enemy. And at 8.30 P.M. Burnside reported to Meade that the enemy on his front did not respect the flag of truce. His medical director was fired upon as he advanced with a white flag, and a continual fire kept up by the enemy during the whole period covered by the flag.[27]

A furious artillery fire was opened on Burnsides lines at midnight, but did us very little damage. To-night orders were given to Potter to retake the hill. As his troops advanced the enemy fell back, after which the position was strongly fortified.

---

25. *O.R.*, vol. 36, part 3, 657.

26. *O.R.*, vol. 36, part 3, 659.

27. *O.R.*, vol. 36, part 3, 681, 684.

Jun 8—Was relieved as Division Officer of the Day by Lt. Col. Ely of the 8th Mich. During the day the 51st P.V.V. and 27th Mich. were placed in the advance line occupied by Christs brigade, built breastworks, and slashed timber in our front. And again during the day the 51st P.V.V. was ordered into Fort Fletcher, and the right wing detailed to throw up breastworks on the outside of the fort, and worked until after dark.[28] Col. Hartranft was to-day commissioned a brigadier general, and I was commissioned Col. Maj. Gen. Crittenden commanding our 1st Division was relieved at his own request, and Brig. Gen. [James H.] Ledlie succeeded him in command. Prv. W. P. Schall Co. D by order of the War Department in S.O. No. 210 was authorized to proceed to his home at Norristown with the remains of his brother, with permission to remain at home three days.

Jun 9—Regiment remained in the fort all day. Received some letters from home, and some official documents from Washington. Made application to Gov. Curtin for a number of commissions to fill up vacancies in the regiment. Rain during the day.

Jun 10—Regiment still occupy Redoubt Fletcher. All quiet last night. Trees are being cut down on the left of the fort to widen the artillery range towards the battery in front of the 18th Corps. The enemy's sharpshooters annoy us some. At 2.45 P.M., the enemy's artillery commenced firing slowly at our fort. Roemer replies occasionally, otherwise all quiet along our lines. Hartranft has advanced his skirmishers about 20 paces to correspond with his new line. Wrote letters to my mother and sister. Received notice from the War Department that my ordnance returns, and accounts with the government were correct, and were closed.

Jun 11—Regiment still occupy the fort. All very quiet. Judging from orders received late this evening, it is very apparent that another flank movement will be made by this army. The order prohibiting the sounding of drum and bugle calls and playing of bands in this command issued some few days ago, was recalled to-day. S.O. No. 83 directs commissaries of subsistence in our division to make sales of supplies to officers on credit, until such times as they may be able to draw pay.

Jun 12—We received marching orders this morning, and left our position Fort Fletcher at 7 1/2 A.M. Passed through Cold Harbor on the road leading towards the James River passing Emmaus Church, and after a march of 20 miles, marching all night, we came to a halt, and went into bivouac along the road, in a very sandy field destitute of trees and everything else. G.O. No. 23 from Burnsides headquarters announces Maj. Gen. Parke U.S.V. as chief of staff, Ninth Army Corps, and the same order announces Maj. J. St. C. Morton, U.S. Engineers, as chief engineer of the corps, to date from May 18/64.[29]

Jun 13—We left our bivouac at 12 M. crossed Matadequin Creek also the White House railroad at Trevilian Station, and after a march of 10 miles went into bivouac at Baltimore Cross-roads at 9 P.M.

Jun 14—We left our bivouac at 3 A.M. passed Gordonsville and Providence Ford, crossed both branches of the Chickahominy River on pontoon boats at Mount Stery, and at 7 P.M. went into bivouac on the plantation of Ex-President John Tyler, some 6 miles from the James River.

Jun 15—Laid in bivouac all day, and the troops had nothing to eat all day, but we had a good rest. At 9 P.M., we left our camp and moved towards the James River and at 11 1/2 P.M., the 9th and 6th Corps crossed the river at Wilcox's Landing and Jones' Bridge. The pontoon bridge was built of 104 boats and the bridge itself was 2000 ft long. We marched all night. Our trains

---

28. Hartranft in *O.R.*, vol. 36, part 1, 952-3.

29. *O.R.*, vol. 36, part 3, 765.

crossed at Cole's Ferry. At the point of our crossing the river is 2,100 feet wide and 80 feet deep, and is 12 miles from City Point and 3 miles from Charles City Court House on the opposite bank is Windmill Point. The point at which we crossed is 20 miles from Petersburg. Our Fourth Division {Ferrero} did not cross with us, but marched to the Chickahominy River.

Chapter 13

Petersburg

June 16–December 31, 1864

After crossing the James River, the Ninth Corps took part in the initial assaults on the Petersburg defenses, then settled down as the armies dug in facing each other. The 51st participated in the attack following the mine explosion (July 30). Here Colonel Bolton was again wounded in the same place where he had been hit at Antietam. However, the surgeons were unable to extract the ball. He was sent home to recuperate and missed the regiment's engagement at the Weldon Railroad (August 19-21). Bolton returned to duty and assumed command of the 51st on October 16.

Jun 16—After marching all night and nearly all day, we arrived in front of Petersburg and about 2 1/2 miles from it on the banks of Harrison's Creek, about 6 P.M., formed line of battle, under the directions of Major Morton, engineer officer of the 9th A.C., on the extreme left of the army, with a regiment of cavalry still further to our left. About one hour later received orders to report to Hancock. Immediately moved forward and occupied works previously held by [Brig.] Gen. [Francis C.] Barlow's division, and remained in this position during the night.[1]

Ferrero's division crossed the Chickahominy and marched to the James River and encamped, relieving the troops of the Sixth Corps. Grant followed the army, crossing the pontoon bridge and followed the road to the front of Petersburg by way of Coch's Mill, Merchants, Hope Chapel and Old Court House. Before dark a general assault was made along the whole line of troops then in position against the enemy's second line, or intrenched position, and proved to be a most brilliant sight. Prv. Nathaniel Vancuran, Co. K, wounded. [Also Pvt. William Stutzman, Co. K, wounded.]

Jun 17—At daylight formed line and moved by the left flank down to the ravine in front and filed to the left up the same until uncovered by the 2d Corps, halted and formed line under direction of Maj. Morton, directly in front of Potter's division.

A short time after moved to the right and formed in two lines in the following order, First line, 2d Mich. 109th N.Y. 37th Wisc. 38th Wisc. Second line 27th Mich. 8th Mich. 51st Penna. At 2 P.M., the command "Forward" was given, and we advanced under a most terrific fire of the enemy's artillery from the left flank. The dust raised by the brigade passing over the

---

1. This entry, as well as those from June 17th and 18th, are taken from Hartranft's report in *O.R.*, vol. 40, part 1, 576-8.

plowed ground on the double-quick and the enemy's shot plowing up the dust made it impossible to see lines as they advanced. The left companies of the left regiment of the first line struck the enemy's pits, and but 18 men out of 95 in those companies made their escape. The remainder of our brigade passed on in front of the enemy's lines, and passed over the 2d Corps line and reformed. As far as our brigade was concerned the attack was a failure. An hour later regimental commanders reported 1,050 men in line out of 1,890, but a few men came in during the afternoon and evening.[2]

Later in the day the 1st Division of the 9th Corps (Ledlie's) and a part of Christ's brigade advanced over the same ground and carried the enemy's line of pits, our brigade moving up at the same time in support on the bank of the ravine. Our brigade remained in this position until daylight. In a second attack of our division at 5.30 P.M. one stand of colors (35 North Carolina) and 100 prisoners were captured. The 51st lost as follows:

Killed:

Pvt. Henry H. Fry, Co. C	Pvt. David Lenhart, Co. E
Pvt. Franklin Hendricks, Co. C	Pvt. Bartley McIlarney, Co. G
Cpl. Wm. Kooker, Co. C	Sgt. Stephen S. Davis, Co. I
Cpl. Joseph Cornag, Co. C	Sgt. Thomas C. Pierce, Co. K

Wounded:

Prv. Lewis Meyers, Co. A (died July 18)	
Prv. Jonathan Webber, Co. A	
Pvt. Jonathan Weeber, Co. A	Pvt. William Kline, Co. E
Pvt. William Buckman, Co. B	Cpl. H. C. McCormick, Co. H
Pvt. Henry Gregory, Co. B	Pvt. Jonathan Hefner, Co. H
Sgt. William J. Osterstock, Co. B	Pvt. John A. Neiman, Co. H (died August 5)
Pvt. William O. Rauch, Co. B	Pvt. John Harris, Co. K (died June 30)
Cpl. J. M. Wein, Co. B	Pvt. Daniel Hoover, Co. K (died June 27)
Pvt. Thomas Sullivan, Co. C	Pvt. Henry Houtz, Co. K
Cpl. Hunter Smedley, Co. D	Pvt. James Marr, Co. K
Sgt. George Diehl, Co. E	Sgt. John Vanlew, Co. K

Deserted:

Prv. Francis Yerger, Co. D

Gen. Hartranft was slightly wounded in the wrist, the ball passing through his pocket, going through a war map he had in his pocket.

Jun 18—We were again drawn up in line of battle at daylight, with about the same formation as yesterday, only that the 51st Penna. was in the first line. We charged at a point on the Suffolk and Petersburg Railroad driving the enemy before us, Maj. Morton directing our course, carrying a compas in his hand. He was shot through the heart and fell dead. We charged in good order and took the railroad cut, and were followed by Raulston's brigade.[3] The enemy's sharpshooters commanded this cut from the right. A traverse was at once built across the cut on the right of the line by tearing up the track and ties.

---

2. From Willcox's report in *O.R.*, vol. 40, part 1, 571.

3. Colonel William C. Raulston took over command of Christ's brigade after Colonel Christ was wounded on June 17.

About 4 P.M., an order was received to advance upon the enemy's works without regard to the troops on our right or left. The enemy's line was about 250 yards in advance. A little stream of water, Poo River, forming a ravine, with trees on the opposite side of the bank intervened. This railroad cut was about fifteen to twenty feet deep, and the sides almost perpendicular. Steps and holes had to be made in the same so as to enable the troops to climb up on the bank, which was commanded by the enemy from his main line. Many, however, were killed and wounded here. The troops of the entire division were in condition to make but a feeble attack; the regiments scarcely averaged 100 men.

Between 5 and 6 P.M., the whole division was out of the cut and in the ravine in advance. The troops were again moved forward to attack, reaching the summit of the opposite bank of the ravine, about 100 yards from the enemy's line. Our line became exposed to the full view of the enemy, whose fire was too severe to attempt any further advance. Our position, however, held and intrenched during the night, and is the nearest point to the enemy's line gained by our army. Our intrenching tools were tin cups, plates and spoons. Poo Creek, or river as called by the rebels, run red with blood and the flag of the 2d Mich. was found floating down the little stream. Yesterday I had a part of my coat-tail shot away by a piece of shell. The 2d Brigade of our division changed its commander three times on the field all having been shot down at their posts. Maj. Morton's body was taken to Burnside's headquarters, and by the orders of Meade his body was ordered to be sent in an ambulance to City Point, where it can be forwarded to Philadelphia, with some suitable officers to attend to the matter. He also adds, I regret the glorious exploits of the Ninth to-day should be dampened by such sad attending events. Our regiment lost as follows:

Killed:

Sgt. Wm. Digman, Co. D

Cpl. Edwiny R. Worth, Co. F

Pvt. Wm. Young, Co. G

Wounded:

Capt. Joseph K. Bolton, Co. A

Cpl. William Smith, Co. A*

Pvt. Jonathan Brooks, Co. A*

Pvt. Chas. Fix, Co. A

Sgt. John W. Meeker, Co. B*

Pvt. Henry Scott, Co. B*

Pvt. Henry Erhard, Co. C* (died July 9)

Pvt. Josiah M. Favinger, Co. C*

Pvt. Joseph Greem Co. C*

Pvt. Abraham Tochler, Co. C*

Sgt. Penrose W. Clare, Co. D

Pvt. Thomas D. Smith, Co. D

Pvt. Jacob S. Boop, Co. E*

Pvt. Henry C. Diehl, Co. E*

Cpl. Henry D. Fox, Co. E*

Pvt. William R. Heckman, Co. E*

Pvt. Barton Kennedy, Co. E*

Lieut. James L. Seebold, Co. E*

Cpl. Thomas S. Mauck, Co. E (died June 20)

Pvt. Henry Miller, Co. E*

Pvt. John Rahback, Co. E*

Pvt. William Schnure, Co. E*

Pvt. Judson Callendar, Co. F

Cpl. George W. Hiltner, Co. F

Pvt. George W. Rodgers, Co. G

Lieut. Jacob Fryburger, Co. K

Jun 19—Our brigade was relieved at 2 A.M. by Potter's division and retired about one half mile and encamped in a woods for some rest. Received a number of letters and papers from home, the first for sometime. Also received some official papers from Washington. All seems comparatively quiet in our front.

Jun 20—Rested all day in the rear. Received a letter from my sister. At midnight ordered again to the front and relieved a division of the 2d Corps. Continued slashing and building abatis. Ferrero's division colored troops was to-day placed in the second line of works in the front occupied by the 9th A.C. Prvs. Henry Furich Co. B and Thomas Hardenstine Co. I wounded, and Copl. Thomas S. Mauch Co. E died of wounds. Prv. Wm. H. Griffith Co. F who had been dropped from the rolls as a deserter was by orders from 9th Corps headquarters restored to duty, to make good the time lost from April 30th. 1863, when dropped to May 26/64, when he returned to duty to his regiment, with loss of all pay and emoluments during that time, this by order of Burnside.

Jun 21—Our brigade has relieved Motts division of the 2d Corps, and the 51st P.V.V. now occupy the most advance line, less than 150 yards from the rebel line. Beans, whisky and potatoes issued to the men, the first for about three months. All very quiet around Petersburg to-day. The President is here and is riding around with Grant visiting the lines, and is being well received by all the troops along the whole line. During the day the 9th A.C. relieved the 2d, 18th, and the 6th Army Corps. The two latter corps were moved across the Jerusalem Plank Road, which the 5th Corps was extended. Prv. James McKenna Co. D was killed to-day, while filling his canteen with water from a spring in a ravine near our pits.

Jun 22—The 51st P.V.V. still occupy the advance line in the rifle-pits and and ordered to be very vigilant, and are now on three quarter rations. Under some difficulties I managed to write a letter to A. L. Russell Adjutant Gen. Penna. for a new flag to replace the one captured from us at Spottsylvania Court-House May 12/64. The enemy are placing abatis in front of their lines in our front, also in front of the 5th Corps, who join us on the left. The fight this evening was in front of the 2d and 6th Corps. At 9.25 P.M. we of the 9th Corps received orders to hold ourselves in readiness to move without a moments delay in event of being called upon to aid in the attack at 3.30 to-morrow morning.[4]

Jun 23—The 51st P.V.V. still occupy the advance line. During the day I received a number of official documents from Washington D.C. Our division are erecting works for artillery within 200 yards of the enemy's main line, and have built abatis along our whole division front under heavy fire. Ferrero was relieved by a part of the 10th A.C. and took position in rear of 2d Division 9th A.C. A part of our division relieved [Brig. Gen. Samuel W.] Crawford's division 5th A.C. The firing on our division front was almost incessant last night, and up to daylight this morning.

Jun 24—I was detailed as Division Officer of the Day, and reported to Col. [Ebenezer W.] Peirce, now commanding 2d Brigade 1st Division 9th A. Corps, who is Corps Officer of the Day. Regiment still occupy the advance line. Ordered to make out our muster-rolls, but find that it is impossible to do so as we are without our regimental and company books and papers. They are now on board of a barge at City Point, together with all of the baggage of the regimental officers, who have not seen their baggage since leaving Warrenton. Later in the day Meade authorized the books and baggage mentioned to be brought up, but wagons and baggage to be returned as soon as possible. The enemy opened their guns along the entire line during the day but did us no damage.

In accordance with S.O. No. 91, Burnside's headquarters, Prv. Jacob Sweeney Co. B and James Powers Co. D were detailed as mounted pioneers, and ordered to report to Capt. Price, Chief Q.M. 9th A.C. near City Point.

Jun 25—The 51st P.V.V. still occupy the advance line, and our whole corps are engaged in strengthening and straightening our lines and getting artillery in position, building abatis, &c.

---

4. *O.R.*, vol. 40, part 2, 319.

I received my commission as colonel of the regiment, also a number of other commissions for the regiment. Lemons, onions, pickels, and dried apples issued to the men. Fifteen men detailed from the regiment to report to the division quarter master for duty.

Jun 26—The 51st P.V.V. still occupy the advance line. Had a very sharp firing on our front during the whole night. Pickles, cabbage, dried apples and whisky issued to the men, but the men declare only a smell of each. The weather is exceedingly hot.

All of the officers in our division are dead broke. The consequence is that Burnside has issued a S.O. that Comy's of Subsistence in the 3d Division are directed to sell subsistence stores to officers, on credit, who may request it, until such time as the regiments be paid.

Jun 27—The 51st P.V.V. still occupy the advance line. This afternoon we received a circular from Gen. Hartranft, ordering the 51st Reg. Penna. Vet. Vol., 109th New York Vols. and 37th Wis. Vols. to be ready to move to the front line of works now held as a picket line immediately after dark this evening. They will be prepared to remain in the front line for 48 hours. One third of the number of men constantly be kept awake and on the alert, and the rest will have their accoutrements on, ready for any emergency. All the men will be kept in the pits. Our line at this point was in the shape of a horse shoe. Our object was to take out and to straighten up this line to the dotted line. The 51st was assigned this task, and right after dark, the regiment commenced while the other two regiments carried sand-bags. They soon gave out, and it remained to the 51st to finish the work, which was done before daylight, without the loss of a man. I was required to report in writing every hour to Gen. Willcox my progress. I alone expended 6,000 rounds of ammunition during the night. Our line is now within 100 yards of the enemys advance line, and that many yards from the battery we are running a mine under. A number of other regiments were put at this work, but failed to succeed. Very heavy firing on both sides all night. A rebel shell exploded within ten feet of my quarters.

Jun 28—The 51st P.V.V. still occupy the advance line. The enemy opened upon us with a mortar battery early this morning. Many shell have dropped in our lines, but without damage. [Sgt. George Carney, Co. I, wounded.]

Jun 29—The regiment pretty well used up, having been on the front line eight days and nights, and by the urgent request of Willcox, are still holding the advance line. The enemy continue to throw shell much to our discomfort. Prv. Samuel Gillespie Co. F killed. [Pvt. Henry Feurich, Co. B, wounded.]

Jun 30—The 51st still occupy the advance line. By the orders of Willcox I mustered the regiment for pay in the trenches under great discomforts and danger, shell dropping around us all day, but no one hurt. Very heavy firing from both sides during the night. Sour-krout, dried apples, lemons, and tobacco issued to the men.

Jul 1—The 51st still holding the advance line. Gen. Hartranft presented me with a pair of colonels shoulder straps. Fresh bread issued to the men. I had a large hole dug in the bank at the foot of the hill in rear of the regiment and built a bomb-prof of railroad sills and railroad iron, placing seven feet of earth on top. The Poo Creek was in front of it. Prv. Wm. H. Shriner Co. H killed. Have received the following:

Adjutant General's Department
Harrisburg, July 1st. 1864.
Major Wm. J. Bolton commanding 51st Regt. P.V.V. Army of the Potomac near Petersburg, Va.,
Major--Your favor of the 22d inst., has just been received. I have already

ordered by telegraph, a new flag for the 51st Regiment P.V.V., and Messrs. Horstman Bro. & Co., to make and forward it to Col. Frank Jordan, Military Adjutant for Pennsylvania, No. 487 11th street, Washington D.C. at the earliest practicable day. Col. Jordan will transmit it to the Regiment without delay.

I congratulate you, Major, that the brilliant record of the 51st is in no degree dishonored by the loss of your flag, under the circumstances so clearly detailed by your letter, but is subject of deep regret that the lives of so many brave men were necessarily sacrificed in defending it.

That portion of your letter, relating to commissions, has been referred to Lieut. Col. S. B. Thomas A.D.C. of the Governor, having charge of the Military Register, who will give it his immediate attention.

With regards to Gen. Hartranft, I am very respectfully yours,
A. L. Russell.
Adjutant General of Pennsylvania.

Jul 2—The 51st P.V.V. still holding the advance line. I was taken very sick during the night. A letter from Daniel H. Stein of Norristown. The night was one of unusual quiet. The enemy are working on their lines, and we can hear them very plainly. We of our division have finished a new covered way to facilitate relieving the pickets. Very warm.

Jul 3—The 51st P.V.V. still holding the advance line. Received a letter from my sister with $25.00 enclosed. [Sgt.] John W. Fair Co.C wounded.

Jul 4—The 51st P.V.V. still holding the advance line.

Jul 5—The 51st P.V.V. still holding the advance line. I was detailed Division Officer of the Day, and reported to Gen. Willcox for orders.

Jul 6—The 51st P.V.V. still holding the advance line. The consolidated morning report of the regiment, for the 8th day of June 1864, as follows: Commission Officers present for duty, 13–Enlisted men present 419. Commission Officers absent, 16.–Enlisted men absent, 463, aggregate number of officers, 29.–aggregate number of enlisted men, 882.–total, 911.

Jul 7—The 51st still holding the advance line. I made an effort to be mustered as colonel, but did not succeed. Received a letter from my sister, and wrote her one. I received through the Adj. Genl's. Department, Harrisburg, Pa., commissions for Lane S. Hart, Jacob P. Brooke, Wm. W. Owen, Allen Fillman, Wm. R. Foster, James L. Seibold, Thomas D. Reed, Geo. H. Smith, and John W. Fair. Firing along our lines was pretty constant during the day and night. [Pvt. John Godley, Co. K, and Cpl. Jacob Truxall, Co. K, killed.]

Jul 8—The 51st still holding the advance line. Received and wrote several letters. The enemy restless and made a charge along our whole line, but were repulsed with heavy loss. Prv. Levi Mattis Co. A killed. During the day a six inch cohorn mortar shell fell within a foot of me, but happened to light in the water, and did not explode. I dug it out of the mud and sent it home. It contains 177 small iron balls. Received commissions from the governor for Geo. Schall and Mark Supplee. We have not had a drop of rain for over one month. Have not seen my trunk since the 4th of May. Very hot.

Jul 9—The 51st P.V.V. still holdind [sic] the advance line. Received a number of letters, and wrote a number. Weather hot, and still no rain.

Jul 10—The 51st P.V.V. still holding the advance line. A little whisky issued to the men in the trenches. Hot and no rain.

Jul 11—The 51st P.V.V. still holding the advance line. A flag of truce appeared on the rebel line near our front, but did not amount to much. Received a letter from Gen. Ramsey, Chief of Ordnance, advising me that my ordnance return was all right. Still no rain.

Jul 12—The 51st P.V.V. still holding the advance line. Received eleven commissions from Gov. Curtin. The noise of railroad trains and steam-whistles was heard quite plain during most of the night. Just before midnight several bright lights were shown from different points on the enemy's lines, but the night passed with the usual picket firing. This morning there was a ringing of bells in the town.[5]

Jul 13—The 51st P.V.V. still holding the advance line. Received a number of papers from home. The cars were running to and fro through the night, on the left side of the town. The rebels fired five shells from the left redoubt (opposite Warren) which fell and exploded in rear of our brigade.[6] Still very hot, and no rain.

Jul 14—The 51st P.V.V. still holding the advance line. Very brisk mortar fire all day.

Jul 15—The 51st P.V.V. still holding the advance line. Priv. Adam Yeager Co. A killed in the trenches.

Jul 16—The 51st P.V.V. still holding the advance line. Very brisk firing all day. Prvs. Wm. M. Stutzman and Daniel Scheets Co. K wounded. After dark the regiment was relieved by the 109th New York, and retired to the rear and occupied their camp near Burnside's headquarters. The regiment had occupied the trenches 26 days and night, constantly under fire, and in that time expended 171,000 rounds of ammunition.

Jul 17—I was detailed as Division Officer of the Day, and reported to Gen. Willcox for orders. Wrote a letter to Hon. Ely Sliffer.[7] Information was received during the day from deserters that Longstreet's Corps would attack on their front to-night, that is, Burnside's left wing and Warren's right. The consequence of this was that the 51st was again ordered to the front after dark, and it was also ordered that all batteries, caissons, limbers, &c not in position to be kept harnassed all night. Laid on our arms all night, awaiting attack.

Jul 18—The regiment returned from the front after daylight, and again re-occupied our old camp. A deserter from the 59th Georgia came into our lines about 12 o'clock last night, and states that orders were issued to the pickets last evening to fire on any man seen going beyond the picket line, that his colonel said no attack would be made on our lines, as so many deserters came into our lines yesterday and told all us all about it. The deserter says that it was generally understood an attack was to be made last night. Longstreet was to assault us in front and Hill would make a circuit in our rear. The day has been a quiet one on our lines.

Jul 19—Company drills, the first for some time. I paid a visit to City Point and took dinner with Mrs. Major Holstein, and Miss Lizzie Brower, at the hospital, and after a pleasant ride reached my camp during the night.

Jul 20—Company drills. Received several letters from home. A detail of men have been employed to-day cutting new abatis, which will be laid soon after dark at points where it is weak. A mortar shell caused an explosion this afternoon in the rebel redoubt on the left of New Market Road. Capt. Roemer threw a shell into a house in the rebel lines this evening, which set fire to the building. The shell was charged with inflammable material, mixed for the

---

5. *O.R.*, vol. 40, part 3, 194-5 (Willcox's report).

6. *O.R.*, vol. 40, part 3, 215.

7. Eli Slifer was Secretary of the Commonwealth of Pennsylvania.

purpose by Roemer. He says "the first shot did the business".[8] The usual amount of firing is going on day and night.

Jul 21—Company drills, received and wrote several letters. There has been to-day great activity on the part of the enemy in front of the Second and Third Divisions of our corps, digging and strengthening their lines. About seventy pieces of abatis timber were put out during the night.[9]

Jul 22—Company drills. Received ordnance papers from Washington. I was to-day mustered as Colonel of the regiment. Capt. Lane S. Hart Co. F promoted Major yesterday and Com. Sgt. Allen H. Fillman promoted 2d Lt. 1st Lt. Jacob P. Brooke Co. F promoted Capt. and 2d Lt. W. W. Owen Co. F promoted 1st Lt.

The rebels in front of Hartranft's brigade attempted to lay some additional abatis, but were prevented by our fire. We have materially strengthened our own within the last forty-eight hours. The picket firing heavier than usual last night.[10]

Jul 23—Company drills, and dress parade. Made out my ordnance return and forwarded them to Washington. Unusually quiet on our line all day and night. New abatis put out. The enemy opened a new mortar battery on Potter's right and threw some shells at our working party in the covered way to the 14 gun battery (Fort Morton) but did no damage.[11]

Jul 24—Company drills, and dress parade. Made out ammunition return and forwarded it to the War department. Regiment inspected.

Jul 25—Company drills. Sent ordnance return to Washington. There has been more than usual shelling by the enemy late this afternoon. The men suffered considerably in the trenches from the rain. Three regiments of Hartranft's brigade had to stand up all night. Received orders to detail from the regiment 100 men with the usual compliment of commissioned and non-commissioned officers for picket duty to report at early dusk on the flat of the creek, and await orders, to relieve the pickets of the 2d Brigade. But when the detail was ready to move from camp, I received another order from Hartranft ordering the whole regiment to the front immediately after dusk, put 200 men on the skirmish line in front of the 2d Brigade and the balance to occupy the trenches of the 2d Regiment Mich. V.V.I. The latter order I obeyed and moved to the new position at 9 P.M., and points designated.

Jul 26—Detailed as Division Officer of the Day and reported to Gen. Willcox and Col. Bliss. Bought a horse from Gen. Hartranft for $160.00. Humphrey's [Brigade] (Second) of our division moved to the left of the army, on the Suffolk Road, and occupied works held by the Second Corps. The changes made by the troops last night and to-night was done so quietly that we met with very little loss. There was incessant musketry by both sides during the night. The enemy's pickets were very active.[12]

Jul 27—Detailed a member of a military commission and met at brigade headquarters.

Jul 28—Met the military commission at brigade headquarters. The musketry and mortar firing is about as usual.

---

8. *O.R.*, vol. 40, part 3, 355.

9. *O.R.*, vol. 40, part 3, 371-3.

10. *O.R.*, vol. 40, part 3, 398.

11. *O.R.*, vol. 40, part 3, 414.

12. *O.R.*, vol. 40, part 3, 481.

Jul 29—Met the military commission at brigade headquarters. Received our new flag through the state commissioner at Washington D.C. A Circular Order was issued to us to-day informing us that the mine would be exploded to-morrow morning at 3.30 by Col. Pleasants, giving the directions to each division commander his orders as to the movement.[13]

Jul 30—The regiment moved to the front to take position at 2 A.M., and a little later our whole four divisions were massed in front of the rebel redoubt known as Redoubt Pegram, or salient, with the 18th A.C. in reserve. After some waiting the fort was exploded at 4.42 A.M. Immediately all of our guns 110 guns and 54 mortars opened along the whole line. The firing was from each piece slow, deliberate, and careful, partaking of the nature of target practice, and was very effective, taking great care in firing over our heads. Ledlie's division 9th A.C. led the charge. The enemy's guns in front of the Fifth Corps were soon silenced, and his fire in front of the Ninth Corps confined to a battery on the hill behind the mine, and to one gun from his work, next south of the mine. The charge was not successful, but we held the crater.

At 8.20 A.M. Hartranft had dug out one gun and placed it in position to fire on the enemy's left flank.[14] At 9.45 A.M., Meade sent orders to Burnside to withdraw, to exercise his own discretion as to the time now or to-night. The enemy had a cross fire on us and it was a difficult matter to get out of the crater. At 1 P.M. the bottom, sides, and nearly all parts of the crater were strewn with dead, dying, and wounded soldiers, causing pools of blood to be formed at the bottom of the crater. It was impossible to get water without great loss of life. Gen. Bartlett ordered a traverse to be cut through the works in order to let the men pass through without being seen by the enemy.

About 2 P.M. the loss of life was terrible. There was death below as well as above ground in the crater. The heat was intense. Two of the captured guns were put in position and turned on the enemy, and were manded by men from the 14th New York Heavy Artillery under the command of Sergt. W. Stanley, but he was killed during the day. About 10,000 rounds of ammunition was carried up by the 51st P.V.V. during the action, part of whom were shot. Burnside did not give the order to retire until 12.30 P.M. and in retreating is where our heavy loss was sustained.[15] I was wounded soon after the explosion, having received a ball in the same place in my face as I did at Antietam. I was carried off the field by Musc. John W. Shillich and Prv. Samuel Taylor, and my wound temporarily attended to by Dr. Rineholdt of my regiment, and then carried through the covered way to the 14 gun battery, placed in an ambulance and taken to division hospital, and the ball probed for by Dr. Wm. C. Shurlock of my regiment, but he failed to locate it, and at sunset was placed in an ambulance and taken to City Point hospital, receiving very kind treatment from Mrs. Major Holstein and Miss Lizzie Brower, who happened to be from my own home.

Our loss in the regiment as follows:

Killed:

Pvt. John F. Ackerman, Co. B   Sgt. James Gibson, Co. K
Lieut. Allen H. Filman, Co. F
Cpl. Josiah Wood, Co. F (acting as orderly to Hartranft)

---

13. *O.R.*, vol. 40, part 3, 596-7. Lieutenant Colonel Henry Pleasants of the 48th Pennsylvania supervised the digging of the now-famous "Mine" under the Southern fort opposite his line.

14. *O.R.*, vol. 40, part 3, 667.

15. *O.R.*, vol. 40, part 1, 575.

Wounded:

Col. William J. Bolton	Pvt. Sutton Kreamer, Co. F
Pvt. William Herbster, Co. A	Pvt. James Hall, Co. G
Pvt. Washington Smith, Co. A	Pvt. Abraham B. King, Co. G
Pvt. Jeremiah Fry, Co. C	Pvt. Daniel Sheets, Co. G (died August 1)
Pvt. Franklin Grubb, Co. C	Pvt. John C. Leamon, Co. H
Pvt. Ellwood Hamilton, Co. C	Capt. George Shorkley, Co. H
Pvt. William Hotchkiss, Co. C	Cpl. John George, Co. I (died August 8)
Sgt. Walter M. Thompson, Co. D	Sgt. Daniel W. Eichman, Co. K
Pvt. Jacob K. Mertz, Co. E	Pvt. Isaiah Henry, Co. K
Lieut. Martin L. Schock, Co. E	Pvt. Samuel Rank, Co. K

Captured:

Pvt. Nelson Y. Mattis, Co. A	Pvt. Jacob Casher, Co. G
Pvt. John W. Sheckler, Co. E	

From the time that Redoubt Pegram was built, the enemy never succeeded in firing but one shot from their guns, and that was fired at the 51st P.V.V. We were too close to them. All the embrasures in the fort were protected by gun-mantilets, nor did they ever thereafter fire a single shot from that point, as we always until the close of the war held our whole original line.

Jul 31—Major Lane S. Hart now in command of the regiment, and the regiment is again occupying their old line in the trenches in front of the crater. I left early this morning, bidding adieu to the hospital at City Point, walking to the landing, and took the steamer *Cincinnati* with the other wounded for Washington D.C. Fortunatly I fell in with a Miss Sharpless from Bloomsburg, Pa., who was a nurse on the steamer. She was very kind to me, and attended to all my wonts while on the steamer. Whisky issued to the men.

Aug 1—I arrived in Washington D.C. at 12 o'clock M., was placed in an ambulance, and taken to Georgetown Seminary hospital. My wound very painful and am suffering inwardly. Regiment still remains on the advance line.

Asst. Surgeon Charles L. Duffell by S.O. No. 30 was to-day detached from the regiment and assigned to duty with the 109th Regiment New York Vols. Received to-day commissions for Owen, Bruce, and Filman.

Aug 2—I remained in bed all day. The ball probed for by the surgeons but they failed to locate it. Feeling very sore in my back. Regiment still occupy the front line.

Aug 3—I am feeling somewhat better. Regiment still occupy the advance line. Whiskey, onions, and cod-fish were to-day issued to the men.

Aug 4—I am feeling much better. Paymaster called at the hospital and paid me $842.44. Regiment still occupy the advance line.

Aug 5—I am feeling much better. Wrote a letter to my mother. Regiment still doing daily duty on the advance line.

Aug 6—I am not feeling very well, and cannot rest. Applied for a leave of absence. Regiment still doing duty on the advance line. Gen. Hartranft has been ordered to relieve the troops of Col. Humphrey's brigade now in the trenches to-night. Col. Humphrey will furnish the number equivalent to the 51st Penn. Vet. Vols. from his brigade.

Aug 7—I am not feeling very well, and rest very little. Regiment still doing duty on the advance line.

Aug 8—I am not feeling very well. Regiment still doing duty on the front line.

Aug 9—I am not feeling very well. Received a letter from my sister. Regiment still on the front line. The enemy has manifested unusual activity throughout the day on our immediate front. Roemer's battery has troubled them somewhat.[16]

Aug 10—I am feeling somewhat better. Regiment still on the front line.

Aug 11—Somewhat better. Received a leave of absence, and left the Georgetown Hospital at 11.15 A.M. arriving in Philada. at 6 P.M. and Norristown at 8 P.M. Regiment still on the front line.

Aug 12—Not very well. Dr. Wm. Corson[17] in attendence but cannot find the ball. Regiment was relieved from the front line, after being on this same front eighteen days, went in bivouac near Burnside's headquarters for a little rest.

Aug 13—Feeling better. Wrote letters to Gen. Hartranft and Quartermaster Samuel P. Stephens. Regiment paid to-day.

Aug 14—Feeling much better. All the regimental baggage brought from City Point, where it had been kept for safety. Found it in a bad condition, particularly the regimental books and papers.

Aug 15—Not feeling very well, and remained in the house all day. Regimental inspection and dress parade, the first for sometime. Lieut. George B. Campbell of the 51st P.V.V. was to-day announced on the staff of Gen. Hartranft as acting Engineer Officer of the Brigade.

Aug 16—Not so well to-day, and remained in the house all day. Company drills and dress parade.

Aug 17—Not so well to-day. Received several letters from friends in the regiment. A general inspection of the regiment.

Aug 18—Feeling a little better. Company drills and dress parade.

Warren moved with his corps this morning to across the Weldon [Rail]road about one mile south of the lead works. He had considerable fighting during the day, suffering some loss and inflicting loss on the enemy. Two of the 9th Corps divisions were relieved by troops of the Eighteenth Corps, and at the same time we of the 9th Corps relieved and occupied the ground held by the Fifth Corps, extending across the Jerusalem Plank Road, and refusing on the left as far as the Williams House.

About 1.30 o'clock this morning a heavy artillery fire was opened from both sides, commenced on the right of the enemy, and gradually worked to the left until the entire front was engaged. In front of the 3d Division (Willcox) heavy mortar shells were thrown. This firing lasted, with more or less fury, until 3.30 o'clock, and in the part of the evening kept up an active musketry fire on this same division.[18]

A detail of 125 men including a full complement of comd and non-comd officers from the 51st P.V.V. has been ordered to report to Lieut. Seydecker at 5 o'clock to-morrow morning at the skirt of woods in rear of the 14 gun redoubt on old 9th Corps front, also another detail of

16. *O.R.*, vol. 42, part 2, 100.

17. Corson was a Norristown physician. He was involved in the abolition movement and the underground railroad.

18. *O.R.*, vol. 42, part 2, 279.

45 men including a full compliment of comd and non-comd officers to report to Lieut. Cuyler at 5 o'clock to-morrow morning at the new works being constructed at head of Norfolk railroad cut and to the left in front of the covered way.

Aug 19—Feeling much better.

The three divisions of the 9th A.C. were sent this morning to re-enforce the Fifth Corps. We left our camp at 2 o'clock A.M., marching through the rain and mud to the Weldon Railroad, near the Yellow Tavern, and in the afternoon the regiment under the command of Maj. Hart, formed in line of battle in a heavy rain storm and remained on the field all night.

Our brigade of the First (Hartranft's) successfully repulsed the first two attacks of the enemy, and our Second Brigade (Humphrey's) gained possession of the line of works from which the Fifth Corps had retired. Our division remained in the front line until the afternoon of the 20th, when it was withdrawn. At 10 P.M., Willcox telegraphed Parke that the corps had did finely to-day, and that Warren had complimented us highly, and that Hartranft and White[19] stood the brunt of Mahone's Division and captured some prisoners, and that Potter had got up in time to save the road of communication.[20]

Maj. Lane S. Hart received three wounds in this action, and of course had to retire, and the command of the regiment fell to the lot of Capt. Joseph K. Bolton. The killed, wounded and captured in the regiment were as follows:

Killed:

Cpl. George M. Aurand, Co. E	Pvt. Christian Sheets, Co. G
Pvt. Alfred Meckley, Co. E	Cpl. Thomas Foster, Co. K

Wounded:

Major Lane S. Hart	Pvt. George Bowman, Co. F
Cpl. John S. Jones, Co. A	Capt. Jacob P. Brooke, Co. F
Cpl. Washington Smith, Co. A	Sgt. Benjamin White, Co. F
Pvt. James M. Doud, Co. A	Lieut. Curtin B. Stoneroad, Co. G
Pvt. Henry McLain, Co. A (also captured)	Pvt. George Dulott, Co. G
Lieut. John W. Farr, Co. C	Pvt. R. C. Hollabaugh, Co. G
Sgt. John W. Fair, Co. C	Pvt. Thomas Moser, Co. G
Cpl. Hugh Lynch, Co. C	Pvt. James T. Kelly, Co. H
Pvt. Christopher Briggs, Co. C	Pvt. H. J. Lingerman, Co. H
Pvt. Jacob Keely, Co. C	Pvt. Thomas Weaver, Co. H
Pvt. James Watter, Co. C	Pvt. Howard E. Gordon, Co. I
Pvt. John Powell, Co. D	Sgt. George W. S. Pennell, Co. I
Pvt. John Roshon, Co. D (died August 22)	Pvt. Thomas Richards, Co. I
Pvt. William Smith, Co. D	Pvt. Lewis Aikey, Co. K
Pvt. Jacob Stadenmayer, Co. D	Pvt. William Poust, Co. K (died Sept. 10)
Sgt. Ellridge G. Maize, Co. E	Pvt. Edward H. Richards, Co. K

Captured:

Pvt. William Horff, Co. A	Pvt. Jonathan Brooks, Co. B
Pvt. John A. Jordan, Co. A	Pvt. Lewis Grupp, Co. B

---

19. Brigadier General Julius White commanded the First Division of the Ninth Corps.

20. *O.R.*, vol. 42, part 2, 320.

Pvt. Samuel F. Knapp, Co. B
Pvt. Jeremiah Cassidy, Co. D
Pvt. Addison Cornog, Co. D
Pvt. Thomas Dunbar, Co. D
Pvt. Stephen Thorp, Co. D
Pvt. Isaac Yocum, Co. D
Pvt. Jeremiah Akey, Co. E
Pvt. Isaac Dolby, Co. E
Pvt. John W. Sheckly, Co. E

Pvt. John Frye, Co. F
Pvt. Samuel Taylor, Co. F
Sgt. Louis Cartuyvel, Co. G
Pvt. George Larrah, Co. G
Sgt. J. J. Peters, Co. G
Cpl. George H. Carey, Co. H
Pvt. Alfred Kunce, Co. H
Pvt. Alfred Kuntz, Co. K

Aug 20—Feeling better. Regiment commenced skirmishing at daylight, through the mud and rain. Remained all day.

Aug 21—Feeling much better. This morning the First Brigade (Hartranft) took up a position and threw up a line of works in front of Blick's House, crossing the railroad. The enemy attacked in the morning at 10.30, but was repulsed. In the afternoon our division was moved to the right and intrenched.

The following men were captured from the regiment:

Lieut. Benjamin P. Thompson, Co. A
Pvt. Augustus Rolley, Co. G
Cpl. Henry G. Dantler, Co. K
Pvt. Solomon Reish, Co. K

Pvt. Henry Underkoffer, Co. C
Pvt. Peter Smith, Co. H
Pvt. Franklin F. Duck, Co. K
Pvt. Alfred Yoke, Co. K

Aug 22—Feeling much better. Regiment still in the intrenchments in line of battle.

Aug 23—Feeling much better. I paid a visit to Philada. and was paid by Maj. Taggart $189.08. During the day the regiment fell back a short distance built some works and threw out pickets.

Aug 24—Much better. Regiment still occupy the intrenchments and building corduroy roads.

Aug 25—Feeling very much better. Our division left their intrenchments at 3 P.M., and marched some ten miles to Ream's Station to support Hancock, arriving on the battle field at dark. We formed line of battle, built some works. Found Hancock's troops very much demoralized and retreating with the loss of some of their artillery. Helped to stay the retreating troops and held the field. Left the works at midnight and moved down the Jerusalem Plank Road.

Aug 26—Feeling very much better. Regiment after marching from midnight of the 25th reached a point within two miles of the Yellow Tavern at 4 o'clock A.M., threw out pickets and took some rest.

Aug 27—Feeling much better. Regiment left their bivouac at the Yellow Tavern moving to the right, relieving part of the 4th Division Ninth Army Corps (colored troops).

Lieut. Benj. P. Thompson who was taken prisoner Aug. 21, was taken to Libby Prison where he was confined about six weeks. From there he was taken to Salisbury N.C. and remained there about two weeks. From there he was taken to Danville Va., and remained about three months and a half, and then taken back to Libby, from which place he was paroled Feb. 22d 1865. A prisoner 185 days.

Aug 28—Feeling very well to-day. Regiment engaged in building a line of breastworks.

The regiment is now in very poor condition for officers, and the consequence is the ten companies have been consolidated into four companies, A and F forming the first company, C and D and I the second, E, H, and K the third, and G and B the fourth. The first is commanded by Lieuts. Schall and Long, the second by Lieut. Thomas, the third by Lieut. Foster, the fourth by Capts. Nicholas and Gilliland. Capt. Joseph K. Bolton in command of the regiment. Lieut. Geo. W. Smith Co. C is Acting Adjutant. Asst. Surgeons Rineholdt and Duffell are absent sick. Gen. White having received a ten days' sick leave, Gen. Hartranft assumed command (temporarily) of the First Division Ninth Army Corps.[21]

Aug 29—Feeling much better. Regiment felling trees and building works. Finished them today and moved our camp.

Aug 30—Feeling very well. Regiment felling trees and building cordoruy roads. Dr. Duffell relieved from duty with the 109th N.Y. Vols., and reported to his regiment for duty. Capt. Brooke left for home on a 20 days leave of absence on account of wounds received in action.

Aug 31—Feeling well. Regiment still felling trees and building corduroy roads. Received a letter from Quartermaster Stephens.

Sep 1—Feeling very well to-day. Went to Phila. and drew from the paymaster, Maj. Taggart, $189.08.

Regiment felling trees and building roads. Parke has been directed by Meade to carry into effect the order of to-day requiring the reorganization of the Ninth Army Corps into three divisions. Consequently by S.O. No. 160, the First Division of this corps was discontinued and the regiments comprising it are transferred to the Second and Third Divisions. Hartranft is to assume command of his original brigade and temporarily the command of the Third Division.[22]

Sep 2—Paid a visit to the Trappe. Regiment felling trees and building breastworks, left unfinished by the colored troops. By G.O. No. 47, Aiken's House, Gen. Hartranft assumed temporarily command of the Third Division Ninth Army Corps.[23]

Sep 3—Feeling much better. Regiment building works for Battery 24, and working on roads. Corpl. Isaac Tolan Co. D and Priv. Owen McBride Co. C deserted to the ememy.

Sep 4—Feeling well. Regiment still building works and working on the roads. The work connecting with the redoubt at the Strong House will be entirely completed this afternoon.

Capt. E. B. Moore of the 138th P.V. has been appointed quartermaster of the 1st Brigade 2d Division, and it has proved a good change, as the butchers of the brigade had been allowed by the former quartermaster to retain for their own use and profit, all the fat, hearts and liver of the beefs killed for the use of the brigade, charging from 50 cents to $1.00 for a heart, and from $1.50 to $2.50 for a liver; but Moore has stopped all that, 25 cents for a heart, and 50 cents for a liver, and nothing for the fat. We are living well now, fresh beef, potatoes, salt fish, cod and mackerel, onions, cabbage, &c with a full ration of whiskey. Men are living in comfort, clean quarters, plenty of good water from wells dug in each company's street.[24]

Sep 5—Getting along very well with my wound. Regiment still building breastworks and working on the roads.

Sep 6—Feeling very well. Regiment still working on the breastworks, day and night. Rained all night.

---

21. *O.R.*, vol. 42, part 2, 560.

22. *O.R.*, vol. 42, part 2, 642-3. See the September 13 diary entry for additional reorganization details as well as a note on the corps organization on that date.

23. *O.R.*, vol. 42, part 2, 669.

24. Following Parker, *51st PA*, 583-4.

Sep 7—Feeling very well. Wrote several letters to friends in the regiment.

Men are felling trees on their front. By S.O. No. 10 1st Brigade 3d Division, Capt. Geo. P. Carman was detached from his regiment and appointed Actg Aide [de] Camp on the Staff of the Col. commanding.

Sep 8—My wound gives me but little trouble. Regiment felling trees and constructing abatis in their front.

Sep 9—Feeling very well. Regiment still constructing abatis in their front.

Sep 10—About 3 o'clock A.M., the rebels attacked the right of our brigade, the fight lasting until 9 A.M. We held our own.

Sep 11—Regiment still felling trees and fortifying.

Sep 12—Regiment still felling trees. and placing abatis in their front.

Sep 13—Regiment still felling trees and constructing abatis in their front. Our regiment was transferred from the 1st Brigade 3d Division, to that of the 1st Brigade 1st Division, Ninth Corps. Willcox has received a leave of absence for fifteen days and temporarily turns over his command to Hartranft. By G.O. No. 39, Ninth Corps Headquarters near Blick's Station, the following changes in designation of the divisions of this corps were announced: 3d Division (Willcox's) to be known as the 1st Division, 4th Division (Ferrero's) to be known as the 3d Division.[25]

Sep 14—Regiment raised the works in their front some two feet. Lt. Mark R. Supplee has been detailed as Lt. of Brigade Ambulences.

Sep 15—Regiment still finished their works.

Sep 16—Whole regiment detailed to raise the works two feet higher on Battery 24. Chaplain Daniel G. Mallory having tendered his resignation on account of ill health, was honorably discharged the service, by S.O. No. 217.

Sep 17—Regiment still at work on Battery 24. The enemy drove in our pickets, and we in turn drove them back.

Sep 18—Regiment still at work on Battery 24.

---

25. *O.R.*, vol. 42, part 2, 808. The corps, still under Parke's command, was now organized as follows:
First Division, Brig. Gen. Orlando B. Willcox
   First Brigade, Brig. Gen. John F. Hartranft: 8th, 27th MI, 79th, 109th NY, 51st PA, 37th, 38th WI, 13th OH Cav (dismounted)
   Second Brigade, Col. William Humphrey: 1st MI Sharpshooters, 2nd, 20th MI, 46th NY, 60th OH, 50th PA, 24th NY Cav (dismounted)
   Third Brigade, Lt. Col. J. H. Barnes: 3rd MD, 29th, 57th, 59th MA, 14th NY Hvy Art, 100th PA
Second Division, Brig. Gen. Robert B. Potter
   First Brigade, Col. John I. Curtin: 21st, 35th, 36th, 58th MA, 51st NY, 45th, 48th PA, 4th, 7th RI
   Second Brigade, Brig. Gen. Simon G. Griffin: 31st, 32nd ME, 2nd MD, 56th MA, 6th, 9th, 11th NH, 2nd NY Mtd Rifles (dismounted), 179th NY, 17th VT
Third Division, Brig. Gen. Edward Ferrero
   First Brigade, Col. O. P. Stearns: 27th, 30th, 39th, 43rd USCT
   Second Brigade, Col. C. S. Russell: 19th, 23rd, 28th, 29th, 31st USCT
Artillery Brigade, Col. John C. Tidball: 7th ME Bty, 11th MA Bty, 19th, 27th, 34th NY Bty, PA Bty D

Sep 19—Regiment still working on Battery 24, and building roads.

Sep 20—Regiment digging and cutting out stumps, to clear a place for guard mounting.

Sep 21—Regiment engaged in cutting stumps. During the night the rebel pickets on our front opened with a rapid fire. The regiment under arms all night.

Sep 22—Regiment cutting stumps, and watching the enemy very closely.

Sep 23—The first Brigade Guard Mounting for one year took place to-day, also the first dress parade.

Sep 24—Regiment detailed to widen the road in rear of the regiment.

Sep 25—Regiment left Battery 24 in the evening, and marched one half mile to the right, and occupied Fort Alexander Hays, where we were relieved from all picket duty, the colored troops doing that duty in front of the fort. The line held by our division is about 2,200 yards long.

Sep 26—Feeling quite well, and am getting ready to leave for the front in a few days.

Sep 27—I spent the evening at Mr. H. S. Stephens and Mr. Von. Tagen, as I intend to leave and join my regiment to-morrow.

Sep 28—I left Norristown, Pa. in company with Lt's Owen and Coulston, for Phila. leaving there at 3 1/2 P.M. for Baltimore.

Sep 29—Lieut's Own, Coulston and myself arrived in Baltimore early in the morning, and left there at 4 1/2 P.M. for Fortress Monroe. Regiment still garrisoning Fort Hays.

Sep 30—Lieut's Owen, Coulston and myself arrived at Fortress Monroe early in the morning and left there at 10 A.M. for City Point.

Regiment still garrisoning Fort Hays. The rebels and the "smoked Yankees" cant agree and the consequence is the regiment is constantly under arms, day and night, and are called out from three to six times of a night. The 79th N.Y. Highlanders are with us. Every night the shot and shell go flying through the air. We have 65,000 rounds of ammunition in the magazine and six days' rations in case we are besieged.

Col. [Samuel A.] Harriman, 37th Wisconsin. in G.O. No. 12, assumed command of the First Brigade First Division, Ninth Army Corps, Col. Christ 50th Penna. having been mustered out of service.[26]

Oct 1—Lieut's Owen, Coulston and myself arrived at City Point, Va. at 6 A.M. and took a train on Grant's celebrated military railroad and reached Fort Alexander Hays at 11 A.M. The boys were all very glad to see us. The usual racket was kept up all day between the rebels and the smoked Yankees. A heavy rain continued throughout the day.

Oct 2—Not feeling very well. I did not assume command. The usual racket between the rebel pickets and the smoked Yankees.

Oct 3—A heavy detail of the regiment working in the fort. The usual racket with the pickets. I rode over to see Gen. Ferrero.

Oct 4—Regiment still working on the fort.

Oct 5—Heavy details working on the redoubts at Pegram, and Clement House.

Oct 6—My wound giving me some trouble. I left Fort Hays and went to Division Hospital for treatment, and about 7 A.M. the regiment left Fort Hays, and took up the line of march, crossed the Weldon Railroad at the Yellow House, marched down the Squirrel Level Road, passed Poplar Grove Church, and went into the works at the Pegram House.

Oct 7—Regiment was paid to-day.

---

26. *O.R.*, vol. 42, part 2, 1138.

Oct 8—Our division (the First) made a reconnaissance to the left, in the vicinity of the Smith House, Hawks House, and Walker House. Returned during the night. We moved by way of the Squirrel Level Road. The enemy was found occupying all the roads coming into Hawks House position except the one we were on. We established a new and advanced picket line. Our casualties in killed, wounded and missing small, 17. By S.O. No. 195, Gen. Hartranft was temporarily assigned to the command of the Third Division Ninth A.C.[27]

Oct 9—I am still in the field hospital. The election commissioners Mr. Samuel Johnson arrived and is the guest of Gen. Hartranft. Hartranft relieved of the command of the 2d Brigade 1st Division by Lieut. Col. Newberry, 24th N.Y. Cavalry.

Oct 10—Still in the hospital. Regiment strengthening our lines, working on redoubts, constructing abatis, and slashing timber.

Oct 11—Lieut. Samuel P. Stephens was detailed from the regiment as quartermaster of the Artillery Brigade, and Lieut. Wm. F. Thomas Co. C appointed to fill the vacancy. Went over to the regiment to vote, and returned to the hospital in the evening. The election was for state officers, and there was a Union majority of eighty-three in the regiment.

Oct 12—The surgeons at the hospital thought that they had located the ball that was in my face, and accordingly they decided to operate for it. My regimental surgeon, Dr. Shurlock, did all the cutting, and cut to the windpipe. He made forty incisions, but failed to find the ball. The cut was sewed up, and I went to bed.

Oct 13—Feel pretty well with all my cutting. Wrote a letter to my sister, and to several others in Norristown.

Regiment still occupy the works at the Pegram House, and slashing timber.

Oct 14—A soldier from our brigade was shot to-day in front of the brigade for deserting.[28] In the afternoon the regiment moved to the left and relieved the colored troops at Fort Sampson.

Oct 15—Regimental inspection, and there was no detail from the regiment for picket duty. Inspection made by the Brigade Inspector, Capt. McCleay. Capt. Jacob P. Brooke, Co. F who had been home on leave, returned.

Oct 16—Feeling all right again. I left the hospital, rejoined the regiment and assumed command. It has been ordered that there shall be no more playing of bands and other music in camp after taps.

Oct 17—Regiment still occupy Fort Sampson. Received ninety drafted men, and assigned them to the different companies. During the day we moved to the right near the Davis House. The Secretary of War is expected to visit our lines, and we have been notified to be ready and appear under arms in the vicinity of our camps and trenches, but at 2 P.M. we were notified not to keep the troops under arms any longer, as the Secretary had left for City Point. Received a letter advising me that Col. F. Beach, through the War Department, had been directed to assign 100 white drafted men to my regiment, but when they reached here there were ten men short, which I was directed to report.

Oct 18—Regiment in the works near the Davis House.

Oct 19—Regiment working on the intrenchments near the Davis House and are doing very little drilling.

---

27. *O.R.*, vol. 42, part 3, 136-7.

28. The deserter was Charles Merling of the 2nd Maryland. See Robert I. Alotta, *Civil War Justice: Union Army Executions Under Lincoln* (Shippensburg, PA: White Mane Press, 1989), 134.

Oct 20—Regiment still in the same position, and working on the intrenchments. Received a letter from my mother.

Oct 21—Regiment still occupy the same position, and are working on the fort. A deserter, who formly belonged to the 2d Maryland was shot a few yards from our camp. He was captured in a fight with his gun in his hands, fighting against us.[29]

Oct 22—Regiment still occupy the works near the Davis House. We received two hundred drafted men, who were immediately assigned to the companies. Two men belonging to the Ninth Corps were drummed around the inside of a hollow aquare, formed by the corps, with the following placards on each: "I deserted in front of the enemy during the fight, and skulked to the rear. I am a coward and have been absent without leave." Pvt. James Powers Co. D was relieved as mounted pioneer.[30]

Oct 23—Regiment still remain near the Davis House.

Oct 24—Regiment remain at the same place. The rebels on our immediate front are cheering for Lincoln, and the bands on both sides played until after midnight. All this time shells were flying through the air from both sides. A beautiful sight, no one hurt on our side.

As we have received a number of drafted men, the order that was issued in August consolidating the regiment into four companies was to-day recinded and we are now having ten companies.

Oct 25—Regiment still near the Davis House.

S.O. No. 211 from Ninth Corps headquarters, directs that the line of works from Fort Fisher to Fort Cummings will be garrisoned as follows: Fort Fisher—45th P.V.V., 31st Maine Vol., Lt. Col. Getchell, 31st Maine Vol. commanding; Fort Walch—58th Mass. Vol., 21st Mass. Vol., 17th Vermont Vol., Lt. Col. Whiton, 58th Mass. Vol. commanding; Fort Gregg—8th Mich Vol., recruits of 51st P.V.V., Lt. Col. Ely commanding; Fort Sampson—3d Md. Vol., Capt. Carter commanding. Troops to be supplied with six days' rations, and 200 rounds of ammunition per man. These regiments are to encamp in the immediate vicinity of the redoubts garrisoned by them, respectively, and expected to picket their entire front.[31] Our brigade reviewed by Gen. Willcox.

Oct 26—Regiment still near the Davis House. Received commissions from Gov. Curtin for Valentine, Stocker, and John W. Meeker, all of Co. B.

Brigade commanders ordered to hold their commands in readiness to march promptly at 3 A.M. to-morrow. Tattoo will be beaten at the usual time this evening and after tattoo the officers will see that the men go to sleep in order that they may have a good night's rest. There will be no reveille in the morning. Troops to be kept well in hand, and aroused without unnecessary noise. The burning of rubbish or dry lumber which is usually burned before a march, is strictly forbidden. There will be no unnecessary fires either to-night or to-morrow morning. The movement to be made as quickly as possible, so as not to excite suspicion of the enemy.[32]

Oct 27—The regiment with the rest of the division, left their camp at 3.30 A.M., taking the road cut through the parapet to the right of Fort Cummings, Warren taking the road on the

---

29. Alotta's book cited above makes no mention of this execution; Bolton may have mistakenly meant the October 14 execution instead.

30. Parker, *51st PA*, 593, noted that three men were drummed out—two were deserters and one was labeled a coward.

31. *O.R.*, vol. 42, part 3, 350.

32. *O.R.*, vol. 42, part 3, 365.

left of Fort Cummings. This movement is a reconnaissance to beyond the Clements House. Soon came up to the enemy's works. The 51st P.V.V. skirmished up to their works, and remained there until 11 P.M. when we were relieved by other troops. The new recruits were left behind, the old vets only taking part. The skirmish line of the enemy was encountered this side of the Watkins House, and was rapidly driven into their works. Our advance was through a heavy growth of timber and underbrush to within 100 yards of the enemy's line of works, when our progress was arrested by slashed timber and abatis.[33]

Our line being established, Parke gave orders to intrench, which was thoroughly done by the morning of the 28th. Our loss was slight. Commanders were ordered to see that the troops sleep with their accouterments on, and that one-third of the officers and men are kept on duty and on the alert during the night. The troops will stand to arms in the trenches fifteen minutes before daybreak in the morning, and remain under arms until half an hour after daylight, ready for any emergency. Slashing to be continued in the morning.

My wound giving me some trouble I did not accompany the regiment in this movement. [Our loss was as follows:]

Wounded:

Pvt. James M. Baker, Co. A	Cpl. Isaac Treat, Co. E
Cpl. George S. Buzzard, Co. A	Pvt. John Camden, Co. F (died November 23)
Pvt. Henry Dersham, Co. E	Cpl. George S. Castleberry, Co. F
Pvt. Jacob Frederick, Co. E	Pvt. Richard A. Cox, Co. F
Sgt. Francis R. Frey, Co. E	Cpl. Joseph Fizone, Co. F
Pvt. William H. Hackman, Co. E	Pvt. Frederick Kreamer, Co. F
Pvt. Peter C. Paul, Co. E	Pvt. George K. McMillan, Co. F
Pvt. Sebastian Searless, Co. E	Cpl. John W. Truscott, Co. F
Pvt. John W. Sheckler, Co. E	

Oct 28—Early in the morning a part of the regiment were sent out on the picket line. At 7 A.M., Parke received orders to prepare to withdraw, in conjunction with the Fifth Corps, to his old position in the vicinity of the Peebles House. This movement was commenced about 1 P.M., our division (Willcox) ordered to bring up the rear. The 51st P.V.V. skirmished all the way back. Our movement was successfully accomplished and by 6 P.M., Parke had all of his command in his old position, and his old picket line established.[34]

Oct 29—Regiment again in their old works, Fort Sampson. Received and wrote several letters.

Oct 30—Regiment still occupy Fort Sampson. We are now having company drills and dress parade, and drilling our new recruits. Some picket firing during the night, and one deserter came in.

Oct 31—Regiment still at the same point. Drills and dress parade.

Nov 1—Regiment still at Fort Sampson. Company drills and dress parade.

Nov 2—Still at Fort Sampson. Company and regimental drills &c.

Nov 3—Regiment still at Fort Sampson. Usual drills and dress parade.

Nov 4—Regiment still garrisoning Fort Sampson, and having our usual drills and dress parade. Received a letter from Maj. Hart. Target practice ordered for to-morrow for the new recruits, 15 rounds per man.

---

33. *O.R.*, vol. 42, part 1, 560 (Hartranft's report).

34. *O.R.*, vol. 42, part 3, 415.

Nov 5—Still at Fort Sampson. Usual drills and dress parade.

Nov 6—Still garrisoning Fort Sampson. Regiment inspected by Gen. Hartranft. Brigade dress parade in the evening. Heavy firing at midnight.

Nov 7—Still at Fort Sampson. Our brigade drilled in the rain for two hours.

Nov 8—Still at Fort Sampson. State commissioners held an election in the regiment for President and Vice President of the United States. Received a letter from Dr. Shurlock. There was 398 votes polled in the 51st P.V.V. McClellan received 145 votes.

Nov 9—Still garrisoning Fort Sampson. Brigade drills and dress parade.

Nov 10—Still in Fort Sampson. Brigade reviewed by Gen. Hartranft.

Nov 11—Still remain at Fort Sampson. Brigade drill and dress parade. I was detailed as Division Officer of the Day. During the day rode out to our picket line, my brother Joe accompanying me, and to our astonishment heard the rebels cheering for McClellan. Presently noticed a rebel beckoning to us, and the same time waving a paper in his hand. I consented to my brother going out to him, to exchange papers. They expressed great disappointment to him in the defeat of McClellan, saying had he have been elected, the war would soon come to a close, and also expressing to him that McClellan was the best man for them. They shook hands and parted.

Nov 12—Still remain in Fort Sampson. Company drills, also Brigade drill and dress parade.

Nov 13—Still in Fort Sampson. Regimental inspection and dress parade. A second line of abatis is now being placed along our entire brigade front, and details from each regiment to do the work.

Nov 14—Still in Fort Sampson. Brigade drill and dress parade.

Nov 15—Still remain in Fort Sampson. The usual drills and dress parade. 12 men detailed and ordered to report to brigade headquarters to act as pioneers.

Asst. Surg. Dr. Charles S. Duffell, expiring to-morrow, the members in a quiet way collected a sum of money among themselves, and procured a handsome silver watch, to present to him as a testimonial of appreciation of his many virtues as a soldier, gentleman, and surgeon. The presentation took place in my quarters this evening, and I was selected to present the gift.

Nov 16—Still remain in Fort Sampson. Company, regimental drills and dress parade. Dr. Charles S. Duffell mustered-out on account of expiration of term of service.

Nov 17—Fort Sampson still our home. Regimental inspection and dress parade.

Nov 18—Fort Sampson still our home. Usual drills and dress parade. Received a letter from my mother. Surg. Wm. C. Shurlock has been detailed by S.O. No. 103 on special duty in 1st Div. Field Hospital.

Nov 19—Still in Fort Sampson. Whole regiment detailed for picket duty.

Nov 20—Fort Sampson still our home. Rained all day. Letter writing the order.

Nov 21—Still remain in Fort Sampson. Rained all day. Received and wrote several letters. Rice issued, the first for six months.

Nov 22—Fort Sampson still our home. Brigade drills and dress parade.

Nov 23—Still occupy Fort Sampson. Company and regimental drills.

Nov 24—Still occupy Fort Sampson. Usual drills and dress parade in the evening. Two apples issued to each man.

Nov 25—Still in Fort Sampson. Usual drills and dress parade.

Nov 26—Still at Fort Sampson. The regiment received a treat to-day from a number of citizens of New York in the shape of roast turkeys, cakes, chickens, and beef; apples, onions, potatoes, tobacco, mince pies. The feast was intended for a Thanksgiving treat, but came two days too late. Some of the turkeys were stuffed with bottles of brandy. I was lucky enough to get one of them, with the following note attached to the neck: "From a lady ninety years old, who when a child, came near being killed by the Tories in the Revolutionary War." One of the barrels was made up by a Miss Louisa Dietz of No. 132 Williams Street, New York, and it was from her barrel my turkey came from. My brother Joe and Capt. Brooke were treated in the same way.

The 207th and 209th Penna. regiments joined our corps yesterday.[35] Usual drills.

Nov 27—Still occupy Fort Sampson. regimental inspection. Cod-fish issued to the regiment.

Nov 28—Still occupy Fort Sampson. Usual drills. Heavy detailed made from the regiment to build a road. Received a letter from Dr. Duffell. The 200th, 205th, 208th and 211th regiments Penna. Vols. having reported for duty with this army, have been assigned to the Ninth Army Corps, and have been ordered to report to Gen. Parke.

The reserve division of the Second Corps has been ordered to-morrow morning to relieve the First and Second Division of the Ninth Corps, who are to relieve the troops of the Second Corps now holding the right of this army. We have been ordered to hold ourselves in readiness to move to-morrow morning, and have been directed not to distroy the huts, stabling, and other shelter they have erected.[36]

Nov 29—Our regiment struck tents and left Fort Sampson at 12 M. took up the line of march, passing the Yellow House, and at 7 P.M. entered and occupied Fort Morton, the center of our line, and directly opposite the "Crater." We took up quarters in the bomb-proofs for the night. A very great change had taken place in the works and surroundings since we left the same spot last August. Traverses had been dug from the fort out to the ravine, near the picket-line. A detail of 120 men sent out on the picket line in front of the "Crater," the very same works the regiment had thrown up on the 17th and 18th of last June. Our First Division occupy the right from the Appomattox to Norfolk Railroad, and the Second Division from the Norfolk Railroad to Battery No. 24, connecting with the right of Fifth Corps at that point.

Nov 30—We not only occupy Fort Morton, but the line of works extending four hundred yards on either side of the Fort, on the right to Battery Haskell, and to the left to the Jerusalem Plank Road. I gave a receipt to-day for all the ammunition in the fort, as has been the custom with change of commanders, satisfying myself of the kind, and amount therein.

The Provisional Brigade of our corps moved from the vicinity of Peeble's House to rear of this corps, and are held in reserve. They are under the command of Brig. Gen. John F. Hartranft.

Dec 1—I was detailed as Division Officer of the Day. Heavy detail from the regiment for picket duty.

Dec 2—One hundred men sent out on picket.

Dec 3—The usual picket detail. Also cutting and hauling wood. The enemy opened with mortars upon Fort Rice and Sedgwick. Our batteries replied.[37]

Dec 4—The usual picket detail. Squad and company drills.

Dec 5—The usual picket detail. Our pickets captured five rebels during the night. Heavy firing from both sides all night. Deserters report the death of the rebel General Gracie by one of our shells.

---

35. *O.R.*, vol. 42, part 3, 704-5.

36. *O.R.*, vol. 42, part 3, 729.

37. *O.R.*, vol. 42, part 3, 789.

By S.O. No. 329 Headquarters Army of the Potomac, corps and other independent commanders will at once cause all their burial grounds to be securely fenced in, each division and independent command to have a separate lot for interment of its dead.[38]

Deserters still continue to come in. Meade has received eleven medals of honor to be distributed to members of the Ninth Corps.

Dec 6—The usual picket detail, 114 men. Brigade drill and dress parade. Mortar shells of all sizes continually dropping around us, rather a hot place to be, but are getting somewhat use [sic] to them.

Dec 7—The usual picket detail. Regimental and brigade drills. Received a dispatch from home, informing me of the death of my father. I at once applied and received a leave of absence to go home. Seven deserters came in on our front.

Dec 8—The usual picket detail. Squad and company drills. I left Fort Morton for Norristown, Pa. at 8 A.M., arriving at Fortress Monroe at 3 P.M., leaving there for Baltimore at 5 P.M. My brother Joe in command. [Pvt. Everet H. Staunton, Co. D, wounded.]

Dec 9—Arrived in Baltimore at 7 A.M., and at Norristown at 5 P.M. The usual picket detail, squad and company drills.

Dec 10—The usual picket detail. Drills and dress parade.

Dec 11—The usual picket detail, and usual drills. Regimental inspection. Red beats issued. The artillery garrison of Forts Haskell and Stedman and Batteries 10, 11 and 12 are ordered to stand to their pieces at 5 A.M., and will remain on the alert till half an hour after daylight.[39]

Dec 12—Attended my father's funeral, a bitter cold day. Usual picket duty and drills. Seven men detailed for duty in hospital of the 9th Army Corps at City Point.

Dec 13—The usual details for picket duty, and the usual drills. Mackerel and potatoes issued. Went to Phila. to see the Paymaster, who paid me $562.68.

Dec 14—The usual picket detail. Brigade and regimental drills and dress parade. Wrote a letter to my brother Joe. There were some movements in the enemy's line during the night indicating a change of troops.[40]

Dec 15—The usual picket detail and drills. I paid a visit to Easton, Pa. The late Provisional Brigade has been organized into two brigades and designated Third Division Ninth Corps. Gen. Hartranft commands the new division.

Dec 16—The usual picket detail and drills. I spent the day in Easton. The enemy this P.M. opened on the Ninth Corps front with their heavy guns, to which are batteries replied with vigor. The enemy are extending their line of chevaux-de-frise in front of their picket line.[41] Meade visited Ninth Corps headquarters to present the medals of honor to the men belonging to the corps.

Dec 17—The usual detail for thr trenches, and drills and dress parade. I returned to Norristown from Easton. The heavy cannonading last evening was caused by the enemy opening upon

---

38. *O.R.*, vol. 42, part 3, 809-10.

39. *O.R.*, vol. 42, part 3, 967.

40. *O.R.*, vol. 42, part 3, 1003.

41. *O.R.*, vol. 42, part 3, 1020-1.

some of our troops drilling on the plain near the Avery House.[42] Maj. Lane S. Hart discharged on account of wounds.

Dec 18—The usual detail for the trenches. Company and regimental inspection.

Dec 19—The usual details for the trenches. Brigade drill and dress parade. I left Norristown to rejoin the regiment, missed the train and had to remain in Phila. over night. One deserter, two refugees, one engineer and a banker came in last night on our front. They are very intelligent and seem to tell correct stories.[43]

Dec 20—The usual detail for the trenches, also the usual drills. I left Phila. at 8 a.m., arriving in Baltimore at 3 P.M., and leaving there at 4 1/2 P.M.

Dec 21—The usual detail for the trenches, and usual drills. I arrived at Fort Morton at 7 P.M. Received a letter from Maj. Lane S. Hart. The enemy have drawn the water from a pond in the vicinity of Fort Stedman since dusk, and their picket firing is more lively than usual. Fort Stedman joins us on our right.[44]

Dec 22—Assumed command of the regiment. The usual picket detail for the trenches, and also the usual drills and dress parade. Four deserters in from the 59th Va.[45]

Dec 23—The usual picket detail. Brigade drill and dress parade. Wrote letters to Judge D. M. Smyser and Maj. Lane S. Hart, Norristown, Pa.

General Orders No. 49, Ninth Corps Headquarters, directs that all officers and men in this command will be required to wear the Corps badge upon the cap or hat. For the Division the badges will be plain, made of cloth in the shape of a shield, red for the first, white for the second, and blue for the third. For the Artillery Brigade the shield will be red, and will be worn under the regulation cross cannon.[46]

Dec 24—The usual picket detail for the trenches. Regimental and company drills and dress parade.

Dec 25—The usual picket detail. Regimental inspection. Took dinner with Gen. Hartranft. Received a letter from my brother John.

Dec 26—The usual picket detail for the trenches. Company drills.

Twenty-five deserters from the enemy, including one commissioned officer, came into our lines this a.m., representing seven brigades. The lieutenant reports that he had arranged matters with sixty men from his brigade to desert next Wednesday, but being fearful that the plot would be discovered came over in advance. Provisions are scarce, no meat issued of late; are issuing codfish. He says we may look for swarms of deserters soon. First Lieut. Redwood, 43d Ala., came in last night. He left Richmond yesterday morning; says that any signal, three shots, this evening, will bring over quite a number of men. Willcox says he will arrange for the signal, if there is no objection.[47]

---

42. *O.R.*, vol. 42, part 3, 1030.

43. *O.R.*, vol. 42, part 3, 1043.

44. *O.R.*, vol. 42, part 3, 1053.

45. *O.R.*, vol. 42, part 3, 1060.

46. *O.R.*, vol. 42, part 3, 1066.

47. *O.R.*, vol. 42, part 3, 1079.

Dec 27—The usual picket detail for the trenches. Company and brigade drills. Parke reports that the experimental signal failed to bring over the deserters as expected. But three came in. They report extra vigilance on the part of their officers. The picket-firing was heavier than usual.[48]

Dec 28—The usual picket detail for the trenches, and usual drills. Seven deserters came in during the night. By G.O. No. 66, 1st Division headquarters, it has been ordered that the badges of this division will be worn by the troops of this command as follows: By enlisted men on the top, and by officers on the left side of the hat, or cap, and when lost or torn off must be immediately replaced.

Dec 29—The usual picket detail for the trenches, drills &c. There was considerable firing, principally mortars, along the line of the Ninth Corps yesterday, and was kept up till 9 P.M.

Dec 30—The usual picket detail for the trenches. Drills and dress parade. Gen. Willcox is in command of the Ninth Corps, in the absence of Parke.[49]

Dec 31—The usual picket detail for the trenches. Regimental and brigade drills. During the pass six day, heavy details have been made from the regiment, engaged in repairing the zig-zags, traverses, and covered ways, leading to the outer line in our front.

48. *O.R.*, vol. 42, part 3, 1085.

49. O.R., vol. 42, part 3, 1104.

Chapter 14

Petersburg

January 1–April 22, 1865

During the final months of the Petersburg siege, the 51st Pennsylvania continued to garrison Fort Morton. The regiment remained relatively unscathed throughout the final operations. It remained behind on the trench line while most of the Ninth Corps assaulted Petersburg on April 2. After performing some additional patrol duty near Petersburg, the regiment, with the corps, was dispatched to Washington following Lincoln's assassination.

Jan 1—The usual detail for picket duty in the trenches, also the usual drills.

Jan 2—We are doing the usual picket duty in the trenches. Company and brigade drills and dress parade.

Jan 3—The usual picket duty in the trenches. The rebels commenced at daylight shelling our lines at a terrible rate, and at noon began to get rather hot. Morton opened with her guns and coehorn batteries. A 200 lb. rebel shell fell on the bombproof magazine in our fort, but did no harm. About dark the firing ceased on both sides, no one hurt on our side.

Jan 4—The usual picket duty in the trenches. Company and regimental drills and dress parade.

Jan 5—The usual picket duty in the trenches, and drills. I was detailed as Division Officer of the Day.

Jan 6—The usual picket duty in the trenches in front of Fort Morton. Usual drills and dress parade.

Jan 7—The usual picket duty in the trenches, and the usual drills and dress parade. Forwarded my ordnance return for the quarter to Washington.

Jan 8—The usual picket duty in the trenches, and also the usual drills. Wrote a letter to my mother. Received a visit from my friend Col. [Matthew R.] McClennan of the 138th Regiment.

Jan 9—The usual picket duty in the trenches, also the usual drills. Capt. Joseph K. Bolton relieved from command of Co. A and ordered to transfer the stores belonging to the company to 1st Lt. John H. Coulston, Capt. Bolton having been commissioned Major of the regiment.

Jan 10—The usual picket duty in the trenches, also the usual drills. A piece of a mortar shell came dashing through my quarters and lodged on my bed.

Jan 11—The usual picket duty in the trenches, and usual drills. Pioneers commenced to build me a bomb-proof in the bank. Five deserters came in on our front, two of them are sergeants.[1] Received permission to move the four companies outside of Fort Morton. The bomb-proofs are untenable, many of them being flooded by the late rain, and the danger of them falling.

Jan 12—The usual picket duty in the trenches. A flag of truce appeared on the rebel works in our front. The matter reported to headquarters, but it amounted to nothing.

Jan 13—The usual drills and picket duty in the trenches. Wrote a letter to my brother John.

Jan 14—The usual drills and picket duty in the trenches. Received and wrote a letter to my mother. My bomb-proof finished, was constructed of pine logs and has six feet of earth on top.

Jan 15—The usual drills and picket duty in the trenches. I paid a visit to my friend Col. McClennan of the 138th P.V. and had a pleasant time.

Jan 16—The usual drills and picket duty in the trenches.

Jan 17—The usual drills and picket duty in the trenches. Heavy rain and we are all washed out. All hands in bad humor.

Jan 18—The usual drills and picket duty in the trenches. Wrote letters to my mother and brother John.

Jan 19—The usual drills and picket duty in the trenches. A white flag was displayed on the rebel works on our front and the fact reported to headquarters. Sometime later a lady crossed into our lines.

Jan 20—The usual drills and picket duty in the trenches.

Jan 21—The usual drills and picket duty in the trenches. Received a letter from my mother.

Jan 22—The usual drills and picket duty in the trenches. Regimental inspection.

Jan 23—The usual drills and picket duty in the trenches.

Jan 24—The usual drills and picket duty in the trenches. I was detailed as Division Officer of the Day, on duty twenty-four hours. Gen. Meade has left for Washington, and Gen. Parke is now in command of the Army of the Potomac, and Gen. Willcox is in command of the Ninth Army Corps.[2]

Jan 25—The usual drills and picket duty in the trenches. Took a ride to the division hospital.

Jan 26—The usual drills and picket duty in the trenches. Eleven deserters came on our front.[3]

Jan 27—The usual drills and picket duty in the trenches. Brigade dress parade.

Jan 28—The usual drills and picket duty in the trenches.

Jan 29—The usual drills and picket duty in the trenches. Col. McClennan paid me a visit. My cook got up a game dinner for us.

During the day a white flag was displayed on the rebel works on my immediate front. Capt. Parker Co. I 51st P.V.V. reported the fact to headquarters as he was in command of the brigade pickets. He was instructed to go and meet the flag, and see what was desired. Capt. Parker and Lt. Col. Hatch who claimed to be Assistant Commissioner of Exchange on the

---

1. *O.R.*, vol. 46, part 2, 97.

2. *O.R.*, vol. 46, part 2, 228.

3. *O.R.*, vol. 46, part 2, 268.

rebel side, met midway between the two lines, on the Petersburg road. Hatch informed Parker that an interview was desired with Grant's chief of staff of the greatest importance, that Alexander H. Stephens, R. M. T. Hunter, and J. A. Campbell was in Petersburg and desired to cross our lines, in accordance with an understanding claimed to exist with Lieut. Gen. Grant, on their way to Washington as peace commissioners, and desired an early answer, and to come through immediately; would like to reach City Point to-night, and if not would like to come throught [sic] at 10 o'clock to-morrow morning.

This at 3.30 P.M. Willcox referred the matter to Parke who is now in command of the Army of the Potomac. Parke at 4 P.M. referred the matter to Ord, as the ranking officer present in the two armies. Ord in turn at 7.15 P.M. referred the matter to Stanton, and informs Parke to inform Hatch to come to-morrow at 10; it is too late to-night. While negotiations were pending, all firing ceased along both lines, and the works on both sides were crowded with troops, and a great many women graced the rebel works, and good feeling prevailed along the lines.[4]

Jan 30—The usual drills and picket duty in the trenches.

The flag of truce was again displayed at the same point. Same good feeling prevailing. Grant and Meade not here, and nothing has been done. Stephens, Campbell and Hunter in substance sent the following to Grant. Sir: We desire to pass your lines under safe conduct and to proceed to Washington to hold a conference with President Lincoln upon the subject of the existing war, and with a vision of ascertaining upon what terms it may be terminated, &c &c.

At 10.30 A.M., Stanton informed Gen. Ord that the President has directed him to inform the three gentlemen that a messenger would be dispatched to them at or near where they now are without unnecessary delay. Later in the day the President directed Ord to procure for the bearer, Major Thomas T. Eckert, an interview with Stephens & Co., and if on his return to him (Ord), he requests it pass them through our lines to Fort Monroe, by such route and under such military precautions as he may deem prudent, giving them protection and comfortable quarters, and not let the matter effect any of his military movements, &c.[5]

Jan 31—The usual drills and picket duty in the trenches. Grant arrived at City Point this morning, and the letter from Messers. Stephens, Hunter, and Campbell placed in his hands, and telegraphed the contents to the President, and sent at the same time a staff officer to receive the gentlemen and conduct them to his quarters to await the action of the President.

The flag of truce has again been displayed on our works at the same point. At 5 o'clock P.M., a large close carriage was seen from our works moving towards us down the Petersburg road, and as it reached the rebel works, a number of gentlemen were seen to alight from the carriage and slowly walked towards our lines, crossing them through that part occupied by the 51st P.V.V. at the trenches and the works occupied by the balance of the 51st, took an ambulance that was in waiting, and rapidly drove to City Point, to Grant's quarters.

All firing has ceased and the best of feeling prevails. The works of both lines were crowded with troops, and both sides watched the proceedings, and after it was made manifest to the troops the meaning of it all, cheer after cheer was given with a hearty will. Capt. Parker was at 4 P.M. relieved from duty in the trenches, and Capt. Wm. W. Owen of Co. D took his place in charge of the brigade picket line, and received the flag.

It is said that if Grant had known of this correspondence in time these gentlemen would not have been received within our lines. This peace commissioners business Grant does not intend to interfere with army movements, for at 7 P.M., Gen. Parke received orders to make preparations to

4. *O.R.*, vol. 46, part 2, 290-1.

5. *O.R.*, vol. 46, part 2, 297, 301-3.

move at short notice with the Army of the Potomac, provided with six days' rations. In case of a flank move the garrison to hold the lines will be reduced to a minimum, and such portions of the Ninth and Sixth Corps as he may select will be left behind. Grant has telegraphed to Meade in Philadelphia to return immediately. Orders received that the troops of our brigade are to form in line at 5 o'clock A.M., and remain under arms until after daylight.[6]

Feb 1—The usual drills and picket duty in the trenches. The flag of truce still displayed at the same point. Lincoln informs Grant that he must let nothing which is transpiring, change, hinder, or delay his military movements or plans, on account of the presence of the peace commissioners, and Grant informed him that there would be no armistice in consequence of the presence of Mr. Stephens and others within our lines. Yesterday about 3 o'clock the enemy opened fire to the front of Fort Stedman and Battery 10; they were replied to by the 19th New York Battery. Very little damage was done by the enemy's fire. Orders issued to be ready to move at a moment's notice. The order to march did not come, but was kept a standing one. Pvt. Harrison Bower Co. H wounded.[7]

Feb 2—The usual drills and picket duty in the trenches.

Feb 3—The usual drills and picket duty in the trenches.

Feb 4—The usual drills and picket duty in the trenches. Received marching orders but did not move.

The Rebel commissioners passed through our lines into their own. Soon after the enemy opened fire all along the line with artillery and musketry, and continued all day and through the night.

Feb 5—Still doing the usual picket duty. A battle in progress on our left.[8] Our whole command under arms all day. Regimental inspection.

At 1 o'clock this morning Parke received orders directing him to hold his command in readiness to move at short notice. The Ninth Corps front extends from the Appomattox to Battery 24, and is held by the First and Second Divisions with the Third Division in reserve. At 1.45 P.M., Parke received orders to send Hartranft's division down the Vaughan Road to report to Genl. Humphreys at Hatcher's Run, arriving and reporting to him at 8 P.M. Col. [Wesley] Brainerd, commanding Engineer Brigade, at City Point, reported with his brigade to Parke during the evening, and was posted as a reserve in the vicinity of the Avery House.[9]

Feb 6—No drilling. The usual picket duty in the trenches. The battle still in progress on our left. The roar of artillery has been incessant all day.

By G.O. No. 13, War Department, an isue of a ration of fish, viz: fourteen ounces of dried fish, or eighteen ounces of pickled fish, will be made to the troops once a week, in lieu of the ration of fresh beef. The same order gives authority to officers actually in the field, who are without means of paying for subsistance stores purchased from the Commissary, and have one month's pay due, to draw for themselves and their authorized private servants present in the field with them, one regular army ration each per day, on ordinary ration returns.[10]

---

6. *O.R.*, vol. 46, part 2, 311-12, 314, 317.

7. *O.R.*, vol. 46, part 2, 341, 347.

8. Bolton heard the sounds of the fighting at Hatcher's Run.

9. *O.R.*, vol. 46, part 1, 315; vol. 46, part 2, 407.

10. *O.R.*, vol. 46, part 2, 421.

Feb 7—The usual drills and picket duty in the trenches. Regiment ordered to have their arms stacked in front of each companies quarters, day and night, and to be ready to stand to arms at the least alarm. Received three commissions from Harrisburg.

Feb 8—The usual drills and picket duty in the trenches. Laid on our arms all night.

Feb 9—The usual drills and picket duty in the trenches.

Feb 10—The usual drills and picket duty in the trenches. Hartranft's division returned during the night, and took up their old position. In the morning the division holding the front lines will extend to the left as far as Fort Howard, and will then be holding the line from the Appomattox to that point.[11]

Feb 11—The usual drills and picket duty in the trenches. Dress parade this evening. Dr. James Cress late Hospital Steward 209th Regt. Pa. Vols. reported to the regiment as assistant surgeon, vice Asst. Surg. Duffell mustered-out.

Feb 12—The usual drills and picket duty in the trenches. Brigade review and dress parade. Was detailed as Division Officer of the Day.

Feb 13—The usual drills and picket duty in the trenches. Regiment inspected by the brigade inspector. The rebels are giving us a good mortar shelling. A ten inch mortar shell struck my bomb-proof, tearing nearly the whole roof off; and another struck in front of my quarters and rolled back to the door. One dropped on the chimney of Dr. Rineholdt, knocking the whole thing down. Another dropped into a tent of Co. C, exploding, tearing it to atoms. Another dropped into the adjutant's quarters, smashing things. Another dropped on the quarters of Co. E & G, displacing the boys. Strange to say no one was hurt, and they were all occupied at the time. This is the worst we have had for sometime.[12]

Feb 14—The usual drills and picket duty in the trenches. Gen. Willcox was granted a leave of absence for twenty day [sic] but has been modified as to read for fifteen days, subject at any moment to recall by telegraph, and is to keep himself within reach of a telegraphic communication, and report to army headquarters his address during his absence.[13]

Yesterday or last evening Pvt. John M. Faul Co. C was killed by a sentenal at the mortar battery in front of Fort Morton, it is said caught in the act of taking some wood belonging to the battery, the ball entering his right shoulder passing through his heart and out of left breast.

Feb 15—The usual drills, and picket duty in the trenches. Whisky issued to the pickets in the trenches. Privates Wm. Search and Cline Summers of Co. K by sentence of G.C.M. We had a fine dress parade this evening.

Two deserters in from Pegram's division report that their army is very much dispirited and starving, and that they know three-fourths of the men in the ranks would make an unconditional surrender now. Horses broken down for want of forage, also say that the two days rations issued them every other day is so small that the men are so hungry when they get it as to eat it all up at one meal; it is only meat and flour. They also report that 600 men laid down their arms a few days ago in the Petersburg line, but were forced back to duty.

Feb 16—The usual drills and picket duty in the trenches. Dress parade.

Feb 17—The usual drills and dress parade in the evening. We are receiving another shower of mortar shelling, and are compelled to keep close to our bomb-proofs. The ground all around us is full of holes.

---

11. *O.R.*, vol. 46, part 2, 521.

12. Parker, *51st PA*, wrote that this shelling occurred on February 14.

13. *O.R.*, vol. 46, part 2, 555.

Feb 18—The usual drills and picket duty in the trenches. Received a letter from Maj. Yerkes, formally of the regiment, now of the 179 P.V.[14] Prv. Henry Gunter Co. C killed.

Feb 19—The usual drills and picket duty in the trenches. Our brigade reviewed by Gen. Willcox this afternoon.

Feb 20—The usual drills and picket duty in the trenches. Deserters on Gen. Ord's front have been on the increase since the return of the Peace Commissioners; more so than on our front. I left for Norristown having received a leave of absence.

Feb 21—The usual drills and duty in the trenches. Fifty-four deserters received to-day, including one captain, one sergeant, and three corporals.[15] I arrived in Baltimore at 7 A.M. and at Norristown 6 1/2 P.M.

Feb 22—The usual drills and picket duty in the trenches. At 7.32 P.M. he received orders to double the guards in the trenches on his left to-night, and to-morrow morning be on the alert to guard against a surprise. Late in the day Gen. Parke was placed in temporary command of the Army of the Potomac. Meade home on account of his son's death. Gen. Potter in command of the Ninth Corps. Orders received to hold our division in readiness to move at a moments notice. The 51st P.V. and 8th Michigan to remain behind to garrison our front in case of a move.[16]

Feb 23—The usual drills and picket duty in the trenches. Seventy-nine deserters came in from the enemy to-day.[17]

Feb 24—The usual drills and picket duty in the trenches. We are receiving the usual mortar shelling. The number of deserters in twenty-four hours, up to 12 last night, was eighty-seven to the Army of the Potomac and forty to the Army of the James, and average of about twelve per day, in addition received at Norfolk. Forty-five have come into the Army of the Potomac since 12 last night, representing every division in our front. Another shotted salute was fired on the Ninth Corps front at 4 P.M.[18] [Pvts. John Blyler, Co. F, and Robert K. Felton, Co. K, killed.]

Feb 25—The usual drills and picket duty in the trenches. Regimental inspection. The enemy only reply to our fire with mortars.

Feb 26—The usual drills and picket duty in the trenches.

Feb 27—The usual drills and picket duty in the trenches. The rebel mortar shelling keeps us within our bomb-proofs.

Feb 28—The usual drills and picket duty in the trenches. Brigade reviewed.

Mar 1—The usual drills and picket duty in the trenches. Regiment paid off. Mus. Edward D. Johnson Co. C promoted Drum Major. Our division the First now occupies the trenches on the right of the Army of the Potomac, its right resting on the Appomattox River, its left extend-

---

14. Major William H. Yerkes of the 179th Pennsylvania Regiment was mustered out of service with his regiment in July 1863.

15. *O.R.*, vol. 46, part 2, 611.

16. *O.R.*, vol. 46, part 2, 642-44.

17. *O.R.*, vol. 46, part 2, 657.

18. *O.R.*, vol. 46, part 2, 668, 678.

ing nearly to Fort Rice, on the left of the Baxter Road. It garrisoned on its front eight inclosed works, batteries, and curtains between. There is also a picket on the Appomattox, extending down the river three miles.

Mar 2—The usual drills and picket duty in the trenches.

Mar 3—The usual drills and picket duty in the trenches, also regimental target practice.

Mar 4—The usual drills and picket duty in the trenches. Are receiving some mortar shelling, keeping within our bomb-proofs.

Mar 5—The usual drills and picket duty in the trenches. Regimental inspection.

Mar 6—The usual drills and picket duty in the trenches. I left Norristown to rejoin my regiment, arriving at Perryville Md. in the afternoon. Could not cross the river, and was compelled to put back to Philada. stopping at the Girard House.

Mar 7—The usual drills and picket duty in the trenches. Was compelled to remain in Philada. on account of the ice blockade.

Mar 8—The usual drills and picket duty in the trenches. Still remained in the city of Philada. on account of the ice blockade.

Mar 9—The usual drills and picket duty in the trenches. I left Philada. for the front, arriving in Baltimore and remaining over night.

Lt. Wm. F. Campbell Co. H, a prisoner of war, rejoined his regiment. By S.O. No. 109 War Department, 2d Lt. Benj. P. Thompson Co. A a returned prisoner of war on parole has been granted a leave of absence for thirty days, at the expiration of which, he is ordered to report in person to the commanding officer of Camp Parole nearest the Department or Army in which his regiment may be serving. Lt. Thompson with a number of others of the 51st was taken prisoner at the Yellow Tavern, Aug. 21st, 1864.

Mar 10—The usual drills and picket duty in the trenches. I left Baltimore at 4 1/2 A.M. for the front.

Mar 11—The usual drills and picket duty in the trenches. I arrived at Fort. Monroe at 12 M. 1st Lt. Wm. F. Campbell Co. H, a returned prisoner of war on parol [sic], has been granted a leave of absence for thirty days by S.O. No. 119 War Department, at the expiration of which time he is ordered to report in person to the Commanding Officer of Camp Parole nearest the Department or Army in which his regiment may be serving.

Mar 12—The usual drills and picket duty in the trenches. Regular monthly inspection by the brigade inspector.

Mar 13—The usual drills and picket duty in the trenches. I arrived at Fort Morton and again assumed command of the regiment. Orders received to send all unnecessary baggage to City Point to be shipped to Alexandria Va., for storage. On the recommendation of Gen. Willcox commanding the division, I was promoted to Bvt. Brig. Gen. U. S. Vols., Lt. Col. Wm. Allebaugh to Bvt. Col., Capt. Daniel L. Nicholas Co. B to Bvt. Major, Capt. Wm. R. Foster Co. E to Bvt. Major.

Mar 14—The usual drills and picket duty in the trenches.

By orders from Hdqrs. Army of the Potomac, General Orders No. 10. In accordance with the requirements of G.O. No. 19, of 1862, from the War Department, and in conformity with the reports of boards convened to examine into the services rendered by the troops concerned, and by the authority of the lieutenant-general commanding Armies of the United States, it is ordered that there shall be inscribed upon the colors or guidons of the regiments and batteries serving in this army the names of the battles in which they have borne a meritorious part, and as hereafter specified, vis:

Fifty-first Pennsylvania Veteran Volunteers

Roanoke Island–New Berne–Camden–Second Bull-Run–Chantilly–South Mountain–Antietam–Fredericksburg–Vicksburg–Jackson–Campbell's Station–Siege of Knoxville–Wilderness–Spotsylvania–Cold Harbor–Petersburg–Weldon Railroad–Ream's Station–Hatcher's Run.[19]

A movement is in no doubt inticipated [sic] in this army. The Ninth Corps is ordered to hold the lines from the Appomattox to Fort Davis and return to the left from this point. This corps will be prepared to move with the same amount of supplies and ammunition as hereinafter specified for the other three. The surplus artillery within this line will be sent to City Point and its defenses. Eight days' hard bread, coffee, sugar, and salt will be carried in the divisional supply train. Ten days' beef on the hoof will be driven in each corps herd. Animals will be foraged for eight days. The allowance of artillery ammunition with the corps will be 270 rounds per gun. Sutlers and all camp followers not allowed on the march to be ordered at once to the rear. All sick in field hospitals to be at once removed to the Depot Field Hospital, City Point.[20]

Yesterday about 3 P.M. the enemy opened fire from rifle batteries on Baxter Road and 8-inch columbiad and mortar batteries near Petersburg Pike. Battery 14, Fort Morton and Avery, and Battery 15 replied to this fire slowly until the enemy ceased. The camp of Capt. [James A.] Cooper in Battery 15 was partially destroyed and the platforms of one of the 10-inch mortars in Fort Morton blown up. No casualties.

My old regiment numbers to-day, 33 sergeants, 7 musicians, and 588 men. My Bvt. Brig. Gen's. commission came through the recommendation of Gen. Parke commanding the corps, instead of through Gen. Willcox, and was recommended March 7, 1865, and heads: for his gallant and meritorious services during the war.

Mar 15—The usual drills and picket duty in the trenches in front of Fort Morton. I was detailed as Division Officer of the Day for the next twenty-four hours. I received a very patriotic letter from Norristown Pa., who signs herself "A niece of Uncle Sam, but not an invalid." Deserters in to-day state that four or five regiments of negroes are near Petersburg. The firing we heard was caused by drilling the negroes in firing with blank cartridges. Negroes were put in the field for the first time last week.

Mar 16—The usual drills and picket duty in the trenches. Regimental inspection.

Mar 17—The usual drills and picket duty in the trenches.

Mar 18—The usual drills and picket duty in the trenches. The 2d, 5th and 6th Army Corps are vacating their works on the left of the 9th Corps, and are moving further to the left, and are making a foray on the enemies right, and part of the 6th, and all of the 9th Corps are now holding the entire line thus vacated, from Petersburg to Hancock's Station. We are ordered to be very watchful.

Mar 19—The usual drills and picket duty in the trenches. We are receiving a terrible shelling at Fort Morton, both from artillery and mortars, continued all day and well into the night. The shelling during the night was grand to behold. The shells in passing from one side to the

19. *O.R.*, vol. 46, part 2, 865-78, for this order. The 51st battle honor list can be found on 874.

20. *O.R.*, vol. 46, part 2, 967.

other, struck each other, watched their flight from our bomb-proofs. Troops laid on their arms all night.

Mar 20—The usual drills and picket duty in the trenches. The enemy again opened on us this morning with a furious shelling. Troops under arms all day and on the alert.

Mar 21—The usual drills and picket duty in the trenches. The shelling not quite so heavy. Under arms all day and night, and outer pickets ordered to be on the alert.

Mar 22—The usual drills and picket duty in the trenches. The "Johnnies" more quiet in our front.

Capt. Wm. Allebaugh Co. C who escaped from a rebel prison, having expressed a willingness to remain in service for the veteran term of his regiment, has by order of the War Department in S.O. No. 129, been remustered for three years, from September 14th 1864, with rank from September 14th 1861, and has been ordered to rejoin his regiment for duty, with permission to delay en route thirty days.

Mar 23—The usual drills and picket duty in the trenches. Laying close to our arms all day and night. Deserters state that a guard is now kept in the rear of the rebel troops to prevent desertions to the rear. They also state that tobacco is stored in Richmond in large warehouses on Washington Street packed with kindling wood, and cotton is stored in the same street, prepared in the same manner. The machinery has been removed from the four cotton mills on the Appomattox above Petersburg. One deserter came in with a negro woman dressed in man's clothing.

Picket firing heavier than usual last night. Seventeen deserters came in on our front. We lost six substitutes last night, four from the 35th Mass. and two from the 45th Penna.

Mar 24—The usual drills and picket duty in the trenches. Matters look threatening. There will be a racket before morning. Sergt. Henry Foreman Co. D wounded.

Mar 25—The usual picket duty in the trenches. The commencement of the end. About 4.30 A.M., the enemy assaulted the Ninth Corps front, with Gordon's Corps, re-enforced by Bushrod Johnson's Division.[21]

It is well to state here the position of the Ninth Corps at this time. Our line extended from the Appomattox on the right, with pickets stretching some three miles down the river, to Fort Howard on the left, a distance of about seven miles. The line was occupied by the First Division, Bvt. Maj. Gen. O. B. Willcox commanding, extending from the Appomattox to Fort Meikel, and the Second Division, Bvt. Maj. Gen. R. B. Potter commanding, extending from Fort Meikel to Fort Howard. The Third Division, Brig. Gen. John F. Hartranft commanding, was held in reserve, its right regiment being posted near the Dunn House Battery, and its left regiment between Forts Hays and Howard. The intrenchments held by Willcox's division and the First Brigade of Potter's, were very nearly as placed when the positions were originally gained by our troops, under fire, and in so close proximity to the enemy that the works was necessarily very defective.

This was especially the case with Fort Stedman, where our line crossed the Prince George Court House Road. This is a small work without bastions, with Battery No. 10 immediately adjoining, the battery open in the rear, and the ground in rear of the fort nearly as high as its parapet. The opposing lines are here about 150 yards apart, the picket lines about fifty yards. This portion of the line was held by the Third Brigade, First Division, Bvt. Brig. Gen. N. B. McLaughlen commanding.

At 4 A.M., the picket line had been visited by the captain of the picket, who found the men on the alert and discovered no signs of a movement by the enemy. Taking advantage of the

21. Much of this account is from Parke's report, *O.R.*, vol. 46, part 1, 316-18.

order allowing deserters to bring their arms with them, the enemy sent forward squads of pretended deserters, who, by this ruse, gained possession of several of the picket posts. They were closely followed by a strong storming party of picked men; this, by three heavy columns. The picket line was overpowered after one discharge of their pieces. The trench guard,though stoutly resisting, was unable to withstand the rush of numbers, and the main line was broken between Batteries 9 and 10, near No. 10. The enemy turned to the right and left hand, the right column soon gaining Battery 10, which is open in the rear, thus acquiring great advantage for an assault on Fort Stedman. The garrison of Fort Stedman, consisting of a battalion of the Fourteenth New York Heavy Artillery under Maj. Randall, made a spirited resistance, but being attacked in front, flank, and rear, was overpowered and most of it captured. The artillery in the fort, consisting of four light 12's, discharged a dozen rounds of canister before being taken. These guns, as well as those in Battery 10, were at once turned upon us.

The enemy then pushed gradually along the lines towards Fort Haskell, driving out the troops holding Batteries 11 and 12, neither of which are inclosed works. It was still quite dark, which circumstance greatly augmented the difficulty of formation to check the progress of the enemy, it being almost impossible to distinguish between friend and foe, and made the use of artillery upon them impracticable at any distance.

At the first alarm, Gen. McLaughlen sent members of his staff to the various positions on his front, and he himself proceeded to Fort Haskell, thence along the line to Stedman. He found that our troops had been driven from Battery 11. He directed Mortar Battery 12 to open on it, and sent for the 59th Mass., and on its arrival recaptured Battery 11 by a bayonet charge. He then proceeded to Fort Stedman and was taken prisoner. Parke dispatched an aide-de-camp to communicate with Willcox and McLaughlen, and ordered Hartranft to concentrate his right brigade and re-enforce Willcox, and ordered Gen. Tidball, chief of artillery, to place his reserve batteries in position on the hills in rear of the point attacked.

Parke, on receiving a report from Willcox and from members of his staff of the state of affairs, ordered up Hartranft's other brigade, and informed Willcox that he would be re-enforced by the Third Division, and directed him to at once reoccupy the works taken. Hartranft concentrated with great promptitude, his left regiment having to move a distance of five miles, he in the meantime gallantly attacking with a regiment of his right brigade, the 200th Penna., assisted by detachments from McLaughlen's and Ely's brigade, of Willcox's division, checking the enemy's skirmishers, who were fast advancing towards Meade's Station, driving them back to the line of works.

The column of the enemy which turned to the left hand after entering our line, proceeded along the trenches in the direction of Battery No. 9, taking the 57th Mass. in flank and rear, and driving them from the trenches. The left of the 2d Mich., the left regiment of Ely's brigade, of Willcox's division, was also somewhat broken, but promptly rallied and fought the enemy over the traverses so stoutly that time was gained to bring up re-enforcements from the right of the brigade, and formed a strong line perpendicular to the intrenchments, and stopped all further advance of the enemy in that direction.

The enemy made several desperate assaults on Fort Haskell, but was bloodily repulsed, and slowly driven back. At 7.30 A.M., we had regained Batteries 11 and 12, and had drawn a cordon of troops around Fort Stedman and Battery 10, forcing the masses of the enemy back into these works where they were exposed to, and suffered greatly from, a concentrated fire from all the artillery in position bearing on those points and reserve batteries on the hill and rear. This cordon was composed of Hartranft's division, with regiments from McLaughlen's and Ely's brigade on either flank.

Gen. Hartranft made his dispositions with great coolness and skill, and at about 7.45 A.M., advance his whole line. His troops, the vast majority of them new men, for the first time under fire, charged with great spirit and resolution, the veterans on the flanks behaving with their accustomed gallantry, and carried the fort with comparatively small loss. Nineteen hundred and forty-nine prisoners, including seventy-one commissioned officers, nine stand of colors, and many small-arms, fell into our hands.

The whole line taken from us was at once reoccupied, and all damage repaired during the following night. We lost no guns or colors. Meade was absent at the time of this attack, and Gen. Parke did not know that he was in command of the Army of the Potomac, until 6.10 A.M. Fort Stedman was called by the rebels Hare's Hill. The force of the enemy consisted of three divisions of infantry, under command of Maj. Gen. Gordon. The great majority of the rebel wounded fell into our hands, and the wounds were all very severe in character. An unusually large number of shell wounds of the thigh and legs, demanded amputation, were seen.

Lt. Henry D. Patterson, First Connecticut Heavy Artillery commanding the guns and mortars in Fort Morton, fired forty-three mortar shells and five 4 1/2-inch percussion shell, some at the Cemetery Hill battery, which was firing on our troops in rear of Fort Haskell, the others were directed on the batteries near the Petersburg pike. The rebels burst a large number of shell in the fort, wounding four men of the Fifty-first Penna., but were of such a light character, that no official report was made of it. I myself was struck with a spent ball in the breast, which did me no harm, and fell at my feet.

At 8 P.M., the number of prisoners received by the provost-marshall was 2,200 taken by the Ninth Corps, and 500 by the Second Corps. At 12 M., Gen. Gordon requested a flag of truce for the removal of the wounded and dead between the lines. Gen. Parke acceded to his request, and authorized Gen. Hartranft to make the necessary arrangements. While the truce was in operation, Gen. Meade informed Parke that if the enemy's parties, while burying their dead, appear incline [sic] to hold intercourse with our troops, he can allow his officers and men to mingle freely with them. At 2.15 P.M., Parke informed Meads [sic] Chief of Staff, Gen. Webb, that five of the captured flags were at Ninth Corps headquarters. At 7.10 P.M., Gen. Hartranft reported to Parke, that during the flag of truce, he had turned over to the enemy 120 dead and 15 badly wounded from which he held a receipt from Gordon's adjutant-general and furnished a list of the names of the rebel wounded and captured officers to Gen. Lewis (rebel). A like list of captured Federal officers was to be furnished by the enemy, but was not made out in time, but to be sent over in the morning, together with our wounded if any in their hands.[22]

Gen. Willcox, in G.O. No. 7, directs that hereafter troops of our division in the trenches will stand to arms promptly at 4 o'clock each morning until further orders and will be kept so until half an hour after daylight, when, if there is no alarm, they can be dismissed. Brig. Gen. John F. Hartranft was promoted to Bvt. Maj. Gen., also Capt. Geo. Shorkley Co. H to Bvt. Lt. Col. to date from to-day. Prv. Chas. Wagoner Co. F killed, and was buried at Meade Station.

Fort Stedman was one of the weakest and most ill-constructed works of the line, being not protected by abatis in the rear, being masked on its right just in rear of Battery No. 10 by a mass of bomb-proofs, rendered necessary by the terrible fire which has habitually had place in this vicinity, and being only about 200 yards distant from the enemy's main line. The parapet had settled greatly during the winter, and in fine, the work was very liable to being carried by a sudden assault. The attack was a complete surprise, and was successful. Maj. Geo. W. Randall, commanding the garrison was captured twice, but made his escape each time. Randall served in my co. as a private in the three months service, and was discharged therefrom through the intervention of Senators John P.

22. *O.R.*, vol. 46, part 3, 153-56.

Hale and Benj. F. Wade to receive promotion as a Lieut. in the Regular Army. Randall is now a Captain in the army. My brother Joe and I paid him a visit yesterday.

About two hours after the first shot was fired, Col. Sam. Harriman of the 37th Wisconsin, but then commanding the brigade, rode up to the fort, and ordered me to send to City Point for horses to haul the guns and mortars out of the fort, or to spike them. He was very much excited. It rather annoyed me and I was wondering what I was there for, and too, with a veteran regiment at my back. Well the horses were not sent for, nor were the guns spiked, and we held the fort. For a time the fort and garrison was completely cut off from division and Corps headquarters,

Mar 26—The usual picket duty in the trenches. Regiment under arms all day and night. Wrote a letter to my sister.

Gen. Parke in G.O. No. 3 from Ninth Corps Headquarters congratulates the corps on this auspicious result. The gallantry and steadiness of the troops engaged, which so brilliantly retrieved a momentary disorder and converted it into a victory, merit and receive his warmest gratitude and commendation. The steadiness and courage of the troops upon the flanks of Fort Stedman, who held their positions, despite the breaking of their lines, are deserving of praise and the General takes occasion to impress upon the Corps the lesson enforced by the example of their brave comrades of the First Division, that a line broken is not carried, and that by prompt rallying and tenaciously holding the position so flanked, the enemy may be made to pay dearly for his temerity.

Our whole corps ordered to be up at 4 o'clock to-morrow morning, ready for any emergency that may arise.

Mar 27—The usual picket duty in the trenches. Standing to arms all day. I was detailed as Division Officer of the Day. Wrote a letter to Capt. Ed. Schall, Norristown.

Mar 28—The usual picket duty in the trenches. We received marching orders, and laid in line of battle all day and night, under a terrible hot fire from the enemies batteries. During the night, the enemy made a general attack along the whole front, particularly in front of Fort Morton. My picket line extended about five hundred feet, the whole detail under the command of Lt. Patterson Co. I. A good portion of the detail were substitutes and drafted men. During the night they were driven in. Lt. Patterson, Corpl. John M. Engle, and two others only remaining to hold the line. Patterson communicated to me so soon as possible. They were soon hunted up, and all the old veterans that could be spared from the fort were sent out with them again to the trenches, giving instructions to shoot down any man who attempted to leave the trenches, giving the order in their hearing. Had no trouble with picket details thereafter. I sent a communication to Gen. Parke recommending that a medal of honor be awarded to Corpl. John M. Engle, Co. I for conspicuous gallantry on the picket line in front of Petersburg.

I received notice through the War Department that the commanding officer of Draft Rendezvous at Philadelphia, Pa., had been this day directed to assign and forward to my regiment one hundred and twenty-five white drafted men, and am to report the number received and date of reception, to Maj. H. Clay Wood, Asst. Adjt. Gen. Washington D.C.

By orders from Gen. Willcox, the trench guards of our division were doubled to-night, and we are enjoined to use the strictest vigilance, the whole command to be under arms promptly at 4 o'clock to-morrow morning.[23]

Mar 29—The usual picket duty in the trenches. The campaign has opened, the fighting on our left terrific. Very heavy cannonading on our immediate front. At 10.45 P.M., the enemy

---

23. *O.R.*, vol. 46, part 3, 233.

threw up a number of rockets and then opened with mortars, and picket firing increased all along the Ninth Corps line. Signal officer reports that between 2 and 5 P.M., about 3,000 infantry and a brigade of cavalry passed our front from Swift Creek, going out on Cox's road towards the left. The enemy appear to be busy on their works on different parts of the line, and considerable stir in Petersburg during the night. Sixteen deserters came in on Potter's front, representing three brigades. We are ordered to stand to arms this p.m., at 4 o'clock and remain so until after dark.[24]

About 10 o'clock when it was dark a rainy night without a moon could be, a furious cannonade, soon joined in by heavy musketry fire, opened on our front and lasted over two hours. The pickets of the 51st in the trenches were again attacked, but nobly held their own. The 8th Mich, on our right and the 109th N.Y. on our left gave way and left the line, leaving our flanks exposed but their officers rallied them and soon again had them in position. At midnight a heavy rain set in and continued all night, and so did the battle. Under arms all night.

Mar 30—The usual picket duty in the trenches. Found time to write a letter to my mother. Very dark and rainy. The roads muddy, and almost impassable for wagons in many places. The dead of yesterday's combat were buried, 50 of our men and 150 of the rebels. At 8.40 P.M., Meade informed Parke that the order to attack to-morrow is suspended, but is ordered to keep a vigilant watch on the enemy and take advantage of any opportunity presenting itself, also to be prepared for orders to assume a threatening attitude and to attack, massing his reserves so situated as to assist in either the defensive or offensive.[25]

Mar 31—The usual picket duty in the trenches. It began to rain at daylight, the roads in a terrible condition from the mud. Towards noon the rain ceased, and the weather became fair. About this time, the Fifth Corps became warmly engaged with the enemy. The enemy showing some uneasiness in our front, and in the afternoon commenced shelling in Fort Morton. Finally Morton with her coehorns, rifled guns, and heavy mortars opened. The rebels concentrated their fire from eight or ten forts on her, making it very hot for us, but those not working the guns kept within their bomb-proofs. We had no one injured. We are all nearly used up on account of the lost of sleep and the constant vigilance, day and night.

Apr 1—The usual picket duty in the trenches. The pickets of our division occupy the trenches before Petersburg, extending from the Appomattox to Norfolk railroad (two miles) and picketing the river. In the night a demonstration was made on the rebel lines, in front of the position occupied by our brigade, in front of Petersburg. The rebels were found in force, and no determined attack was made. [Pvt. Simon Dobson, Co. A, wounded (died April 3).]

In accordance with instructions from Gen. Meade, commanding the army, Gen. Parke, commanding Ninth Corps, issued orders as follows: An assault upon the enemy's works in front of Fort Sedgwick will be made at 4 A.M. to-morrow by the Second and Third Divisions and the First Brigade of the First Division. Hartranft, commanding Third Division, will mass his division in rear of the line between Fort Sedgwick and Fort Rice by 3 A.M. Potter, commanding the Second Division, will withdraw his division from the line and mass it in rear and to the left of Fort Sedgwick and on the left of the Third Division at the same time. Willcox, commanding the First Division, will withdraw his First Brigade from the line and mass it on the right of the Third Division at the same time. Willcox and Potter will leave their picket line out and garrisons in the forts.

24. *O.R.*, vol. 46, part 3, 247.

25. *O.R.*, vol. 46, part 3, 312.

At 4 A.M., the entire picket line will advance, endeavoring to hold all ground gained and the assaulting columns will charge. Strong pioneer parties, provided with spades and axes, will be arranged by the commanders of divisions. Willcox will hold his other two brigades in readiness to advance upon the enemy's works in his front on the receipt of orders. They will not be withdrawn from the line till further orders. Quartermaster's commissary of subsistence and medical departments will make their dispositions accordingly. After 3.30 A.M., Ninth Corps headquarters will be at the Avery house.

At 10.15 P.M., Parke was instructed to feel the enemy's line with skirmishers and open with artillery along his line. We learn that Sheridan has captured 4,000 prisoners and many guns. At dusk reports came from Sheridan, that he had routed the enemy at all points at Five Forks, capturing all his artillery and claims to have captured 6,000 or 7,000 prisoners, cavalry doing splendidly. The enemy are going to the rear fast. The infantry flanked them; the cavalry took breast-works. We are nearing the end.[26]

Apr 2—The usual picket duty in the trenches. General assault on the enemy's works in front of Petersburg; First Brigade of our division massed in front of Fort Sedgwick, reporting to Gen. Hartranft; Second and Third Brigades, with Fifty-first Penna. of First Brigade, at 4 A.M., made demonstrations along the whole division line; fighting throughout the day.[27]

The position of the Ninth Corps confronting that portion of the enemy's line the longest held and most strongly fortified, is held by a second and inner line, we find unable to carry. Parke, during the early morning, informed Meade that he was being pressed by the enemy. The troops left in the defenses at City Point under [Brig.] Gen. [Henry W.] Benham and [Brevet Brig.] Gen. [Charles H. T.] Collis, were ordered up to Parke's support. At 3 A.M., Parke established his headquarters at Fort Rice, and at the same time Genls. Potter and Hartranft formed the assaulting column between our main line and picket line without alarming the enemy, whose picket line was in close proximity.[28]

---

26. *O.R.*, vol. 46, part 3, 429.

27. Much of this account is from Parke's report, *O.R.*, vol. 46, part 1, 1016-8.

28. The Ninth Corps was now organized as follows:
Provost Guard: 79th NY
First Division, Brevet Maj. Gen. Orlando B. Willcox
    First Brigade, Col. Samuel Harriman: 8th, 27th MI, 109th NY, 51st PA, 37th, 38th WI
    Second Brigade, Brevet Col. Ralph Ely: 1st MI Sharpshooters, 2nd, 20th MI, 46th NY, 60th OH, 50th PA
    Third Brigade, Col. James Bintliff: 3rd MD, 29th, 57th, 59th MA, 18th NH, 14th NY Hvy Art, 100th PA
    Acting Engineers: 17th MI
Second Division, Brevet Maj. Gen. Robert B. Potter
    First Brigade, Brevet Brig. Gen. John I. Curtin: 35th, 36th, 58th MA, 39th NJ, 51st NY, 45th, 48th PA, 7th RI
    Second Brigade, Brig. Gen. Simon G. Griffin: 31st ME, 2nd MD, 56th MA, 6th, 9th, 11th NH, 179th, 186th NY, 17th VT
Third Division, Brevet Maj. Gen. John F. Hartranft
    First Brigade, Lt. Col. William H. H. McCall: 200th, 208th, 209th PA
    Second Brigade, Col. Joseph A. Mathews: 205th, 207th, 211th PA
Artillery Brigade, Brevet Brig. Gen. John C. Tidball: 7th ME Bty, 11th MA Bty, 19th, 27th, 34th NY Bty, PA Bty D
Cavalry: 2nd PA Cav

The assaulting force was in column of regiments in the following order: On the right of the Jerusalem Plank Road with left resting on the road. The Third Division, the advance regiments being the 207th Penna. Col. Cox commanding, followed by the 205th Penna. Maj. Morrow commanding, the 211th Penna. Col. Dodd commanding, and the 208th Penna. Col. Heintzelman commanding; the two remaining regiments of the division, the 200th and 209th Penna. were held in reserve behind the works.

On the right of this column was Harriman's brigade of the First Division in the following order; 38th Wis. Col. Bentliff commanding, 109th N.Y. Lt. Col. Pier commanding, and the 8th Mich. Maj. Doyle. The remaining regiments of the brigade, the 27th Mich. and 37th Wis. remained in reserve in rear of the intrenchments. On the left of the plank road, and connecting on the right with Hartranft's division, Potter's division was formed, Griffin's brigade in the advance, supported by Curtin's brigade. Six regiments from the division were left to garrison the forts on its line. Storming parties, accompanied by pioneers provided with axes to clear away the abatis and chevaux-de-frise, proceeded each column. Details of artillerymen to work any guns that might be captured were also in readiness.

Gen. Parke, with the view of leading the enemy astray as to the real point of attack directed Willcox to make a strong demonstration on his front, as before stated. About 4 A.M., the artillery opened vigorously along the whole line firing for some minutes. Promptly our skirmishers were pushed out along the whole line. The 51st Penna. Vet. Vols. left to hold Harriman's brigade front, captured some of the enemy's skirmishers near the Crater, and Col. Ely, commanding the brigade next the river, not only carried their picket line but even about 200 yards of the main line, but could not hold it for any length of time. At about 4.30 A.M., the signal was given for the main attack in front of Fort Sedgwick, and the column moved swiftly and steadily forward. In a moment the enemy's picket line was carried. The stormers and pioneers rushed on and under a most galling fire cut away and made openings in the enemy's abatis and chevaux-de-frise. They were closely followed by the assaulting columns, undeterred by an exceedingly severe fire of cannon, mortar, and musketry from the enemy's line, pressed gallantly on, capturing the enemy's works in their front with 12 guns, a number of colors, and 800 prisoners. Harriman's column re-enforced by the two reserve regiments swept up to the right until the whole of what was called by the enemy "Miller's Salient" was in our possession.

Potter's column swept down to the left. Potter was severely and dangerously wounded shot in the body, low down. He was taken to the Jane's House, and well cared for. This part of the enemy's line was heavily traversed, and they fought from traverse to traverse. The captured guns were at once turned upon the enemy. The fort captured was Fort Mahone and the main line almost as far right as the sand-bag battery; also a portion to the left of the fort. A heavy explosion occurred a little after 3 A.M., in the heart of Petersburg.

This fighting was all done before daylight, and no further attempt was made to advance, but attention was turned to securing what we had gained, and restoring the organization of the troops, much shattered by the hard fighting and the advance over broken ground in the darkness. The captured line was promptly made tenable as possible and the troops got in readiness for another forward movement.

At 7.40 A.M., Parke received orders directing him to hold on to all he had got, and not to move or advance unless he sees his way clear. About this time the enemy made an attempt to get up a charge on us, but our fire was so hot that they did not get many men outside their lines. At this time we held a distance of about 400 yards on each side of the Jerusalem Plank Road, including several forts and redans. The enemy made no further movements, excepting of being very busy planting guns and keeping up an incessant and murderous fire of sharpshooters, until about 11 o'clock, when he made a heavy and determined assault on the captured line, but we repulsed him at all points with much loss. At intervals the enemy made heavy and desperate attempts to recapture his lost works, but without success.

At about 3 P.M., the enemy succeeded in regaining a few traverses on the left, which gave them a flank fire upon a small detached work on the left of the plank road, held by one regiment of Curtin's brigade, and occasioned its temporary abandonment. The work was retaken by Gen. Collis.

Between 4 and 5 P.M., [Brevet Brig.] Gen. [Joseph E.] Hamblin arrived with a brigade from the Sixth Corps, and was directed to report to Gen. Hartranft, by whom he was placed in support of the left of his line. These re-enforcements having rendered Parke's line secure, he was disposed to make another effort to drive the enemy from his position in the rear, but the exhausted condition of his troops forced him to abandon the idea. He contented himself by strengthening his line as much as possible, whenever practicable transferring the enemy's chevaux-de-frise to the front of the reversed line, and on the right connecting with a cross line the extreme point we held with our main line.

Desultory firing continued nearly all night. Our batteries on the right fired at intervals all night at the bridge across the Appomattox. The troops were instructed to exercise the greatest vigilance for the purpose of detecting the expected evacuation of the enemy, or any other movement of his. There were brought to division hospitals of the Ninth Corps from the scene of this assault 1,114 wounded, including 21 rebels.

Prv. Lucius Lake Co. A seriously wounded, and Prv. Joseph Parely Co. H killed by the premature explosion of one of our shells. [Also Pvt. Gabriel Fay, Co. B, wounded.] I received orders to make frequent details to supply the picket line with ammunition and ordered to keep on hand at least 5,000 rounds on hand constantly.

Apr 3—The regiment still in the trenches of the whole brigade line, also garrisoning Fort Morton and the lines to the right and left of it. About midnight huge fires were seen springing up in all directions in and around Petersburg and towards Richmond, and about 2 A.M., Fort Darling, at Drury's Bluffs, blew up, making a heavy report, and about 3 A.M., everything indicated the evacuation of the city.

Selecting Prv. Thomas Troy Co. I, known in the regiment as "Scout," I ordered him to try and make his way into Petersburg, and he was very willing to make the attempt. Returning in much less than an hour, with the intelligence that the enemy hadn't all left yet, but were leaving fast. He also managed to get some liquor. On the strength of Tom's report, I immediately ordered the pickets in the trenches over the works, deploying them as skirmishers, under the command of Lieuts. Geo. H. Smith and Ed. Evans, they skirmished their way into Petersburg, capturing a large number of prisoners, returning about 9 A.M., bringing with them some mementoes, among which was a hose-carriage bell, which they gave to me. Had they had had the regimental colors with them, they would certainly have been the first on the public buildings. At 6 A.M., I mounted my horse and rode into the city, remaining an hour or two. I recommended that Troy should be awarded a medal of honor for distinguished gallantry during the morning of the 3d of April 1865, in ascertaining the movements of the enemy, bringing the first reliable information of the evacuation of Petersburg.

Soon after 4 A.M., we succeeded in penetrating their lines at all points nearly simultaneously, capturing the few remaining pickets. The Second Brigade, Ely's of our division, was the first to enter the city, near the Appomattox, and to Col. Ely the formal surrender of the city was made by the authorities; and at 4.28 A.M., the flag of the First Michigan Sharpshooters was raised on the court house, and guards were posted throughout the city. Maj. Lounsberry of the 2d Mich. was met in front of the court house by three citizens bearing a flag of truce and a communication from the mayor and common council tendering the surrender of the town and requesting that persons and private property be respected. But the major would listen to no proposition until the "old flag" was floating from the highest point of the court house steeple.

The enemy had fired the bridges, but with the aid of the negroes, who manded the fire-engines, our troops extinguished the flames in time to save the main structures and skirmishers were at once across the river, picking up stragglers and other prisoners. In two hours, notwithstanding the presence of troops from every corps, including colored troops, Petersburg which had been besieged by our army nearly ten months, was as quiet, and property and persons as safe as in Washington. The enemy left 150 of his badly wounded in a well-appointed hospital located in the suburbs, and known as the "C. S. Hospital," with two medical officers.[29]

Gen. Parke, with two divisions of the Ninth Corps, moved to the right of Wright, the supply trains to follow on the Cox Road. Hartranft has the fire-engines at work trying to save a bridge. Our division, Willcox's has been ordered to occupy Petersburg, to guard it and the railroad. Consequently the 51st P.V.V. prepared to move from Fort Morton and the trenches where we had been for the pass nine months and twenty days, without any intermission.

The following in an extract from my report:

"Having extended my regiment the whole length of the brigade line I instructed them in case of attack to be prepared at any moment to move to any point on the line. Our casualties were during the day 1 man killed and 1 mortally wounded; this being done by our own shells. On the morning of the 3d instant, suspecting the evacuation of the enemy, I sent a scout to ascertain the truth or falsity of my suspicion. He soon returned and reported that he had penetrated to the enemy's rear line, finding one man to every forty yards of the line. I ordered the officer of the picket to advance in front of the Crater; they met with no opposition and soon gained Cemetery Hill. At this point the picket officer sent to me for the colors, which I refused to send; however, they advanced and claimed to have been in the city twenty minutes before the national colors had been placed upon any buildings. They also claim to have captured some fifty prisoners."[30]

Apr 4—The weather still continues pleasant. No detail for the trenches this morning, that is a thing of the past. The men of the regiment, since yesterday have been sleeping on the ground in and around Fort Morton, awaiting orders to move. They have been under arms day and night for over one week without obtaining an hour's unbroken rest in all that time, part of which was cold and rainy weather.

About noon we shouldered our muskets and marched over the works to Petersburg, and halted for about an hour at the outskirts of the city. After resting a short time, we entered from the side opposite the works we had captured. While marching along we were greeted by the colored population with songs and joyous exclamations. We march through the city without halting and encamped on the outskirts of a suburban village called "Halifax," at the southwestern part of Petersburg, where stood a very valuable mineral works said to belong to the Confederate Government, said to be under the charge of a Mr. B. A. Birchett, who informed us that the works were valued at about eight millions of dollars (Confederate scrip) we suppose. The mineral stock was chiefly Galena (lead) copper and iron ores, and quite a number of

29. *O.R.*, vol. 46, part 1, 1018-9, 1048.

30. Bolton's report was included in Col. Harriman's report in *O.R.*, vol. 46, part 1, 1044.

boxes marked Perkimon mines. Some silver ore was also about the place. I made my headquarters in the office of the works. We were not long in finding in the laboratory several hundred rifles and muskets, and a large amount of ammunition, which had been placed there on the afternoon proceeding the evacuation.

At 6.30 A.M., Gen. Wright was ordered to move up to the Cousins House at Winticomac Creek. At 7.45 P.M., Parke received at E. A. Puckett's House, sixteen miles from Petersburg, a dispatch dated at 2.15 P.M., to take the first cross-road to the Cox Road, and not to pass the Sixth Corps, and to guard the South Side Railroad as far as the rear of the army back to Sutherland's Station, leaving a detachment of not less than one brigade at each post. Willcox will protect the road at Sutherland's Station. One of Hartranft's brigade [sic] was halted at Browder's crossing of railroad, and his other brigade at Mrs. Crowder's, forks of Ford's Road and Cox's Road. Our brigade still remains in Petersburg, and is encamped inside the old rebel line of works, but outside of the town, between the Jerusalem and Boydton Plank Roads, and is guarding all the approaches to the town between and including those roads. Col. Ely is still in command of the city.[31]

Apr 5—The regiment left their quarters at the leadworks at 1 P.M. Our division pickets were relieved by the troops of Gen. Ferrero and the division took up the line of march to Sutherland's Station, on the South Side Railroad, ten miles from Petersburg, marching by the Cox Road. After marching ten miles, went into bivouac. At midnight again moved off marching all night.[32]

Apr 6—We passed through Sutherland's Station and after marching all day, reached Wilson's Station about 6 p.m., and went into camp on the plantation of Col. Hobbs, who has been in the rebel army. Gen. Willcox has been directed to extend his advance to Wellsville, covering well the roads approaching the railroad at or near that place.[33]

Apr 7—I was detailed Division Officer of the Day. There being a nice lawn in front of the Hobbs' mansion, I concluded to pitch my tent there, within a few feet of the high steps of the mansion. Hobbs, as well as his whole family became dissatisfied, but the spot just suited me, and the tent stayed there, and the regimental colors floated in front of my quarters, much to their dislike.

The boys soon found out that there was a flour mill on the plantation, and we were not long in making use of some of its contents, both for man and beast. The brigade commander sent me a note informing me that five of my men had been arrested in a near by woods with some beef, and orders me to investigate the matter.

Apr 8—The regimental staff officers and myself took dinner in the Hobbs' mansion. The whole family very sulky. We each paid $1.50 for our meals, a very mean dinner. Two thousand rebel prisoners encamped near us, a hard looking crowd.

Parke ordered to send forward troops enough to make a full division at Burkesville for the purpose of furnishing escorts to prisoners and guards to public property. Also ordered to detail one commissioned officer and forty men to report as guard at Burkesville Junction to the officer in charge of the general cattle herd. The Ninth Corps now stretches out from Sutherland's to Burkesville, some fifty miles.[34]

---

31. *O.R.*, vol. 46, part 3, 555-6.

32. *O.R.*, vol. 46, part 3, 581.

33. *O.R.*, vol. 46, part 3, 607.

34. *O.R.*, vol. 46, part 3, 649.

At 10 P.M. received marching orders, struck tents, and commenced our march along the railroad marching all night in the direction of Blacks and Whites. The Hobbs family seemed delighted at our departure. Just before leaving camp at the Hobbs mansion, I was ordered to move my regiment at once, three miles above Wellsville, and picket the roads one mile to the left of that point and to the right as far as Blacks and Whites.

Apr 9—We arrived at Blacks and Whites Station at 3 A.M., and all the companies of the regiment were detailed to guard the railroad, the line extending over two miles. I made my headquarters in a double one story frame house. The owner, a widow Mrs. Mary C. Jones, and a married daughter occupied the house. The daughter's husband was in the rebel army. The house contained four rooms. Mrs. Jones kindly gave me the use of two rooms, and kept them clean. She kept slaves and a large number of small huts were on the plantation.

Willcox has appointed Lt. Col. F. W. Swift, Seventeenth Michigan Vols. provost marshal of the district occupied by the troops of this command. At daylight, the disposition of our [division] was as follows: The First Brigade extended from one mile above Wilson's Station to Blacks and Whites. The Second Brigade extended up to Ford's Station and guard Ford's Station. The Third Brigade from Ford's Station to one mile above Wilson's Station. The 51st P.V.V. relieved Hartranft's [division].

Willcox sent a scouting party as far as Jones' Bridge, on Nottoway River, under command of Capt. Manning. His scouts were fired upon several times by bushwhackers. Met rebel soldiers on their way in to give themselves up. The people driving their herds and horses across Nottoway River. Negroes coming in in numbers. They are stealing and pillaging. The people along here are all taking the oath of allegiance, and ask protection. At Wilson's Station, 8,000 prisoners, with their guard, arrived last night, without food. Willcox supplied them from his train.[35]

I received a note from a Mrs. E. A. Boling, requesting me to send her a safeguard. Also received one from a Mrs. Mary McFarley, emploring for a safeguard, informing me that her residence on the road that goes to the mill, a white house a mile and a half from Blacks and Whites. Also a letter from a Mr. Wm. B. Irby, wishing to take the oath of allegiance.

Bvt. Lt. Col. Geo. Shorkley promoted to Bvt. Col.

Apr 10—Regiment still guarding the railroad. The cars continue to carry large numbers of rebel prisoners from the front to Petersburg; 2,000 to 4,000 pass daily. The road is in a terrible running order, and the trains scarce exceed a speed of five miles per hour. A large number of our own troops are continually passing from the front towards Petersburg. Wrote a letter to my sister and received a number of government documents.

Willcox, commanding our diviion, in a circular order, has ordered inclosed works of dimensions for garrisons of at least 200 men and two guns each will at once be thrown up at Ford's, Wilson's and Blacks and Whites Stations. The works will be surrounded by abatis, which will be so planted, about seventy-five yards from the works, as not to obstruct the view of the ground immediately beyond. Brigade commanders are to locate the works and complete them as soon as possible.[36] This we do not understand. We all thought that the war was about over, also our digging days.

I paid a visit to the Nottaway County Poor House, and a poorer house is not easily found. It contains some fifteen or twenty inmates, and what they live on God only knows. They are dirty and ragged, and living in abject misery.

---

35. *O.R.*, vol. 46, part 3, 675-6.

36. *O.R.*, vol. 46, part 3, 693.

Apr 11—Regiment still guarding railroad. Received three commissions from Harrisburg, Pa., for Capt. Wm. S. Melick, First Lt. Jacob Hawk, and Second Lt. John Vanlew, all of Co. K.

Apr 12—Regiment still guarding railroad. 150 men detailed to work on the fort at Blacks and Whites. What this fort is for, is more than any military genius can tell. Cars continue to haul prisoners pass our camp.

Apr 13—Regiment still guarding railroad. 200 men detailed for the fort. Wrote a letter to Gen. Hartranft, at Nottoway Court House.

Apr 14—Regiment still guarding railroad. Two commissioned officers and 150 men detailed to work on the fort.

In the evening we had dress parade, the occasion being the presentation of a gold watch and chain to Bvt. Maj. Gen. John F. Hartranft. The regiment was formed in a hollow square, the brigade band being present. The address was made by myself, and was responded to by Gen. Hartranft.

The excitement and hilarity in the army for the pass few days have been intense. All are looking for a speedy termination of the war. No one, then, but those who witnessed can have any idea of the deep gloom which spread through the whole army, when, at midnight, I received a dispatch from Corps Headquarters, announcing the assassination of Abraham Lincoln.

Apr 15—Regiment still guarding railroad. Another heavy detail to work on the fort.

Apr 16—Regiment still guarding railroad. Another heavy detail for work on the fort. Labor all for nothing.

Apr 17—Regiment still guarding railroad, and working on the fort.

Apr 18—Regiment still guarding the railroad, and doing work on the fort. Wrote a letter to my mother. The troops of the Ninth Corps extend along the whole of the line of the railway between Petersburg and Farmville, a distance of sixty-nine miles.

Apr 19—Regiment still guarding the railroad and working on the fort. Hartranft called to see me to-day. At 9 P.M. Grant ordered Meade to send the Ninth Corps to Washington as rapidly as their places can be filled by such other troops as he may designate to take their place, the shipment to commence at once.[37]

Apr 20—Was detailed as Division Officer of the Day. The whole corps received marching orders to proceed to City Point. We were relieved by the Fifth Army Corps. From City Point we are to proceed to Washington with instructions to report to Gen. Grant. Struck our tents at 10.30 A.M. and at 12 M. left Blacks and Whites Station, and at dark came to a halt at Ford Station and went into bivouac for the night.

Just four years ago to-day, I left my home for the war. Just one year ago to-day lacking three days, this army struck their tents at Annapolis Md. (April 23d 1864) and at once commenced the campaign against Lee, and to-day, a very singular coincident, we received orders to strike tents, with orders to march with our faces turned toward home.

Apr 21—We left our bivouac at 6 A.M. and came to a halt at 5 P.M., and went into bivouac two miles from Petersburg. The 2d and 3d Brigades of our Division embarked at City Point.

Apr 22—We left our bivouac at 5 A.M., marched through Petersburg, arriving at City Point at 10 A.M., and immediately embarked on board of the S. S. *Cossack*, leaving there at 5 P.M., and steamed down the James River, dropped anchor in the stream at 7 P.M. for the night.

---

37. *O.R.*, vol. 46, part 3, 832.

Chapter 15

Final Duty

April 23–August 2, 1865

After moving to Washington, the 51st served in the District of Alexandria for the rest of its term of service. The regiment participated in the Grand Review (May 23), then waited impatiently for its mustering-out, which occurred on July 27. The soldiers returned to Harrisburg and were discharged from state service on August 1.

Apr 23—Hoisted anchor at 5 A.M., arrived at Fort Monroe at 9 A.M., steamed up the Chesapeake Bay and into the Potomac River, running all night. Capt. Wm. Allebaugh Co. C promoted to Lt. Col.

Apr 24—Arrived in front of Washington at 6 A.M., dropped anchor and awaited orders, which came when we again hoisted anchor and steamed down the river to Alexandria, disembarked, marched through the city about three miles and encamped on the Fowles' farm, near the Fairfax House. We are now under the orders of [Maj.] Gen. Christopher C.] Augur, commanding Department of Washington.

Apr 25—We left our camp this morning and went into camp near Fort Lyons. Our connection with the Army of the Potomac has ceased.

Apr 26—We left our camp at 7 A.M., marched through Alexandria, crossed the Potomac River over the Long Bridge, marched through Washington and Georgetown, arriving at Tennallytown at 4 p.m., and bivouacked along the roadside. I received a large mail from home.

Apr 27—We changed our camp and moved into a woods. After clearing away the underbrush, it has made a fine camping ground. Commenced to make out our muster rolls.

Apr 28—Companies engaged on their muster rolls. We received a visit from Maj. Hart, Florence Sullivan, and Chris. Blounce.[1] Brigade dress parade, first for some time.

Apr 29—Companies still engaged on their muster rolls. Wrote a letter to Benj. F. Hancock.[2] Have just received the following order:

---

1. Florence Sullivan was a Norristown hat and clothing store owner and county prothonotary, while Christopher Blounts was a manufacturer of woolen goods.

2. Benjamin F. Hancock, the famous general's father, was a Norristown lawyer.

Special Orders   Hdqrs. District of Alexandria.
No. 2   Ninth Army Corps
                               April 29, 1865.

1. The Fifty-first Pennsylvania Veteran Volunteers, Col. William J. Bolton commanding, now serving with the First Division, Ninth Army Corps, is hereby transferred to the Third Division, Brevet Major General Hartranft commanding. Col. Bolton will at once report with his regiment accordingly.

   x   x   x   x   x   x   x   x   x

By command of Maj. Gen. John G. Parke,
Jno. C. Youngman, Asst. Adj. General.

Gen. Augur, commanding Department of Washington, has ordered Parke to have Gen. Hartranft report at his headquarters at once.[3]

Apr 30—Regiment mustered for pay.

May 1—Regiment left their camp at Tennallytown at 9 A.M., marching through Georgetown and Washington, crossed the Potomac over the Long Bridge, marched through Alexandria and went into camp on the outskirts of the city, and reported to Gen. Hartranft our arrival.

May 2—I was assigned to the command of the Third Division, Ninth Army Corps, by virtue of seniority of rank, in the absence of Gen. Hartranft. In pursuant to instructions from Headquarters, District of Alexandria 9th A.C., the 51st Penna. Vet. Vols., 215th Penna. Vols., 197th Ohio Vols., and 155th Indiana Vols., will form a brigade, and will be designated as the Provisional Brigade 3d Division 9th Army Corps, Col. Wm. Wister 215th Regt. Penna. Vols. assumed command. Lt. Wm. F. Thomas Co. C was appointed Acting Asst. QrMr. of the brigade.

May 3— Not feeling very well.

May 4—I was relieved of the command of the 3d Division by Bvt. Brig. Gen. John I. Curtin.

May 5—Not feeling very well. Wrote a letter to my sister. Company drills and dress parade.

May 6—Regiment left their camp at 12 M., marched three miles out to the Mount Vernon Road, and went into camp in a peach orchard.

May 7—Received a large mail from Norristown. Heavy detail made from the regiment to guard rebel prisoners. In S.O. I named our camp "Camp Andy Johnson." Company drills and dress parade.

May 8—Regiment still guarding rebel prisoners. Company drills and dress parade.

May 9—Regiment relieved from guarding rebel prisoners. Regimental and company drills and dress parade. By G.O. No. 3, Parke's headquarters: "The Officers will wear the badge of mourning on the left arm, and on their swords; and the colors of their Commands and Regiments will be put in mourning for the period of six months." The Provisional Brigade has become defunct. The 215th Penna. 155th Indiana, and 169th Ohio Regiments have orders to report at Dover, Delaware.

May 10—Company drills and dress parade. By the orders of Parke, no visitors are permitted at Mount Vernon on Sundays.

May 11—Company drills and dress parade.

May 12—Company drills and dress parade.

---

3. *O.R.*, vol. 46, part 3, 1013-4.

May 13—Company drills and dress parade. Received a letter from Maj. Wm. H. Yerkes.

May 14—Regimental and brigade reviews by Gen. Curtin. Dress parade.

May 15—Company and regimental drills, and dress parade.

May 16—Company and regimental drills, and dress parade. Received a letter from my mother.

May 17—Was detailed as Division Officer of the Day. Company drills and dress parade. Wrote a letter to my mother.

May 18—Company and regimental drills. It has been ordered by Gen. Augur that a suitable number of experienced and competent officers to be detailed at once in each brigade, to make a thorough inspection of the regimental and company records therein, particularly muster rolls and clothing accounts of enlisted men and all that relates to their bounties and claims for pensions. Officers to make daily reports.

May 19—Company drills and dress parade. Received a pass and paid a visit to Washington and remained over night.

May 20—Paid a visit to the U.S. Arsenal in Washington, and attended the Court Martial there siting, trying the assassins of Lincoln. Had a full view of the court, and the prisoners. Returned to camp in the evening. Regiment turned in all of its ammunition. I was appointed on a board of officers and made president of the board, to decide what officers were to remain in the service, to meet at division headquarters.

May 21—Company drills and dress parade.

May 22—Regiment left their camp at 5 o'clock A.M., and proceeded to Washington, arriving there at 2 o'clock P.M., and went into bivouac on Capitol Hill, to be in readiness for the Grand Review.

May 23—The troops began taking their position early in the morning, and when the signal gun was fired, one hundred thousand troops moved off to pass in review. It was a drama of dazzling splendor and the day was all that could be expected. There was myriads of smiling faces to welcome our return. After passing the reviewing stand, the regiment with the rest of our division, turned off at the Circle, through K Street, and crossed the Potomac at the foot of High Street, Georgetown, taking the lower road pass Arlington House, to Columbia Pike, arriving at our camp at 4 o'clock P.M., pretty well tired out.

The following is the order in column of the troops of the Ninth Army Corps as arranged for the review:

Maj. Gen. John G. Parke, commanding, and staff; cavalry escort (detachment Second Pennsylvania Cavalry), Lieut. D. R. Maxwell commanding.

First Division, Bvt. Maj. Gen. O. B. Willcox.
First Brigade, Col. Samuel Harriman.
38th Wis., Col. James Bintliff.
27th Mich., Col. Charles Waite.
17th Mich., Lt.Col. F. W. Swift.
37th Wis., Lt.Col. John Green.
109th N.Y., Capt. Z. G. Gordon.
79th N.Y., Maj. A. D. Baird.
Second Brigade, Bvt. Col. Ralph Ely.
1st Sharp'ers, 2d Mich., Lt.Col. A. W. Nichols.

46th N.Y., Lt.Col. Adolph Bocker.

50th Penna., Lt.Col. W. H. Telford.

20th Mich., Lt.Col. C. A. Lounsberry.

60th Ohio, Lt.Col. M. P. Avery.

Third Brigade, Bvt. Brig. Gen. N. B. McLaughlen.

3d Md. Battalion, Bvt. Col. G. P. Robinson.

14th N.Y.H.A., Col. E. G. Marshall.

57th Mass., Lt.Col. J. M. Tucker.

59th Mass., Capt. Frederick Cochran.

100th Penna., Col. N. J. Maxwell.

Second Division, Brig. Gen. S. G. Griffin.

First Brigade, Col. Sumner Carruth.

39th New Jersey, Col. A. C. Wildrick.

48th Penna., Col. I. F. Brannon.

7th Rhode Island, Bvt. Col. P. Daniels.

45th Penna., Bvt. Col. T. Gregg.

58th Mass., Lt.Col. J. C. Whiton.

36th Mass., Lt.Col. T. L. Barker.

35th Mass., Lt.Col. John W. Hudson.

51st N.Y., Col. J. G. Wright.

Second Brigade, Col. Herbert B. Titus.

11th N.H., Col. Walter Harriman.

56th Mass., Col. S. M. Weld, jr.

179th N.Y., Col. Wm. M. Gregg.

17th Vermont, Col. F. V. Randall.

31st Maine, Col. Daniel White.

186th N.Y., Lt.Col. E. J. Marsh.

2d Md., Lt.Col. B. F. Taylor.

6th N.H., Lt.Col. P. P. Bixby.

9th N.H., Maj. Geo. H. Chandler.

Third Division, Bvt. Brig. Gen. John I. Curtin.

First Brigade, Col. A. B. McCalmont.

51st Penna., Col. William J. Bolton.

208th Penna., Lt.Col. H. T. Heintzelman.

209th Penna., Col. T. B. Kaufman.

200th Penna., Maj. Jacob Rehrer.

Second Brigade, Col. J. A. Mathews,

207th Penna., Col. R. C. Cox.

211th Penna., Lt.Col. W. A. Coutter.

205th Penna., Lt.Col. W. F. Walter.

Artillery Brigade, Bvt. Brig. Gen. J. C. Tidball.

34th New York Battery, Bvt. Maj. Jacob Roemer.

7th Maine Battery, Capt. A. B. Twitchell.

19th New York Battery, Capt. E. W. Rogers.

Battery D, Penna. Vol. Artry., Capt. S. H. Rhoads.

11th Massachusetts Battery, Capt. E. J. Jones.

27th New York Battery, Capt. J. B. Eaton.

Dwight's division Nineteenth Army Corps, Brig. Gen. Wm. Dwight commanding, marched with the Ninth Corps, under the command of Parke.[4]

May 24—No drilling, all hands took a good rest. Received a letter from my mother. Sherman Army 100,000 veterans under the command of Gen. Sherman passed in review before the President, an imposing military spectacle.

May 25—Company drills and dress parade. Paid a visit to Mt. Vernon with some lady friends, Miss Rupert and the Miss Robinsons.

May 26—I was appointed president of a board of officers to determine on what officers should remain in the 1st Brigade, 3d Division 9th A.C.

Under instructions from headquarters Armies of the United States, Gen. Hancock has ordered Gen. Augur to send at once to the coal regions of Schuylkill County Pa., a small regiment of infantry, under a discreet and reliable commander, with instructions to maintain order among the operators and miners in the collieries of the New York and Schuylkill Coal Company, and all the collieries there furnishing coal for the supply of government, and protect the persons and property of all persons working, or willing to work, in these collieries. In consequence of this order, Parke has selected the 201st Pa. Regiment to be put en route for the coal regions, and has also directed that the 202d Penna. Vol. be prepared to move to Fort Delaware without delay.

In consequence of this order, I received orders to report at Fort Ellsworth at day-light to-morrow morning with my regiment to relieve the 201st Regt. Penna. Vols. We will be under the temporary command of Brig. Gen. John P. Slough, Military Gov. of Alexandria.[5]

All enlisted men belonging to our division whose term of service expire subsequent to Oct. 1st, 1865, are to be transferred to the 51st P.V.V. Thirty-five men from the 205th, 207th, 208th, 200th, 209th, and 211th Penna. Vols. with their proper Muster and Discriptive Rolls, and accounts of pay and clothing accompanying them, were received in the regiment to-day. All ammunition in the cartridge boxes of our division was turned in to-day to the Ordnance Officer, and accounted for upon the return as expended. It is to be destroyed to prevent accident.

May 27—Regiment broke camp and moved off at daylight through the rain to Alexandria, Va., and took up position at the head of King Street, and occupied the frame huts of the 201st Penna. Vols., just vacated by them. A heavy detail made immediately to patrol the city.

May 28—Regimental inspection, and dress parade. I spent the evening in the City of Alexandria, and paid a visit to the old slave pen.

May 29—Company drills and dress parade. Wrote letters to my mother and sister.

May 30—Company drills and dress parade. Regiment was paid off to-day. I received $1,046.15. Corp. Isaac Frick Co. E and Uriah Dungan Co. F detailed for clerical duty at the headquarters of the Military Governor.

May 31—Company drills and dress parade. Regiment still doing parole duty in Alexandria, and will continue to do so, as long as we will remain here.

Jun 1—The day was observed by the Army as a day of humiliation and prayer on account of the murder of President Lincoln. In accordance with G.O. No. 101, War Department, upon all honorable muster-out and discharge from the service of the United States, all volunteer soldiers desiring to do so, are hereby authorized to retain their arms and accoutrements, on paying therefor their value to the Ordnance Department. The payment will be made under

---

4. *O.R.*, vol. 46, part 3, 1188-90.

5. *O.R.*, vol. 46, part 3, 1220-1.

the regulations of the Ordnance Department, to the officer or representative thereof, at the rendezvous in the State to which the troops are ordered for payment and final discharge.

Jun 2—Company drills and dress parade. All of the drafted and substitute men were mustered-out by Lt. Wm. S. Hodgkins, 3d division staff. All of these discharged men left this morning, under the command of Capt. Jacob P. Brooke, for Harrisburg, Pa., to receive their pay and final discharge.[6]

Jun 3—Company drills and dress parade.

Jun 4—Company drills and dress parade.

Jun 5—Company drills and dress parade.

Jun 6—Company drills and dress parade. Surg. Wm. C. Shurlock mustered-out. To-day Gen. Meade recommended John F. Hartranft to be full major general

Jun 7—Company drills and dress parade.

Jun 8—Company drills and dress parade. In company with several other officers I paid a visit to Washington to witness the review of the Sixth Army Corps, Maj. Gen. H. G. Wright commanding. On my return to Alexandria I found the following order awaiting me:

General Order   Headquarters Military Governor
No. 233   Alexandria, Va., June 8th 1865.

During the temporary absence of the General commanding, Colonel William J. Bolton 51st Penna. Vet. Vols. will command the troops of the Seperate Brigade, known as the command of the Military Governor of Alexandria, Va., with headquarters at the Headquarters of the Military Governor.
       By command of Brig. Gen. Slough
           Rollen C. Gale, Capt. and A. A. Genl.

Jun 9—Company drills and dress parade. Pickeled onions, peppers, potatoes and tobacco issued to the regiment.

Jun 10—Company drills and dress parade. I drove out to the camp of the 51st P.V.V. at the head of King Street and spent the evening with the boys.

Jun 11—Regimental inspection and dress parade. Col. McClennan of the 138th Regiment paid me a visit. We took dinner at the Philadelphia House. Lieut. Col. Allebaugh has orders to turn in all surplus ordnance stores in his possession to the Chief Ordnance Officer, Department at Washington.

Jun 12—Company drills and dress parade.

Jun 13—Company drills and dress parade. Lt. Col. Allebaugh has been directed to have the guard detailed from the 51st P.V.V. on duty at the Cameron Run and Edsall Block House, inspected by a commissioned officer on Tuesday and Friday of each week and report in writing to headquarters Military Governor the result of such inspection.

Jun 14—Company drills and dress parade.

Jun 15—Company drills and dress parade. Received a letter from Surgeon General Phillips of Pennsylvania in reference to the appointment of a surgeon for the regiment in the place of Surgeon Shurlock mustered-out.

---

6. Nominal list included 150 names of men from all ten companies.

Jun 16—Company drills and dress parade. Dr. M. F. Bowes of Snyder Co. Penna. has been assigned to the 51st P.V.V. vis Surgeon Shurlock mustered-out, and has been ordered to report to the commanding officer of the regiment by the Surgeon of the State, Joseph A. Phillips.

The Artillery Brigade of the Ninth Army Corps, having been discontinued, Lt. Samuel P. Stephens, who has been acting as Quartermaster of the Artillery Brigade, has been ordered to rejoin his regiment.

Jun 17—Company drills and dress parade.

Jun 18—Company drills and dress parade.

Jun 19—Company drills, regimental inspection, and dress parade. George Fortner of Alexandria, Va., presented to me a silver cup as a token of friendship.

Jun 20—Company drills and dress parade.

Jun 21—Company drills and dress parade. Lt. Henry Jacobs, Co. F, detailed for duty in the city as Officer of the Patrols.

Jun 22—Company drills and dress parade. Surgeon Manning F. Bowes reported for duty and was mustered-in.

Jun 23—Company drills and dress parade. Paid a visit to Washington, going up in a government tug.

Jun 24—Company drills and dress parade. Received a number of letters from home, and wrote several.

Jun 25—Company drills and dress parade. Regimental inspection.

Jun 26—Company drills and dress parade.

Jun 27—Company drills and dress parade. Lieut. Samuel P. Stephens, R.Q.M. has been appointed A.A.Q.M., 3d Division 9th A.C., relieving Maj. J. K. Cilley, A.Q.M., who has been ordered to Rochester, N.Y.

Jun 28—Company drills and dress parade.

Jun 29—Company drills and dress parade.

Jun 30—Company drills and dress parade.

Jul 1—Company drills and dress parade.

Jul 2—Regimental inspection and dress parade.

Jul 3—Company drills and dress parade. I was to-day relieved of the Military Governorship of the City of Alexandria by Gen. Slough, and again assumed command of the regiment.

Jul 4—All drills suspended. Dress parade in the evening. By order of Gen. Augur, all duty in our department, excepting the necessary guard duty and fatigue duty, was suspended between Reveille and retreat, and all indulgence promotive of enjoyment and not inconsistent with the requirements of military discipline and good order, was granted to the troops.

Jul 5—Company drills and dress parade.

Jul 6—Company drills and dress parade. Received a large number of letters from Norristown.

Jul 7—Company drills and dress parade. Wrote letters to Mrs. Hill and Mrs. Harry, Norristown, Pa.

Jul 8—Company drills and dress parade. By the orders of Gen. Parke Lieut. Samuel P. Stephens, A.A.Q.M. 3d Division 9th A.C. will immediately turn over to the Depot Q.M. at Alexandria, Va., all the public property in his possession, after which he will report to the Commanding Officer of his Regiment for duty.

Parke has also in S.O. No. 64 detailed Capt. John Lougharn Company I, New York Vols., as Special Inspector for the 51st Pa. Vet. Vols. and 79th New York Vet. Vols. the results to be reported daily to the Asst. Inspector General.

Jul 9—Company drills, regimental inspection and dress parade.

Jul 10—Company drills and dress parade. The regiment is indulging in another one of those generous feelings in the way of presentations. The fortunate one is Capt. Wm. F. Thomas of Co. C. His men presented him with a splendid Silver Hunting Case American Watch. Lieut. John W. Fair of the same company made the presentation.

Since the Grand Review in May, we have been expecting orders to be sent home. Since we have been here, the men of the regiment have been detached for various duties, but are now being returned to the regiment every day, an indication of the near approach of the order for home. Quite a number of the officers and men have had their wives down here for a few weeks on a visit. Among the number were Mrs. Thomas, Mrs. Parker, Mrs. Santo, Mrs. Tompkins, and Mrs. Cartyvel. The health of the Regiment is good, notwithstanding the hot weather.

Jul 11—Company drills and dress parade. By S.O. No. 69, Headquarters Provost Marshal General, Defences South of the Potomac, Alexandria, Va., Lieut. George H. Smith Co. C and Lieut. Henry Jacobs Co. F were detailed as Officers of the Patrol and ordered to report to Captain J. E. Wurtzeback. Pro. Judge, Alexandria, Va.

Jul 12—Company drills and dress parade.

Jul 13—Company drills and dress parade. Received a pass and paid a visit to Washington, returning in the evening.

Jul 14—Company drills and dress parade.

Jul 15—Company drills and dress parade.

Jul 16—Regimental inspection and dress parade.

Jul 17—Company drills and dress parade.

Jul 18—Company drills and dress parade.

Jul 19—Company drills and dress parade. Received a letter from Dr. Wm. C. Shurlock.

Jul 20—Company drills and dress parade.

Jul 21—Company drills and dress parade. Received orders this morning to make out our muster-out rolls. It will be an immense job. Every name that ever appeared on any of the former rolls, from original muster-in, have to be accounted for on nine seperate rolls. Nine rolls for the field and staff, and nine for each company.

Jul 22—All men detailed from the regiment doing duty in Alexandria have been ordered to rejoin their regiment, being relieved by the 2d District of Columbia regiment. All drilling now dispensed with, only dress parade in the evening.

Jul 23—Companies working on their muster-out rolls and discharge papers.

Jul 24—Companies working on their muster-out rolls and discharge papers. I was engaged nearly all day in signing the discharge papers.

Jul 25—Companies still working on their muster-out rolls. I was engaged nearly all day in signing the discharge papers. Gen. Willcox issued his farewell address to his old division.

Jul 26—The regiment still working on their muster-out rolls. Received a letter from my mother. My farewell address read to the regiment on dress parade, which was the last one:

Headquarters 51st Regt. P.V.V.
Alexandria, Va., July 26th, 1865.

Officers and men of the 51st Regt. Penna. Vet. Vols.

In a very few days this organization will cease to exist. Our mission has been fulfilled, the armed hosts of the enemy no longer defy us, our long fatiguing marches and hard fighting and weary watching for the enemy, day and night, are things of the past. You have, by your patriotic devotion, assisted in establishing a country, one, grand glorious, and indeed free. For nearly four years I have been associated with you, and for over one year of that time I have had the honor to be your commander. I would not be doing myself or you justice without giving expression to my feelings. A thousand thanks are due to both officers and men for your prompt obedience to all my oders, and my love is increased by the remembrance of your bravery and gallantry as you have so often displayed on many a bloody field. But alas! many of our organization now sleep in the valley of the dead; they sleep in honored graves. And it is with pleasure that we can think of their many virtues, their valors in the field, and their cheerful voice in camp, and hope that they have received their golden reward in heaven. When all looked gloomy, you wore cheerful faces; and when orders were exacting, you always cheerfully obeyed. When fighting against overwhelming odds, and by superior numbers compelled to retreat, you have ever evinced that noble, praiseworthy characteristic of a good soldier, "repulsed, but not whipped," "defeated but not conquered." I feel sad to part you; we may never meet again. You are about tor eturn to your homes, and assume the garb and customs of private citizens. I am a young man; there are many amongst you who are old enough perhaps to be my father; time has whitened your hoary locks. I cannot part with you without urging that if you have acquired bad habits, incidental to camp life, to make a firm resolve to break off at once, and show to your friends at home that you can be as good and law-abiding citizens as you have been good, brave, and exemplary soldiers.

I need not particularize separately your many deeds; they all have been fairly won. The records you bear on your silken colors have been honestly won by the blood of your companions, and the deep scars many of you bear upon your persons. You need no marble shaft to commemorate your many valorous needs; your scars, your sacrifices, and the noble acts of gallantry you have displayed, will be your monument. Posterity will applaus you as the redeemers of our country, the worls will admire your self-sacrificing devotion to your country.

I now bid you farewell, and when the war of this life is over with us, when we shall have performed our last earthly mission, may we all meet in heaven is the earnest prayer of the colonel commanding.

With my kindest wishes for your future prosperity, I bid you farewell.

Wm. J. Bolton,
Colonel 51st P.V.V.

Jul 27—Muster-out rolls, discharge papers, completed and signed, and the regiment mustered out of the United States service to-day by Capt. Edwin Earp, of the 1st Massachusetts Heavy Artillery, Assistant Commissary of Musters for the District of Alexandria.

Most of the men retained their guns and equipments. at a cost of six dollars per set to each man. There were only a few who declined to retain those articles that had become associated with them so long, in all their trials, privations, dangers, troubles, and pleasures, and they were principally the "raw recruits."

Jul 28—The regiment broke camp this morning and at 2 P.M. marched to the foot of King Street, amid the congratulations of its many friends who thronged the streets on both sides, embarked on board of a steamboat for Washington D.C. there disembarking, marched to the Soldiers Rest and took supper, after which they marched to the Baltimore Depot, where we had to lie until dark, embarked on the cars, arriving in Baltimore during the night.

By S.O. No. 82, Headquarters District of Alexandria & Ninth Army Corps, I was directed to march the regiment to Washington, and proceed to Harrisburg, Pa. and report the command to the Chief Mustering Officer of the State, but instead of marching to Washington, we chartered a steamboat at our own expense, and steamed up the Potomac to Washington.

Jul 29—Regiment arrived in Baltimore early in the morning, disembarked and marched to the depot of the Northern Central Railroad, and took cars for Harrisburg. Our transportation were all open cars, and our ride was anything but a pleasant one, sparks and dust filling our eyes and burning our clothes.

Jul 30—Regiment arrived in Harrisburg in the afternoon, disembarked at Fort Washington, marched across the river. The city was gayly decorated, many arches were thrown across the streets, one in particular a very large one, had the names of all the states inscribed upon it. We marched under this one on our way to the Soldiers Rest, where we took our supper.

After supper we marched to Camp Curtin and went into camp. I received a notice from the Paymaster that the distance traveled by the men from Alexandria to Harrisburg had not been stated on the rolls. This was immediately attended to before morning.

Jul 31—We turned over to the state all books, regimental papers, unserviceable arms, and those not retained by the men, and the flags belonging to the state, and are making final arrangements for our muster-out of the state service and pay. At 5 P.M. I received a telegram from Gen. Hartranft at Norristown, that the Supt. of the Reading Railroad has agreed to run the regiment down to Norristown by extra train.

Aug 1—The regiment was mustered-out of the State service, received their discharge papers and were paid off. The pay off all the men required $230,000.

Aug 2—The five Montgomery County companies, A, C, D, F and I, left Harrisburg for Norristown at 3 A.M. arriving in Bridgeport at 8 A.M., where we received the congratulations of our many friends, and after a great deal of hand shaking, the line of the procession to receive us formed and it moved in the following order:

> Brevet Major General John F. Hartranft and Staff
> Norristown Band
> Discharged soldiers of the 51st P.V.V.
> Co. E, 95th Regt., and company of Independent Engineers
> Discharged soldiers of 138th P.V.
> Town Council of Norristown
> Fifty-first Regiment P.V.V. commanded by Col. William J. Bolton
> > Lieut. Col. William Allebaugh
> > Major Joseph K. Bolton

> Quar. Mas'r. Lieut. S. P. Stephens
> Adjutant J. A. Santo
> Captain Henry Coulston, Co. A
> Captain Jacob P. Brooke, Co. F
> Captain W. W. Owen, Co. D
> Lieut. Geo. Patterson, Co. I
> Captain Wm. F. Thomas, Co. C

Norristown Hose Company No. 1
Montgomery Hose Company No. 2
Humane Engine Company No. 1
Citizens on foot and in carriages.

The route moved over was across the bridge and up DeKalb Street to Lafayette, down to Mill, up to Main, up Main to Barbadoes, and countermarch to Swede, out to Jacoby, down to DeKalb, down to Odd Fellow's Hall.

When the regiment reached the front of the Hall, they were welcomed in a speech by Benj. F. Chain, Esq., to which I responded in a few sentences. The regiment then marched into the hall, where an ample repast had been prepared by the committee of rec eption. After partaking of it they were finally dismissed. A number of arches were thrown from curb to curb on the principal streets containing appropriate mottos, and the town generally decorated. The next day all the officers returned to Harrisburg to settle their accounts with the government and receive their final pay.

The following poem was written for the occasion:

Welcome Home—At Last
To the 51st Regt. P.V.V.

Brave boys, dear brothers! may that day be near
When you, the Victory won, no more shall roam:
When all the land, from sea to sea, shall hear
"The War is Ended—Victors, Welcome Home!"
Herald, Feb. 9, 1864.
That day has come—that glorious Day is here!
It blooms in peace and Victory through the land,
New England's mountains catch the echoing cheer
That rings on far Pacific's golden strand.
Peace! Peace, at last! We tremble, now, no more
O'er news of battle-days, o'er lists of slain—
No longer cheer or weep at fate of war.
No longer blush beneath our banner's stain.
The white is spotless as our country's fame,
No traitor's fingerprints its pureness mars.
Nor turns the crimson deeper with our shame—
No Longer is the shadow on the stars.
It waves, it reigns—the blessed Flag we love!

O'er every sister in the band of States!
And she who watcheth e'er its stars above,
America, our Mother, smiles and waits.
She waits to see the welcome we would speak
To you, her soldiers, who have won the fight.
Our hearts are full of welcome! all too weak
And words, to tell our thanks and joy aright.
We owe you, under God, the Nation's life,
And, more than life, the Nation's honor, too.
Pledged to sweet Freedom's cause you dared the strife—
True to your vow, to-day we welcome you.
Ah, soldiers, in the peaceful years to come,
We still will pay a Nation's thanks to you.
When sleeps the trumpet's blare, the beat of drum,
Still next our hearts, will wear the Army Blue!
And in our hearts enshrined, the People's Heart—
We wear th e memory of those who sleep,
Who sleep beneath the Flag. The People's Heart
Shall ever o'er them loving guardiance keep.
Rest, rest, my brothers! Dearest, bravest, best!
Rest in our love beneath the hallowed sod.
Where'er ye lie, sweet angels watch you rest,
Your memory be to us, your souls to God!
Rest, rest, O Conquerors! Mid your laurels, rest!
Kinglierr than purple is the Army Blue,
Such robe, such rest, a king hath never blest.
As we to you, may God to us, be true!
But joy returning Victory! joy to you!
Shake out the flags in golden air of noon!
We hail you proudly, for we know you true,
And God hath sent by you the longed-for boon.
The blessed boob of Peace with Victory crowned—
Brave Boys, dear brothers! you no more shall roam:
Take, take, 'mid loud huzzas and bugle's sound.
From lip and hand, our heartfelt Welcome Home!

August 1, 1865. Octavia.

The first stanza of this poem, dated February 9th 1864, was the last stanza by the same writer, of a poem written on the return of the 51st P.V.V. on their veteran furlough.

Appendix

Field, Staff, and Company Officers of the
51st Pennsylvania, 1861-65[1]

Field and Staff

Colonel John F. Hartranft; promoted to Brigadier General of Volunteers, 6/8/64

Lieutenant Colonel Thomas S. Bell; killed at Antietam, 9/17/62

Major Edwin Schall; promoted to Lieut. Col., 9/17/62; killed at Cold Harbor, 6/8/64

Captain William J. Bolton; promoted from Capt., Co. A, to Major, 9/17/62; to Colonel, 6/26/64

Captain William Allebaugh; promoted from Captain, Co. C, to Lieut. Col., 4/23/65

Captain Lane S. Hart; promoted from Captain, Co. F, to Major, 7/12/64; discharged, 12/17/64, on account of wounds received at Weldon Railroad, 8/19/64

Captain Joseph K. Bolton; promoted from Captain, Co. A, to Major, 1/15/65

Adjutant Daniel P. Bible; resigned 6/5/62

1st Lieutenant George Shorkley; promoted from Co. H to Adjutant, 6/6/62; to Captain, Co. H, 4/22/64

2nd Lieutenant Martin L. Schock, Co. E; promoted to 1st Lieutenant and Adjutant, 5/2/64; discharged on account of wounds, 11/2/64

2nd Lieutenant Jacob H. Santo, Co. H; promoted to 1st Lieutenant and Adjutant, 1/15/65

Quartermaster John J. Freedley; promoted from 1st Lieut., Co. C, 10/17/61; resigned, 5/11/63

Commissary Sergeant Samuel P. Stephens; promoted to 1st Lieut. and Regimental Quartermaster, 5/13/63

Surgeon J. A. Livergood; transferred to 101st PA, 11/20/61

Surgeon John A. Hosack; transferred from 101st PA, 11/20/61; resigned, 7/30/63

Surgeon William C. Shurlock; transferred from 100th PA, 3/9/64; mustered out of service, 6/65

Surgeon Manning F. Bowes; assigned to regiment, 6/65

Assistant Surgeon James D. Noble; resigned, 7/21/62

Assistant Surgeon John B. Rineholdt; mustered out of service, 6/5/65

Assistant Surgeon Charles F. Duffell; mustered out of service, 11/16/64

Assistant Surgeon James Cress; mustered out of service with regiment, 7/27/65

Chaplain Daniel G. Mallory; resigned, 7/27/63; recommissioned, 4/8/64; discharged by special order, 9/2/64

---

1. This list is taken from the roster in Parker, *51st PA*, 622-88. The remarks for each officer do not include all casualties (such as when wounded) if such statistics did not affect the man's rank.

Sergeant Major C. Jones Iredell; drowned, 8/13/62

Sergeant Major Curtin B. Stoneroad; promoted to 2nd Lieut., Co. G, 6/25/64

Sergeant Major George C. Gutelius; promoted to 2nd Lieut., Co. E, 1/14/65

Sergeant Major Levi Shingle; promoted from Sergeant, Co. C, 1/14/65

Quartermaster Sergeant Louis Cartuyval; mustered out with regiment, 7/27/65

Quartermaster Sergeant William L. Jones; committed suicide, 12/12/62

Quartermaster Sergeant Christopher Wyckoff; promoted from Corporal, Co. F, 12/13/62; discharged by special order, 3/8/65

Commissary Sergeant Levi Bolton; promoted from Corporal, Co. A, 12/3/64

Commissary Sergeant Thomas H. Parker; promoted to Captain, Co. I, 12/2/64

Commissary Sergeant Allen H. Fillman; promoted to 2nd Lieut., Co. F, 7/22/64

Hospital Steward Martin L. Dunn; mustered out with regiment, 7/27/65

Drum Major Edward D. Johnson; mustered out with regiment, 7/27/65

Company A

Recruited in Montgomery County

Captain William J. Bolton; wounded at Antietam, 9/17/62; promoted to Major, 9/17/62

1st Lieutenant Joseph K. Bolton; promoted to Captain, 9/17/62; to Major, 1/15/65

2nd Lieutenant Abraham L. Ortlip; promoted to 1st Lieut., 9/17/62; resigned, 4/20/64

1st Sergeant John S. Moore; promoted to 2nd Lieut., 9/17/62; to 1st Lieut., 5/3/64

Pvt. John H. Coulston; promoted to Corporal, 1/21/62; to 5th Sergeant, 9/17/62; to 4th Sergeant, 9/28/62; to 1st Sergeant, 10/1/63; to 2nd Lieutenant, 5/3/64; to 1st Lieutenant, 10/1/64; to Captain, 1/15/65

Pvt. Benjamin P. Thompson; promoted to Corporal, 1862; to 3rd Sergeant, 1/21/62; to 2nd sergeant, 9/17/62; to 1st Sergeant, 10/1/64; to 2nd Lieutenant, 10/1/64; to 1st Lieutenant, 12/18/64

Company B

Recruited in Northampton County

Captain Ferdinand W. Bell; killed at Fredericksburg, 12/13/62

2nd Lieutenant Daniel L. Nicholas; promoted to Captain, 12/14/62

2nd Lieutenant John H. Genther; promoted to 1st Lieut., 12/14/62; appointed brigade quartermaster in 1863; mustered out, 10/9/64

1st Sergeant Valentine Stocker; promoted to 1st Lieut., 10/30/64

2nd Lieutenant Robert M. Burrell; discharged for disability, 5/2/64

Sergeant John W. Meeker; promoted to 2nd Lieut., 10/30/64

Company C

Recruited in Montgomery County

Captain William Allebaugh; captured at Spotsylvania, 5/12/64; promoted to Lieut. Col., 4/23/65

1st Lieutenant John J. Freedley; promoted to Regimental Quartermaster, 10/17/61

2nd Lieutenant Davis Hunsicker; promoted to 1st Lieut., 10/17/61; killed at Antietam, 9/17/62

1st Sergeant William F. Thomas; promoted to 2nd Lieut., 9/19/62; to 1st Lieut., 5/13/64; to Captain, 4/24/65

2nd Lieutenant Thomas J. Lynch; promoted to 1st Lieut., 9/19/62; killed at Spotsylvania, 5/12/64

1st Sergeant George H. Smith; promoted to 2nd Lieut., 8/8/64; to 1st Lieut., 4/25/65

Sergeant John W. Fair; promoted to 1st Sergeant, 10/8/64; to 2nd Lieut., 5/17/65

Company D

Recruited in Montgomery County

Captain Edward Schall; resigned, 4/14/63

Captain William W. Owen; promoted from 1st Lieut., Co. F, to Captain, 9/1/64

1st Lieutenant Lewis Hallman; promoted to Captain, 4/14/63; transferred to Invalid Corps, 8/6/64

Sergeant John Gilligan; promoted to 1st Lieut., 8/12/64

Sergeant Samuel Fair; promoted from Sergeant, Co. C, to 2nd Lieut., 10/8/61; died 9/21/62, of wounds received at Antietam

2nd Lieutenant Jonathan Swallow; resigned, 3/15/64, on account of wounds received at Fredericksburg, 12/13/62

Sergeant Isaac Fizone; promoted to 2nd Lieut., 5/3/64; killed at Cold Harbor, 6/3/64

Sergeant David Long; promoted to 2nd Lieut., 6/25/64

Company E

Recruited in Union County

Captain George H. Hassenplug; discharged by special order, 6/11/64

1st Lieutenant John A. Morris; promoted to assistant quartermaster and transferred to General Burnside's staff, 3/16/63

2nd Lieutenant William R. Foster; promoted to 1st Lieut., 9/10/63; to Captain, 7/13/64

1st Sergeant Francis R. Frey; promoted to 1st Lieut., 1/13/65

1st Sergeant Martin L. Schock; promoted to 2nd Lieut., 1/12/64; to 1st Lieut. and Adjutant, 5/2/64

1st Sergeant James L. Seebold; promoted to 2nd Lieut., 5/2/64; to 1st Lieut., but not mustered, 6/12/64; discharged by special order, 12/10/64

Sergeant Major George C. Gutelius; promoted to 2nd Lieut., 1/14/65

Company F

Recruited in Montgomery County

Captain Robert E. Taylor; resigned, 7/27/62

1st Lieutenant Lane S. Hart; promoted to Captain, 7/28/62; to Major, 7/21/64

2nd Lieutenant Joseph C. Reed; promoted to captain and commissary of subsistence, 7/22/62

1st Sergeant Jacob P. Brooke; promoted to 1st Lieut., 7/29/62; to Captain, 7/22/64

Sergeant William W. Owen; promoted to 2nd Lieut., 7/23/62; to 1st Lieut., 7/22/64; to Captain, Company D, 9/1/64

1st Sergeant Howard Bruce; promoted to 2nd Lieut., 9/2/64; to 1st Lieut., 10/31/64

Sergeant Henry Jacobs; promoted to 2nd Lieut., 11/1/64

Commissary Sergeant Allen H. Fillman; promoted to 2nd Lieut., 7/22/64; killed at the Crater, 7/30/64

Company G

Recruited in Centre County

Captain Austin B. Snyder; resigned, 2/12/62

1st Lieutenant William H. Blair; promoted to Captain, 2/12/62; commissioned Colonel, 179th PA, 12/19/62

2nd Lieutenant Peter A. Gaulin; promoted to 1st Lieut., 2/12/62; to Captain, 1/11/63; resigned, 3/16/64

Sergeant John R. Gilliland; promoted to 2nd Lieut., 3/1/62; to 1st Lieut., 1/11/63; to Captain, 6/5/64; mustered out of service, 10/16/64

1st Sergeant Thomas D. Reed; promoted from Co. E to 1st Lieut., 11/23/64; to Captain, 2/11/65

Sergeant George B. Campbell; promoted to 2nd Lieut., 1/11/63; to 1st Lieut., 6/5/64; mustered out of service, 10/16/64

1st Sergeant John Gunsalles; promoted to 2nd Lieut., 1/11/63; to 1st Lieut., 2/13/65

Sergeant Major Curtin B. Stoneroad; promoted to 2nd Lieut., 6/25/64; to Captain, 10/20/64, but not mustered; discharged, 12/31/64, for wounds received at Weldon Railroad, 8/19/64

Sergeant George Decker; promoted to 2nd Lieut., 2/13/65

Company H

Recruited in Union, Lycoming, and Snyder Counties

Captain James M. Linn; resigned, 4/4/64

1st Lieutenant George Shorkley; promoted to Adjutant, 6/6/62; to Captain, 4/22/64

2nd Lieutenant James G. Beaver; promoted to 1st Lieut., 6/6/62; killed at Antietam, 9/17/62

Sergeant William F. Campbell; promoted to 2nd Lieut., 6/6/62; to 1st Lieut., 9/18/62; mustered out of service, 4/28/65

1st Sergeant Hugh McClure; promoted to 1st Lieut., 5/15/65

1st Sergeant Aaron Smith; promoted to 2nd Lieut., 10/23/62; discharged from service, 11/7/63

1st Sergeant Jacob H. Santo; promoted to 2nd Lieut., 4/15/64; to 1st Lieut. and Adjutant, 1/15/65

Sergeant David C. Brown; promoted to 2nd Lieut., 3/16/65

Company I

Recruited in Montgomery County

Captain George R. Pechin; resigned, 6/21/62

1st Lieutenant George W. Bisbing; promoted to Captain, 6/23/62; died, 6/7/64, of wounds received at Spotsylvania, 5/12/64

2nd Lieutenant George Schall; promoted to 1st Lieut., 6/23/62; mustered out of service, 10/24/64

Commissary Sergeant Thomas H. Parker; promoted to Captain, 12/2/64

1st Sergeant Lewis Patterson; promoted to 1st Lieut., 5/21/65

1st Sergeant Mark R. Supplee; promoted to 2nd Lieut., 6/23/62; mustered out of service, 11/15/64

Sergeant George W. Patterson; promoted to 2nd Lieut., 5/21/65

Company K

Recruited in Union and Northampton Counties

Captain John E. Titus; resigned, 9/10/63

1st Lieutenant Josiah Kelly; resigned, 7/25/62

2nd Lieutenant J. Franklin Beale; resigned, 12/28/61 recommissioned, 9/29/62; re signed, 4/7/64

1st Sergeant George P. Carman; promoted to 2nd Lieut., 12/28/61; to 1st Lieut., 7/26/62; to Captain, 9/10/62; mustered out of service, 11/12/64

Sergeant William S. Mellick; promoted to 1st Sergeant, 12/28/61; to 1st Lieut., 12/19/64; to Captain, 4/18/65

1st Lieutenant John B. Linn; resigned, 3/9/63

1st Sergeant Jacob Fryburger; promoted to 1st Lieut., 3/11/64; discharged, 10/3/64, for wounds received at Petersburg, 6/18/64

1st Sergeant Jacob Hawk; promoted to 1st Lieut., 4/18/65

2nd Lieutenant Frank B. Sterner; killed at Spotsylvania, 5/12/64

Sergeant John Vanlew; promoted to 2nd Lieut., 4/18/65

Bibliography of the 51st Pennsylvania

Barrett, Eugene A. "The Civil War Services of John F. Hartranft." *Pennsylvania History* 32 (1965): 166-86.

_____. "John Frederic Hartranft: Life and Services." Ph.D. Dissertation, Temple University, 1950.

_____. "John Frederic Hartranft: Life and Services." *Bulletin of the Historical Society of Montgomery County* 7 (April 1951): 295-378; 8 (October 1951): 12-44.

Beaver, Jacob G. Letters. In James A. Beaver Papers. Pennsylvania State Archives.

Bell, Thomas S. Papers. Chester County Historical Society.

Benfer, David. Diary, January 1863-January 1865. United States Army Military History Institute.

Bolton, William J. "War Journal." Civil War Library & Museum.

Chain, B. Percy. "Report of Presentation of Battle Flag of the 51st Regiment, Penna. Volunteers." *Historical Sketches: A Collection of Papers Prepared for the Historical Society of Montgomery County, Pa.* 6 (1929): 71-75.

Clifton, Allen J. Letter, June 23, 1862. United States Army Military History Institute, Civil War Miscellaneous Collection.

Clifton, J. Leonard. Letters, July 31-August 13, 1862. United States Army Military History Institute.

Davis, Thomas P. Letters, June 1862. United States Army Military History Institute, Civil War Times Illustrated Collection.

Dix, Mary S. (editor), " 'And Three Rousing Cheers for the Privates': A Diary of the 1862 Roanoke Island Expedition." *North Carolina Historical Review* 71 (January 1994): 62-84. Edited version of the Gangewer diary cited below.

Fisher, Louis C. "Buying Molasses." *National Tribune*, March 6, 1919.

_____. "Traded Muskets." *National Tribune*, May 7, 1891.

Gambone, Albert M. *Major-General John Frederick Hartranft: Citizen Soldier and Pennsylvania Statesman*. Baltimore: Butternut & Blue, 1995.

Gangewer, Henry W. Diary, November 1861-April 1862. United States Army Military History Institute, Civil War Miscellaneous Collection.

Hartranft, John F. "The Stone Bridge at Antietam. How It was Carried and at What Cost." *Grand Army Scout and Soldiers Mail*, November 22, 1884.

Henry Family Papers. Letters, October 1862-July 1865. United States Army Military History Institute, Boyer Collection.

Hunsicker, Davis and Charles. Letters, 1861-62. Historical Society of Montgomery County.

Jacobs, Henry. Letter, July 9, 1864. United States Army Military History Institute, Civil War Miscellaneous Collection.

Linn, James M. Papers. Bucknell University.

_____. "The Burnside Expedition. Annals of the 51st Pa. Vol." *Lewisburg Chronicle*, most issues of February 3, 1894-June 22, 1895.

_____. "The Campaign of the 51st Pa. at Vicksburg." *Lewisburg Chronicle*, December 31, 1885; January 7, 14, 28, February 25, 1886.

_____. "The 51st Regiment Pennsylvania Volunteers at Newberne." *Philadelphia Weekly Press*, September 1, 1886.

_____. "Itinerary of the 51st Regt. Penna. Vols." *Lewisburg Chronicle*, January 21, February 18, April 18, 1893.

_____. "The Ninth Army Corps. Annals of the 51st Pa. Vol." *Lewisburg Chronicle*, most issues of June 29, 1895-February 8, 1896.

Linn, John B. Letter, December 30, 1862. United States Army Military History Institute, Centre County Collection.

Newspaper Letters from Soldiers in the 51st:
    Bellefonte *Democratic Watchman*
        1862: February 13; March 13, 27
    Bellefonte *Central Press*
        1862: January 10; March 7; June 6; September 26; October 24
    Clinton Democrat (Lock Haven)
        1861: September 12, 26

Easton Argus
   1863: February 26
Harrisburg *Patriot and Union*
   1862: August 13
Herald and Free Press (Norristown)
   1861: November 12, 26; December 3, 10, 17, 24
   1862: January 14; February 4; March 4, 18, 25; April 8, 15, 29; May 25;
      June 3; July 1, 15, 22, 29; August 12; September 30
   1863: February 10; May 5; December 8
   1864: April 26; May 17, 24; June 14, 28; July 12, 19; August 9, 23, 30
Mifflinburg Telegraph
   1862: July 15, 22, 29; August 12; September 30; December 23
   1863: September 3
Miltonian (Milton)
   1862: February 7; April 4
National Defender (Norristown)
   1862: January 7, 14; February 4; March 4; April 22; May 13, 20, 27;
      June 17; July 8; August 19; September 30; October 14, 21;
      November 4, 11, 18; December 2, 16, 23
   1863: January 13, 20, 27; March 17; April 28; May 26; June 2, 9, 16;
      July 21, 28; August 25; September 1; November 24; December 1
   1864: January 12, 26; February 2, 9; April 5, 26; May 17, 24; June 7;
      July 21, 28; November 1
Montgomery Ledger (Pottstown)
   1861: December 10
   1862: September 30
   1863: July 14
Pennsylvania Daily Telegraph (Harrisburg)
   1862: May 15
Philadelphia *Daily Evening Bulletin*
   1863: May 27
Philadelphia Press
   1861: December 19
   1862: March 12
Union County Star and Lewisburg Chronicle
   1861: September 27; November 22, 26; December 6, 17, 24, 27
   1862: January 3, 14, 17; February 4, 7, 14, 25; March 4, 14, 21; April 1, 4, 15;
      May 9, 23, 27; June 17; July 15, 29; December 12, 16, 19, 26
   1863: February 20, 24; March 10, 13, 31; April 17; May 5, 12; June 5, 16, 30;
      July 10, 14, 21; August 25
   1864: February 2, 12; April 26; May 24; June 10, 28; July 1, 15, 26
   1865: March 31
West Chester *Village Record*
   1862: March 1; October 4

Parker, Thomas H. *History of the 51st Regiment of P.V. and V.V., From Its Organization at Camp Curtin, Harrisburg, Pa., in 1861, to Its Being Mustered Out of the United States*

Service at Alexandria, Va., on July 27th, 1865. Philadelphia: King & Baird, Printers, 1869; reprint edition, Baltimore: Butternut & Blue, 1999.

Parsons, Phyllis V. (editor). "Drum! Drum! Drum!" *Pennsylvania Folklife* 28 (Spring 1979): 27-37.

_____. "The Schillich Diary." *Bulletin of the Historical Society of Montgomery County* 21 (Spring 1979): 326-57.

Parsons, William T. (editor). "Letters from the 51st." *Bulletin of the Historical Society of Montgomery County* 13 (Fall 1962): 195-238.

Reed, M. G. "How the 51st Pa. Took the Bridge." *National Tribune*, June 10, 1886.

Richards, E. V. "At the Burnside's Bridge." *National Tribune*, September 9, 1909.

Roach, Harry. "Images of the 51st Pennsylvania Infantry." *Military Images* 3 (January-February 1982): 10-13.

_____. "John F. Hartranft: Defender of the Union." *Military Images* 3 (January-February 1982): 4-9.

Schall, Edwin. "A Soldier's Story. The Battle of Roanoke Island." *Philadelphia Weekly Times*, July 14, 1877.

Schillich, John W. Diaries, 1861-65. Historical Society of Montgomery County.

Scholl, John J. "Battle of Camden, N.C." *National Tribune*, November 7, 1889.

Sekel, Edwin R. W. Letters, 1861-64. Historical Society of Pennsylvania.

Shorkley, George. Papers. Bucknell University.

Smith, Montgomery S. "The 51st Pa. at Antietam." *National Tribune*, January 20, 1910.

Society of the 51st Pennsylvania Veteran Volunteers. *Record of Proceedings of the First Annual Reunion, Held at Norristown, Pa., Sept. 17, 1880.* Harrisburg: Lane S. Hart, Printer, 1880.

_____. *Record of Proceedings of the Second Annual Reunion, Held at Lewisburg, Pa., Sept. 14, 1881.* Harrisburg: Lane S. Hart, Printer, 1882.

_____. *Sixth Annual Meeting of the Association of the 51st Regiment P.V. Dedication of Monument at Antietam Bridge, October 8th, 1887.* N.p., n.d.

Index

Allebaugh, William, 203, 247, 249, 261

Annapolis, MD, 16, 17, 189

Antietam Creek, MD, 85-87, 89, 90

Appomattox River, VA, 245

Augur, Christopher C., 261, 263

Babcock, Orville E., 147, 148

Baseball, 69

Big Black River, MS, 125, 126, 132

Bodey, George, 194

Bolton, Joseph K. (brother), 19, 26, 76, 89, 133, 137, 157, 161, 202, 228, 230, 236, 238, 241

Bolton, William J., 13, 14, 26, 32, 76, 86, 87, 89, 90, 91, 92, 93, 94, 102, 108, 115, 118, 129, 130, 135, 137, 152, 155, 157, 166, 190, 194, 198, 202, 205, 207, 211, 214, 220, 221, 224, 225, 226, 227, 229, 232, 233, 235, 238, 246, 247, 248, 251, 256, 257, 258, 260, 262, 266, 267, 269

Buford, John, 73, 74

Burnside, Ambrose E., 27, 34, 37, 41, 42, 45, 46, 50, 58, 61, 63, 64, 68, 79, 80, 81, 83, 84, 86, 87, 89, 97, 105, 110, 131, 133, 134, 144, 150, 153, 154, 155, 159, 188, 191, 193, 194, 198, 201, 202, 203, 205, 206, 211, 212, 213, 221, 225

Butler, Benjamin F., 16, 17

Chantilly, VA, 77

Crittenden, Thomas L. 202, 214

Curtin, Andrew G., 13, 30, 214, 223, 234

Curtin, John I., 262

Ellsworth, Ephraim E., 20

Engle, John M., 252

Ferrero, Edward, 86, 93, 103, 112, 114, 137, 144

Foster, John G., 50, 159

Franklin, William B., 22, 23

Frederick, MD, 81

Fredericksburg, VA, 98, 100

Grant, Ulysses S., 123, 125, 129, 131, 132, 201, 206, 243, 244, 260

Hart, Lane S., 226, 228, 239

Hartranft, John F., 13, 21, 22, 23, 27, 30, 60, 86, 93, 94, 100, 102, 107, 110, 114, 115, 127, 132, 137, 149, 150, 153, 157, 171, 191, 192, 202, 205, 214, 218, 221, 224, 228, 230, 231, 236, 238, 249, 250, 251, 253, 257, 258, 262, 266

Hawkins, Rush C., 56

Heintzelman, Samuel P., 22, 75

Hooker, Joseph, 80

Howard, Oliver O., 23

Jackson, MS, 126, 127, 128, 129

Johnston, Joseph E., 123, 125, 126, 127, 129, 132

Kearny, Philip, 77

Kentucky, 111-120, 137-140

Kitty (camp cook), 76, 90, 91

Knoxville, TN, 151, 153, 158, 159

Ledlie, James H., 214, 225

Lexington, KY, 115

Lincoln, Abraham, 193, 244

Longstreet, James, 149, 150, 154, 155, 159, 160

Manassas Battlefield, VA, 75-76

Manassas Junction, VA, 75

McClellan, George B., 79, 84, 87, 89, 236

McDowell, Irvin, 13, 23, 24, 78

McLaws, Lafayette, 150

Meade, George G., 225, 230, 238, 242, 246, 251, 253, 260, 266

Memphis, TN, 122

Morgan, John H., 117

North Anna River, VA, 208

North Carolina, 37-65 , 68

Octavia (poet), 171, 271-272

Ord, Edward O.C., 126

Parke, John G., 37, 54, 122, 123, 125, 127, 131, 132, 159, 198, 228, 230, 242, 243, 246, 248, 250, 251, 252, 253, 255, 257, 258, 262

Pennsylvania, towns, cities and features,

Bridgeport, 14, 25, 27, 171, 188, 270

Camp Curtin, 15, 27, 188, 270

Harrisburg, 13, 25, 27, 91, 188, 270
Norristown, 13, 14, 25, 27, 91, 140, 141, 171, 187, 188, 205, 207, 227, 246, 270
Philadelphia, 15, 91, 140, 227, 247
Petersburg, VA, 220, 245, 253, 254, 255, 256, 258
Poe, Orlando M., 145, 153
Pope, John, 71, 72, 73
Potter, Robert B., 155, 156, 159, 228, 246, 249, 255

Rapidan River, VA, 197
Reno, Jesse L., 34, 37, 56, 57, 58, 71, 72, 73, 75, 80, 81, 82, 83, 90
Richmond, VA, 210, 249, 256

Schall, Edwin, 30, 35, 94, 107, 133, 137, 141, 149, 154, 159, 170, 171, 188, 189, 191, 202, 207, 211
Sherman, William T., 125, 127, 129, 131, 132
Sigel, Franz, 74, 75
Slemmer, Adam J., 19
South Mountain, MD, 81-83
Spotsylvania Court House, VA, 201
Stevens, Isaac I., 77

Tennessee, 143, 158
Thanksgiving (1864), 236-237

Units, Confederate
3rd Georgia, 57, 58, 59, 91
26th North Carolina, 205
31st North Carolina, 44

33rd North Carolina, 50
35th North Carolina, 218
37th North Carolina, 205
Black units, 248
Units, Union
Army of the Ohio, 158, 159
Army of the Potomac, 79, 81, 89, 105, 202, 208, 242, 244, 246, 251
Army of the Tennessee, 130, 132
Army of Virginia, 71, 79
IX Corps, 69, 80, 81, 83, 84, 85, 87, 97, 106, 110, 115, 117, 123, 127, 129, 132, 138, 188, 189, 190, 191, 192, 197, 199, 206, 207, 208, 211, 225, 238, 239, 242, 244, 246, 248, 249, 254, 258, 260, 263
Coast Division, 34, 37, 38, 52, 63, 69
3rd New Jersey Cavalry, 193, 194
21st Massachusetts, 44, 45, 56, 57, 62, 77
35th Massachusetts, 82, 141
1st Michigan Sharpshooters, 188, 189, 192, 256-257
2nd Michigan, 198, 202, 203, 219, 250
17th Michigan, 82, 198, 202
27th Michigan, 214
9th New York, 44, 47
51st New York, 44, 45, 77, 86, 89, 127
4th Pennsylvania Volunteer Infantry, 13, 15, 16, 22, 24, 25, 27, 50, 78, 91, 205

48th Pennsylvania Volunteer Infantry, 166, 189
51st Pennsylvania Volunteer Infantry, 27, 28, 30, 33, 37, 43, 56 44, 45, 47, 49, 50, 51, 53, 57, 58, 61, 62, 63, 68, 71-72, 73, 74, 75, 76, 77, 81, 82, 86, 87, 89, 91, 94, 98, 100, 102, 103, 116-117, 125, 126, 127, 128, 129, 130, 135, 137, 138, 140, 142, 144-145, 147, 151, 152, 154, 158, 160, 162-164, 165, 166-168, 170, 171, 187, 188, 189, 190, 198, 200, 202, 205, 206, 209, 210, 211, 214, 218, 220, 222, 225, 229-230, 234, 235, 246, 248, 251, 252, 253, 254, 255, 257, 260, 262, 269
Wayne Artillerists (Company A, 4th Pennsylvania), 13, 31
Signal Corps, 42
Invalid Corps, 147

Vicksburg, MS, 123, 124, 125, 132

Washington, DC, 17-18, 20
Weldon Railroad, VA, 228
Wilderness, VA, 198, 200
Willcox, Orlando B., 23, 113, 193, 198, 201, 202, 212, 221, 228, 231, 242, 245, 247, 248, 249, 250, 251, 253, 254, 255, 257, 258, 259, 268